HOW ECONOMICS SHOULD BE DONE

Wherever possible, the articles in these volumes have been reproduced as originally published using facsimile reproduction, inclusive of footnotes and pagination to facilitate ease of reference.

For a full list of published and future titles in this series and a list of all Edward Elgar published titles visit our website at www.e-elgar.com

How Economics Should Be Done

Essays on the Art and Craft of Economics

David C. Colander

Distinguished College Professor
Middlebury College, USA

and

Huei-chun Su

Institute for New Economic Thinking
University of Oxford, UK

EE | **Edward Elgar**
PUBLISHING

Cheltenham, UK • Northampton, MA, USA

Published by
Edward Elgar Publishing Limited
The Lypiatts
15 Lansdown Road
Cheltenham
Glos GL50 2JA
UK

Edward Elgar Publishing, Inc.
William Pratt House
9 Dewey Court
Northampton
Massachusetts 01060
USA

A catalogue record for this book
is available from the British Library

Library of Congress Control Number: 2017947243

This book is available electronically in the **Elgar**online
Economics subject collection
DOI 10.4337/9781786435903

ISBN 978 1 78643 589 7 (cased)
ISBN 978 1 78643 590 3 (eBook)

Printed and bound by CPI Group (UK) Ltd, Croydon, CR0 4YY

Contents

**PART IV   PRAGMATIC METHODS FOR DOING ECONOMICS AS A
PROFESSION**

Acknowledgements

The editors and publishers wish to thank the authors and the following publishers who have kindly given permission for the use of copyright material.

American Economic Association for articles: David Colander (1992), 'Retrospectives: The Lost Art of Economics', *Journal of Economic Perspectives*, **6** (3), Summer, 191–8; David Colander, Peter Howitt, Alan Kirman, Axel Leijonhufvud and Perry Mehrling (2008), 'Beyond DSGE Models: Toward an Empirically Based Macroeconomics', *American Economic Review: Papers and Proceedings*, **98** (2), May, 236–40.

Cambridge University Press for article: David Colander (2000), 'The Death of Neoclassical Economics', *Journal of the History of Economic Thought*, **22** (2), June, 127–43.

Duke University Press for excerpt: David Colander (2015), 'Framing the Economic Policy Debate', in Alain Marciano and Steven G. Medema (eds), *Market Failure in Context: Annual Supplement to Volume 47, History of Political Economy*, Part 2, 253–66.

Eastern Economic Association for article: David C. Colander (1993), 'The Macrofoundations of Micro', *Eastern Economic Journal*, **19** (4), Fall, 447–57.

Erasmus Journal for Philosophy and Economics for article: Huei-Chun Su and David Colander (2013), 'A Failure to Communicate: The Fact–Value Divide and the Putnam–Dasgupta Debate', **6** (2), Autumn, 1–23.

Jeffrey Frankel for article: David Colander (1987), 'Why Aren't Economists as Important as Garbagemen?', *Journal of Economic and Monetary Affairs*, **1** (1), July, 11–18.

MIT Press for excerpt: David Colander (2016), 'Complexity Economics and Workaday Economic Policy', in David S. Wilson and Alan Kirman (eds), *Complexity and Evolution: Toward a New Synthesis for Economics*, Chapter 15, 285–98.

Oxford University Press, USA for excerpt: David Colander (2016), 'Creating Humble Economists: A Code of Ethics for Economists', in George F. DeMartino and Deirdre N. McCloskey (eds), *The Oxford Handbook of Professional Economic Ethics*, Part VIII, Chapter 36, 737–49.

Taylor and Francis LLC (www.tandfonline.com) for article: David Colander (2003), 'Post Walrasian Macro Policy and the Economics of Muddling Through', *International Journal of Political Economy*, **33** (2), Summer, 17–35.

Taylor and Francis Ltd (www.taylorandfrancis.com) for articles and excerpt: David Colander (1994), 'Vision, Judgment, and Disagreement among Economists', *Journal of Economic Methodology*, **1** (1), 43–56; David Colander (2010), 'Moving beyond the Rhetoric of Pluralism: Suggestions for an "Inside-the-Mainstream" Heterodoxy', in Robert Garnett, Erik K. Olsen and Martha Starr (eds), *Economic Pluralism*, Part I, Chapter 2, 36–47; David Colander (2011), 'How Economists Got it Wrong: A Nuanced Account', *Critical Review: Capitalism and Economics after the Crisis*, **23** (1–2), 1–27; David Colander (2013), 'The Systemic Failure of Economic Methodologists', *Journal of Economic Methodology*, **20** (1), 56–68.

Preface

David Colander

The methodology of the positive science of economics is a well explored subject. That hasn't provided much help for economists since most of what economists do is not science; it's applied policy. Trying to use the methodology of science to guide applied policy work causes serious problems; it undermines both the science of economics and applied economic policy work.

Because of the focus on scientific methodology, there has been very little work done on the methodology of that applied policy work. I'm one of the few economists who write about it; I call it the methodology of the art and craft of economics to distinguish it from the methodology of the science of economics.

The essence of my argument is that positive economic science methodology, with its strict scientific empirical rules, is not the methodology that applied economists use, nor is it the methodology that they should use. They pay lip service to it, but following it is impossible given the realities of the data and the complexities of the real-world problems they are dealing with. The methodology they use is a much looser methodology that deviates from scientific methodology by necessity; it is a methodology that integrates value judgments and that makes many decisions based on heuristic models and rough empirical guesses, not on formal models or scientific-level empirical evidence.

Focusing on scientific methodology encourages economists to hide, or at least to obscure, those deviations, and is part of the reason many people think that the science of economics is ideologically tainted. Because economic methodologists have focused on scientific methodology the question that isn't addressed is whether the deviations from that scientific methodology currently being made are the best deviations to make. That question should be front and center in discussions of applied policy economic methodology.

What the methodology of applied policy economics should be primarily about is the compromises that are needed to actually do applied policy work. In my methodological work I've argued that (1) it is ok for economists to do much of what they are doing, as long as they don't pretend to be doing something else, and (2) if economists recognize that they have to use heuristics in applied policy work, they will likely make better deviations.

The decisions of how best to incorporate the necessary deviations from scientific methodology in applied policy work cannot be determined by outside methodologists – they are decisions that can only be sensibly made by practicing economists. Moreover, those decisions are constantly changing as analytic and computational technology changes. So applied policy methodology is constantly evolving and in flux. It should be thought of not as a set of invariable rules, but as a sensibility that governs ongoing decisions.

The idea for this book originated with Alan Sturmer at Edward Elgar; he has been pushing me to put together a collection of my essays on applied policy methodology for well over a decade. I responded – yes it was a good idea – but, as is the case with many good ideas, I never quite got around to it. What made this book possible is that Huei-chun was willing to work with me in putting it together.

I am delighted to be working with Huei-chun, whom I first met when I attended her presentation at a 2009 conference in Amsterdam where I gave a keynote address. I usually attend some of the other sessions when I speak at a conference, and her paper title looked interesting, so I sat in. I was very impressed. She had a solid understanding of both moral philosophy and economic issues, and could convey her ideas simply and clearly. Thus, it didn't come as a surprise to me when I later learned that she had won the History of Economics Society Joseph Dorfman Best Dissertation Award for 2007, and the 2006 Society of the Development of Austrian Economics' Don Lavoie Memorial Essay Competition Prize. I found her book, *Economic Justice and Liberty: The Social Philosophy in John Stuart Mill's Utilitarianism* (Routledge, 2013) a tour de force.

She isn't as well-known as she could be because, like many superb young women scholars, Huei-chun faced the dilemma – how to blend family and work. (It is a dilemma that culturally, and physically, is less binding on men.) So despite her enormous talent, she partially withdrew from academic work to focus on raising her family. Luckily for me, she wanted to keep her toes in economics, and so, as time permitted, we started working together on a variety of papers, one of which is reprinted in this volume, and ultimately on this project.

This collection has given me a chance to reflect back on my research over the past 40 years and to consider how my ideas have evolved over the years. The result is this volume which I think nicely captures my evolving views on applied methodology. It begins with an introduction by Huei-chun, which gives context to my arguments. It concludes with an annotated bibliography that should be useful to anyone who wants to go further into my work.

Authors' acknowledgements

Books, even ones that are collections of past works, take lots of work, much of it not done by the authors. So there are many people to thank. They include Edward Elgar and Alan Sturmer, who long ago suggested the project and, each year at the ASSA meetings – first Edward and then Alan – with their notebooks in hand, reminded Dave of the project, and nudged him to move forward on it. The book would not have existed without them. Then there are the publishers of the original articles, who kindly gave permission for the articles to be reprinted in this volume. We thank them all. We also would like to thank our families, Huei-chun's husband, Otto, and their two boys, Cornelio and Tiberio, and Dave's wife, Pat. They put up with our academic pursuits with a smile and encouragement, even when publishing deadlines interfered with the joint pleasures of life, and we thank them for it.

Huei-chun would also like to thank Philip Schofield, Director of the Bentham Project at University College London and Eric Beinhocker, Executive Director of the Institute for New Economic Thinking at the University of Oxford. Professor Schofield's steadfast support and the honorary affiliation with UCL he provided were invaluable in supporting her to carry on academic work even when family took most of her time. Once the boys were a bit older, allowing Huei-chun to return part time to work, Eric Beinhocker, Executive Director of INET at Oxford, was also very supportive of the project. He made it possible for Huei-chun to focus on finalizing the manuscript while juggling between family and work. We thank them both.

Once the manuscript was turned in to Elgar, the Elgar organization started up, and did their usual excellent job in processing it. Thanks are due to Erin McVicar for her role in preparing the project at its early stages and Jenni Gardner for project managing the process of clearing the formal copyright permissions. Elgar Publishing has a wonderfully efficient publishing organization, and it didn't surprise us at all when they were named the 2017 Independent Publisher of the Year.

Introduction

Huei-chun Su

David Colander has been writing about economic methodology for over 30 years, but he goes out of his way to emphasize that he does not see himself as a methodologist. In one of our private email exchanges on a well-known economic methodologist's work, he told me that it looks interesting but is a bit too deep for his interests. As far as I know him, this is just a polite way of saying that he won't spend much time on that methodologist's work as it is irrelevant to what he sees himself as an economist/educator doing. Indeed, he once complained openly in a review on a book written by two philosophers of science that:

> Like economic theory, methodological arguments have a habit of taking off on their own into a philosophical quagmire through which most economists cannot travel, and from which most economists who try, do not return.
>
> Just as economics has become remote from the real-world economy, so too has economic methodology become remote from what economists do. Methodology has become an end in itself, quite separate from a description of what is done in economics, or a prescription for what should be done. (Colander, 1997, p. 141)

Colander's interests in what is done and what should be done in economics led him to write about methodology from the perspective of an economist and economist watcher, not from the perspective of a philosopher or methodologist of economics. For him, useful methodological discussion for most economists has a strong practical purpose; the profound philosophical questions that tend to attract methodologists have never been the focus of his methodological writing, and he argues that they are quite irrelevant for most economists.

Colander does not deny the importance of fundamental philosophical questions to methodology. But he argues that what economics needs much more is some rough and ready hands-on guidance on the workaday economic problems that economists experience as they do their research. Methodologists who do not deal with such workaday problems have essentially removed most of their usefulness to the profession.

Despite his limited engagement with formal methodologists, it would be a mistake to think that Colander's writings on methodology are not of significance to them, because if he is right, his arguments present serious challenges to the standard economic methodology literature at a foundation level. There are at least two challenges raised by Colander's methodological work which methodologists should not neglect. The first challenge concerns the subject-matter of the methodology of economics and the role of economic methodologists; the other concerns the nature of economics. They are related and the second challenge is particularly crucial, because if Colander is right about the nature of most economists' work, then their current practice is based on a shaky ground. If it is indeed true, as Colander claims, that the nature of the problems which most economists are dealing with is not science, then it also implies that the majority of methodologists who treat methodology of economics solely as methodology of science have failed to get the grand question concerning the nature of their discipline right.

In Colander's view, the relevant methodology is embedded in the workaday activities of economists: one cannot understand economists' methodological practices through abstract methodological discussion; one can only understand economists' work by understanding their craft, the institutional incentives they face, and the specific problems they are trying to solve. Colander argues that, generally, these problems are not pure theoretical or formal empirical problems; they are practical policy problems that require a topic-specific methodology that generally differs from the methodology deemed as 'scientific' by philosophers of science or methodologists. To constrain economists' methodology to fit a precisely determined scientific methodology does not make sense. Doing so, Colander argues, has caused a problem of cognitive dissonance to economists. He argues that currently the standard practice of academic economists involves serious methodological mistakes which result in various problems, such as the disconnection between models and reality and the neglect of needed value judgments. His explanation for why economics is making such mistakes is that economists are attempting to conform to two conflicting goals – to follow a scientific methodology and to do solid policy analysis. Since the two methodologies are different, if one has to meet both criteria, the only answer is the cognitive dissonance that economists demonstrate in justifying their approach. It is such questions that Colander wants methodologists to engage. He believes that methodologists should be telling economists they are making such methodological mistakes, and offering ways to avoid them. But that doesn't happen in most literature on economic methodology. The difference in his views regarding what methodologists should do, and what they actually do, is so huge that he decided to leave behind almost the entire economic methodology literature of the twentieth century and follow his own route.

A continuation of the Mill–Keynes tradition
Colander's methodological approach may appear eccentric in the landscape of the modern methodology literature, but it is not so unconventional if seen from a longer-term perspective in the history of economics. As he emphasizes, the methodological approach he advocates is not unique to him, but is, in fact, part of long tradition that is to be found in Classical economic writing. Specifically, he sees his methodological approach as a continuation of the Mill–Keynes approach, updated for developments in computational and analytic techniques. According to Colander, the Classical methodological tradition he has been following fully understood the limitation of scientific methods in providing answers to practical policy questions and hence had a much better balance between scientific methods and other methods when approaching this type of question. His claim is that this Classical approach was lost, unfortunately, in the neoclassical period as economists tried to be more scientific than was possible when dealing with policy issues. That desire to meet scientific standards led them to spend too much of their time analysing issues abstractly and developing models that deviated far from the real-world problems faced by policy makers. Methodologists followed suit. They focused only on whether economists were following scientific methodology, not whether they were following a reasonable methodology.

In Colander's view, most of what economists do is applied economics, which is, following John Neville Keynes, neither normative nor positive economics; instead it belongs in a third category – the art of economics. This tripartite division of economics guides Colander's thinking about methodology and can be seen as one of the foundation stones on which he builds his arguments of methodology. Only when one understands the way Colander divides economics can one make sense of his claims for economic methodology.

In this tripartite division of economics, positive economics is part of science. So economists doing positive economics should take guidance from scientific methodologists on the appropriate methodology for positive economics. Normative economics is a part of moral philosophy. So economists doing normative economics should take guidance from moral philosophers on the appropriate methodology for normative economics. Applied economics is a blend of both of these, and it is here where most economists need pragmatic methodological guidance. Such pragmatic methodological guidance is largely missing in the literature.

Methodology based in engineering, not science

For Colander, applied economics is best thought of as engineering, not as science.[1] Following Billy Vaughn Koen, Colander makes a clear distinction between engineering and science and subsequently between the engineering methodology and scientific methodology. In engineering, the primary goal is to solve real-world problems; in science, the primary goal is to find the truth. It is the difference in goals that leads to the difference in methodology.

By engineering methodology, Colander means 'the strategy for causing the best change in a poorly understood or uncertain situation within the available resources' or 'use the best available engineering heuristics to solve problems' (Chapters 4, 9 and 17, this volume). It uses any information available. In contrast, the scientific methodology focus is on knowledge that meets generally accepted scientific criteria. The requirement rules out historical knowledge, intuition, and guesstimates. That scientific methodology doesn't work best for engineers who have to come up with an answer to a problem.

When given a problem to solve, engineers need to arrive at an answer even if some facts are unknown to them or certain observed phenomena cannot be explained by existing scientific theories. The way they fill the gap between scientific knowledge and solutions is to make judgments based on all the information and tools they have; judgments that do not and cannot meet strict scientific standards. Thus, for example, if only a small amount of data is available, they will use that data to provide a rough estimate, at the best level of confidence they can, increasing the fudge factor to account for the limited accuracy. In making these judgments engineers will introduce whatever evidence they can, and then, through experimentation, attempt to gain better understanding of the underlying properties through experience with building the actual product, or with tailored experiments designed to better understand the relationship.

Engineers often use backward induction thought experiments, hypothesizing from the desired end product to the underlying relationships needed to get them there. Then they try a small experiment to see if it works in practice. If it does there must be some scientific foundation for it, even if it has not yet been discovered. Engineering is very much a creative exercise that precedes science as much as it is built on science. This entire process of working directly with a specific goal, separate from finding the truth, is what Colander calls the engineering methodology, and it is that methodology that Colander argues that applied economists should follow and methodologists should focus on.[2]

Complexity vision and economics

A final introductory comment that should be made about Colander's methodology concerns its relationship to complexity economics, which Colander argues is the future of economics (Colander, 2005). The fact that abundant yet diverse work in the literature has been associated with complexity economics leaves it unclear what exactly constitutes complexity economics. In Colander's use of the term, it involves a complexity vision of the economy, a scientific complexity theory of the economy and a complexity approach to policy analysis.

With a complexity vision, one sees the economy as a complex evolving system undergoing continual evolutionary change; that is, the economy is seen as an interconnected collection of co-evolving, adapting agents interacting at a variety of time/space scales, evolving in complicated ways in which path dependencies, novelty, and emergent structures play a major role. This is a vision shared by many economists who see themselves as doing complexity economics.

The element in Colander's version of complexity economics that is less commonly noticed is its importance for applied policy. According to Colander, the approach adopted by policy-focused complexity economics moves away from thinking that general abstract models are going to lead to direct policy results. Instead, in policy-focused complexity economics, the researcher has a vision of the economy, which he or she uses as a general guide, and the researcher refines that vision with multiple models designed to answer one of the multitude of questions relevant to the policy at hand. This complexity approach, which has, at its core, a loose vision, rather than a narrow well-defined theory, he argues, is much more conducive to his pragmatic methodology than is the current Walrasian general equilibrium vision, which most economists consider the core of economics.

Another difference between complexity economics and much modern standard economics structured around a Walrasian general equilibrium vision is that Walrasian modern economics attempts to analyse economies with a set of analytic and computational tools that were state-of-the-art analysis decades ago, but which no longer are. Complexity economics embraces new analytic and computational technologies. In Colander's view, the adoption of complexity economics, and its new analytic and computational technologies, will lead to the adoption of the methodological position he advocates, because recognizing the complexity of the system undermines the ability of a researcher to rely on a single precisely-specified general theory to anywhere near the degree to which modern economics relies on Walrasian general equilibrium theory.

This view of changing analytical and computational technology allows Colander to see the art and craft applied policy methodology he advocates not only as the methodology of past Classical economics, but also as the methodology of the future. Colander argues that complexity economics will become seen as a continuation of Classical economics updated for new analytic and computational technology, with neoclassical economics being seen as a diversion.

Note that despite being highly enthusiastic about complexity economics as a scientific program, Colander does not consider it the major task for most economists to study it. To study it rigorously requires high-level mathematics that is often not suited to policy questions and to the training and ability of most economists. Colander argues that the policy research program in complexity economics will be a pragmatic combination of current practices modified to incorporate new analytic and computational technology, interpreted within a complexity evolutionary framework.

According to Colander, it will likely take decades for the complexity scientific research program to replace the current Walrasian scientific research program both because researchers are vested in the current program, and because the complexity research program is still in its infancy. Thus, were one to argue that applied economics was only applied science, then the complexity vision would have no effect on policy. But Colander argues that that is not the case. He argues that we do not need to wait for a paradigm shift to occur in the scientific branch of economics in order to adopt a new methodological approach for applied economics. A policy research program shift often precedes a scientific research program shift. According to Colander, the complexity policy research program, based on data science, agent-based modeling techniques, and increased use of non-linear dynamics is changing the way applied economic research is done, and will eventually change the science of economics.

Structure of the book and articles selected
Colander has written 80 or 90 articles related to methodology. In this book, I have selected 17 of those articles that give the reader a sense of his approach. The articles are organized into four parts. Part I puts together the articles that provide a framework underlying Colander's methodology and introduces Colander's methodology for economic policy within that framework. Part II introduces Colander's view on the methodology for microeconomics. Part III looks at Colander's methodology for macroeconomics. Part IV looks at some broader issues.

Part I: Methodological framework and methodology for economic policy as art
I begin with a fun piece, 'Why Aren't Economists as Important as Garbagemen?' that was written in 1987 when Colander started forcefully arguing that what academic economists were studying had gradually drifted away from the real economic world. While he had written other methodological articles before then, this article can be seen as the starting point of Colander's series of writing on reflecting the methodology of economics and the economics profession.

Intriguingly, for Colander, the main reason why much of economists' research has lost contact with the real world is not because economists have attempted too little. On the contrary, it is because they have been trying to do something unachievable – to avoid all value judgments in their analysis. In his own words, 'economics tries to do too much – to be too objective, to be too fair. The only way economics can do that is to make it irrelevant, and that's what it has done' (Colander, 1991, p. 7). The discussion in Chapter 1 thus served as Colander's first broadside attack on welfare economics. After 30 years, the core of Colander's argument remains the same and it is applicable to current applied economics in general. The relevance of the article for today is largely due to his insights into the nature of economists' role in society. How economists perceive their role will determine what they do as economists.

In Chapter 1, Colander argues that economists today do not play a more direct role because they have a fundamentally incorrect view of the nature of their role. Specifically, he argues against what he calls the 'outside perspective', that is, a perspective whereby economists view themselves as outside the economy when judging how well the economy is functioning. The outside perspective has made the natural/unnatural dichotomy pervasive in economic terminology and policy analysis. In Colander's view, this natural/unnatural division is not a helpful way of looking at society. In fact, it often causes confusion as if the division itself can serve as an appropriate basis for evaluating policies. It is not incidental that the neo-liberal thought can easily latch onto the mainstream economics to become the dominant economic thinking over the past decades; with the outside perspective, the laissez faire policy conclusion is preordained. Ironically, the main reason for economists to adopt the outside perspective is to avoid value judgments in their analysis. Their attempt to be objective has resulted in a paradoxical situation. On the one hand, economists have made their research irrelevant. On the other hand, their seeming neutral position has led to an outcome opposite to their intention – the natural/unnatural narrative following from the outside perspective has been used uncritically to support certain policy standpoints. If, as Colander argues, the criterion of objectivity required by science has been unduly imposed by economists onto their policy analysis, it implies that in order to make economics relevant again, economists have to liberate themselves from the straightjacket of scientific methodology when doing applied policy analysis.

After the first publication of 'Why Aren't Economists as Important as Garbagemen?', Colander continued analysing methodology in a series of papers trying to provide a theory of why what happens in economics happens. He used what he called an 'economic approach to methodology', that is, an approach that examines how economists' research behavior has been influenced by the institutional incentives under the assumption that economists are primarily self-interested people, rather than assuming that economists always aim to search for the truth regardless of the institutional incentives, as most approaches to scientific methodology implicitly do. It is close to a sociological analysis of economists' behavior. Chapter 2, 'Vision, Judgment, and Disagreement among Economists', is one of those articles adopting such an economic approach of reasoning and provides insights into the essential role of vision and judgment in not only choosing among policies but also in selecting among assumptions and models, which was traditionally believed to be value-free.

Chapter 2 starts with a challenge to a common view that there is too much disagreement among economists. For Colander, significant disagreement is both to be expected and desirable given the nature of the questions economists ask. The real problem for him is that economists often disagree about the things they should agree about, and agree about things they should disagree about. In the chapter Colander argues that disagreements among economists are often due to the differences in vision of how an economy operates and the differences in judgments about how the political system would implement a policy or on what effect the policy will have on existing institutions. Yet economists often shy away from this type of difference, because those differences are deemed subjective or non-scientific and cannot be captured in formal models. Colander calls this fear of discussing difference in judgment and vision 'artiphobia'. Partly as the consequence of the artiphobia, economists spend enormous amounts of time disagreeing about what Colander considers relatively minor modeling issues. This chapter explains the formulation of this artiphobia among economists by analysing institutional incentives that guide economists' actions. It argues that this type of differences cannot be resolved by formal empirical testing: only when economists accept an open treatment of the disagreements can we better handle the debates about policy.

To have a good sense of the term artiphobia introduced in Chapter 2, it needs to be read in the context of Colander's writing. Chapter 3, 'Retrospectives: The Lost Art of Economics', is the first article in which Colander directly argued that applied economics should be treated as art, rather than science. It presents Colander's methodological argument within a historical context, showing how his interest with methodology is blended with his interest in history of economic thought. In it Colander returns to Friedman's famous article on positive economics, in which he cites J.N. Keynes as his forerunner. What Colander points out is that Keynes's view was fundamentally different than Friedman's and Friedman and economic methodologists have totally lost sight of a central part of Classical and Keynes's methodology – the view that there is a tripartite division of economics, not a bipartite division. Following Keynes, Colander argues that the study of economic policy belongs in the art of economics, not in the positive science of economics nor in the normative branch of economics. This division of economics sets the stage for Colander's later writing on the methodology of economics. He doesn't claim to be making new arguments; he is simply restating Classical economists' arguments.

With all the methodological debate about Friedman's essay, how could methodologists have missed that simple division and sleight of hand by Friedman? Chapter 4, 'The Systemic Failure of Economic Methodologists' provides Colander's answer to that question. Academic methodologists were lost in their own little debates and weren't worried about applying their arguments to economics, but were more interested in making esoteric points and winning academic debates. To do that, they found it useful to take implicit neutral positions on economists' work. They didn't say – this approach does not make sense if one's goal is to answer policy questions; they instead tried to fit economists' work into a scientific methodology.

Colander challenges that neutral standpoint held by many methodologists, and argues that, by trying to maintain a neutral stance, and not making judgments, economic methodologists have shirked their moral responsibility to the economics profession and to society. In this chapter one can see clearly Colander's standpoint regarding the responsibility of economic methodologists to make judgments and make the basis for those judgments clear. In this chapter Colander also elaborates on what he means by an engineering methodology, and why he believes that engineering methodology is the appropriate methodology for the study of economic policy.

Colander is often known as a critic of modern mainstream economics. Unlike many other critics calling mainstream economics neoclassical economics, Colander is wary of using the label neoclassical economics to refer to the economics he is criticizing. In his view, economics has changed significantly over the past one hundred years since the term 'neoclassical economics' was initially coined by Thorstein Veblen in 1900. He argues that the moniker cannot capture the ever-changing dynamics of economics nor can it capture the diverse content of what economists are doing today. More importantly, the inconsistent, sometime even schizophrenic, use of the term neoclassical economics is detrimental to constructing effective methodological discussion. For Colander, calling current economics neoclassical economics does not add anything to, and often obscures, our understanding of the current failings of economics. From the methodological point of view, adopting a new classifier that can provide a more accurate picture of economics today is a crucial step forward in order to better understand the methodological problems of current economics and to enhance the effectiveness of conversation in the methodological literature.

Chapter 5, 'The Death of Neoclassical Economics', is another fun piece to read. It provides Colander's explanation of why the term neoclassical economics should die. The chapter was initially his presidential address to the History of Economics Society in June 1999, but its theme goes beyond the realm of history of economics. It argues that what defines modern economics is not content, but method, that is, the modeling approach to problems. 'Modern economics', according to Colander, 'is economics of the model'. Note that this is a descriptive definition, not a prescriptive one. It does not suggest that all economists should do is modeling; it simply describes the phenomenon that modeling is the central element of modern economics.

That said, Colander indeed conveys a prescriptive message in this article regarding how to use models. After examining how the use of models has changed over time in both micro and macro, Colander praises the modern movement to applied modeling, but he also raises the alarm about the undue weight economists gave to formal empirical testing of models. In his view, it is not possible to test many of the applied models economists use in a formal manner without being ad hoc, given that the assumptions of those models are themselves ad hoc. But he doesn't see this as a real problem to modern applied economics because in his view applied economics should be treated as engineering, not science, and it follows that applied models can still be meaningfully tested in an informal empirical way that works for the needed engineering knowledge. To Colander, the real serious problem of modern applied economics is the way economists try to avoid the semblance of ad hoc pontificating by structuring their models in scientific clothing.

Part II: Methodology for microeconomics
In Colander's view, abstract modern theory and models are extremely useful for a subset of policy problems in micro that involve constrained optimization. Examples include allocation problems and algorithmic shadow price models. The problem is that there are many other problems where economist's standard models aren't that useful, and economists haven't distinguished these from those where it is useful. The problem has two dimensions. First, the dominant optimal control framework is not suitable for studying numerous problems and questions that belong in a micro framework. For example, what policy should one follow if tastes are partially endogenous, if people are highly uncertain about what their goals are, if a number of people find markets morally unacceptable, or if results of a policy could be changed by changing the institutional structure? Or what policy should we follow when people's views of the goals of policy differ widely? The optimal control framework is not especially helpful with such questions. Second, even in those areas where the control framework of analysis seems appropriate, the application of theory or model to the policy often goes consistently wrong. These are normal occurrences and Colander argues economists need methodological guidance on how to use their models in real world situations.

In Chapter 6, 'Applied Policy, Welfare Economics and Mill's Half-Truths', Colander argues that that methodological guidance for applied economics has already been provided by J.S. Mill. He argues that the economics profession needs to return to Mill's earlier methodological approach, which held a strict separation between policy and theory and saw models as aids to judgment, not as definitive guides to policy. This chapter first examines how this traditional methodological view got lost in the development of economics in the twentieth century and then suggests how the understanding of this difference in methodology between the classical and modern approaches may affect economics policy training.

Chapter 7, 'A Failure to Communicate: the Fact–Value Divide and the Putnam–Dasgupta Debate', co-authored by Colander and myself, can be seen as an extension of the argument in Chapter 3 and an application of the Mill–Keynes approach to understanding some of the contemporary economic policy work. It is often believed by philosophers that the fact–value dichotomy has impoverished the ability of welfare economics to evaluate economic well-being and that it is impossible for economics to be free from ethical values. Hilary Putnam, for one, is a strong advocate for such a view. His view led to a long-lasting debate between him and Partha Dasgupta. By exploring and disentangling the debate between these two leading scholars, this chapter demonstrates that the so-called fact–value divide is a pseudo-problem in the Putnam–Dasgupta debate, and that there is much more agreement between good economists' methodology and philosophers' desired methodology than generally recognized.

Chapter 7 reiterates the argument in Chapter 6, and uses the works of Mill and J.N. Keynes to clarify the mixing up of the art–science distinction and the logical positivist fact–value dichotomy. In the Mill–Keynes tradition, the separation of applied economic policy analysis from the scientific branch of economics is meant to enhance the quality of the latter by improving the understanding of economic phenomena through adopting appropriate methods for the question at hand.

Chapter 8, 'Framing the Economic Policy Debate', analyses how the currently dominant frame of economic policy came to exist. It does so by examining the history of economics from the perspective of analytic technology. In doing so, Colander argues that the rise of the 'market failure' policy frame in the 1930s is highly related to the introduction of multivariate calculus into economic theory at the time.

The reason why modern microeconomics has been focused on analysing efficient allocation problems rather than other aspects of economic policy cannot be separated from the fact that the allocation problem can be easily portrayed as a LaGrangian constrained optimization problem. Looking in this light, Colander argues that the market success policy frame variants based either on Buchanan and Tullock's government failure policy frame or on Stigler and Coase's promarket policy frame are merely adjustments, not alternative frames to the market failure policy frame developed by Samuelson and Lerner. Moreover, given the analytic technology, the market failure frame was more teachable and better fit the evolving pedagogical needs of the economics profession at the time. After analysing how the rise and dominance of the market failure policy frame is tied to analytic technology, Colander suggests how the changing analytic technology can open up the possibility for movement away from the market failure policy frame.

As the economics profession evolved, Colander's thinking of methodology also has evolved. While the core ideas in Colander's methodology have remained mostly the same over the decades, new elements have been added in response to the recent development in economics. Chapter 9, 'Complexity Economics and Workaday Economic Policy', brings Colander's reasoning to his latest framework which emphasizes the importance of explicitly recognizing the economy's complexity within economics and within economic methodology. Colander argues that a complexity evolutionary framework will supplement the Walrasian general equilibrium framework for thinking about policy. That change is not dependent on a paradigm shift, because the policy framework is not dependent on the existing scientific paradigm in economics.

In Colander's view the tendency of methodologists and economists to think of economic policy as a direct application of economic science has made them miss the importance of the complexity revolution, which currently is a much greater revolution for policy than it currently is for science. The standard argument is that since complexity is not ready to become the new paradigm in economics, it has few implications for applied policy. For many economists, the story about complexity economics ends here. Colander challenges this common view shared by economists. He argues that once one recognizes that applied policy is engineering, rather than direct application of science, the importance of the complexity revolution is clear. Thus, the complexity framework still can free applied policy analysis from the Walrasian general equilibrium paradigm because in that complexity framework abstract theory has little direct relevance to workaday economics. This article also shows how the acceptance of complexity framework can supplement the standard allocation policy with formation policy, a set of policies designed to influence the ecostructure within which individuals operate. It uses distribution policy as an example to demonstrate the difference between complexity policy and the standard policy.

Part III: Methodology for macroeconomics
For Colander, the complexity vision is applicable to both microeconomics and macroeconomics. However, accepting this vision means that the appropriate methodology for each is different. Given the dominance of the current general equilibrium paradigm, the complexity vision has particular importance for macroeconomic policy. Unlike in micro, where the general equilibrium models are applicable to certain problems, in macro the dynamic complexity of the macro economy makes it next to impossible for economists to capture the macro economy with precise formal models. It follows that the attempt to develop specific general equilibrium theories to predict how macro economy works is doomed to fail. Nevertheless, this does not mean that economists cannot develop applied macro theories. It only means that their applied theories will be highly limited and ad hoc. Thus, when discussing macro theory, economists should make it clear that they are talking about heuristic theories and not presenting their models as pure scientific theories.

Chapter 10, 'The Macrofoundations of Micro', discusses a methodological perspective that Colander calls a 'macrofoundations-of-micro' perspective, a then newly emerging perspective when the article was published in 1993 for the first time. By perspective or vision, Colander means 'a way of putting reality together'. This perspective can be seen as a reverse of the microfoundations-of-macro perspective, the dominant approach in macroeconomics since 1970s. The basic premise of the old perspective was that if an aggregate model were to assume any individual behavior, that behavior had to follow from a microeconomic choice theoretic framework. In contrast, the new perspective maintains that before there is any hope of undertaking meaningful micro analysis, one must first determine the macro context within which that micro decision is made, as well as the micro context for macro results.

More than twenty years after the article was written, the arguments in this chapter remain relevant to today's economics, especially with the rise of complexity economics. Between these two perspectives, it is the macrofoundations-of-micro perspective that fits better with the complexity vision of economy. In the past, economists used to perceive the economy as a mechanical system consisting of homogeneous atomic individuals. In such a system, the aggregate properties at the macro level was simply the adding-up of the properties of individuals at the micro level; there is no qualitative transformation from micro to macro. It follows that as long as we understand micro, macro can be understood with the same logic. But in recent years, more and more economists started to accept that emergent phenomena at the macro level generated by the interaction of individuals cannot be approached by the traditional microfoundations-of-macro perspective. This has significant implications for the way in which rationality is thought about; all rationality becomes context dependent. Although placed in Part III on the methodology for macro, this chapter also has implications to the methodology of micro. It argues that the macrofoundations-of-micro perspective should complement the microfoundations-of-macro perspective. In so doing, not only the way macro is done will change, but also the way micro is thought about, since much of what economists currently teach as micro is outside of its macro context, and hence missing important complexity that creates a non-removable systemic uncertainty.

Colander has called his complexity interpretation of macroeconomics *Post Walrasian macroeconomics*, where by Post-Walrasian he means work that comes after Walrasian economics and that takes the complexity of the economy seriously, rather than assuming it away. He has written a number of articles and edited two books on Post Walrasian macroeconomics. The first edited volume (1996) focuses on outlining the problems with the Walrasian agenda; the second one (2006) goes further to specify a positive program that constitutes a Post Walrasian macro research agenda.

Chapter 11, 'Post Walrasian Macro Policy and the Economics of Muddling Through', is one of Colander's early writings on how an acceptance of Post Walrasian economics would significantly change the focus of macro policy discussions. In this chapter, Colander makes a contrast of what he calls 'muddling through' approach to policy in Post Walrasian economics with the traditional 'economics of control' approach to policy based in Walrasian economics. The two differ in how they relate theory to policy. The muddling through approach is a search for rules of thumb that work temporarily in a specific institutional environment since no universally agreed-upon model of the economy is available in Post Walrasian economics. It is essentially a pragmatic exploration of better, not optimal, policy in the environment in which policy makers do not know the underlying outcome-generating mechanism of the economy. In contrast, Walrasian economics assumes infinitely bright policy makers who face a full information environment. Hence, it is possible for them to take the economics of control approach, that is, a precise calculation of optimal policy by maximizing a social welfare function subject to constraints. Colander argues that, by moving from the latter to the former, economists will change the way they apply models to real problems and will be able to broaden the goals of policy from efficiency to distribution.

The financial crisis of 2008 led to significant criticism of contemporary economics and of the economics profession. Many people were asking and trying to answer why economics has failed to warn us. Paul Krugman in a well-known *New York Times Magazine* article 'How Did Economists Get It So Wrong?', suggested that Classical economists were blinded by the beauty of mathematics, and that Keynesian economics is the path of the future. Chapter 12, 'How Economists Got It Wrong: A Nuanced Account', is Colander's response to Krugman's argument.

Colander argues that Krugman's story is too black and white. He argues that the evolution of economic thinking is much more nuanced than Krugman portrays it. According to Colander, the systematic failure of the economics profession is closely related to their belief that the complexity of real-world economy can be captured by a unified model. In his view, both New Classical economics and Neo Keynesian economics suffer from that same problem of blending policy and theory, that is, using the conclusions of theoretical models as direct guides for policy precepts. It follows that what the economics profession needs to do is not to switch from New Classical economics to Keynesian economics as Krugman argues, but to return to the Classical tradition in the sense that it recognizes that the economy is a complex system and it is far too complex to be captured by any unified model. In this tradition, economists should not draw policy implications directly from models, including the most complex models. Models can be, at best, only rough guides to policy; they cannot determine policy.

Chapter 13, 'Economists, Incentives, Judgment, and the European CVAR Approach to Macroeconometrics', covers a wide range of issues discussed in this volume, including the institutional incentives for economists and the real forces behind the evolution of economic theories. By placing this article in Part III, we attempt to draw the attention of the reader to the contrast between the methodology of DSGE and the methodology that follows from a complexity view of macro – an empirically based co-integrated vector autoregression (CVAR) approach. Colander's argument that the data-first approach of CVAR is more reasonable than the theory-first approach of DSGE is forceful and needs to be taken seriously by anyone who believes that economic theories should not be detached from the reality as they currently are. In this chapter, Colander argues that doing good empirical work requires judgment that cannot be captured in the information normally reported in a published article and that if the CVAR approach doesn't get accepted as widely as DSGE, the reason is not that it isn't a better way to undertake macro policy analysis, but rather because it doesn't fit the current institutional structure of academic economics. The current structure tends to encourage publishing for career advancement, rather than understanding advancement, and the CVAR approach is less likely to lead to a 'publishable' article because it builds in the need for researcher judgment. For Colander, institutions guide methodological choices and can distort them from what an outside observer would say are reasonable ones. One can only understand a field's methodology if one understands the incentives built into its institutional structure.

Chapter 14, 'Beyond DSGE Models: Toward an Empirically Based Macroeconomics', is a joint article by Colander and four other well-known macroeconomists who share Colander's vision of how macro should be done. This short article was written as a type of Post Walrasian manifesto and presented at the American Economic Association meetings. It outlines the problems with current DSGE macro models and explains why having a complexity vision of the economy leads to a quite different way to do macro. It concludes by arguing that this new way of doing macro would be much more empirically based, following a data-first approach. It would use theory to interpret data rather than to guide and limit the search for data.

Part IV: Pragmatic methods for doing economics as a profession
The first three parts of the book deal with the methodology of doing economics relevant for both micro and macro. Part IV focuses on methodology in a broader sense. It sees methodology as embedded in the institutions of economics and argues that the only way to change economics is to change the institutions.

The development of economic theories and the economics profession has never been as simple as the story that the best always wins out. Some economists may genuinely be unaware of the problems of the methods they are using. But for most of them, sticking to what they are doing generally is the best choice for their professional career. They have no incentive to make changes to their practice as economists. After all, being an economist is not just about pursuing the truth or the best knowledge about the economic world. All individuals are driven by a blend of broad social goals and private individualistic goals. Institutions determine how that comes out. Changes will only come about through policies based on a deep understanding of those institutional structures which led to the current situation of the economics profession.

The occurrence of the financial crisis in 2008 gave many the hope that economics would change. Colander has never been one of them. He was pessimistic about the possibility of change because of his above institutional and sociological view regarding economics and the economics profession. After the financial crisis, Colander gave testimony at two different Congressional hearings for the House Science and Technology Committee. Chapter 15, 'Written Testimony of David Colander', is the second testimony, in which he tries to persuade those who have the power over economic research funding to make structural changes to economics professions. This chapter first explains how economists failed society in the financial crisis in 2008. Colander focuses on two causes: first, the problems of the DSGE model; and second, the way in which the DSGE model has been used in guiding policy: Each of these two points is discussed more extensively by chapters in Part III. Then the chapter turns to the main theme of Part IV – the role of institutional incentives in shaping the development of modern economics and how those institutional incentives can be changed. It explains how the success of the DSGE model came as the consequence of the existing institutional incentives. The chapter concludes with two proposals for the National Science Foundation to change the way funds are allocated to economic research.

Like all other institutions and systems, there are strong forces preventing the economics profession from making the enormous effort needed to overhaul itself. Before the external institutional environment changes, it would be unrealistic to expect that most economists would have incentives to adopt new methodology. Does that mean there is nothing individual economists can do? Colander believes that keeping up a constructive and effective conversation with economists in the inner circle is important. He considers the approach currently used by critics or economists who are outside the mainstream as an approach that will not resonate with the mainstream circle. In several articles, Colander suggests some pragmatic approaches for those who see themselves as heterodox economists in order to establish better lines of communication with the mainstream economists.

Chapter 16, 'Moving beyond the Rhetoric of Pluralism: Suggestions for an "Inside-the-Mainstream" Heterodoxy', is one of the articles with the goal stated above. In this chapter, Colander first points out how the approach used by many self-described heterodox economists stops dialog with mainstream economists. In its place he advocates that heterodox economists consider an alternative strategy, which he calls an inside-the-mainstream heterodoxy. According to Colander, the best of the mainstream group are open-minded to new ideas and he encourages heterodox economists to direct their arguments to this open-minded group. His position is grounded on a rule that 'the only ones who are allowed to break to the rules are those who have demonstrated a full command of them'. Colander makes it clear that his suggestions are not directed at all heterodox economists, but he hopes his approach will be considered by some of the younger heterodox economists as a pragmatic alternative to current heterodoxy.

The financial crisis in 2008 triggered the public's concern regarding not only the competence of economists in doing their job but also their integrity. From the movie, *Inside Job*, one gets the impression that economists are ethically challenged because they take payments for writing papers that say what the funders of their research want them to say. In the last chapter of this volume, 'Creating Humble Economists: A Code of Ethics for Economists', Colander takes issue with that view, and suggests that the more serious ethical problem of economics has to do with lack of humility. By this, Colander means that economists have a tendency to convey more scientific certainty in their policy positions than the theory and evidence objectively would support. Colander's solution to this is to see economists as engineers, rather than as applied scientists. His hypothesis is: if it is true that economics is essentially engineering, then a code of ethics for engineers should nicely translate into a code of ethics for economists. As a preliminary attempt, Colander arrives at a code of ethics for the economics profession by adopting the code of ethics for the National Society of Professional Engineers with a global change of the word 'engineer' to 'economist'. Colander argues that adopting a variation of an engineering code of ethics, which is an individual action oriented code, could create a professional ethic that is stronger and more inclusive than a code that deals with moral judgments such as 'opposing oppression' and 'giving voice to the needs and aspirations of the dispossessed'. Ultimately, Colander hopes that such a code will help to create humble economists.

Annotated bibliography and list of book reviews
The articles included in Parts I–IV should be seen as an introduction to, and a brief summary of, Colander's policy methodology. The ideas presented in them are further developed in other work. At the end of the book, I provide an Annotated Bibliography that can be used as a guide to further reading. In addition, there are other useful materials if the reader wishes to learn more about Colander's methodology. In some of his review essays, Colander made important arguments concerning methodological issues. Thus, I also include a list of book reviews by Colander which are relevant to the methodological issues discussed in this volume. Moreover, Colander has made a number of methodological points in his textbooks, especially in his principles text. His ongoing regular column 'Colander's Economics with Attitude' in the *Eastern Economic Journal* since 2013 is also a valuable source for those who are interested in keeping up with Colander's latest thinking about methodology. Each column is freely available on the website of the journal.

The richness in Colander's writing on economic methodology has inspired me to work on a book like this so that anyone who is interested in the methodology of economics would not miss his work and could approach it in a more systematic manner. Enthusiastic as I might be, I want to emphasize that the articles presented in this volume should be seen as a stepping stone, not a sorcerer's stone. Their role is to stimulate thought, not to provide final answers. Colander is comfortable with that. 'Pragmatic' and 'humble' are key concepts that characterize Colander's methodological prescriptions and also characterize his methodology. For him, ultimately, it is best to consider all methodology a heuristic that is to be judged only on its usefulness for the question at hand. That gives Colander's methodology its pragmatic sense. It is also humble – it doesn't try to answer deep questions nor does it pretend it could. Instead, it attempts to answer workaday questions that all economists face as they go about their work. More importantly, Colander sees that his approach must also be turned on itself; if everything is a heuristic, then so too is his methodology. It is not a deep truth, but simply a heuristic to be used when useful, and dumped when not.

Notes
1. In Colander's original writing, he contrasted engineering with applied science and argued that applied economics is engineering, not applied science. By applied science, he meant the application of scientific theories in the narrowest sense of application, that is only the theories derived from those methods which meet so-called scientific criteria can be applied to solving practical questions. In other words, methods like using judgments based on intuition or common sense are not legitimate methods. It is in this sense that Colander differentiated engineering from applied science. As this meaning of applied science is different from the daily loose use of the term by the public, and some engineers do see engineering as applied science but not science, I replace Colander's

own term 'applied science' with 'science' in this introductory chapter to avoid confusion. The reader should bear this in mind when they come across the term 'applied science' later in Colander's articles.

2.   In a broader sense, Colander, following Koen, argues that science also follows an engineering methodology, but that it is an engineering methodology with a specific sub-goal – to discover the truth. He describes scientific methodology as a set of heuristics that have developed to guide researchers searching for the 'truth' and engineering methodology as a set of heuristics that have developed to guide researchers searching for answer a problem. The specific heuristics will differ as the problems addressed differ.

References

Colander, D. (1991), 'Introduction', in his *Why Aren't Economists as Important as Garbagemen? Essays on the State of Economics*, Armonk, New York: Sharpe Publishing, pp. 3–16.

Colander, D. (ed.) (1996), *Beyond Microfoundations: Post Walrasian Macroeconomics*, Cambridge: Cambridge University Press.

Colander, D. (1997), Review of *Beyond Rhetoric and Realism in Economics: Towards a Reformulation of Economic Methodology* by Thomas A. Boylan and Paschal F. O'Gorman, London: Routledge, 1995, in *Economics and Philosophy*, **13** (1), 140–42.

Colander, D. (2005), 'The Future of Economics: The Appropriately Educated in Pursuit of the Knowable', *Cambridge Journal of Economics*, **29** (6), 927–41.

Colander, D. (ed.) (2006), *Post Walrasian Macroeconomics: Beyond the DSGE Model*, Cambridge: Cambridge University Press, pp. 46–69.

PART I

METHODOLOGICAL FRAMEWORK AND METHODOLOGY FOR ECONOMIC POLICY AS ART

[1]

WHY AREN'T ECONOMISTS AS IMPORTANT AS GARBAGEMEN?

David Colander

Say that all garbagemen got together and went on strike. What would the effect on society be? The answer is clear: Society would be a mess. Now say that all economists got together and went on strike. What would the effect on society be? Most people's answer would be, "None. Things would be just about the same with or without economists." Hence the question: Why aren't economists as important as garbagemen?

That rhetorical question sets up an unfair comparison. To contrast the two roles adequately, one would need to qualify the comparison in innumerable ways, but it does highlight economists' lack of a direct role in the everyday functioning of the economy.

Many of the articles in this issue discuss what economists' role is not. The Survey of Legislative Assistants and Stephen Quick's article point out that economists do not play a significant role in the development of laws; James Harasimow-icz's Survey of Economic Journalists points out that economists do not play a significant role in transmitting ideas to journalists. The article by Robert Zevin points out that, when economists appear as consultants, their role is often a cameo—their advice is used if it supports what the proponents want and totally ignored if it does not. Moreover, as discussed by Alfred Malabre and documented by Terry Plum, an entire movement in economics—supply-side economics—can develop, influence policy, and fade away with little or no input from economists. Put simply, economists are not directly involved in the functioning of the economy.

In this lack of direct involvement, economics differs from many other professions. For example, in the above comparison, were one to replace economists with doctors, lawyers, or engineers, one's answer would be different; although these groups are still not as directly important as garbagemen, they play a more integral role in the everyday functioning of society.[1]

Economists' role could be different; there are numerous more active roles economists could play. For example, they might follow the lawyer pattern and play

---

1. No value judgments are being made here about what type of role a group should play. Shakespeare may have been right: Society might be better off if lawyers played no role. My point is simply that if lawyers were eliminated, it would have an immediate effect on the economy; if economists were eliminated, it would not.

a "certification" role: Any law Congress passed that affected the economy and any decision business executives made that significantly affected the economy, such as plant closings or price changes, might require certification as "economically healthful" by a council of economic advisors. Thus, before a tax cut could be instituted or a major public works program begun, the proposals would need to be ruled upon by an independent economic judiciary.

A less-directly involved role might be modeled on doctors' or engineers' roles. If a doctor says you need an operation, you might get a second opinion, but if the two doctors concur, you are likely to have the operation. To some degree, this currently happens with economists, but, more often than not, economists' experience instead parallels that discussed by Zevin. Economists' specialized knowledge is used to support already decided-upon positions, is ignored, or is used in a "cover your backside" role.[2] Somehow, policymakers simply do not believe that economists' specialized knowledge is a necessary input into the decision-making process.

It is not surprising that economists are not perceived in the same light as doctors or lawyers. Whereas a majority of doctors and lawyers practice medicine and law, the majority of Ph.D. economists teach; few economists "practice" economics. This means that when doctors and lawyers teach, they are teaching how to "do" law and medicine; when economists teach, because they are not "doing" economics, what they teach is not necessarily determined by what economists do.

At many community colleges and less prestigious four-year colleges, where faculty are given course loads of four or five courses per semester, economists have no time for anything but teaching. At the more prestigious four-year colleges and at universities, that teaching function is complemented by a research function that takes as much, or more, of the economists' time as does their teaching. A "normal teaching load" is two to three classes meeting a total of three hours per week for two fifteen-week semesters. That is a total of 225 hours per year or about 4.5 hours per week with four weeks off for vacation. At research universities, teaching loads are about half that. Academic bureaucracy, course preparation, grading, and following the literature take varying amounts of time, but assuming economists devote twenty hours a week to these activities during the school year, at the higher level schools, economists can devote half their time to research. Economists' role in the functioning of society comes from this research.

When economists talk to other economists about their work, it is this research that they are talking about. Graduate schools are designed primarily to prepare economists to conduct this research, and economists' indirect influence on the policies and activities of government and business stems in large part from this

---

2. If an individual can argue to his boss that he relied upon the best (interpret "most expensive") advice, he cannot be blamed when things go wrong.

research. Considering the nature of this research clarifies why economists' role is indirect. Their research is basic, rather than applied, and even the applied research is generally presented in a form that is unintelligible to noneconomists; little or no interpretation is provided. Its effect on policy, if it has an effect, occurs through interpreters.

Focusing on basic research is not necessarily bad; nor does engaging in these pursuits mean that economists' role is smaller than other professionals. It does, however, make their role indirect. Keynes may well be right; economists' long-run indirect role may be of major importance for the economy: Monetary policy, fiscal policy, and the market itself are tombstones to earlier economists' scribblings. Economists' research has also provided an empirical basis that will underlie future policy changes and that limits others in their excessive claims for new policies. For example, although economists did not play a direct role in the supply-side revolution, their empirical work provided a counterweight to supply-side enthusiasm. Thus, economist-bashing is not in order.

Despite their successes, there is a lingering concern about the relevance of much of that research. When teaching others about a subject becomes the main activity of a profession, the subject matter can become more and more removed from what the profession is teaching about. The subject can become self-contained; it can lose its focus, and the research can become elaborate mind games designed to give students hoops to jump through and economists activities to keep them occupied, rather than contributing to our economic understanding. There are indications that this has happened in economics. The questions economists debate seem to many to be the modern-day equivalent of such scholastic questions as "God is omnipotent; can He create a rock so heavy He cannot lift it?" While debating these "important" questions, economists leave the "unimportant" questions of policy implementation to lawyers, politicians, and special interest groups.

Economists' role has not always been indirect. When economics began, teaching was a sideline; economists wrote for policymakers rather than for economists. Classical economists used contextual heuristic arguments that required a reader to bring to the reading of their work a sensitivity to institutions, politics, and moral considerations. They would make arguments that "made sense" to a normal lay reader and were designed to convince that reader.

As economics evolved in the nineteenth and twentieth centuries it moved away from the contextual argumentation that required the reader and writer to share a sense of the institutional framework and into noncontextual argumentation in which the assumptions and institutional framework of their argument were precisely spelled out. Economists came to wear two hats and used contextual or noncontextual arguments, depending on the audience. By the late 1960s, the formal techniques necessary to undertake the noncontextual arguments had become so great that younger economists were no longer being trained to know about real world institutions, a requirement if one is going to talk seriously about policy.[3]

Unless an economist has inherent or independently acquired abilities in communicating ideas to the outside world, becoming an economist is like joining a priesthood sworn to communicate only among its members. For economists, if one's arguments can be understood by outsiders they are obviously too simple; and if one's work has direct policy relevance, one must be doing something wrong.[4] With such beliefs, it is little wonder that economists are less important to the everyday functioning of the economy than are garbagemen.

Many economists, citing the reasons given above, argue that this separation between economists and the public is necessary. They argue that physicists and mathematicians are not required to communicate with the general public; why should economists? I agree with this argument for a small few in the profession, but there are many more economists than theoretical physicists, and most are not working on the borders of our understanding. Thus, in the case of the majority of economists, I disagree; their role should be similar to that of doctors or engineers. For them, communicating their research to the general public should be an important consideration.

ECONOMISTS' PERCEPTION OF THE ROLE IN SOCIETY

Economists do not play a more direct role because they have a fundamentally incorrect view of the nature of their role. In his article, Robert Heilbroner nicely captures the way economists view society. They are trained to be detached—to view themselves as outside the economy—looking down from above. From that perspective, they make judgments on how well the economy is functioning. This is in direct contrast to individuals who view society from their own perspective: When faced with a problem, most people ask, "How will it affect me?" Economists ask, "How will it affect society?" Economists see themselves as outside judges.

Placing any group in an outside position "judging society" is a dangerous undertaking. One is left with the problem: Who will judge the judges? Economists have taken this concern to heart and have worked hard at eliminating their own individualistic perspective and replacing it with "society's perspective." As Heilbroner argues, economics has not been totally successful in eliminating values from its analysis, but it has been partially successful.

---

3. In a survey of graduate students that Arjo Klamer and I did, three percent of the students thought institutional knowledge was important to getting on the fast track in economics; 68 percent thought it unimportant.

4. When Robert Lucas, a top theoretical macroeconomist, was asked what he would do if he were appointed chairman of the Council of Economic Advisors, he quipped, "I would resign."

Unfortunately, economists' Don Quixote-like quest for the ideological purity of a value-free perspective has come at a cost. In trying to achieve the impossible—avoiding all value judgments in their analysis—they have eliminated their direct role in policy.

In order to stay out of the fray, economists have retreated into pure theory and basic research, leaving others the "unimportant" role of interpreting the "pure theory" and applying the ideas to society. It is as if a judge, for fear of bringing his own, rather than the law's, perspective to a case, will decide only hypothetical cases.

Taking an outside perspective and attempting to remain value-free is wrong, but not, as Robert Heilbroner suggests, because it is impossible. The fact that it is impossible to be totally value-free does not mean that economists should not attempt to be as value-free as possible. It is wrong because it is too heavy a burden for any group to bear. Economists are not the judges of the economy; society is. Economists are inside society; their existence as a group reflects society's investment in protecting, modifying, and changing economic institutions.

Viewing economists from an inside perspective changes the nature of their role. They are not gods who have little need to communicate with policymakers; a bit of ideological impurity will not destroy their role. Their role is to study the economy and to present their conclusions (derived from maintaining as outside a perspective as possible) and to argue their case to the public as strongly as they can. If the public accepts it, fine; if not, that is also fine. Their work is simply one input into the decision-making process; it is not the final pronouncement. Recognizing this more limited role for economists is humbling for them, but it also frees them to take a more active direct role in policy formation without their current excessive concern that they might include some of their own value judgments in their prescriptions.

THE PROBLEM WITH AN OUTSIDE PERSPECTIVE

The problem of taking an outside perspective can be seen in economists' thinking about the economy. Taking an outside perspective, one is godlike and is led inevitably to one of two positions: that one should keep one's hands off society—laissez-faire—or that one should change society because one knows best. Both these positions are mistaken and do not capture the role economists should be playing in society.

Liberal economists have been willing to argue, generally implicitly, that they know best. Logically, this position cannot be held simultaneously with the position that individuals are rational and know best, but liberal economists do not push economic logic to extremes. They find room for new ideas and policy initiatives in economics even while using both the assumption of individual rationality and an "outside" perspective. But they can do so only by making logical jumps that conservatives delight in pointing out.

A few, generally conservative, economists push economic logic to its extremes and arrive at the conclusion that there is no room for economic policy. Examples of this reasoning pervade economics; they include some versions of the invisible hand theorem, aspects of the public choice literature, the Coase theorem, New Classical economics, and the efficient market hypothesis. What all these arguments have in common is that they lead to a laissez-faire policy prescription because economists begin with an assumption that individuals are rational and that whenever they can make a gain from trade they will. Economists then ask what possible role there might be for government intervention, which makes everyone better off than they would be on their own. Because any action worth doing would already have been done by rational individuals, given the assumption, the laissez-faire conclusion is preordained.

Now, I am not arguing that government intervention is good and laissez-faire bad. I am simply arguing that the laissez-faire conclusions and all the theorems and arguments associated with them are tautologically correct if the judge is viewing society from an "outside" perspective. They are also irrelevant. The arguments state no more than "what is, is."

To see why the outside perspective is wrong, consider a similar problem of perspective in making judgments about the ecological system. The ecological system is evolving. What role should humankind play in that evolution? The "outside" perspective places humankind outside of nature. From this outside perspective, if an animal or plant changes the environment, that is as it should be—nature's way. If humans change the environment—say, by devising a new chemical process—that is unnatural and, by implication, bad.

On a logical level, why should humans' actions be any less "natural" than animals' actions? If humans are unnatural, then they have been unnatural forever, and their actions, including domestication of plants and animals—agriculture, reading, and thinking—are unnatural. But were humans not to have taken such actions, society would not be what it is, and what we are calling natural would not exist. Relying on natural/unnatural categorization places humankind outside of nature when, in fact, men and women and their ways of dealing with life are as much part of the natural processes (whatever they are) as are animal, vegetable, and physical operations.

In order to undertake policy, actions must be divided into good actions and bad actions, but the division is not synonymous with the natural/unnatural division. All policy actions that humans suggest are not unnatural and therefore bad, but that is the logical conclusion that one inevitably arrives at if we use the "outside" rather than the "inside" perspective.

Because economists take an outside perspective, that same natural/unnatural dichotomy pervades economic terminology. They use terms such as "the natural rate of interest" and "the natural rate of unemployment" in much the same way that people use "natural food": as a way to convey that the phenomenon is as it should be. But just as is the case with ecology, the separation of actions into two sets, natural and unnatural, is not a helpful way of looking at society.

I am not arguing that the outside perspective should not be the economists'. I am simply arguing that in their analysis they must remember that they ultimately remain inside the economic system. Having decided what is best from their attempt at taking an outside perspective, they must play an inside role in implementing their proposals, convincing others that their policy proposals are good for society. Doing so is as much a part of the economists' function as providing an understanding of the economy. Unless economists convince society that their policy recommendations are best, their policy recommendations are not best. Economists cannot stand on any moral higher ground. Their ideas are as subject to the intellectual marketplace as lawyers' and politicians'.

The inside perspective avoids the logical problems of suggesting policy changes from an outside perspective. It answers the question of how, if individuals are doing everything in their power to make themselves as well off as possible, a policy government could implement could make people better off. From an inside perspective, laissez-faire policies cannot be deductively arrived at from the model. If laissez-faire were optimal, society would not have designated a group of people— economists—to study how to improve the economy. One might conclude that a laissez-faire policy is preferable, but it is a conclusion to be arrived at in comparison with other policies; it is not a priori.

From within, economists cannot say, on the basis of what is natural (or efficient) and what is not, "The government should, or should not, intervene." "This policy should be introduced." "This policy should not." In making judgments from an inside perspective, these criteria no longer pertain; there are no outside criteria to judge by. Efficiency is no longer an end in itself; it is simply one attribute of a policy that economists can use to convince policymakers of its desirability. Instead of stating that "this policy is best because it is more efficient," their arguments for a policy will be on the basis of the policy's effect on society. Their arguments will be more like: "This policy will change society in this way." "Here is what society will be like with this policy." "Here is what society will be like without this policy." Their arguments will include all aspects of a policy, including income distribution effects, administrative costs, and political feasibility.

CONCLUSION

Learning how to play this inside role would change the nature of economic education. Students would learn how to argue, how to write, and how to make contextual, as well as noncontextual, arguments. They would learn how to explain their ideas, how to modify theoretical notions, and how to make them fit into the political and social realities. Similarly, what the research economists do would change, and the pure research about the ''important'' questions would be supplemented by the research about the ''unimportant'' questions, such as what policy firms or government should undertake.

Changing perspective will not make economists more important than garbagemen. Garbagemen are naturally more important than most other groups in society. The change will, however, play a role in increasing economists' direct impact on society, not to the level of lawyers (God help us [society] should that happen), but perhaps to the level of doctors or dentists. Keynes once said, ''If some say we could manage to get ourself thought of as humble, competent people, on a level with dentists, that would be splendid.'' Changing to an inside perspective would be one small step for humility and competence. Whether that step will make society better off is debatable, but it will make economics a more meaningful profession.

2

Journal of Economic Methodology 1:1 1994

Vision, judgment, and disagreement among economists

David Colander

It is often said that if you laid all economists end to end, they still wouldn't reach an agreement. The implication of that and similar statements about economists is that there is too much disagreement among economists. I disagree; in my view, given the nature of the questions economists ask, significant disagreement is both to be expected and desirable.

Unfortunately, while I believe that the total amount of disagreement may be approximately the right amount, I also believe that the areas and reasons for disagreeing are often wrong. In my view, we often disagree about the things we should agree about, and agree about things we should disagree about.

For example, on the one hand, economists generally agree to use a mainstream model that, in my, and in many economists', view (even those who use it), does not relate to the real world, and embodies innumerable *ad hoc* assumptions. Here is an example in which more disagreement would seem warranted. On the other hand, economists spend enormous amounts of time disagreeing about what I consider relatively minor modeling issues – such as whether the Pigou effect logically exists, or what is the shape of the LM curve. I consider these relatively minor issues because the answer to them does not make a large difference to our policy advice.

The different models that economists use, and the different policies that economists recommend, are not dependent on minor modeling issues; they are dependent on differences in vision of how an economy operates, and in differences in judgments about how the political system would implement a policy, or on what effect the policy will have on existing institutions. But most economists' debate concerns minor issues of modeling. It is as if economists use disagreements about minor modeling issues to mask differences in vision and judgments about the dimensions of economic problems that cannot be precisely quantified.

ARTIPHOBIA

This fear of discussing differences in judgment and vision can be called

                                                    1350–178X

artiphobia. Economists have a fear of being considered artists, who use judgment and vision to come to a conclusion, rather than being considered scientists. Artiphobia shows up in many ways. One recent example is a 'slam sheet' on my introductory textbook prepared by a competing textbook author.[1] One of the major reasons why this competing author believed people should not use my book is that 'Colander takes a whimsical approach to principles. In his view economics is more art than science.'

Similar views of my treatment of J.N. Keynes' tripartite art/positive economics/normative economics distinction have been conveyed to me by economists who share my view that many of the differences among economists concern differences in judgment and vision, and not differences that can be captured in formal models. But they object to, or at least strongly discourage me from, using the term 'art' to capture that judgment and vision aspect of economics. They believe, probably correctly, that for me to tell economists that much of what they do is art will insure that my views will not be taken seriously. Actually, I have no problem with dropping the term art; labels are unimportant. I mention the reaction my treatment provokes because it helps explain the perverse nature of economists' disagreement; our disagreements are generally on matters of judgment about the relevance of models, not technical issues within those models. But such disagreements are not allowed to be expressed explicitly since they might be considered artistic disagreements. Instead, the disagreements get reflected in disagreements about models – disagreements that 'obviously' fall in science.

THE NEED FOR VISION AND JUDGMENT IN SELECTING AMONG *AD HOC* ASSUMPTIONS

To see what I mean about the importance of differences in vision in determining a theory, consider the economic problem in its full complexity: You have five billion people – all pursuing ends that are partially endogenously determined – interacting in a variety of institutional settings – using a large variety of differentiated inputs and ever-changing technologies – to arrive at some undetermined output. What will be the nature of that interaction, and what output will it lead to?

Faced with the problem of designing a core model of the aggregate economy to capture that interaction, imagine someone put the following propositions to someone:

1   That we forget about the multitude of inputs, and use a model with only two – capital, a fixed input, and labor, a variable input.
2   That we assume away technological complexities leading to infinitely varied adjustment costs and focus only on diminishing marginal returns.

3   That we use a representative agent approach to analyzing aggregate phenomena, eliminating questions of strategic interdependence.
4   That we talk about money as a fixed concept, even though we're not sure which of the constantly changing empirical measures of money to use.
5   That we assume, for the sake of analytic convenience, that tastes are exogenous.
6   That, again for the sake of analytic convenience, we assume a simple utilitarian psychological basis for our analysis of individual decision making.
7   That when talking about the aggregate economy we aggregate up millions of different goods into an aggregate output concept, and that we can assume technical efficiency of the aggregate production function.
8   That we assume costs of rationality are zero, and people can make rational decisions intertemporally and across the full domain of goods.
9   That we can assume a unique aggregate equilibrium.

I could continue with this list, but the list I have just given should be sufficient to make my point. Given the complexity of the problem to be solved, disagreement, in the sense of diversity of research programs, should be expected.[2] That isn't what one sees. While there are small pockets of non-mainstream critics – such as Institutionalists, Post Keynesians, Austrians, and Radicals – the large majority of the profession makes up an almost hegemonic research program in which most researchers accept the broad outlines of assumptions, and then modify one or another slightly or ask questions that can be structured within the standard model.

I believe the reason we don't see major disagreements is that such disagreements would involve differences in vision and judgment. The guiding light in choosing among assumptions cannot be pure logic – the decisions are too complicated for formal logic. Instead one must rely on vision to choose that combination of simplification and admission of complexity – the *ad hoc* assumptions – that produces a model that leads to relevant insights, and that is convincing to others. Yet there is almost no discussion of disagreement about economists' vision.

The evolution of the Keynesian revolution is a case in point. There were many ways in which the Keynesian challenge to neoclassical economics could have been structured; it could have been seen as a vision fundamentally different from the Classical vision – one involving multiple aggregate equilibria, strategic interdependence, and dynamic path dependency. The way it was structured was within a unique aggregate equilibrium framework in which the only difference between Keynesian and Classical was a fixed nominal wage assumption. This meant that Keynesian economics was simply a special case of the Classical model. All the disagreements between Keynesians and Classicals were forced to be placed in this fixed wage framework, and thereby many of the issues raised by the Keynesian revolution were trivialized. Why? Because structuring the question this way made it fit a relatively simple model, whereas other frameworks raised far more fundamental questions.

THE NEED FOR JUDGMENT IN CHOOSING AMONG POLICIES

The policy debates, similarly, involve disagreements on issues that are not central to the reasons the profession disagrees. In policy, the true debate generally relates to judgments about non-quantifiable effects. Yet, economists' debate about policy is generally formulated in terms of applied models and empirical specification. For example, we see that most economists' discussion of economic policy focuses on efficiency and on quantifying 'efficiency'. But efficiency is not an end in itself; it is not even a meaningful concept except as a description of achieving some other goal. The implicit assumption used in economics is that more consumption – higher standards of living – makes people happier, with little discussion of how that 'more consumption' leads people to be happier, or what problems that might involve, or whether the process of fulfilling these desires creates further desires.

Let me give a specific example. One of the most powerful economic policy arguments I have seen lately is made by Charles Murray. Murray, who is not an economist, used standard economic arguments to argue that public welfare is bad for people because it destroys the social fabric of society. He reasoned that, given current US institutions, because people do not have to face the consequences of their actions – having to feed their children, for example – the number of unwed mothers has increased significantly, and will continue to increase. Eventually, he argued, the institution of the family will be destroyed. Many economists agree in part with Murray's argument, but discussions about the effect of public welfare on the structure of the family have not filled the economists' journals because the argument cannot be quantified and placed in a formal model. How does one specify the 'efficiency' of the family? More generally, institutions cannot be easily modeled so they are typically left out of economists' models.

Resolving questions about assumptions and on differences in judgment has little to do with formal empirical tests as economists usually conduct them. As Thomas Mayer (1993), and Edward Leamer (1978, 1991) have convincingly argued, given the nature of observation in economics, empirical tests at this level are inevitably indecisive. Numerous theories and judgments can be interpreted as consistent with the data.

One example of the way in which statistics are used can been seen in a recent study of the effect of the social security system on savings rates. Martin Feldstein (1974) published a study in a major economic journal providing empirical support for his position that the existence of an unfunded social security system in the US was significantly decreasing the savings rate. Two researchers (Leimer and Selig 1982) tried to replicate his study, but could not. It was found that a data input error had led to the result, and that, when that error was corrected, Feldstein's model showed that the unfunded social security system had a positive, not a negative, effect on the savings rate! Did this result cause Feldstein to change his policy proposals? No. Instead he redid his empirical study, adjusting the model, and came out with a slight negative effect of social security on the savings rate.

The point of this example is not that a data input mistake was made, although as Dewalt *et al.* (1986) have shown, such mistakes happen relatively often. The point is the way in which 'empirical evidence' is used. To structure a model that will capture the effect of social security on the savings rate, enormous *ad hoc* assumptions must be made to develop the data. These *ad hoc* assumptions make it impossible for the empirical analysis to be definitive. Feldstein knew that, and he, correctly, did not change his policy position when the data input error was found. His policy position was based on a much broader combination of vision and judgment. But in the study he did not make his argument based on that vision and judgment; instead a position based on judgment was translated into formal empirical evidence that looked scientific and definitive, but was not and could not be.

Admitting that most policy conclusions are arrived at by a combination of judgment, vision, formal and informal empirical evidence, and a knowledge of history and institutions, has a cost; it raises what might be called the 'expert question'. Why should policy makers, or anyone, rely on economists' judgment rather than someone else's? I believe the answer to this question should be the following: One should rely on economists' judgment because they have studied the history and the institutions and have training in interpreting the empirical evidence. This training in judgment makes them better qualified than most other people to offer advice on policy, and, when one understands the economists' reasoning, it will be more convincing than other people's reasoning. The answer to which the current structure of the profession directs economists is that the mantle of science legitimizes economists' policy pronouncements. Instead of admitting that policy decisions must be made on informed judgment, and that judgment is best left to experts, the economics profession has chosen to look impressive, and to try to 'snow' policy makers.

INSTITUTIONS, ECONOMISTS, AND DISAGREEMENT

Economists are not born with artiphobia; it is bred into them through selection mechanisms, limiting who becomes an economist and who advances as an economist, and through constant institutional reinforcement. Thus, the artiphobia explanation of the perverse nature of economists' disagreement is only a surface explanation. To explore beneath that surface and explain why this perversity of agreement exists, one must explore the incentives in the academic institutional environment within which economists operate.

I believe that institutional structure channels their self-interested behavior into what might be called microdisagreements – disagreements that don't really matter – and away from macrodisagreements – disagreements about core issues – which would significantly change their analysis. The reason is that the microdisagreements avoid the appearances of an art, whereas macrodisagreements would be considered directly as differences in judgment and thus would fall into what I have classified as an art.

AN ECONOMIC APPROACH TO AGREEMENT

To see my argument about how and why institutions reinforce economists' artiphobia, it is useful to consider the question of agreement and disagreement among economists within an economic framework. In this framework there are costs and benefits to agreeing and to disagreeing. Individuals weigh those costs and benefits and choose their optimal private level of disagreement. When it is in a person's interest to agree, he or she agrees, even if what he or she is agreeing about is quite intuitively disagreeable and far fetched. And, when it is in a person's interest to disagree, he or she disagrees, even if the disagreement is about something relatively small. Thus the institutional structure that determines the costs and benefits of agreeing is central to an understanding of the nature of disagreement in economics.

The recent round of GATT talks provides an example of this economic cost–benefit analysis of agreement and of the importance of institutional structure. These GATT talks dragged on interminably, with the same issues being discussed over and over again. They went on two years longer than planned. Why the continued disagreement? Clearly part of the reason has to do with the contentiousness of the issues involved. But the economic approach to agreement directs one to consider the incentives created by the institutional structure: What were the costs and benefits of agreeing and disagreeing?

To answer that question, consider where the talks were held: in the pleasant surroundings of Geneva over expensive meals. Given these surroundings, the benefits of disagreeing to the participants were high, and the costs were low; the economic approach suggests that the disagreement would be continued as long as possible. Had those talks taken place in Buffalo in winter (and all the excellent restaurants in Buffalo had been closed down), the GATT talks would have come to a quick resolution.

GATT, of course, is as much about political as it is about economic agreement. But the issues are the same for any economic issue, be it one of theory or of policy. People agree and disagree when it is in their interest to do so, and the institutional structure within which they operate determines their interest.[3]

The statement that agreement depends on the costs and benefits of agreeing is, as is much economic analysis, logically correct, but empirically vacuous, in the sense that it simply pushes the analysis back to what determines the costs and benefits. Thus in no way am I arguing that the economic approach is sufficient. The economic approach simply provides a framework of analysis that is useful in the same way that Arabic numerals are useful: One can build an elegant, logically correct system of analysis around them which sheds more light than would an analysis built around some other number system, such as the Roman system. Similarly with economic analysis.

INCENTIVES FOR AGREEMENT AND DISAGREEMENT

What the economic approach does is to direct us to look at how institutions structure the incentives for agreement and disagreement of economists. How will agreeing or disagreeing on an issue help an economist achieve his or her goals within the institutional framework where he or she operates?

The institutional framework within which academic economists operate is one of tenure and quantitative publication requirements based upon rankings of journals. Advancement in the profession depends on publication. It follows that if a disagreement can be stated and resolved in print, it is much more valuable for the participants than if that same disagreement is settled elsewhere. For example, there is little incentive for one economist to call up another with whom he or she disagrees, and try to work out the disagreements over the phone. Thus, there is much disagreement based on misinterpretation. This interpretative disagreement could be relatively easily resolved by letter, or by phone, but instead it fills the pages of journals with models which are not getting at the true nature of the disagreement.

One of the most insightful pieces in economics that I have seen was Arjo Klamer's *Conversations with Economists (1984)*. In that book Klamer published his interviews with various top macroeconomists, asking questions about debates New Classicals were having with Keynesians. What was amazing to me about these conversations was how little effort was made by these economists to actually specify the precise nature of their agreement and disagreement with their 'opponents'. Often one side's view of the arguments was quite different than another side's. Each side had a caricature of the other side, and it debated that caricature, not the other side. The only serious interaction among these competing sides occurred in formal journal articles, and that required maintaining a caricature of the other side. No serious attempt was made to resolve the differences efficiently. The economic approach to agreement explains this phenomenon; discussing the issues privately would have reduced private benefits of disagreement.

A second way in which the academic institutional structure influences the nature of the disagreement among economists is that it focuses that disagreement on technical and formal empirical issues, and away from issues of judgment. Technical and empirical disagreements look more impressive, and can generate more 'resolvable disputes'. The problem with disputes in judgment and vision are that they are unresolvable in articles. Thus, self-interest channels disagreement away from disagreement of judgment and vision, and toward 'resolvable disputes' about technical matters.

The publication institutions are not structured for major disagreements about assumptions – they are much more structured for definable disagreements, given the major assumptions. Such technical and empirical disputes have another advantage; since they do not resolve the issue, they leave open the possibility of re-examining the issue again and again, creating more grist for articles leading to tenure and promotion. One of the most telling remarks was made to me by an extraordinarily bright, but relatively unknown, Oxford economist who combined judgment with technical expertise. When I asked him why he wasn't better known he said that it was because when he tackled a subject, he answered it to the degree it could be answered; thus, his work stopped research in a topic.

Let me give an example of the profession's proclivity to avoid fundamental disputes, an example that involves the use of macroeconometric models. In 1972 Robert Basmann (1972) strongly condemned the structure and use of macroeconometrics in general, and the Brookings model in particular, arguing that it was pretending to be something that it wasn't and that it lacked a scientific basis. This was a challenge to the major assumptions. His critique was essentially ignored. Reflecting on Basmann's criticism, Lawrence Klein *et al.* (1991) again dismissed Basmann's critique, reiterating Fromm and Klein's (1972) statement that if one 'took Basmann's critique seriously, inductive science must perish' (p. 79). This is one of many examples. A disagreement that cuts to the core is ignored, not because it may or may not be correct, but because the institutional structure strongly discourages such major disagreements.[4]

WHY ARTIPHOBIA DEVELOPED

The institutions that determine the incentives for agreement and disagreement are not *ad hoc*. They have developed for reasons and, if they work effectively, they should be designed to create incentives so that disagreements are optimally resolved. But there is no reason why one should expect optimal institutions to develop, and there is a strong reason why one should expect that suboptimal institutions will develop. The reasoning that supports me here is similar to the reasoning that public choice theorists use in explaining why government spending programs become too large.

The costs and benefits of developing institutions tend to reflect the needs of individuals within the institutions, rather than the needs of society. The reason is that the benefits of creating institutions, while overall large, are broadly distributed and small on a societal per-person basis, but are relatively large on a per-person basis for the individuals who work within those institutions. Thus, as a general rule, institutions develop that have, from society's point of view, incentives that direct people's private interest away from society's interest. This might be called The Theorem of Perverse Institutions.

Academic economic institutions are more perverse than most institutions because they were designed around a technology that did not pan out. In the 1950s it was believed that econometrics was going to provide a technological change that would transform the nature of disagreement among economists by providing definitive tests of theories. Much of the modern structure of economic argumentation and methodology that I find perverse was designed around that belief. That methodology directed researchers toward highly formal analysis – structured in a way that would be susceptible to empirical tests. Incoming economists were taught what might be called 'classical econometric intuition'. They were taught to replace their own intuition with a refined intuition based on econometric empirical tests. They were taught to limit arguments to those susceptible, at least in principle, to formal econometric testing, and to structure arguments in a formal way so that eventually they can be resolved by empirical testing.

Unfortunately, econometric testing has proven far less definitive than was initially hoped. Dealing with this failure has been difficult for the economics profession. The institutional incentives in the profession are to base your argumentation and analysis on this econometric testing, and not on debatable judgment and sensibility. Yet, most of the issues at debate concern judgment and sensibility, and are not susceptible to formal empirical tests. The problems this creates are predictable. When industry has designed its structure around a technology, and that technology doesn't pan out, there will inevitably be serious problems.

INSTITUTIONAL SCREENING EFFECTS

Another way in which the institutional structure has played a role in structuring the nature of disagreement in the profession is in its effect on the personality of the individuals within the profession. In this world there are contentious people who will make big challenges, and there are uncontentious people who will focus their energies more narrowly. Similarly, there are people who excel in broad vision, and judgment, and those who excel in more technical areas. The screening process that selects which people go into a field, and which do not, plays a big role in determining the nature of agreement and disagreement in a profession.

Currently, the economic profession's institutional screening process channels a particular type of individual into economics, and that, I believe, is another reason why disagreements in economics take the form that they do.

Consider the following four candidates applying for a top graduate economics program:

Candidate A1: an economics major – a bright generalist. GPA – 3.9; GREs: math – 740; English – 760; two courses in calculus and one in statistics; wide range of extracurricular activities. Relatively uncontentious; he generally goes along.

Candidate A2: an economics major – a bright generalist. GPA – 3.9; GREs: math – 740; English – 760; two courses in calculus and one in statistics; wide range of extracurricular activities. Relatively contentious; she challenges everything.

Candidate B1: a physics major. GPA – 3.9; GREs: math – 790; English – 620; minors in both mathematics and economics; seven courses in math; few extracurricular activities. Relatively uncontentious; she generally goes along.

Candidate B2: a physics major. GPA – 3.9; GREs: math – 790; English – 620; minors in both mathematics and economics; seven courses in math; few extracurricular activities. Relatively contentious; he challenges everything.

All four of these candidates are what I would consider excellent candidates. A strong profession would be made up of a combination of the four types; their interaction and disagreement would strengthen the profession. Unfortunately, the current institutional structure does not bring such disagreement among these four types about for two reasons. The first reason has to do with the probability of acceptance.

My reading of the current selection process used in top graduate schools is that Candidates B1 and B2 have a higher chance of getting into a top graduate program with financial support. That, of course, depends on who is on the selection committee, and, generally, I believe that the 'A' candidates can get into a top school if they have strong undergraduate faculty support. Specifically, I would suspect that with some phone calls, some strong letters of recommendations, and some luck in who is on the selection committee, both the A candidates could get in, and possibly could get financial support. Still, there is a bias toward B type candidates; they are the ones most graduate schools would prefer because they are the ones most likely to excel initially.

Let us now consider the choice from the candidates' side.

Candidates A1 and A2 are most likely have a wide range of choices in business, in law, or in business school. Their choices may narrow down to something like the following: (1) a $45,000 job on Wall Street with significant opportunities to be challenged; (2) law school without support, but with high earning expectations in the future; and (3) a Ph.D. economics program for which they may have barely obtained financial support, and in which it is almost assured that they will have an extraordinarily difficult time in their first two years. Given these opportunity costs, very few of type A candidates will choose economics, and of those that choose it, type A1 candidates are more likely to choose it and stay with it through the first two years than are type A2 candidates.

The choices facing type B candidates will likely be quite different. They may be choosing between a graduate physics program and a graduate economics program. Of these two they will probably see the graduate physics program as the intellectually more challenging, but may be enticed by a higher level of financial support to go into economics. Type B1 candidates are more likely to choose economics than are B2 types; in physics one is asking questions about the nature of matter, and the sky is no limit. The subject matter of economics is tame relative to physics.

A few type A2 and B2 candidates will get their Ph.D.s. They, however, will likely be weeded out of academic careers at the two-year, four-year, or six-year review stage of the tenure process, which gives highest weight to work that exhibits technical mastery, and not to policy issues related to judgment. Any economist who really tries to challenge the underlying foundations of the assumptions will almost assuredly be weeded out. Major contributions take gestation time and the tenure and promotion system in academic economic institutions does not allow such long gestation periods.

The result of this selectivity bias is that the interaction among the various types of students never materializes. Type B1 candidates predominate in the profession, and the approaches that are used are not challenged by the contentious generalists or contentious mathematically inclined students. This selection system causes the institutional structure to be self reinforcing, and brings about the current state of affairs in the profession. I am known as a critic of graduate school; a major reason I am is that its screening weeds out individuals that I believe the profession needs.

CONCLUSION

The economics profession is not in a crisis. It is simply in a slow decline, as is suggested by the declining number of US citizens receiving Ph.D.s in economics over the last twenty years. Eventually, the problems in the profession will cause the current institutional structure to break down, or to change, to better accommodate disagreement in judgment. But any change is unlikely to occur anytime soon.

Nonetheless, the current institutional structure of the profession has short-run costs. To be sincere in one's disagreements, as I believe economists are, and simultaneously to hide the true nature of the disagreement requires a certain detachment from the analysis. Hiding the true nature of the disagreement makes it impossible to arrive at intuitively satisfying resolutions to debates. Moreover, it makes the resulting research less valuable than it could be.

Another effect of the institutional structure in the profession is that it strongly discourages disagreement based on judgment and sensibility, where much of the disagreement about economic theory and policy resides, and that it encourages economists to surround themselves with like-minded economists, rather than encouraging interaction and debate with economists who have differing sensibilities and judgments. This leads to geographical pockets of agreement.

For example, in a survey asking students their views on the statement: 'Can fiscal policy be an effective tool in stabilizing policy?' only 6 percent of Chicago students agreed with the statement; 60 percent of Yale students strongly agreed with it. Or alternatively, 70 percent of the Chicago students strongly agreed with the proposition that a minimum wage increases unemployment among young and unskilled workers; only 15 percent of Harvard students strongly agreed to that. On a third issue, 84 percent of Chicago students strongly agreed with the proposition that inflation is primarily a monetary phenomenon; 7 percent of MIT students strongly agreed. This clustering of agreements strongly suggests that the interchange of ideas is not taking place, and that empirical work is not eliminating the disagreement.

It is my belief that a more open treatment of the reasons for disagreement would encourage discussions to proceed beyond formal empirical testing, and focus more on informal evidence. This more open treatment of reasons for disagreement would accept that evidence will often be limited or inconclusive, and that much disagreement is likely. But it would lead to more precise statements of where and why economists disagree, and to more intuitively satisfying states of, if not resolutions to, debates.

Middlebury College

NOTES

1   A slam sheet is a list of reasons a professor should not use a competitor's book. Slam sheets are not compiled by most textbook authors; most prefer to highlight the strengths of their book. They are compiled by a few textbook authors whose egos and incomes are significantly intertwined with their own introductory books.

2   The competition among these competing paradigms need not be based on disagreement as much as on following different leads. By that I mean that a group considers the choices made by the other group legitimate, and complementary to their own approach.

3   The economic model of disagreement and the above discussion of the private costs and benefits of disagreeing cannot be applied to a 'representative agent' model of economists. The reason is that there is a distribution of optimal disagreement in a field. The overall amount of disagreement depends on the character, independence of thought, personality, training, and ability of economists. An individual's optimal amount of disagreement depends on the total amount of agreement in the field. When most economists agree, there are enormous gains to be had in disagreeing. Thus, the odd contrarian can do very well for him or herself.

4   Part of the reason for this dismissing of fundamental critiques is the legitimate need to get on with what one is doing. In 1972, perhaps temporarily dismissing Basmann's critique made sense – in the hope that future work would show the attributes of the chosen path. But in 1992, to continue to ignore such criticisms, in spite of the failure of many econometric models, suggests a problem in the profession.

REFERENCES

Basmann, R.L. (1973) 'The Brookings quarterly econometric model: science or number mysticism?' and 'Arguments and evidence in the Brookings-S.S.R.C. philosophy of econometrics', respectively, chapters 1 and 3 in K. Brunner (ed.) *Problems and Issues in Current Econometric Practice*, College of Administrative Science, Ohio State University, Columbus, Ohio.

Bodkin, Ronald G., Klein, Lawrence R. and Marwah, Kanta (1991) *A History of Macroeconometric Model-Building*, Aldershot: Edward Elgar.

Dewalt, William, Thursby, Jerry and Anderson, Richard (1986) 'Replication in economics: the *Journal of Money, Credit and Banking* project', *American Economic Review* 76 (September): 587–603.

Feldstein, Martin (1974) 'Social security, induced retirement and aggregate capital accumulation', *Journal of Political Economy* 83(5) (Sept./Oct.): 905–26.

Fromm, G. and Klein, L.R. (1972) 'The Brookings econometric model: a rational perspective', in K. Brunner (ed.) *Problems and Issues in Current Econometric Practice*, College of Administrative Science, Ohio State University, Columbus, Ohio.

Klamer, Arjo (1984) *Conversations with Economists*, Totowa, NJ: Rowman and Allanheld.

Klamer, Arjo and Colander, David (1990) *The Making of an Economist*, Boulder, Co.: Westview Press.

Klein, L. *et al.* (1991) 'Lessons from half a century of macroeconomic modelling', in R.G. Bodkin, L.R. Klein and K. Marwah *A History of Macroeconomic Model-Building*, Aldershot: Edward Elgar.

Leamer, Edward (1978) *Specification Searches: Ad Hoc Inferences with Non-experimental Data*, New York: John Wiley.

—— (1991) 'Let's take the con out of econometrics', *American Economic Review* 73 (March): 31–43.

Leimer, Dean and Selig, D. Lesnoy (1982) 'Social security and private saving: new time-series evidence', *Journal of Political Economy* 90 (3) (June): 606–29.

Mayer, Thomas (1993) *Truth vs. Precision in Economics*, Aldershot: Edward Elgar.

3

Journal of Economic Perspectives—Volume 6, Number 3—Summer 1992—Pages 191–198

Retrospectives
The Lost Art of Economics

David Colander

This feature addresses the history of economic words and ideas. At a minimum, the hope is to deepen the workaday dialogue of economists. At best such discussion may cast new light on ongoing questions. If you have comments or criticisms about this column or suggestions for future topics or authors, please write to Joseph Persky, c/o Journal of Economic Perspectives, Department of Economics (M/C 144), The University of Illinois at Chicago, Box 4348, Chicago, Illinois 60680.

Introduction

Economists generally divide economics into two distinct categories—positive and normative—but how applied economics fits within these categories is unclear. This paper argues that applied economics belongs in neither normative nor positive economics; instead it belongs in a third category—the art of economics. Currently, many economists are trying to use a methodology appropriate for positive economics to guide their applied work, work that properly belongs in the art of economics.

This three-part distinction is not mine, but dates back to a classic book, *The Scope and Method of Political Economy* (1891) by the father of John Maynard Keynes, John Neville Keynes. What is particularly ironic about losing the art of economics is that it was lost while in plain sight. By that I mean that in the United States at least, the entrenchment of the positive/normative distinction

■ *David Colander is Professor of Economics, Middlebury College, Middlebury, Vermont.*

dates back to Milton Friedman's (1953) "Methodology of Positive Economics," where Friedman cites J. N. Keynes as his reference for the positive/normative distinction. But Friedman actually quotes J. N. Keynes' discussion of a *three-part* distinction. Friedman writes (p. 3):

> In his admirable book on *The Scope and Method of Political Economy*, John Neville Keynes distinguishes among "a positive science ...a body of systematized knowledge concerning what is; a normative or regulative science ...a body of systematized knowledge discussing criteria of what ought to be...; an art ...a system of rules for the attainment of a given end;" comments that "confusion between them is common and has been the source of many mischievous errors"; and urges the importance of "recognizing a distinct positive science of political economy."

Friedman's essay (and most post-Friedman economic methodological work) discusses the methodology appropriate for positive economics. But using Keynes' tripartite division, most economists' work does not belong in positive economics. If one accepts Keynes' three-part division, Friedman's and most subsequent methodological discussions are not relevant to a major portion of economists' work. Friedman placed Keynes' tripartite distinction in the open and then he lost it.[1]

In his book, Keynes argued that economists' failure to distinguish the art of economics as a separate branch from positive and normative economics would lead to serious problems. One hundred years later, he has turned out to be clairvoyant.

Science, Art, and Applied Economics

Keynes placed his discussion of the art of economics under the heading "Applied Economics" (p. 55). According to Keynes, positive economics is the study of what is and the way the economy works; it is pure science, not applied economics. Normative economics is the study of what should be; it is not applied economics. The art of economics is applied economics. It relates the lessons learned in positive economics to the normative goals determined in normative economics.

The methodology Keynes finds appropriate for the art of economics is fundamentally different than the methodology he finds appropriate for normative economics or for positive economics. He wrote:

[1]A likely reason why Keynes' tripartite distinction was not central to Friedman's essay is that the reference to J. N. Keynes was a late addition to the essay. According to Daniel Hammond (March 1991), early drafts of Friedman's essay did not include any positive/normative distinction, let alone a tripartite one. In fact, the term "positive economics" did not make it into the title until the final draft.

[F]ew practical problems admit of complete solution on economic grounds alone.... [W]hen we pass, for instance, to problems of taxation, or to problems that concern the relations of the State with trade and industry, or to the general discussion of communistic and socialistic schemes—it is far from being the case that economic considerations hold the field exclusively. Account must also be taken of ethical, social, and political considerations that lie outside the sphere of political economy regarded as a science [p. 34]...

We are, accordingly, led to the conclusion ...that a definitive art of political economy, which attempts to lay down absolute rules for the regulation of human conduct, will have vaguely defined limits, and be largely non-economic in character [p. 83]...

The main point to notice is that the endeavour to merge questions of what ought to be with questions of what is tends to confuse, not only economic discussions themselves, but also discussions about economic method. The relative value to be attached to different methods of investigation is very different, according as we take the ethical and practical standpoint, or the purely scientific standpoint. Thus it would be generally agreed that, in dealing with practical questions, an abstract method of treatment avails less and carries us much less far than when we are dealing with theoretical questions. In other words, in dealing with the former class of questions, we are to a greater extent dependent upon history and inductive generalization.

Again, while economic uniformities and economic precepts are both, in many cases, relative to particular states of society, the general relativity of the latter may be affirmed with less qualification than that of the former. "Political economy," says Sir James Steuart, and by this he means the art of political economy, "in each country must necessarily be different"; and, so far as practical questions are concerned, this is hardly too strong a statement. On such questions there is nearly always something to be said on both sides, so that practical decisions can be arrived at only by weighing counter-arguments one against another. But the relative force of these arguments is almost certain to vary with varying conditions.... We are not here denying the relativity of economic theorems, but merely affirming the greater relativity of economic precepts. Unless the distinction between theorems and precepts is carefully borne in mind, the relativity of the former is likely to be over-stated [pp. 63–65].

As these quotations show, Keynes saw applied economics as the art of economics and believed that the appropriate methodology for the art of economics is different from the appropriate methodology for positive economics. The profession has not followed Keynes' division and, as he warned would happen, the distinction between precepts and theorems has often been overstated, and implications from economic theory have been drawn which do not follow, causing others to overstate the relativity of the theories of economic science. Explicitly recognizing the art of economics would make a major difference in the methodological conventions of economics.

The Art of Economics and Positive Economics

Positive economics suffers from the lack of an art of economics because, if a separate art is not delineated, positive economic inquiry faces pressures to have policy relevance, which is constraining to imaginative scientific enquiry. Positive economics is abstract thinking about abstract problems which might someday have some relevance, but immediate relevance is simply a side issue of no concern to the positive researcher. Imagine, for example, if theoretical physics were required to maintain policy relevance. Einstein's thought experiments would have been seen as a waste of time.

Few observers would deny that most economic inquiry today is abstract thinking about abstract problems. But abstract is not necessarily imaginative. Much of the current abstract thinking is the mundane application of technique to precisely defined problems; such work seldom leads to significant advances in science. If positive economics were freed from policy relevance, imagination would be enhanced.

The Art of Economics and Today's Applied Economics

The current version of applied economics suffers from the lack of an art of economics because it feels compelled to use methodology imported from positive economics. Thus, most current applied work in economics initially employs a formalistic method of argumentation and exposition which leads to exact results.[2] The formalistic results are then modified by political and sociological dimensions (or, at least, a sentence at the end of the work states that the results need to be so modified). These dimensions are addenda, made after the formal analysis is complete.

This sequencing loses interconnections between the various dimensions and leads to much work that is needlessly precise. The reason is analogous to the law of significant digits—the results of an analysis can only be as exact as the least precise part of the analysis. Since the sociological and political dimensions are extraordinarily imprecise, *making applied economic theory precise adds nothing to the precision of the final conclusion.*

For example, economists have analyzed the optimal tariff and the optimal tax and have come up with enormously precise results (usually specified in long equations). These economists agree that before the analysis can be applied to the real world, the imprecise historical, institutional, political, social, and

---

[2] A majority of graduating Ph.D.s classify themselves as "applied theorists." Applied theory is exactly what the art of economics is, and according to Keynes it is largely non-economic in character. Yet Ph.D. theses are generally required to follow a positivist methodology.

distributional dimensions must be added back to the analysis. But if the final policy recommendation is no more precise than these dimensions, the economic precision has served no purpose. Actually, it may have served a negative purpose since some interconnections among dimensions are likely lost in the process.

Many economists implicitly think of applied work of the type I am suggesting as subjective and normative; they implicitly equate positive economic analysis with objective analysis. That's wrong. All economic analysis—positive, normative and art—should be as objective as possible. Good applied economic work tells people how to achieve the goals they want to achieve as effectively as they can. No normative judgments about those goals need be made, and the analysis should remain objective. Even normative economics should be objective. It should discuss society's goals, and the reasons why these goals should be followed. It may be harder to maintain objectivity in the art of economics, but that simply suggests that one must work harder.

The Art of Economics and Empirical Economics

Applying the methodology of the art of economics to empirical work would also bring about significant changes. Most empirical work done by academic economists is currently very formal, technical, econometric analysis. Often the researchers' knowledge of the institutions they are studying is limited to computer printouts of large data sets. Empirical tests are also formal and results are expected to fall within 95 percent or 99 percent confidence intervals. This might be appropriate for empirical work in positive economics; it is not appropriate to empirical work in the art of economics.

In the art of economics, because of the interconnection of sociological and political dimensions of the problem, precise tests are impossible. Judgment dependent on institutional and historical information is required. This means that in the art of economics a wide range of observation and empirical exploration is appropriate. Often simple statistics, tables, charts, and case studies are the appropriate modes of expression for empirical work in the art of economics.

The purpose of empirical work in the art of economics is not to test theories; it is to apply theories to real-world problems. The appropriate methodology for such applications involves sociological and political observations and, to stay within the confines of precision established by the law of significant digits, is generally not precise.

Empirical work in positive economics should be designed to test whether a theory should be tentatively accepted; such empirical tests may have little or no relevance in applying a theory to a real-world problem. Empirical work in the art of economics should be designed to apply a theory by adding back the contextual reality. The two types of empirical work are fundamentally different. Current practice does not differentiate between the two.

The Art of Economics and Normative Economics

Reintroducing the art of economics would free normative economics from dealing with economic policy and allow a deeper consideration of what policy goals are appropriate. The art of economics would accept some set of goals determined in normative economics, and discuss how to achieve those goals in the real world, given the insights of positive economics.

Reshaping Economic Education

Explicit recognition that most economists' work falls under the classification of the art of economics would change the way economics is taught at both the undergraduate and graduate level. The appropriate methodology for the art of economics is much broader, more inclusive, and far less technical than the methodological approach for positive economics that underlies current teaching practices. The art of economics requires a knowledge of institutions, of social, political, and historical phenomena, and the ability to use available data in a reasonable way in discussing real-world economic issues. These aspects of economic knowledge have been purged from the graduate curriculum in economics. Only 3 percent of the graduate students at top universities stated that having a thorough knowledge of the economy is very important to succeeding as an economist, while 68 percent of them said that that knowledge was unimportant (Klamer and Colander, 1990). If economists accepted that the appropriate methodological conventions were those of the art of economics, graduate training would change significantly. Most students would be taught to interpret, use, and apply theory, not to develop it.

The blurring of the distinction between positive and normative economics occurs early in students' careers. Introductory textbooks commonly divide economics into positive and normative, and then conclude that anything involving a value judgement belongs in the normative category (for example, Samuelson and Nordhaus, 1989, pp. 10–11; McConnell and Brue, 1990, p. 6). Since any statement about what policy should be followed must necessarily involve a normative goal, these definitions place all policy considerations outside of positive economics.

Having so classified economics, these books then proceed to discuss economic policy issues, focusing on economic efficiency and giving the impression that discussions of efficiency belong in positive economics. However, achieving economic efficiency is not an end in itself, but is a debatable, normative goal which often will conflict with other normative goals society might have.

Only if teachers of economics introduce the third division—the art of economics—will the distinction between normative and positive economics become clear. Separating out the art of economics allows one to point out that objectivity in the art of economics is not achieved by avoiding value judgments, but, rather, by making clear what are the value judgments upon which one is basing the policy recommendation.

The Art of Economics and Debates about Policy

Economists raised with the positive/normative distinction tend to argue, as the Samuelson and Nordhaus textbook put it, "The major disagreements among economists, however, lie in normative areas." However, if economists are being objective, either their own normative views should not enter into their analyses, or they should state what those normative views are, and why those normative views should be used. In either case, it is difficult to see normative areas as the source of disagreement. I believe many or most of the debates about economic policy are not debates about normative issues; they are debates about how best to achieve an agreed-upon normative end.

Friedman (1953) was clearer about the reasons for differences among economists' policy recommendations. He states (p. 4):

> I venture the judgment, however, that currently in the Western world, and especially in the United States, differences about economic policy among disinterested citizens derive predominantly from different predictions about the economic consequences of taking action—differences that in principle can be eliminated by the progress of positive economics—rather than from fundamental differences in basic values, differences about which men can ultimately only fight.

The problem with this statement is the inserted phrase, "differences that in principle can be eliminated by the progress of positive economics." This phrase assumes that policy conclusions flow directly from positive economics. However, as Keynes argued, the art of economics is contextual and as much dependent on non-economic political, social, institutional, and historical judgments as it is on economics.[3] Thus, advances in positive economics generally will not help settle policy differences among economists because those policy differences result primarily from different judgments about political and social dimensions of policy implementation, not about differences in underlying theory.

Conclusion

Recognizing that what most economists do belongs in the category of the art of economics, and taking seriously the appropriate methodology for that

---

[3]Larry Boland (1991) makes a similar point about this problem with Friedman's methodology.

category, would fundamentally change the economics profession. But as a realist, I recognize that few practicing economists will heed this or any other methodological discussion; they do what they do.

However, historians of thought do take methodology seriously and this paper is a criticism of much of the economic methodological literature. That literature has refined the methodology of positive economics ad infinitum, but those refinements are irrelevant to most economists because most economists don't do positive economics. They do applied economics, and the relevant category for applied economics is the art of economics. Keynes had definite views of what the appropriate methodology for the art of economics is; I agree with him. Many in the profession may disagree, but that is where the methodological debate should focus. The economics profession is overdue to begin a serious discussion on the appropriate methodology for the art of economics.

■ *The author would like to thank Roger Backhaus, Mark Blaug, Larry Boland, Daniel Hammond, Thomas Mayer, Cordelia Reimers, Carl Shapiro, Joseph Stiglitz, and Timothy Taylor for helpful comments on earlier drafts of this paper.*

References

Adams, Walter, James W. Brock and Norman P. Obst, "Pareto Optimality and Antitrust Policy: The Old Chicago and the New Learning," *Southern Economic Journal,* July 1991, *58*:1, 1–14.

Blaug, Mark, *The Methodology of Economics.* Cambridge: Cambridge University Press, 1980.

Boland, Larry, "Positivism in Economics and Accounting," unpublished manuscript, Simon Fraser University, April 1991.

Colander, David, "The Best as the Enemy of the Good." In Colander, David, "Why Aren't Economists As Important As Garbagemen? Essays on the State of Economics. Armonk: M. E. Sharpe, Inc., 1991, 31–37.

Friedman, Milton, "The Methodology of Positive Economics." In *Essays in Positive Economics.* Chicago: University of Chicago Press, 1953.

Hammond, J. Daniel, "Early Drafts of Friedman's Methodological Essay," unpublished manuscript, Wake Forest University, Winston-Salem, NC, March 1991.

Keynes, John Neville, republished 1955 in *The Scope and Method of Political Economy,* 4th edition. New York: Kelley and Millman, Inc., 1891.

Klamer, Arjo, and David Colander, *The Making of an Economist.* Boulder: Westview Press, 1990.

McConnell, Campbell R., and Stanley L. Brue, *Economics: Principles, Problems, and Policies.* New York: McGraw-Hill Publishing Co., 1990.

Samuelson, Paul A., and William D. Nordhaus, *Economics,* 13th edition. New York: McGraw Hill Book Company, 1989.

[4]

Journal of Economic Methodology, 2013
Vol. 20, No. 1, 56–68, http://dx.doi.org/10.1080/1350178X.2013.774848

The systemic failure of economic methodologists

David Colander*

Department of Economics, Middlebury College, Middlebury, Vermont

This paper argues that economic methodologists failed to point out to the profession or to policy makers that the method macroeconomists (and applied economists generally) were using was problematic, and therefore bear a portion of the blame for macroeconomics' failure to prepare for the recent financial crisis. The reason they did not was systemic; they did not see doing so as their job. The paper argues that the systemic failure of the economics profession in the financial crisis and the systemic failure of economic methodologists reflect the same cause. Both groups see their primary role as detached scholars or as scientists providing abstract understanding, not as engineers whose primary role is to provide insight and analysis for individuals attempting to achieve better real-world outcomes. Rather, they see themselves as detached scholars. This paper argues that the roles should be reversed – the economics profession's primary goal should be achieving better real-world outcomes, and its secondary goal should be better understanding of the economy for the sake of understanding.

Keywords: methodology; engineering; systemic failure; macroeconomics; value judgments; intuition

In Colander (2009, 2011), I argued that one of the causes of the recent financial crisis was a systemic failure in the economics profession. In this paper, I argue that one of the causes of the economics profession's systemic failure was a parallel systemic failure of economic methodologists. Specifically, I argue that economic methodologists failed the economics profession by not actively pointing out to the economics profession or to the general public that, if an economist's primary goal was to provide policy advice to society, then the standard methodology being used by applied macroeconomists had serious problems.[1]

I see methodologist's failure as a systemic failure because the reason they did not point out to the profession or to policy makers that the method macroeconomists (and applied economists generally) were using was problematic was systemic; they did not see doing so as their job. They did not see their job as trying to affect economists' methodology or even to make judgments about whether it was good or bad. Instead, they saw their job as trying to understand that methodology. Thus, when Solow (2007, pp. 235–236; 2008) bluntly stated that the modern macroeconomics was best seen as a 'rhetorical swindle' that 'seems to lack all credibility,' we saw no organized group of economic methodologists either supporting or attacking Solow. His strong statements about fellow economists were seen as a breach of academic decorum, acceptable because of his wit and fame, but not an issue that methodologists should actively weigh in on.

The systemic failure of the economics profession in the financial crisis and the systemic failure of economic methodologists reflect the same cause. Both groups see their primary role as detached scholars, or as scientists providing abstract understanding, not as

---

*Email: colander@middlebury.edu

engineers whose primary role is to provide insight and analysis for individuals attempting to achieve better real-world outcomes. Criticism of the economics profession's failure in the crisis, and my criticism of economic methodologists in this paper, is based on the belief, which I believe is generally held by members of society, that the roles should be reversed – the economics profession's primary goal should be achieving better real-world outcomes, and its secondary goal should be better understanding of the economy for the sake of understanding.

The issue is one of primacy of engineering or scientific goals, not whether engineering and science are related. Obviously, they are related; both indirectly contribute to the other's goal; better scientific understanding improves real-world outcomes, and solving real-world problems leads to better abstract understanding. But primacy is important because the primary goal determines methodology, and an engineering methodology tailored to solve problems is different from a scientific methodology designed to discover truth. If engineering is not applied science, and applied economics is primarily engineering, applied economists should be judged by an engineering methodology, not by a scientific methodology.[2] Economic methodologists have not done that.

Economic methodologists' interpretation of their primary role as detached scholar searching for the truth is reflected in whom they see as their primary audience. Just as applied macroeconomists see other macroeconomists as their primary audience, economic methodologists see other methodologists, not the public or policy makers using economists' advice, as their primary audience. This tendency to write for one's peers leads scholars to see themselves as detached scholars whose job is to discover the truth, not as active participants in policy determination whose job is to see that society gets better real-world outcomes. Writing primarily for one's peers separates the actual real-world outcome and the scholar's work. Thus, following a scientific methodology, macroeconomists did not see themselves as bearing any significant responsibility for the financial crisis.[3] While Solow's views that macroeconomics were studying the wrong models may be shared by many in the economics profession, one would not discover such shared views from reading most mainstream economists', or economic methodologists', work because, from a scientific methodological standpoint, it is not clear whether Solow is right. However, from an engineering methodological standpoint, it is hard to come to any conclusion other than Solow's.

Because macroeconomists see themselves as detached scholars – macroeconomic scientists – they do not take responsibility for what happens in the macroeconomy. Similarly, economic methodologists do not take responsibility for what macroeconomists do. Methodologists *do not* see their primary job as seeing to it that applied policy economists are using the best methodology they can to solve real-world problems. Since it is not their job to see that economists use the best methodology, methodologists do not see themselves as bearing any responsibility if the method actually used by macroeconomists proves inappropriate, just as macroeconomists do not see themselves as bearing responsibility for the economic crisis.

I am quite willing to accept that macroeconomists' and economic methodologists' detached approach may reflect the state-of-the-art scientific method. If an economist's goal is understanding for the sake of understanding, then I am willing to accept that there is no systemic failure. But, in my view, scientific understanding is not the primary goal that society wants from macroeconomics or from economic methodologists. Society primarily wants help from economists in solving the problems it faces. What I am arguing is that the scientific methodology is the wrong methodology to use, or to judge macroeconomists' work in reference to, if the primary goal is solving the macroeconomic problems society faces. The appropriate methodology for that goal would be an engineering methodology.

In the next part of the paper, I will outline a general engineering methodology and contrast it with an applied scientific methodology, discussing how economists' and methodologists' research and role would change were they to see themselves as primarily engineers rather than as primarily scientists or philosophers of science. Then, I will discuss institutional modifications that could change the situation to achieve what I believe would be better outcomes.

The engineer's general method

The general methodology of science has been extensively explored by scholars. The general methodology of engineering has received little discussion. The reality is that engineers do not spend a lot of time writing about abstract methodological issues. Instead, there seems to be general acceptance of a general engineering methodology as spelled out by Koen (2003). Koen defines the engineering method as 'the strategy for causing the best change in a poorly understood or uncertain situation within the available resources'. Koen argues that this definition is operationally equivalent to a second definition – *use the best available engineering heuristics to solve problems.*

Since Koen sees no part of knowledge as infallible, heuristics includes all theories and models, and any other aid, such as intuition, experience and expert knowledge that may usefully lead to a solution. In engineering, nothing is off the table. By explicitly calling the models and aids that an engineer uses to arrive at a conclusion, heuristics, he calls attention to any model's problems and encourages a methodological openness in inquiry that is open to all evidence and arguments.

Koen does not discuss what the appropriate heuristics are for particular problems or even for a particular sub-branch of engineering. Such specifics are to be decided by the engineering community working on the problem, not by a specialized methodologist. Koen argues that engineering fields will come to decisions about the appropriate heuristics and will characterize a certain set of heuristics as the 'state-of-the-art' heuristics. He argues that these heuristics will be changing, and discussion of them will be part of what every engineer does. Thus, while abstract methodology is not much discussed by engineers, practical methodology is constantly discussed. It is integrated into what engineers do, so all engineers are simultaneously engineers and methodologists. Methodology is an important part of engineering, but it is a narrow applied micro methodology of best practices for particular areas, with a very loose general methodology that can probably best be described as an educated common sense methodology. Koen calls it a 'universal method.'

This engineering methodology is quite different from an applied science methodology that applied economists use, and that economic methodologists judge them in reference to. A scientific methodology is focused on understanding for the sake of understanding and the 'truth'; an applied scientific methodology is focused on applying the truths one has found in science to real-world problem. Applied science methodology uses engineering knowledge as a stepping stone to scientific knowledge, which is close to truth as can be reasonably asked for.

An engineer is not specifically interested in truth; he or she is interested in solving problems; the approach an engineer uses may be based on science, but it need not be. An engineer makes no claim for the heuristic he or she is using being the truth or even being a correct representation of the problem. Truth is not an issue of importance to an engineer except as it relates to the solution of the problem at hand. Engineering is all about heuristics. Heuristic knowledge may include scientific knowledge – scientific knowledge is knowledge that has been developed using a scientific heuristic and that meets generally accepted scientific criteria – but heuristic knowledge is not limited to applied scientific knowledge. It also includes a variety of sources of understanding that experience has shown to be useful.

The particular branch of engineering, and the particular problem the engineers are trying to solve, will determine how important the scientific heuristic is and how important other heuristics are. There is no one overriding engineering heuristic. The difference between thinking about applied economics as applied science and as engineering can be seen by considering what is at the core of the model used. Applied science sees scientific knowledge at its core. It excludes all non-scientific knowledge. The engineering core includes all applied science but can include non-scientific knowledge in the core as well as established scientific knowledge. Historical knowledge, intuitive knowledge and guestimates are all allowed as foundations for engineering models. This larger core opens up the analysis to a wider range of acceptable models than does applied science.

Let me consider the difference in terms of macroeconomic theory. From an engineering standpoint, to try to understand what policies to use to guide the macro economy, it seems reasonable that interactions of heterogeneous agents are likely to be important; in a model with interacting heterogeneous agents, there will likely be herding, fads and bubbles. We have some intuition and observations of how such interactions might affect the macro economy, and a variety of *ad hoc* models, but we have no scientific knowledge of how they do. The heterogeneous agent models are too rudimentary at this point to warrant being called scientific models. Thus, the reigning academic methodological approach to macroeconomics holds that any macro model must use a scientifically acceptable Dynamic Stochastic General Equilibrium (DSGE) model (see, for example, Chari and Kehoe [2006, 2008] who argue that any macro model that does not use a DSGE framework should not be seriously considered). It was general acceptance of this argument by the profession that led to the use of the DSGE model as the foundation of modern macroeconomics.

I am not arguing that modern macroeconomists do not recognize the importance of heterogeneous agents; they are developing such models on the 'to do' list (Kocherlakota, 2010). But I am arguing that their applied scientific methodology holds that until formal models of interacting heterogeneous agents are developed within an acceptable formal DSGE framework, the informal models of how heterogeneous agents might affect policy results are outside of the science of economics, and this is not what applied macroeconomists should study or use. Thus, in the science of macro, informal models based on loose insights about interactions of heterogeneous agents have no place. They would be *ad hoc* and not scientific. If modern macroeconomists used an engineering methodology, such informal models not only would be allowed but also could and should be a core focus of macroeconomists' research. Whether the models were *ad hoc* or scientific would be irrelevant.

The relation between engineering problems and applied economics problems

If one were to take the standard definition of economics given in most principles textbooks – the study of the allocation of scarce resources among alternative ends – and develop from that a related definition of applied economics, the textbook definition of applied economics one would come up with would be something like the following – *the strategy for causing the best change within the available ends*, where 'best change' means achieving a goal with the least amount or resources. Such a textbook definition of applied

D. Colander

economics is very close to Koen's definition of engineering, with two fundamental differences. The first is that Koen's definition emphasizes 'poorly understood or uncertain' situations, and the applied economics definition does not. The second is that Koen specifically includes the engineer's time as a scarce resource, whereas in an economist's standard definition, limitations in the economist's time to study the problem are generally not taken into account. Both distinctions are important and are derived from Koen's thinking of engineering not as applied science, but more as 'applied objective analysis.'

Koen carefully points out that, while there is a connection between engineering and science, engineering is not applied science; rather, science should be seen as applied engineering. By that he means that science is the application of the engineering methodology 'Use the best available engineering heuristics to solve problems' to a particular problem – the problem of understanding for the sake of understanding or for 'finding the truth.' For an engineer, abstract truth is not that important, except as it contributes to an understanding of what works and will continue to work for the real-world problems he or she is trying to solve. Thus, a central difference between a scientist and an engineer involves different goals. Engineering primarily concerns how to best solve a problem or achieve a specified goal.[4] Finding the truth or understanding for the sake of understanding is a side benefit. The primary goal of science is to find the truth; any applied usefulness is a side benefit. The methodology of each is designed to achieve the primary goal. Thus, the methodology of science is concerned with rules that help a scientist find that truth. The goal of an engineer is to find a solution to a specified problem – to achieve a goal in the best way possible, and the methodology of engineering is concerned with the heuristics that help an engineer do so.

This difference in goals accounts for the two differences in the definitions of applied economics and engineering. The engineering definition explicitly takes into account the time allotted to finding a solution to a problem, because it is concerned with finding a solution to that problem. Koen emphasizes that solving problems takes the engineer's time, and embodies that in his methodological prescription. Engineering problems have deadlines – and at some point an engineer must come up with a workable solution to a problem; thus, one can only understand engineering methodology by understanding how one manages one's scarce time, and you can only judge an engineering solution in reference to the amount of time and other resources the engineer had to arrive at that solution. The pressures of time means that there is no blanket condemnation of *ad hoc* models or of rough and ready guesses within models.

In almost perfectly understood situations, the engineering and scientific methods may asymptotically approach each other, and the better the situation is understood, the closer the two methods are likely to be. But Koen emphasizes that engineers deal with 'poorly understood and uncertain' situations, and the less understood, and more uncertain, the situation, the more likely the methods will differ. That is why engineers do not care a lot about the fine points of scientific methodology; the marginal contribution to a better understanding of a fine point of scientific methodology is unlikely to have a high payoff in the situations that engineers are dealing with.

These different goals lead to fundamentally different ways of going about scientific research and engineering research. An engineer uses science when he or she deems it appropriate, but when science does not have an answer to a part of the question that is needed to come to a policy recommendation, or to achieve a goal, the engineer finds the best objective answer he or she can, and uses that answer until a better answer is found. The engineer does not claim that his/her is the right answer, or the truth. The question the engineer focuses on is: does the answer he or she has found work for this particular problem. It is to emphasize the known fallibility of engineer's approach that Koen calls the engineering method a heuristic, and his proposed method a heuristic as well. In doing so, he makes no claims to it being an absolute standard, but simply a working standard that describes what good engineers do.

His emphasis on uncertainty reflects a descriptive, not a prescriptive reality. Engineers are almost inevitably concerned with uncertain situations, and achieving some goal. If the goal and the method of solving the problem were certain, it would be a manufacturing problem, or a mathematical problem, not an engineering problem.

How will the adoption of this engineering methodology change applied economics?

Now that I have distinguished an engineering methodology from a scientific methodology, let me discuss why I believe economists would serve society much better if they followed an engineering methodology rather than a scientific methodology in guiding their applied research.

Once one considers the researcher's time as a scarce resource, the scientific heuristic, which is designed to uncover truth, often is the inappropriate heuristic. It simply requires too much time and effort to come to a workable solution for uncertain and poorly understood problems. Engineering heuristics do not carry out any part of the analysis to a higher degree of precision than the weakest link of the chain of reasoning. This is often called the significant digit heuristic. Since most problems faced by engineers and by applied economists have highly uncertain elements, scientific precision is usually not appropriate for the relevant heuristic. Instead, engineers use rules of thumb with large fudge factors, which become precise only for those problems where precision is easily achievable and needed. This is *not* what applied economists do when they follow an applied scientific methodology, as should be clear in the macroeconomic DSGE example. The scientific methodology puts science first. It directs economic thinking toward first solving abstract problems, and then relating that abstract solution to real-world problems; the engineering methodology puts applied work first. It directs economists toward first solving imprecise real-world problems, and only secondarily relating that solution to abstract problems.

The acknowledged switch from an applied science methodology to an engineering methodology may seem minor, but such a switch would lead to major changes to the way in which applied economics is practiced. Specifically, it will lead to five changes in how applied economics is done.

More careful specification of the real-world goal of the research

An engineering methodology would require applied economists to much more carefully specify the real-world policy goal of their applied research. Only if the goal of the research is better scientific understanding would an economist follow a scientific methodology. If the goal of the research is to solve some other problem, the looser engineering methodology would be employed, and the precise nature of the problem to be solved would determine the methodology used.

Incorporate value judgments

An engineering methodology would use a much broader and looser methodology that would blend economic and non-economic considerations. All aspects of the problem necessary to arrive at an actual answer would be included in an applied economist's research. Thus, for example, if judgments about tradeoffs of individual's welfare were necessary, the economic engineer would develop as objective a method of making those judgments as possible. Earlier economists, who took a more engineering approach, were quite willing to develop models involving interpersonal welfare comparisons (Colander, 2007b). For example, Fisher (1927) and Frisch (1932) developed a statistical method of making interpersonal comparisons of wants; they justified their models by pragmatism. Fisher posed the rhetorical question about whether the necessary assumptions can be used, and answered: 'To all these questions I would answer "yes" – approximately at least. But the only, or only important, reason I can give for this answer is that, in actual practical human life, we do proceed on just such assumptions.' He continues: 'Philosophical doubt is right and proper, but the problems of life cannot, and do not, wait' (Fisher, 1927, pp. 179–180). Maximizing a non-operational social welfare function is not a policy goal of engineering research.

An engineering methodology would lead to a quite different way of doing applied economics, one that embraces, rather than avoids, value judgments because value judgments must be made to arrive at policy recommendations. Science rightly avoids such value judgments, and with applied economics based on the science of economics, applied economics has a tendency to avoid them as well. The scientific methodology guiding applied economics work explains why the economics profession has gone to great length to avoid value judgments. An engineer would not avoid value judgments but instead would attempt to make them as transparent as possible, so that other individuals using the economist's suggested solution can see whether the value judgments used match their value judgments. The reason is that in order to talk about economic policy, we need to know the goals of individuals and society. What policy is presented as best depends heavily on the value judgments we make. Using an engineering methodology, economists' recommendations would be presented as being explicitly contingent on the underlying value judgments.

Discussions of value judgments involved in particular solutions would be a central element of discussion of applied economists. This would mean that an applied economist would not provide a definitive answer, but rather a particular answer from his point of view. Koen writes:

> A fundamental characteristic of an engineering solution is that it is the best available from the point of view of a specific engineer. Theoretically, then, best for an engineer is the result of manipulating a model of society's perceived reality, including additional subjective considerations known only to the engineer constructing the model. In essence, the engineer creates what he thinks an informed society should want based on his knowledge of what an uninformed society thinks it wants.

An applied economist using an engineering methodology would do the same. Whereas science avoids all issues involving value judgments, engineering embraces value judgments because they cannot be avoided and still arrive as a solution.

More informal empirical work

An engineering methodology would integrate empirical work into economic analysis differently than is currently done. Modern economists' strong reliance on scientific standards of significance in its applied work would decrease. Many economists today have a tendency to think of applied economic research as applied econometrics, and they approach most applied problems by bringing their econometric skills to bear on it. They choose problems and research topics accordingly.[5] This follows from their applied science methodology. That strategy would change if they saw themselves as engineers. For an engineer, arriving at an answer to a question might involve back-of-the-envelope calculations, input from other specialties, guestimates and individual judgment – whatever is needed to provide a policy solution to the problem at hand. In deciding how to allocate scarce research time for thinking about the problem, the state-of-the-art engineering heuristic follows the weakest link principle – it allocates marginal research resources to that part of the problem that seems to be the weakest link, regardless of whether that aspect of the problem is scientific or not.

Using an engineering methodology, applied economics would not be thought of as econometric analysis; econometrics would simply be one of the many empirical tools that comprise applied economics. Case studies, exploratory data analysis, interviews with specialists and any other technique that might shed light on the problem would be part of applied economics. Using Deirdre McCloskey's terminology, engineering economics would rely on oomph, not 'it' statistics, and would vary the degree of statistical precision needed with the time available to arrive at a solution, the degree to which policy goals can be precisely specified, the importance of the empirical measure to solving the problem and the nature of the problem. Each branch of applied policy economics would develop its own empirical heuristic, rather than there being a single empirical heuristic centered on statistical significance measures.

More reliance on intuition

An engineering methodology would involve a greater focus on intuition and back-of-the-envelope calculations, and on a practitioner's understanding of the problem, not an outside observer's. Policy work would involve much greater focus on design and actual implementation, not on abstract solutions. The science branch and the engineering branch would be blended, and Bernanke's (2010) statement that even as the economy crashed the underlying macroeconomics could not be criticized would be seen as an inappropriate. If the economy crashed, applied economics cannot plead that the science of economics was not at fault; if the economy crashed, the economics profession failed society.

Less abstract, more practical, goals of research

An engineering methodology would have different output measures than applied economists currently use. The primary output measure would be the implementation of the actual program, not a research paper. One could still have scientific economists exploring models with little relevant to policy, but they would make it very clear that their models had no direct policy relevance. Measuring output in terms of research papers is a scientific convention, not an engineering convention. Output of applied economists would more likely be measured in terms of projects worked on, and contributions to problem, just as engineers do now.

Elsewhere (Colander, 2010), I have described that the change in research economists seeing themselves as engineers rather than scientists would do as a change from *hands-off* to *hands-on* research. Hands-off research involves writing abstractly about approaches to problems; it involves doing econometric studies relevant to problems and criticizing other economists' approaches. Hands-on research would give a much greater focus to actually trying to solve problems as opposed to advice from afar. Economists would spend less time criticizing other economists and more time coming up with alternative solutions. As Koen writes 'The argument about which heuristic is preferable is not done primarily by discussing their relative merits, but rather by demonstration.'

The acceptance of an engineering methodology would mean that workable mechanism designs would become much more a focus of what applied economists do. There might be general regulatory designs, market-based designs and tax-based designs, and those would be analyzed in terms of how they work in practice, not how they work in the abstract. The debates within applied economics would switch to practical applied economics – more institutional in nature and less abstract theoretical.

Other changes to the profession

Besides the above changes, there would also be changes in pedagogy and the teaching of economics. Economists' training would be much more closely tied to what applied economists do, and far less concerned with both models and methods. Economic education would spend much more time preparing students to solve real-world problems and less time on how to write academic papers, or how to develop and solve abstract models (see Colander [2010] for a further discussion).

J.M. Keynes once said that he hoped one day economists would be thought of in the same way as dentists. You have a problem with your teeth – you go to the dentist to solve it; you have a problem with the economy, you go to an economist to solve it. The suggestions in this paper are very much in line with that view. Using an engineering methodology, economists' suggestions about policy will be presented much more humbly than they currently are. The subjective and *ad hoc* nature of the engineering method would be recognized and accepted, and any model used would not be portrayed as representing the correct model, but simply as a useful model for one set of particular problems.

There will, of course, still be economists who are primarily economic scientists, not economic engineers. For them, economists' current methodological approach would likely remain, since their primary goal will be to find the truth, not to solve a particular problem. They would not take a primary interest in the implications of their research for policy (Gerard Debreu is a good example of such a theoretical economic scientist). But such scientific economists would likely be only a small part of the profession. In a profession guided by an engineering methodology, most economists would be applied economists, and as such methodological generalists, not methodological specialists. Whereas currently economists require formal models because they see themselves as scientists who are adhering to a scientific method, engineering economists would be happy with *ad hoc* informal models that seemed to work. An economic engineer would see himself as more of a generalist and would not be constrained by a scientific method.

The economic engineer would use many different methods that would likely vary with the particular problem he or she is working on, the time he or she has to find a solution and the nature of the problem. At times their focus might be philosophical questions having to do with goals; at other times their focus may be on judgment questions, having to do with how best to incorporate value judgments into their policy solution. At other times it might focus on institutional questions having to do with implementation, or historical questions having to do with how similar problems occurred in the past.

A throwback to classical methodology

Were applied economics to adopt this engineering methodology, it would not represent an entirely new approach. In many ways, it would be a movement back from the scientific methodology adopted in the 1950s that centered around the Walrasian general equilibrium model and welfare economics, moving directly from models to policy, to a classical methodological approach, where applied policy economics was strictly separated from the science of economics. Within classical methodology, applied economics had a different methodology than did positive economics. Keynes, in his summary of the classical methodological approach, wrote

> [F]ew practical problems admit of complete solution on economic grounds alone ... [W]hen we pass, for instance, to problems of taxation, or to problems that concern the relations of the State with trade and industry, or to the general discussion of communistic and socialistic schemes – it is far from being the case that economic considerations hold the field exclusively. Account must also be taken of ethical, social, and political considerations that lie outside the sphere of political economy regarded as a science [p. 34] ... We are, accordingly, led to the conclusion ... that a definitive art of political economy, which attempts to lay down absolute rules for the regulation of human conduct, will have vaguely defined limits, and be largely non-economic in character. (1891, p. 83)

The role of the methodologist and methodology in the economic engineering

The above discussion has focused on how the role of an applied economist would change if the profession adopted an engineering methodology. Let me now turn to how I see the role of an economic methodologist changing. First, it changes who is an economic methodologist. In the engineering model, methodology is embedded in the heuristics of applied researchers, so every applied economist would be concerned with what might be called micro methodology – the consideration of methods that worked for solving the type of problems they are trying to solve. So applied economists will discuss methodology much more – this is a heuristic that works for this particular type of problem, this one does not – than they currently do.

As methodology becomes embedded in applied economics, the role of the methodological specialist will change. They too will likely be applied economists as well as economic methodologists, and their research will focus more on discussing whether specific heuristics used in this particular sub-area might usefully transfer to the heuristics used in other areas. Their research would be far less likely to focus on abstract issues. Methodologists would simply be a group of economic engineers whose goal is to assist other engineers in finding the best heuristic. They would work with practicing economists, not write about practicing economists.

How to change the profession

A key difference between an engineering methodology and a scientific methodology is that a researcher using an engineering methodology is working on solving a particular problem. That holds for economic methodologists as well, and the problem I am attempting to solve is how to get economists to see themselves as using an engineering methodology rather than a scientific methodology. That will not be done by writing papers such as this one for other economic methodologists. In my view, economists fully recognize the problem and often joke about it. Walter Heller's definition of an economist as 'a man who, when he finds something works in practice, wonders if it works in theory' captures that understanding. But under current institutions, they have no incentives to change.

Contrary to what some heterodox economists claim, the economics profession is not in crisis – far from it, it is highly successful in recruiting students and in being respected by the public. The experience with the financial crisis hardly dented it at all. My message for economic methodologists who consider themselves applied engineering methodologists trying to make the profession better, as opposed to philosophical methodologists who are trying to understand what economists are doing, is that the only way the system will change is if the incentives change. The ones with the power to change incentives, and the ones whom I believe want change in the economics profession, are policy makers and the funders of economic research. Therefore, the engineering methodologist's intended audience should not be other economic methodologists, but rather policy makers and funders of economic research.

In Colander (2009), I have outlined the design of a system that would significantly change in what applied academic economists do and lead them to use an engineering rather than a scientific methodology. The proposal for change is directed not at academics but at funders of academia – various levels of government, foundations and individuals. The change essentially involves making full outside funding of research a requirement for a much larger percentage of the academic profession than it currently is and separating out the implicit funding for research built into current academic institutions. As opposed to applied academic researchers being given a goal of solving some abstract problem – providing knowledge and letting the applied academic researcher determine what issue he or she will study – as the current system does, academics need to be given the goal of assisting society in solving particular problems.

This change can be accomplished in a number of ways. One method I developed is for governments and foundations to fund some part of university research indirectly by providing vouchers to groups who want applied research done, rather than directly. I proposed that funders divide funding into 'hands-on' (applied) research funding and 'hands-off' (scientific) research funding, as they choose (Colander, 2009). The 'hands-off' research vouchers would go to scientific funding agencies such as National Science Foundation (NSF). The 'hand-on' research vouchers would go to non-profits and other organizations that needed problems solved.

Say that 5% of a state's funding of a university was given in the form of 'hands-on' research vouchers to the non-profits or government agencies who could use assistance of academics, and that 5% of the professor's pay was paid only when he or she acquired a voucher. (The percentage of an academic's pay could be expanded over time to include the full amount of the time the academic is expected to spend on hands-on research.) The non-profits could then use those vouchers to hire academics when they help them solve problems. The academic would then turn over the voucher to the university who would get the funding if the university agreed that it would use that voucher as a measure of the researcher's hands-on research.

Depending on to which groups the funding agency gives the research vouchers, the change in funding would involve a major change in research incentives. If the funding agencies give the vouchers to scientific foundations, such as the NSF, then it would involve little change. If, however, they gave it to non-profit agencies, such as a development agency, or non-profit agencies, it would involve significant change. Rather than trying to solve abstract problems, the academic doing research for a development agency would involve in solving real-world problems. The higher the percentage of money going to hands-on vouchers, the greater the amount of hands-on research. (This plan is spelled out in more detail in Colander [2009]). This change would replace academic publication as a measure of research with research vouchers, putting more emphasis on service and solving problems. I proposed the creation of an online consulting market in these vouchers, with academics checking to see what jobs needed doing and how many vouchers they would receive for it. They could use students to help them in their research, possible paying them some percentage of these vouchers, so that these vouchers could help reduce student tuition.

There are other ways to achieve similar ends and well, and in other work (Colander, 2010) I have explored some of these. They involve changes in research funding mechanism that would give funders much more control over the nature and type of research that academic economists do, and allow for more funding of hands-on research.

Conclusion

Seeing oneself as an engineer and not as a scientist would have a useful humbling effect on economists, but it would also free them up to apply economics in ways that currently they cannot. Recognizing that you are working on heuristics, and not offering the truth, frees one to be more imaginative and expansive in one's thinking. It would reduce the tendency for economists to herd since there is far less tendency to search for a single truth. For example, because of my particular historical circumstances, I have been lucky to have had the luxury to let an engineering methodology guide my work, and few would regard me as herdable.

My work is seen as idiosyncratic by most economic methodologists – as a strange admixture of wild ideas, conjecture and reporter level research. It is engineering research much more than scientific or philosophical research. Such research is not seen as appropriately scientific for a methodologist, or for an economist. It is the type of research that a funding group would be more interested in than an academic group. This is to be expected. The natural consumer of an economic engineering methodologist's research would not be other methodologists; rather, it would be groups that hire economists, groups that fund economists and the groups that give research grants to economists to achieve some end. But methodologists do not write for such groups. We should. These funding groups are the ones who can best decide whether economists are fulfilling their goals or not. Economists cannot objectively decide. Thus, it would make sense for each of these groups to have their own economic methodological consultants who could advise them on how to structure incentives for economists to bring about their desired ends. The engineering methodologist's goal would be to design incentive systems facing economists so that their research reflects the desires of the funding agency.

I have been lucky because with few people following my approach, my work can stand out. If more economists were doing what I am doing, I have no doubt that they would do it much better than I do it. But they do not do it because they have few incentives to do it. Were a young economic methodologist to do it, he or she would likely not remain an academic economic methodologist. That is why I argue that methodologists failed society, and why that failure is a systemic failure, not an individual failure.

In summary, economists are not playing as positive a role in society as they should. Economic methodologists should see as one of their important roles as improving the efficiency of economists – designing changes that will lead economists to play a more positive role. But they are subject to the same forces as are economists, and the incentives that lead economists away from most efficiently solving problems also lead methodologists to fail to point out the problems.

Notes

1. The systemic failures result from a deeper systemic failure in academia, which has separated it from the society that supports it, but I will not address that broader systemic failure here other than to note that the failures discussed here are paralleled in other areas of academia.
2. The argument carries over to much of what 'scientists' of all sorts do; much of what scientists do is engineering. The distinction is important not because it matters whether one is called an engineer or a scientist. It matters only because different methodologies are appropriate for each.

If applied economists accepted that they should use engineering methodology, I would have no problems with calling them scientists.

3. One can see this in the discussions of top economists. For example, Eric Maskin states, 'I don't accept the criticism that economic theory failed to provide a framework for understanding this crisis …' (as cited in Taylor, 2010). Similarly, Ben Bernanke argues that the mistakes that were made were primarily engineering or management mistakes, not mistakes in the fundamental science of macroeconomics, which he argues is sound. He writes, 'The recent financial crisis was more a failure of economic engineering and economic management than of what I have called economic science' (Bernanke, 2010).

4. Whereas an engineer is not a scientist, a scientist can be seen as an engineer, and scientific methodology can be thought of as a sub-area of engineering methodology, in which the goal is to find the truth.

5. In my interviews with graduate students (Colander, 2007a), students pointed out that data availability determined the research they focused on, not the importance of problems. One stated that the difference between an economist and a sociologist was that an economist studied unimportant problems about which he could say something precisely, whereas a sociologist studied important problems about which he could not say anything precisely. Were an engineering methodology to be followed, an economist would study important problems being as precise as he could be but not more so.

References

Bernanke, B. (2010). *Implications of the financial crisis for economics* [Speech]. Princeton University. Retrieved from http://www.federalreserve.gov/newsevents/speech/bernanke20100924a.htm, September 24.

Chari, V. V. & Kehoe, P. (2006). Modern macroeconomics in practice: How theory is shaping policy. *Journal of Economic Perspectives*, *20*(4), 3–28.

Chari, V. V. & Kehoe, P. (2008). Response to Solow. *Journal of Economic Perspectives*, *22*(1), 247–250.

Colander, D. (2007a). *The making of an economist redux*. Princeton, NJ: Princeton University Press.

Colander, D. (2007b). Edgeworth's hedonimeter and the quest to measure utility. *Journal of Economic Perspectives*, *21*(2), 215–226.

Colander, D. (2009). *The making of a European economist*. Cheltenham: Edward Elgar.

Colander, D. (2010, Unpublished). *Creating the right blend of economists*. Paper presented at the Society of Government Economists. Middlebury College Working Paper.

Colander, D. (2011). Is the fundamental science of macroeconomics sound? *Review of Radical Political Economics*, 43, 302–309.

Colander, D., Kirman, A., Goldberg, M., Sloth, B., Juselius, K., Haas, A., & Lux, T. (2009). The financial crisis and the systemic failure of the economics profession. *Critical Review*, *21*(2/3), 249–267.

Fisher, I. (1927). A statistical method for measuring 'marginal utility' and testing the justice of a progressive income tax. In J. Hollander (Ed.), *Economic essays contributed in honor of John Bates Clark*. New York: Macmillan (on behalf of the American Economic Association).

Frisch, R. (1932 [1978]). *New methods of measuring marginal utility*. Philadelphia, PA: Porcupine Press.

Keynes, J. N. (1891). *The scope and method of political economy*. London: Macmillan.

Kocherlakota, N. (2010, May). Modern macroeconomic models as tools for economic policy (2009 Annual Report). The Region, The Federal Reserve Bank of Minneapolis.

Koen, B. V. (2003). *Discussion of the method*. New York: Oxford University Press.

Solow, R. (2007). Reflections on the survey. In D. Colander (Ed.), *The making of an economist redux* (pp. 234–238). Princeton, NJ: Princeton University Press.

(2008). The state of macroeconomics: Comment. *Journal of Economic Perspectives*, *22*(1), 243–238.

Taylor, T. (2010). Recommendations for further reading. *Journal of Economic Perspectives*, *24*(2), 227–234.

5

Journal of the History of Economic Thought, Volume 22, Number 2, 2000

THE DEATH OF NEOCLASSICAL ECONOMICS

BY

DAVID COLANDER

The term "neoclassical economics" was born in 1900; in this paper I am proposing economist-assisted terminasia; by the powers vested in me as president of the History of Economics Society, I hereby declare the term neoclassical economics dead.[1] Let me be clear about what I am sentencing to death—it is not the content of neoclassical economics. As I will discuss below, it is difficult to determine what that content is, and even if I wanted to kill the content, I have no role in determining content. The role of historians of thought is to record, not determine, content. What I am declaring dead is the term.

Historians of thought, especially those of us who write textbooks and teach, have some influence over terminology. One of our important jobs is to provide students and non-specialists with insight into what the content of economics is. One of the ways we do so is through classifying—creating terminology that provides students and non-specialists an entree into debates that would otherwise be too complicated to understand. We adopt classifying terminology and give it definitional content. It is historians of thought who are the primary arbiters of descriptive terminology and, hence, we can have a role in changing that terminology. Therein lies the basis for my decree of death.

I. ON CLASSIFICATION

Classifying is not for the faint of heart nor the perfectionist; it requires you to mix what, in a deeper sense, are unmixables, to blend into composites that which does not blend. When you do this, you've got to hold your nose to avoid the resulting reaction, both from researchers who feel mistreated and from other historians of thought who rightly point out the innumerable sensibilities the classification has violated. But classification is necessary, and what we hope is that with the classification, those students who don't go on to further studies will have a better understanding than they otherwise would have had, and that those

---

There is a bug—the Y2K bug—that comes along at the turn of the millennium and bites otherwise sane people, leading them to pontificate about grand issues. Individuals, such as me, who have a natural proclivity to pontificate are especially susceptible, so I ask your forbearance at the beginning; this paper was written under the influence.

[1] Actually it is not clear to me that I have the power to do so, but since my term is almost over, I will assume that before impeachment proceedings can be completed, I will be out of office.

ISSN 1042-7716 print; ISSN 1469-9656 online/00/020127-17 © 2000 The History of Economics Society

students who continue their studies will learn the problems with the classifications, transcend them, and forgive us our compromises that mislead.

Historians of thought have seldom given serious specific consideration to the general characteristics of good classification.[2] Should one focus on temporal dimensions? Should one use terms that tie together the similarities, or terms that emphasize the differences? What is the ideal terminology?

While I certainly don't have the answers to these questions, I do have a few observations and suggestions. The first observation is that since classifications are usually employed to compare one set of thoughts with another, there is one degree of freedom in making classifications. This means that the reference school can be called anything. For example, the longevity of the term "classical" is not so much because the term is good, but is more because it has been the numeraire for other classifications. The neoclassical and New Classical classifications only make sense in relation to Classical, but in itself "Classical" could have been anything. Had economics chosen a different reference term we could be talking about "the New Ricardians" or the "New Marketeers."

The second observation is that most of the classifications economists use have developed serendipitously. A term is used and repeated by a couple of people, and suddenly it is "in use." Such serendipitous terminology generally has a short-run focus—it refers to what immediately preceded it. That's why we see lots of new, neo, new neo, and post (with and without hyphens) modifications of schools.

Let me suggest five classification criteria that I think are important:

1. A classification should help organize thinking about the issues to which it refers, and it should do so in a way that is understandable to the non-specialist.

The reasoning for this criterion is fairly obvious. The whole purpose of the classification is to help non-specialists understand complicated debates. Based on this criterion, the term "Classical" is not an especially good term.

2. A classification should seem natural and intuitive to most practitioners, and acceptable to those thus classified.

Ultimately, assuming we are talking about an existing school, it is the individuals being classified who will have to say if a classification captures their thinking. If they object to it, it will not be likely to last. Luckily, when classifying historical schools, most practitioners are dead and cannot object.

3. A classification should work well over time.

Classifications that are most useful remain appropriate over a fairly long period of time. This criterion does not bode well for any classification with the prefix

---

[2] Joseph Schumpeter (1954) is an exception; he deals with the issue in his discussion of the problems of periodization.

new or neo. Seen against a short term horizon, defining something as "new whatever" makes a lot of sense, since people have a good idea of "whatever" is. But as time goes by, that "whatever" is forgotten and the "new whatever" is less clear. Moreover, what is new in one time period soon becomes old. But, when that happens, the classification often has become sufficiently used so that it is part of the language and difficult to replace. To describe the next development you've got to move to "new new," "neonew," or maybe "neoneo." The same problems exist with the terms modern and post modern.

4. A classification should be used to describe content, not to harbor some ideological content.

The argument for this proposition is, again, fairly obvious; one wants a general criterion that is as value neutral as possible. The "Dummies" would not be a good classification.

5. A classification should have a consistent definition.

Classifications exhibit network externality characteristics. The value of the term is in the image, the set of articles and ideas, that a term brings up in people's minds. A good classification has a standard definition, so when people hear it, they know what is meant by it. It should not mean different things to different people. When a single classification means different things to different people, confusion will result.

   If a classification doesn't meet these five criteria it will clutter the terminological landscape; if it does, then the name can serve a useful purpose: it can complete a picture, and make clear not only the ideas of the group being described, but, like the final piece of a puzzle, also make the others' work clearer. Otherwise, the classification will confuse, not clarify. Just as a piece of a puzzle in the wrong place will obscure a picture rather than complete it, so, too, will a loosely used term.

   All fields have classification problems. In art, for example, one finds some good classifications: impressionism, expressionism, and minimalist bring to mind the art to which they are referring. Of course, art has some bad classifications too. Who knows what is meant by modern or post modern?[3]

II. WHY THE NEOCLASSICAL CLASSIFICATION SHOULD DIE

Given my acknowledgment of the problems of any classification system, the problems with the term neoclassical must be especially onerous to call for its death. In my view they are. The use of the term neoclassical to describe the economics that is practiced today is not only not useful, but it actually hinders understanding by students and lay people of what contemporary economics is. The term may still have a role in intertemporal comparisons, but if it is to do so,

---

[3] It might be argued by a cynic that that ambiguity is precisely the image the terms are meant to bring forth.

it is even more important to have the neoclassical era end at some point.[4] Economics has changed enormously from 1870 to now, and is continually changing. To serve an intertemporal purpose, the term "neoclassical economic school" has to die.

Let me be clear about what I see as the largest problem with the use of the term. The problem is its use by some heterodox economists, by many non-specialists, and by historians of thought at unguarded moments, as a classifier for the approach that the majority of economists take today. We all, me included, fall into the habit of calling modern economics neoclassical when we want to contrast modern mainstream economics with heterodox economics. When we like the alternative, the neoclassical term is often used as a slur, with our readers or listeners knowing what we mean. Of course, historians of thought are far better at avoiding this "slur" use than are others. The worst use, and the place one hears the term neoclassical most often, is in the discussions by lay people who object to some portion of modern economic thought. To them bad economics and neoclassical economics are synonymous terms.

There is much not to like in current economics; but slurring it, by calling it neoclassical economics, does not add to students' understanding of the current failings of economics. Economists today are not neoclassical according to any reasonable definition of the term. They are far more eclectic, and concerned with different issues than were the economists of the early 1900s, whom the term was originally designed to describe. If we don't like modern economics, we should say so, but we should not take the easy road, implicitly condemning modern economics by the terminology we choose.

III. EVOLUTION OF THE TERM NEOCLASSICAL

The story of the evolution of the term neoclassical is a story of metamorphosis. Let me briefly recount its history. The root term, Classical, was coined by Karl Marx (1847) as a description of David Ricardo's formal economics; Marx contrasted Classical with vulgar or romantic economics, by which he meant "economics close to the people." Various writers used the "Classical" terminology and, as they did, the term eventually became a general classifier for the economics of the period running somewhere between 1776 and 1870. Thus we could talk about the evolution of thinking from the mercantilist to the Classical period.

Historians of thought have raised numerous issues about the use of the term Classical. One issue is, when did the Classical period begin? Schumpeter, following Marx, starts the Classical era with Ricardo. He places Adam Smith with the mercantilist pamphleteers, taking the Classical period as 1790 to 1879.[5] Most histories of thought include Smith as a Classical economist. Most writers put the end of the Classical period a bit earlier—in 1870—and start the

---

[4] As I will discuss below in my treatment of the history of the neoclassical classification, that intertemporal role is questionable, too.

[5] Schumpeter considers the issue of classification of Classical economics carefully. In a footnote (p. 379) he remarks that there were three uses of the term Classical. (Elizabeth Schumpeter, who edited the book from his notes states that this section was unfinished.)

neoclassical period with Carl Menger, but such beginning and ending issues, unless they involve a writer of the stature of Smith, are of minor importance. Another issue is whether a single term can encompass such disparate thinkers as Smith and Ricardo. In some ways it would have been much more helpful to have had a separate Smithian school whose focus was on growth, and a separate Ricardian school whose focus was on distributive shares.

From Classical To Neoclassical

In the 1870s there was a qualitative change in some economists' approach to doing economics. During this time utilitarianism and marginalism rose in importance, and deductive models with utilitarian foundations became more fashionable. To capture this change, it was helpful to develop a new classification to distinguish that approach from the earlier Classical approaches based on the labor, or cost, theories of value. The term that developed was neoclassical.

The term neoclassical was initially coined by Thorstein Veblen (1900) in his "Preconceptions of Economic Science."[6] As Veblen used the term, it was a negative description of Alfred Marshall's economics, which itself was a type of synthesis of the marginalism found in Menger and W.S. Jevons with broader Classical themes in Smith, Ricardo, and J.S. Mill. Thus, from the beginning, the term was used by an outsider to characterize the thinking of another group. When Veblen coined it, it was not meant as a description of mainstream economics. In the early 1900s, economics was divided and, in the U.S. at least, neoclassical thought was not mainstream; institutionalism was more embedded than neoclassical thought. Veblen's terminology caught on, and the term neoclassical came into general use and can be found in the writings of W.C. Mitchell (1967), J.A. Hobson (1925), and Eric Roll (1938, 1942).

Hicks (1932, 1934) and Stigler (1941) extended the meaning of neoclassical to encompass all marginalist writers, including Menger, Jevons, and J.B. Clark. Most writers after John Hicks and George Stigler used the term inclusively. Thus it lost most of its initial meaning. Instead of describing Marshallian economics, it became associated with the use of calculus, the use of marginal productivity theory, and a focus on relative prices. As has been noted by a number of authors, while the neoclassical terminology makes some sense for Marshall, who emphasized the connection of his approach with the Classical approach, it makes far less sense for the others, such as Jevons, who emphasized the difference between his views and those of the Classicals. Some have suggested that anti-Classical would have been preferable.

J.M. Keynes (1936), as was his way, disregarded existing usage and developed his own. He lumped Classicals and neoclassicals together, calling them all Classicals—suggesting that the distinctions in pre-Keynesian work were of minor importance. Keynes's use added yet another dimension to the Classical classification: it was a term that was to be contrasted with Keynesian. In the third edition of his principles textbook, Paul Samuelson (1955) built on Keynes's

---

[6] See Tony Aspromourgos (1986) for a discussion. See also Sasan Fayazmanesh (1998).

classification and turned it around on Keynes by developing the neoclassical synthesis. In the neoclassical synthesis, Keynes's dispute with Classical economists was resolved. This use of the term neoclassical as an alternative to Keynesian models provides another confusion because it adds another reference point that brings to mind different elements of thought than would other comparisons.

IV. CURRENT USE OF THE TERM

The most lavish users of the term neoclassical are heterodox economists. (I can always tell when I am around heterodox economists by the number of times I hear the term.) For the most part, mainstream economists don't use the term; when they do, it is used almost unthinkingly, as in "neoclassical growth theory" or "neoclassical synthesis."

The current use of the term by historians of thought is schizophrenic and inconsistent. Most books follow Stigler's lead and include Jevons, Marshall, Léon Walras, Menger, and similar writers as neoclassical economists, thus starting the neoclassical period in 1870 and ending it around 1930. Consistent with this usage, many history of economic thought texts, mine included, are divided into sections: pre-classical, classical, neoclassical, and modern.

That use has its problems, but they fall within the normal set of problems of any classification. My objections to the term neoclassical involve its use to juxtapose modern mainstream economics with heterodox economics, which is another use historians of economic thought make of the neoclassical classification.

Let me give a couple of examples. Roger Backhouse (1985) discusses the neoclassical period as extending from 1890 to 1939. (It is one of his central divisions.) He contrasts that period with the modern period. But then he concludes his book by contrasting modern economics with heterodox economics. There, he talks about "a neoclassical research program" and writes "for all its limitations, and there are many, neoclassical economics has, over the past century, been successfully applied to an ever-wider range of problems" (1985, p. 414). Somehow, neoclassical economics didn't end in 1939, but became merged with modern economics.

In their text, Robert Ekelund and Robert Hebert (1997) emphasize the early work of Augustine Cournot and Jules Dupuit in their discussion of neoclassical economics. Thus their neoclassical period starts at about 1840. They are unclear as to where it ends; they trace the development of "early neoclassical economics," a term that suggests that there is a "later period." They continue that view in the discussion of twentieth-century paradigms where they state that "neoclassical economics blossomed" (p. 404). Thus it would seem that neoclassical economics became the modern orthodoxy.

Stanley Brue (1994) distinguishes the marginalist school of Jevons and Menger from the neoclassical school of Marshall, F.Y. Edgeworth, and J.B. Clark. Neoclassical economists include Edward Chamberlin and Joan Robinson. He then starts the mathematical period in 1935, although he states that that "mathematical economics" does not constitute a separate school of economics (p. 361).

THE DEATH OF NEOCLASSICAL ECONOMICS   133

Mark Blaug (1985) does not use the neoclassical term to describe marginal-ism, but he does use it in two ways, first when discussing macro theory (p. 632), and, second, when he is criticizing modern theory.[7]

As a textbook author, I am sympathetic to the inconsistent use of neoclassical. In popular parlance the term neoclassical is used in two quite separate ways: (1) to describe the economics from 1870 to the 1930s, and (2) to describe modern economics in reference to heterodox thinking today. Textbook authors have a natural tendency to use it in that same way. Unfortunately, the two uses make logical sense only if modern economics is essentially the same in the earlier time period as it is today. You can't have it both ways. Either modern economics is part of neoclassical economics or it isn't.

I quite agree that certain aspects of neoclassical economics remain as part of modern economics. That is true of any field—the new approach accepts certain parts of the previous approach. But, in my view, modern economics is funda-mentally different from neoclassical economics and, if students are to understand modern economics, they must understand that. In our choice of terminology it is more helpful to students to emphasize the differences between modern economics and neoclassical than it is to recognize the similarities.

Modern economics involves a broader world view and is far more eclectic than the neoclassical terminology allows. To capture that eclecticism, modern economics must be given a much broader, and more sympathetic classification, including the penumbra surrounding the core ideas. Thus, the argument I am making is that, for outside observers to understand what is happening in economic thinking today, it is necessary to distinguish a new school of economics that can be contrasted with neoclassical economics in the same way that neoclassical economics was contrasted with Classical economics.

I'm not sure when we should say neoclassical economics died. The most logical cutoff would be somewhere between 1935 and 2000. The date cannot be pinpointed because its death was gradual—a slow transition rather than a sudden epiphany. Game theory made its appearance in 1946. In many ways, the two books that tied up the loose ends and captured the essence of neoclassical economics, Hicks's *Value and Capital* (1939) and Samuelson's *Foundations* (1947), were culminating works—they put all the pieces of marginalism to-gether. Important work thereafter was modern. The very fact that the economics of the 1950s was able to include Keynesian economics as its macroeconomics demonstrates an enormous change in method, approach, and content of econom-ics. Keynesian macroeconomics has few of the characteristics attributed to neoclassical economics.

I should make it clear that I am not alone in declaring the neoclassical terminology dead; some historians of thought, such as Jürg Niehans, don't use the term at all. Even some of those who use it question its usefulness. For example, Mark Blaug writes: "Neoclassical economics transformed itself so radically in the 1940s and 1950s that someone ought to invent an entirely new label for post-war orthodox economics" (1998, p. 2).

---

[7] For example, in his methodological postscript he writes "the besetting methodological vice of neoclassical economics was the illegitimate use of microstatic theories (p. 701).

Hicks (1983, pp. xiii-xiv), who helped broaden the use of the term to include all marginalists in his *Value and Capital* had second thoughts, and in 1983 he suggested that the term neoclassical be killed. And finally, the two writers who have explored the history of the term in depth, Tony Aspromourgos (1986) and Sasan Fayazmanesh (1998), both conclude that the term should die.

Attributes of the Neoclassical School

To make the comparison between neoclassical and modern more concrete, let me list briefly the primary attributes of neoclassical economics that are found in most history of thought texts and contrast them with the primary attributes of modern economics.

1. Neoclassical economics focuses on allocation of resources at a given moment in time.

This attribute is embodied in Lionel Robbins's definition—the allocation of scarce resources among alternative ends—which became the standard definition of neoclassical economics.

2. Neoclassical economics accepts some variation of utilitarianism as playing a central role in understanding the economy.

The movement to demand and subjective choice theory, and away from supply considerations, was a hallmark of early neoclassical thought. While initially the focus was almost entirely on utilitarianism and demand, the focus quickly evolved to a view that demand was only one blade of the scissors.

3. Neoclassical economics focuses on marginal tradeoffs.

Neoclassical economics came into existence as calculus spread to economics, and its initial work was centered around the marginal tradeoffs that calculus focused on.

4. Neoclassical economics assumes farsighted rationality.

In order to structure the economic problem within a constrained maximization framework, one has to specify rationality in a way consistent with constrained optimization. Specific rationality assumptions quickly became central to the neoclassical approach.

5. Neoclassical economics accepts methodological individualism.

This assumption, like the two before it, is closely tied to the constrained maximization approach. Someone must be doing the maximizing, and in neoclassical economics it was the individual. One starts with individual rationality, and the market translates that individual rationality into social rationality.

6. Neoclassical economics is structured around a general equilibrium conception of the economy.

This last attribute is more debatable than the others. Schumpeter made the general equilibrium conception of the economy central to his definition of neoclassical economics. I agree it is important, but if it were absolutely central it would eliminate Marshall from the neoclassical school. However, Schumpeter is right in the following way: in order to make neoclassical economics more than an applied policy approach to problems (something Schumpeter wanted to do) one needs a general unique equilibrium conception of the economy. Formal welfare economics is based on this general equilibrium conception.

V. MODERN ECONOMICS AND THE SIX ATTRIBUTES

My argument against the use of the neoclassical term to describe modern economics is that modern economics does not require adherence to these six attributes. It is much more eclectic. The movement away from neoclassical economics can be traced to the 1930s, when large components of neoclassical theory were being abandoned by cutting edge theorists as they attempted to forge a new economics.

Let me consider each of the six attributes, giving examples of where modern economics parts company with neoclassical economics.

1. Focus on allocation of resources at a given moment in time.

The interest in allocation of resources at a given moment in time ended long ago, the problems solved. Been there, done that. The focus of research quickly turned to allocation over time. In the 1990s, for example, growth has been a key topic. New growth theory is decidedly mainstream and decidedly non-neoclassical. In fact, it is generally contrasted with neoclassical growth theory.

2. Acceptance of utilitarianism.

Few modern economists today accept utilitarianism; most see it as a quaint aspect of the past. One sees very little operational use of utility theory in modern economics. Critics of my view might claim that, in principles and intermediate books, versions of utilitarianism still reign, but they are presented for pedagogical reasons, not because utilitarianism is the reigning approach of modern economists.

3. Focus on marginal tradeoffs.

While many undergraduate texts still present economics within a marginal framework, that is not the way it is presented in graduate schools or the way top economists think about issues. In fact, by the 1930s, in cutting-edge theory, calculus was already being dropped, having been mined for its insights, and math was moving to set theory and topology as economists tried to expand the domain of the economics to include a wider variety of topics. In modern graduate microeconomics, game theory has almost completely replaced calculus as the central modeling apparatus.

4. Assumption of farsighted rationality.

The decrease in the focus on utilitarianism has been accompanied by a decrease in the far-sighted rationality assumption. In modern economics, bounded rationality, norm-based rationality (perhaps established through evolutionary game theory), and empirically determined rationality are fully acceptable approaches to problems.

5. Methodological individualism.

While individualism still reigns, it is under attack by branches of modern economics. Complexity theorists challenge the entire individualistic approach, at least when that approach is used to understand the aggregate economy. Evolutionary game theorists are attempting to show how such norms develop and constrain behavior. New Institutionalists consistently operate out of a framework at odds with methodological individualism.

6. General equilibrium.

The existence of a unique general equilibrium is still the predominantly held view, but that is primarily because general equilibrium models are seldom used. In theory, multiple equilibria work is ongoing, and equilibrium selection mechanisms are an important element of study. Schumpeter made the existence of a single equilibrium the requirement of science, and neoclassical economics never seriously considered the problem of multiple equilibria.[8] In modern economics, theoretical economists are quite willing to consider multiple equilibria, as can be seen in the work of Michael Woodward (1991). It is true that modern work in policy generally avoids any discussion of multiple equilibria, and that is one of the contradictions in modern economics, but the multiple equilibria topic is no longer out of bounds.

VI. TOP MODERN ECONOMISTS

My argument is not that neoclassical economic ideas are not still used; they are. My argument is only that they are not constraining attributes; they are not requirements of what a current economist must do to have a reasonably good chance for success. One can work in a quite different vein and still be considered

---

[8] Schumpeter writes: "Multiple equilibria are not necessarily useless, but from the standpoint of any exact science the existence of a uniquely determined equilibrium is, of course, of the utmost importance, even if proof has to be purchased at the price of very restrictive assumptions; without any possibility of proving the existence of (a) uniquely determined equilibrium—or at all events, of a small number of possible equilibria—at however high a level of abstraction, a field of phenomena is really a chaos that is not under analytical control" (1954).

mainstream. Consider the following names: David Romer, Buz Brock, Richard Thaler, William Baumol, George Akerlof, Joe Stiglitz, David Card, Alan Krueger, Paul Krugman, Ken Arrow, Amartya Sen, Thomas Shelling, etc. I could go on, but these should make my point. Each is considered a top modern economist, but each operates outside the "neoclassical framework" in portions of his work.

Now one could argue that the economists listed above are actually heterodox economists who are deviating from the neoclassical core that is modern economics. But such an argument would be wrong. First, these researchers do not see themselves as heterodox economists, and thus classifying them as heterodox would violate the criterion that a classification should be acceptable to its practitioners. Second, all of them are highly respected economists with jobs at, or offers from, top graduate schools. If the term heterodox is to be meaningful, it should be defined as an approach to problems that is not accepted as legitimate. Thus, my litmus test of heterodox economists is their ability to get jobs at major graduate schools. Marxist and Institutionalist economists are heterodox economists; those on the above list are not. The reality is that, when it comes to content, modern economics is open to new ideas. (I'm not saying totally open, but I am saying at least begrudgingly open.) There are disagreements about content, and about how consistent with general equilibrium theory models should be, but in terms of content, there is significant flexibility, especially at the cutting edge.

VII. THE CENTRAL ATTRIBUTE OF MODERN ECONOMICS

If content does not define modern economics, what does? It is method. The same modern economics that is enormously broad in its acceptance of various assumptions and content is extremely narrow when it comes to method. As Robert Solow (1997) spells out, and as Niehans (1990) emphasizes, *the modeling approach to problems is the central element of modern economics*. Solow writes:

> Today, if you ask a mainstream economist a question about almost any aspect of economic life, the response will be: suppose we model that situation and see what happens ... There are thousands of examples; the point is that modern mainstream economics consists of little else but examples of this process (1997, p. 43).

Modeling is not seen as an end in itself; there is a continual discussion of the need to empirically test, and the formal modeling is undertaken in large part to make the models empirically testable, and applicable to policy, with formal statistical techniques.

Given the changes in economics, the "study of the allocation of scarce resources" definition of economics no longer describes what economists do. A better definition would be, "The study of the economy and economic policies through empirically testable models." An alternative definition comes from Keynes: "Economics is the science of thinking in terms of models joined to the art of choosing models which are relevant to the contemporary world." The point of these new definitions is that they do not consider content; they consider the approach used. Modern economics is economics of the model.

VIII. A MODEL FOR EVERY PURPOSE

To say that modern economics follows a modeling approach is not to say that other periods did not use models. Economists have always used models. But there is a distinction in how the models are used. To see the distinction between modern economists' use of models and earlier economists', it is useful to distinguish between pure theory models and applied policy models. Formal modeling has always been the essence of the pure theory of economics—the metaphysics, or science, depending on one's view. For example, François Quesnay, Ricardo, Cournot, and Walras all simplified their views to develop a theoretical model. Modern pure theory has evolved from the general equilibrium theory of Walras to the general equilibrium of Arrow/Debreu, but the modeling approach has not changed. These pure theory models are highly formal and mathematically deep. But such formal models are not the type of models that the large proportion of economists deal with.

It is in applied policy where modern economics differs from earlier econom-ics. In previous time periods, economists such as Smith or Marshall kept the theory in the back of their minds and thought about the policy problem as an art. Their models were kept in the background, and reasonableness—critical thought—was emphasized in applying the models. Applied policy belonged in what J. N. Keynes (1897) called the "art" of economics. In the art of economics the pure theory model served as a backdrop, but one approached problems in an informal way. Formal empirical testing of such loose models was impossible, but one could easily include non-quantifiable variables and sensibilities in one's policy consideration.

In modern economics that has changed. There is no art of economics in which policy problems are addressed in an informal manner. Modern applied policy models must be specified in a way that can be directly empirically tested, at least in principle. While such models are informal by mathematical standards, they are formal by artistic standards, which is why some observers call modern econom-ics formalist.

Ironically, the modern modeling approach grew out of the Keynesian macroe-conomics of the 1930s and Marshall's practical policy approach to problems. It is a blend of the Keynesian and Marshallian visions of economics with the twist that the models are specified in such a way that they are subject to econometric testing. But in specifying the models so that they are subject to econometric testing, the current approach fundamentally alters the Marshallian approach to policy. The simplified models are moved up to center stage, and the judgment, embodying the blending of the assumptions kept in the back of ones mind which lead to the model's results, are moved to a side stage.

Another aspect of modern applied policy modeling is that, with the exception of work in computable general equilibrium, these models pay almost no heed to consistency with general equilibrium theory. New work in micro emphasizes the development of a variety of practical models, such as the asymmetric pricing model, that are relevant for specific problems, but make no claim that, and give little thought to whether, they are general-equilibrium consistent. Modern applied microeconomics consists of a grab bag of models with a model for every purpose.

Practical models were not always divorced from pure theory models. In the 1950s and 1960s, it was hoped that practical models would be guided by general equilibrium theory. Thus, when Arrow/Debreu proved the existence of a general equilibrium in 1957, there was hope that the pure science of economics would progress in tandem with the practical application of that science. By the 1970s economists recognized that the Arrow/Debreu general equilibrium work was not going to get to the promised land. That recognition freed economists to deal with practical policy models that were inconsistent with general equilibrium theory.

In my view, that recognition accounts for the developments of new growth theory, new trade theory, and other partial equilibrium models that are inconsistent with formal general equilibrium models. They are practical models, which can be loosely tested empirically and which shed some light on issues. Shedding some light on a problem is all that the practical track of modern economics requires. Solow (1997) calls this approach "loose fitting positivism." The difference in view can be seen in the change in approach to increasing returns. Whereas in 1939, when the general equilibrium hope was still alive, Hicks commented that assuming increasing returns could lead to the "wreckage of the greater part of general equilibrium theory" (1939, p. 84), in the 1980s and 90s Paul Krugman, and other new trade, industrialization, and growth theorists proceed as if it is not even an issue. They simply assume away the problems that multiple equilibria and increasing returns raise.

Whereas in micro the evolution has been toward a grab bag of models, the evolution in macro has been different. Modern macro started in the 1940s as a grab bag of ad hoc models inconsistent with general equilibrium theory. Throughout the 1950s and 1960s macroeconomics was the essence of pragmatic eclectic modeling. Macro models focused on consumption functions and quantity theories, based on general aggregate relationships, dominated the field. In these models there was no demand for micro foundations.

That state of affairs was challenged by the New Classical revolution, which argued that Keynesian economics needed micro foundations and had to be consistent with general equilibrium. In the 1980s, New Classical economics had a brief day in the sun by adding farsighted rationality to existing macro models and justifying that addition with a call for consistency with general equilibrium assumptions. In my view it succeeded in becoming important primarily because it offered a relatively easy modeling criterion that led to numerous papers and theses. Its applicability was always in doubt.

By the early 1990s, the New Classical revolution had played itself out; most economists recognized that general equilibrium could not be applied directly to the economy. New Keynesian models incorporated farsighted rationality, but they were primarily partial equilibrium models. Neither New Classical nor New Keynesian models were especially insightful and, in the 1990s, the theoretical focus of attention in macro shifted to growth. Practical and macro modeling was returned to the real-world practitioners, and applied macroeconomics returned to pragmatic, ad hoc modeling.

IX. PROBLEMS WITH MODERN APPLIED ECONOMICS

In many ways the modern movement to applied modeling is laudable. It is empirical and is an attempt to avoid the pontificating that characterized earlier periods. Modern applied modeling looks to the empirical evidence through models. But it also has problems. Since the connection with general equilibrium theory has been eliminated, there is no theoretical core limiting assumptions. New Classicals criticized the lack of a theoretical core in Keynesian macro; that criticism led to its success. Put bluntly, modern applied economics is essentially data mining with some semblance of "scientific empirical testing" added to make it seem less ad hoc. Don't get me wrong; there is nothing wrong with data mining; you can find out much about the economy in the data. My point is that when you data mine, you undercut your ability to formally statistically test the results in a formal manner. If the assumptions of the model are ad hoc, then the results are ad hoc. That doesn't mean that the models can't be informally empirically tested and compared with reality, but the major thrust of modern economics is on formal empirical testing of the models. They avoid the semblance of pontificating by structuring their models in scientific clothing. Thus, in my view, modern applied economics has serious problems.

The problem is exacerbated by incentives within the profession for publishing; these incentives lead to assumptions for the ad hoc pragmatic models often being chosen based on their likelihood of getting published, which requires "nice" results and empirical statistical applicability, rather than their reasonableness. These problems are serious, but they are not the problems of neoclassical economics. In fact, they are problems that developed because modern economics has moved away from the neoclassical assumptions and become more eclectic.

X. THE BIRTH OF THE NEW MILLENNIUM ECONOMICS

A theory can be replaced only by another theory; a term can be replaced only by another term. The staying power of the term neoclassical can, in many ways, be explained by the absence of an alternative. Unless another term is forthcoming and becomes generally accepted and used by historians of thought and other observers, the term neoclassical will continue forever.

A number of alternative terms have been proposed. Xiaokai Yang and Siang Ng (1994) have proposed "new Classical" to describe modern work. The problems with this are (1) the term has already been used to describe an approach to macro; (2) it is unclear whether modern theory is "Classical" in any meaningful sense; (3) the use of the "new" classification is shortsighted and leads to long-run confusion. Stanley Brue's term for modern economics, "mathematical economics," doesn't work because (1) it is not descriptive of much of what is done—most policy models use little deep mathematics; (2) it misses the empirical testing aspect of the modeling; (3) practitioners such as Solow don't like it. The "formalist" classification fails for similar reasons.

Jürg Niehans has come the closest in classifying the modern era when he called modern economics "the era of modeling." It is descriptive and acceptable to most practitioners (Solow emphasized the modeling aspect of modern economics in his description). Its problems are that it fails to capture the nature of the modern applied policy modeling, specifically its tendency to simplify in an ad hoc manner and then empirically test. As I stated above, economists have always modeled; what distinguishes approaches is the nature of the modeling. Ad hoc modelers, or eclectic modelers, would be more descriptive.

My proposal for what to call modern economics is "New Millennium Economics." In doing so I am following Schumpeter's lead in classify schools by temporal terms. The advantages of doing so are the following: (1) The term fits in with the millennium rage; (2) it is forward looking, and thus does not have to deal with the issue of what economics was from 1930 to 2000; some can see it as a transition period; others can see it as the early beginning of New Millennium economics; (3) it is ideologically neutral; it does not come with the excess baggage of Classical or Keynesian or neo, new terminology; (although it will have to be changed when 3000 rolls around); (4) it is easily broken up—there can be an early twenty-first century and a late twenty-first century branch.

XI. CONCLUSION

Let me conclude by briefly talking about changes I see occurring in the future. The changes will be driven by developments in theory that allow modern economics to come to grips with the disconnect between their practical ad hoc models and their pure theory general equilibrium models. This can be accomplished in two ways. Either the underlying pure theory can change, or applied policy work can change. I see both occurring.

In pure theory there are two complementary directions research is taking. One is the development of a general equilibrium theory based on evolutionary game theory, supplemented by experimental economics. This approach "solves" the multiple equilibrium problem by adding an analysis of equilibria selection mechanisms. That work has the potential to change the way we think about general equilibrium theory by providing a richer foundation from which to build practical models.

The other direction is the work of complexity theorists. Their work provides an alternative to a general equilibrium foundation. In the complexity approach, one takes the position that something so complex as the aggregate economy cannot have formal analytic foundations; hence our understanding of it must proceed through alternative means. In complex systems, order spontaneously develops as patterns emerge. Simplicity of complex systems is to be found in the study of dynamics and iterative processes, not in structural simplicity. In the complexity approach, everything is data mining, but it is a highly sophisticated data mining done under specific rules—rules which are just now developing. It

142   JOURNAL OF THE HISTORY OF ECONOMIC THOUGHT

is still a modeling approach, but it is done with computer simulations.[9] The ever-falling costs of computing will push this approach forward in the twenty-first century.

The other change that I see occurring is in how one tests practical models and in how one decides on assumptions. Here I see experimental economics as playing a central role. Experimental economics offers a way of choosing among various equilibria that result from game-theoretic models. I believe it is because of the hope provided by experimental economics that game theory is succeeding now whereas before it did not. Thus, I regard the experimental economics movement as an important development in modern economics. Experimental economics provides a whole new way of testing and applying economic models. Because it does, experimental economics will grow significantly and be an important pillar of twenty-first century economics. Although currently, by my graduate school standards, experimental economics is not yet mainstream, I predict it soon will be.[10]

While I think there will be many changes in economics over the coming century, pragmatic modeling, the major focus of what economists do, is here to stay; it will be the hallmark of New Millennium Economics. Current economics is institutionally stable; it can get enough funding to keep its practitioners doing what they are doing. There will be an evolution, not a revolution. It was in thinking about how to tell the story of that evolution that I came to the conclusion that the term neoclassical must die. Modern economics is fundamentally different from neoclassical economics, and if we are to tell the story of modern economics effectively, we must have a term for modern economics that makes that point.

REFERENCES

Aspromourgos, Tony. 1986. "On the Origin of the Term 'Neoclassical." *Cambridge Journal of Economics* 10 (30): 265–70.
Backhouse, Roger. 1985. *A History of Modern Economic Analysis*. New York: Basil Blackwell.
Blaug, Mark. 1985. *Economic Theory in Retrospect*. New York: Cambridge University Press.
———. 1998. "The Formalist Revolution or What Happened to Orthodox Economics After World War II." 98/10 Discussion Paper in Economics. University of Exeter (October).
Brue, S. L. 1994. *The Evolution of Economic Thought*, 5th ed. New York: Dryden Press.
Colander, D. and Landreth, H. 1994. *History of Economic Thought*, 3rd ed. Boston: Houghton Mifflin Company.
Ekelund, R, Jr., and Hebert, R. 1997. *A History of Economic Theory and Method*, 4th ed. New York: McGraw-Hill.
Fayazmanesh, Sasan. 1998. "On Veblen's Coining of the Term 'Neoclassical'." In Sasan Fayazmanesh and Marc R. Tool, eds., *Institutionalist Method and Value: Essays in Honour of Paul Dale Bush*, vol.1. Aldershot: Edward Elgar.

[9] One individual stands out at the center of both approaches: John von Neumann. His 1928 and 1937 papers, and his 1944 book with Oskar Morgenstern on game theory, pointed the way to expanding general equilibrium via game theory; his work on artificial life and computers is at the foundation of the complexity approach to economics.
[10] The reason experimental economics hasn't become mainstream is that the training required to do it well is so fundamentally different from the training for doing standard deductive economics. This means that integrating it into the curriculum is not a marginal process; it is a jump process.

THE DEATH OF NEOCLASSICAL ECONOMICS   143

Hicks, J. R. 1932. "Marginal Productivity and the Principle of Variation." *Economica* 12 (February): 79–88.

——. 1934. "Leon Walras." *Econometrica* 2 (October): 338–48.

——. 1939. *Value and Capital*. Oxford: Clarendon.

——. 1983. *Classics and Moderns: Collected Essays on Economic Theory*, vol. III. Oxford: Basil Blackwell.

Hobson, J. A. 1925. "Neo-Classical Economics in Britain." *Political Science Quarterly* 40 (September): 337–83.

Keynes, J. M. 1936. *The General Theory of Employment, Interest, and Money*. New York: Harcourt Brace Jovanovich.

Keynes, J. N. 1897. *The Scope and Method of Political Economy*. New York: Macmillan.

Machlup, Fritz. 1963. *Essays on Economics Semantics*. Englewood Cliffs: Prentice Hall.

Marx, K. 1847. *The Misery of Philosophy*.

Mitchell, W. C. 1967. *Types of Economic Theory*, 2 vols., edited by Joseph Dorfman. New York: Kelley.

Niehans, Jürg. 1990. *A History of Economic Theory: Classic Contributions, 1720–1980*. Baltimore and London: The Johns Hopkins University Press.

Roll, E. 1938. *A History of Economic Thought*. New York: Prentice-Hall, 1942.

Samuelson, P. 1947. *Foundations of Economic Analysis*. Cambridge: Harvard University Press.

——. 1955. *Economics: An Introductory Analysis*, 3rd ed. New York: McGraw-Hill.

Schumpeter, J. A. 1954. *A History of Economic Analysis*, edited by E. B. Schumpeter. London: George Allen and Unwin.

Screpanti, E. and S. Zamagni. 1993. *An Outline of the History of Economic Thought*. Oxford: Clarendon Press.

Solow, R. M. 1997. "How Did Economics Get That Way and What Way Did It Get?" *Daedalus* 126 (Winter): 39.

Spiegel, H. W. 1991. *The Growth of Economic Thought*, 3rd ed. London: Duke University Press

Stigler, G. J. 1941. *Production and Distribution Theories*. New York: Macmillan.

Veblen, T. 1900. "Preconceptions of Economic Science." *Quarterly Journal of Economics* 14 (February): 261.

Von Neumann, J. 1928 "Zur Theorie Der Gesellschaftsspiele." *Mathematische Annalen* 100: 295–320.

Von Neumann, J. and O. Morgenstern. 1944. *Theory of Games and Economics Behavior*. Princeton NJ: Princeton University Press.

Woodward, Michael. 1991. "Self-fulfilling Expectations and Fluctuations in Aggregate Demand." In G. Mankiw and D. Romer, eds., *New Keynesian Economics*. Cambridge, MA: MIT Press.

Yang, Xiaokai, and Siang Ng. 1994. "Specialization and Division of Labor: A Survey." Seminar Paper 24/95, Department of Economics, Monash University (December).

PART II

METHODOLOGY FOR MICROECONOMICS

6

8 Applied policy, welfare economics, and Mill's half-truths
David Colander

8.1 INTRODUCTION

The argument in this chapter is a simple one. It is that sometime around the 1930s the economics profession's use of models in thinking about economic policy changed. The result has been a tendency to draw unwarranted policy implications from models and theory, such as occurred in the recent financial crisis. The chapter argues that to prevent such misuse of models from occurring, the economics profession needs to return to the earlier methodological approach, which recognized the complexity of the economy and the relative simplicity of our formal models.

Up until the 1930s what might be called the Classical method predominated in applying models to policy.[1] This method assumed that the economy was too complicated for formal modeling, and that any formal model would have to be seen as providing at best what John Stuart Mill called half-truths (Mill, 1838 [1950]). These half-truths from models would have to be integrated into a much broader implicit theory before they could be applied to real-world policy. Because this broader implicit theory was so complicated, it was accepted that economists would focus only on the economic portion of that broader theory, leaving it to other social scientists, or to economists who were operating outside the science of economics, to add the other elements necessary to draw policy results from economic models. This meant that for Classical economists, welfare economics was not, and could not be, a stand-alone field. Only when these other elements were added could one arrive at policy conclusions.

Classical economists who specialized in methodology recognized that economists would have a tendency to justify their policy prescriptions by claiming the imprimatur of economic science. To help insure against that, Classical economic methodology maintained a strict separation between the science of economics and economic policy analysis. Science was concerned with understanding for the sake of understanding, and was not concerned with policy. This meant that if there was any welfare economics which gave prescriptions for policy, it was not part of the science of economics.

174   *The Elgar companion to recent economic methodology*

The Classical method reflected a skepticism of models and theory, and of what economics could contribute to policy. As an advocate of this Classical method, Lionel Robbins stated: 'What precision economists can claim at this stage is largely a sham precision. In the present state of knowledge, the man who can claim for economic science much exactitude is a quack' (Robbins, 1927, p. 176).

Put in modern context, Classical economists saw the economy as a highly complex and interrelated system that was impossible to model formally. This did not mean that they did not use models; it simply meant that they saw a model's results being blended together with philosophical views, feelings, sensibilities and institutional knowledge to arrive at a policy conclusion. For Classical economists applied policy was an art, not a science.

We can see this separation of policy from models early on in Classical methodological writing. For example, Nassau Senior, the earliest Classical economist who took a strong interest in methodology, writes:

> [An economist's] conclusions, whatever be their generality and their truth, do not authorize him in adding a single syllable of advice. That privilege belongs to the writer or statesman who has considered all the causes which may promote or impede the general welfare of those whom he addresses, not to the theorist who has considered only one, though among the most important of those causes. The business of a Political Economist is neither to recommend nor to dissuade, but to state general principles, which it is fatal to neglect, but neither advisable, nor perhaps practicable, to use as the sole, or even the principle [*sic*], guides in the actual conduct of affairs. (Senior, 1836 [1951], pp. 2–3)

For Senior, and for most early Classical economists concerned with methodology, the economic science of the time was a branch of logic. In the pure science of economics at the time one did theory, which meant that one developed theorems from almost self-evident principles. But, as Senior makes clear, economic theory was not meant to guide policy directly. To move from the theorems developed in the science of economics to the precepts of policy-relevant economics, Classical economists believed that one had to rely on commonsense judgment and institutional knowledge, and that discussing policy involved different skills than did doing economic theory.

This theory–policy divide can also be found in J.N. Keynes's famous summary of economists' methodology at the turn of the nineteenth century (J.N. Keynes, 1891). Like Senior, J.N. Keynes saw the pure science of economics, which he called positive economics, as a relatively narrow branch of economics, which needed to be strictly separated from the applied policy branch – which he called the art of economics. He argued that the two branches needed to be separated because they had quite different methodologies. He writes: 'a definitive art of political economy, which attempts to lay down absolute rules for the regulation of human conduct, will have vaguely defined limits, and be largely non-economic in character' (J.N. Keynes, 1891, p. 83).

8.2   'NEOCLASSICALS' FOLLOWING CLASSICAL METHODOLOGY

This separation of applied policy from the science of economics did not end with Classical economists. It also characterized the approach of numerous economists who are often classified as neoclassical. These include Alfred Marshall, Lionel Robbins, John Maynard Keynes and even A.C. Pigou. In my view, in terms of method (by which I mean methodological views about how economic theory and models relate to policy), all four of these writers belong much more in a Classical tradition than in what has become known as a neoclassical tradition. By that I mean that they maintained the same strict separation between policy and theory that Classical economists did, and saw models as aids to judgment, not as definitive guides to policy.

Consider Marshall and Pigou. While it is true that Marshall and Pigou both developed more formal models than did most earlier Classical economists, and used those models in discussions of policy, it is also true that they were very careful to add a large number of qualifiers that could change the results of the model. Like their Classical ancestors, they both saw economic policy as an art that involves issues outside the domain of economics, and not as a set of prescriptions that followed directly from models. They were careful in their writings to emphasize the limitations of their models. For example, in the core text of Marshall's *Principles* he carefully specifies the limitations of the models rather than developing the analytics of the models. Often, he placed his formal analytics in appendices, not in the core chapters. His *Principles* was designed to teach students how economists thought about policy issues, and to introduce them to some models that could help integrate economic reasoning into their thinking. His textbook was not designed to teach students about how to model the issues formally. Put another way, he was teaching students to be 'consumers' of theory, not 'producers' of theory.

Pigou, the economist most associated with the term 'welfare economics', also carefully limited the applicability of his models. He tells his readers that his analytic work provides only 'vague judgments' and 'instructed guesswork'.[2] He specifically does not draw definitive policy conclusions from his models. For example, in Pigou (1935) he argues that his formal model showing that certain policy actions will improve welfare 'only takes us a little way' in arriving at a policy view. He points out that there are many other issues that the model does not take into account, any of which could reverse the policy argument following from a model. He further states:

> The issue about which popular writers argue – the principle of laisser-faire versus the principle of State action – is not an issue at all. There is no principle involved on either side . . . Each particular case must be considered on its merits in all the detail of its concrete circumstance. (Pigou, 1935, 127–128)

Contrary to popular opinion, Lionel Robbins also falls into this Classical methodological tradition of not drawing policy conclusions from formal models.[3] In his Ely Lecture (Robbins, 1981), Robbins reflects back on how his famous 1932 essay (Robbins, 1932) was incorrectly interpreted by the profession. He states explicitly that the economics profession needs a separate branch, which he calls political economy, to deal with policy. He writes that this policy branch of economics 'depends upon the technical apparatus of analytical Economics; but it applies this apparatus to the examination of schemes for the realization of aims whose formulation lies outside Economics' (Robbins, 1981, p. 8).

It was not only in microeconomic policy that the Classical methodology of strict separation of models and policy continued beyond what is generally thought of as the Classical period. It was also in macroeconomic policy. By that I mean that J.M. Keynes also followed this Classical method, and carefully did not derive policy conclusions from his models.[4] Instead, he used many different models and arrived at a policy conclusion through reasoned judgment. He writes:

> Economics is a science of thinking in terms of models joined to the art of choosing models which are relevant to the contemporary world . . . Good economists are scarce because the gift for using 'vigilant observation' to choose good models, although it does not require a highly specialized intellectual technique, appears to be a very rare one. (Keynes, 1938)

In summary, the economist's method through the 1930s was a method that separated applied policy work from formal models and theories. Applied economics was seen as an art that used economic models, but that also involved much more than those models. To arrive at any policy conclusion, one had to go beyond economic models. In the Classical method, any 'theory' of welfare economics was not a theory to be applied directly to policy. Instead, it was a guide to reasoned thought about applied policy issues. The results of theory were meant to be used with caution, judgment and knowledge of the institutional details. No policy conclusion followed directly from economic theory or from economic models. Consistent with this applied policy approach, discussions of applied policy were to carry warning labels about the limitations of the models. This approach did not mean that economists, in their role as private individuals or statesmen, could not or should not arrive at policy conclusions. What it meant was that if they did so, they should make it clear that they were not claiming economic science as underpinning their arguments.

8.3   THE ABANDONMENT OF THE CLASSICAL METHOD AND THE RISE OF THE NEOCLASSICAL METHOD

Beginning in the 1930s, that Classical 'strict separation' methodology became less and less strict, and by the 1970s it was replaced in the textbooks with a more direct approach of connecting models and policy. Instead of maintaining a strict separation between models and policy, and emphasizing the importance of broader issues in arriving at policy conclusions, models and policy prescriptions became blended into one. To contrast this direct blending of models and policy with the above described Classical methodological approach, I call it the neoclassical methodological approach.

The neoclassical method does not seem ever to have been formally defended in methodological writings, as the Classical method was. It simply evolved over time, as the strict separation qualifications that the Classical methodologists emphasized faded from memory and practice. A full explanation of why this occurred is beyond the scope of this chapter, but my initial thoughts are that the change was associated with a change in the institutional structure within which economists worked, and with the development of empirical methods, which allowed economists to hope that the models could be chosen on the basis of statistical tests, and hence could have empirical foundations that would not necessitate the subjective judgment that Classical economists believed that it did.

The change in institutional structure involved the development of economics as a separate discipline with its own separate training. Up until the 1930s, a majority of those who wrote on economics were not in economics departments. They either were not primarily employed as academics, or were in broader political philosophy departments. Increasingly after the 1930s that changed; economics became a separate academic discipline, and training in economics became narrower as it focused more on pure economic issues, and less on the broad social science and philosophical issues that characterized earlier training. As that narrowing happened, methodology no longer became a topic that economists studied. Instead, economists' work became more focused on the technical issues of modeling. As that happened the extensive discussions of scope and method of economics, which contained the caveats on the use of models in Classical writing, disappeared, either because the writers assumed that economists knew these caveats, and hence they did not require further discussion, or because such methodological issues were not for economists to discuss.

This institutional reason for the change was supplemented by a technological change in how economic analysis was done. Beginning in the 1930s, empirical methods of testing models expanded. This allowed economists to hope that the precision of the models could be increased beyond a 'sham precision'. With developments in econometric theory, there was hope that economics could become a positive science, in which theories and models could be tested, and shown to be true or false. That hope was largely unfulfilled, but the hopes for empirical work likely played a role in changing the economic method guiding applied policy work. If models could be selected on scientifically acceptable empirical grounds, then they could be considered scientific truths, and implications for policy could be drawn from those truths.

It was during this shift from Classical to neoclassical methodology that the formal subfield of welfare economics, which drew relatively firm policy precepts from economic models, developed. Welfare economics moved beyond Marshall's partial equilibrium approach in which models were used as a tool for reasoning about particular policy issues. In the Marshallian approach to applied policy the reasoning chains were kept short, and one would continually emphasize the limitations of the models. In the new welfare economics approach to policy this Marshallian partial equilibrium framework was replaced with a Walrasian general equilibrium framework. This Walrasian framework that pictured the economy as a system of 'solvable' simultaneous equations was much more mathematical than the Walrasian approach, and it drew out policy conclusions from models based on long chains of reasoning, with little to no discussion of the limitations of the models as they related to real-world policy.

These developments led to an enormous burst of creative technical work that extended the partial equilibrium models of Marshall to general equilibrium models. The limitations against using long lines of reasoning to arrive at policy conclusions faded away. In the 1930s and 1940s work in this area advanced economic theory enormously, and a wide range of theoretical issues were cleared up in the writings of economists such as John Hicks (1939), Paul Samuelson (1947) and Abba Lerner (1944). It was a change from a Marshallian economic vision of the economy as a complex system too complicated to model fully to a Walrasian economic vision that was captured by a formal model.

It was during this time period that most of the qualifications of models that Classical economists had emphasized were moved to the back of economists' minds. As I argue in 'The Sins of the Sons of Samuelson' (Colander and Rothschild, 2010), with each successive generation the qualifications about the use of models faded further and further back, and by the 1960s Classical methodology had been replaced by neoclassical methodology in young economists' thinking and in the textbooks.

Of the three economists mentioned above, Abba Lerner was the most likely to draw policy conclusions directly from models and, in many ways, the policy discussion in his *Economics of Control* (1944) served as the template for the teaching of both micro and macro policy starting in the 1950s and continuing until today. Lerner drew specific policy conclusions from his theoretical models in microeconomics and provided few discussions of nuances or limitations.[5] He framed microeconomic policy as a technical issue of meeting the appropriate marginal conditions that were to become the fundamental theorems of welfare economics. Instead of students being taught that models provided half-truths, they were taught that by following the rules of welfare economics that equated marginal social costs with marginal social benefits, policy makers could lead society to a Pareto optimum. These rules, which were known as the Lange–Lerner rules, became the guiding rules of welfare economics, and have become the central frame of undergraduate micro theory in the textbooks.

Similarly, Lerner framed macroeconomic policy as a technical issue of meeting what he called the rules of functional finance (Lerner, 1944). These rules structured macroeconomic policy as following directly from an IS/LM type model, which led to specific policy actions: if income is below what is desired, use expansionary fiscal policy; if income is above what is desired, use contractionary fiscal policy. Use monetary policy to set interest rates so as to yield the optimal amount of investment.

Lerner's rules of both microeconomic policy and macroeconomic policy, because of their simplicity and clearness, became the template for the textbook presentation of both micro and macro policy discussions.[6] These policy rules that Lerner developed were not presented in the texts as general guidelines to be used in combination with non-economic considerations, as were the policy precepts found in Marshall and Pigou. Instead, Lerner's policy rules were presented as firm rules following directly from economic theory. Models were presented as forming the basis of policy – the blueprints that governments should follow – if government wanted to work in the social interest. For example, in the introduction to his *Economics of Control* Lerner writes:

> [we] shall concentrate on what would be the best thing that the government can do in the social interest – what institutions would most effectively induce the individual members of society, while seeking to accomplish their own ends, to act in the way which is most beneficial for society as a whole . . . Here we shall merely attempt to show what is socially desirable. (Lerner, 1944, p. 6)

Unlike Marshall, and Pigou (1920), who carefully discussed the limitations of economic models when arriving at policy conclusions, following Lerner, the new pedagogical presentation of applied policy aggressively related theory and models to policy conclusions. The new pedagogical presentation did not make the Classical distinction between precepts (derived from the art of economics embodying value judgments in the theory) and theorems (derived from pure theory, and quite irrelevant for direct policy application).[7] Lerner's work was the core of much graduate teaching in the late 1940s. Then, as others expanded the models and developed more complicated models that showed the limitations of the arguments, Lerner's work simply became a stepping stone to a much wider range of increasingly complex models taught in graduate school. It remained, however, the central framework of undergraduate presentations of economic policy in both micro and macro, and thereby provided the frame that most economists who do not specialize in welfare economics bring to policy analysis.[8]

I am not arguing that the limitations of that framework were not known or understood. Although in Lerner's presentation, and in the textbook presentations of welfare economics that followed from it, there was little to no discussion of the nuances of application, in more technical advanced work there was a clear exposition of the limitations. Specialists in welfare economics fully understood that the formal models had little value for actual direct policy guidance. For example, in his *A Critique of Welfare Economics*, I.M.D. Little (1950) showed the limitations of the welfare economics as a guide for policy. Similarly, J. de V. Graaff concluded his famous consideration of welfare economics, *Theoretical Welfare Economics*, with the statement: 'the possibility of building a useful and interesting theory of welfare economics – i.e. one which consists of something more than the barren formalisms typified by the marginal equivalences of conventional theory – is exceedingly small' (Graaff, 1957, p. 169). Unfortunately that advanced work was not imprinted on the minds of most economists in the way that the limitations of the models for policy analysis were imprinted on Classical economists.

The decreasing emphasis given to the limitations of economic models for policy can also be seen in the evolution of the presentation of advanced social welfare theory, which abandoned the Pareto optimality approach to welfare economics found in Lerner's approach and replaced it with a social welfare function approach (Bergson, 1938). Analytically, the social welfare function approach was a major improvement; it solved the Hume's dictum problem that one cannot derive a 'should' from an 'is'. It recognized that to derive policy recommendations that involve value judgments, one must explicitly state what underlying value judgments one starts from. But it did so primarily in theoretical expositions, not in real-world applications. By that I mean that while this social welfare function approach helped to clarify the formal structure of the micro policy model, and more correctly specified the analytics of what policy implications could be drawn from the analytics of the model, it nonetheless lost many of the nuances about limitations of applying models to reality that the earlier strict-separation Classical method had maintained. Consider Bergson's initial discussion of the social welfare function (Bergson, 1938). In it, he distinguishes an economic welfare function, in which only economic variables are considered, from a social welfare function, in which all the variables which affect welfare are taken into account.

He emphasizes that his 1938 discussion is of an economic welfare function, not of a social welfare function, which means that he accepts that the economic welfare function approach is only a partial analysis which needed to be combined with insights of other social sciences and philosophy to arrive at a policy conclusion. He justifies his focus on economic variables in his article with the following argument: 'For relatively small changes in these variables, other elements in welfare, I believe, will not be significantly affected. To the extent that this is so a partial analysis is feasible' (Bergson, 1938, p. 314)

But Bergson went even further than that, and later questioned whether a useful separation could be made. In a later article (Bergson, 1954), he expanded on this distinction where he discusses new developments in welfare theory. In this article he repeats his earlier argument that welfare analysis 'must rest on "value judgments" no matter how broad or narrow the scope' (Bergson, 1954, 249) He also writes that his 'own ethical thinking has evolved in the course of time'. He states: 'If value criticism of a deep sort can be meaningful, I still feel that it is also largely philosophic, at least in the present primitive state of psychology.' He concludes: 'I cannot imagine any sensible alternative to ethical counseling.' By this, he meant that the conclusions of any of economic models could not be translated into policy without their being placed in a broader philosophical and ethical context. Welfare economics as a separable branch of the science of economics could not exist, and policy advocacy had to integrate ethical and value considerations. The economics profession did not follow Bergson; instead, it moved further and further away from any discussion of broader issues and concentrated on drawing direct policy conclusions from formal economic models.

What is relevant about Bergson's qualifications and differentiation between the economic welfare function and the social welfare function were soon lost and forgotten in most economists' discussions of applied policy and in the textbooks. To my knowledge, no textbook differentiated an economic welfare function from a social welfare function and made the point that Bergson made that economic welfare was only a small part of social welfare, and policy had to be decided on social welfare grounds, not on economic welfare grounds. Instead microeconomists have translated their economic models' results into direct policy recommendations with few of the broader qualifications that were emphasized in the Classical and Bergson's method.

More advanced critiques of the economic welfare function frame, such as Graaff's and Bergson's, or later Amartya Sen's (1970), seldom made it to the textbooks even in watered-down form, and thus between the 1940s and 1960s there was a major change in how economics was taught and how most economists thought about applied policy. Robert Solow (1997) makes this difference in pedagogy clear in his comparison of 1940s textbooks and textbooks beginning in the 1960s. He writes that books through the 1940s were discursive in nature. He states: 'Most provide more institutional descriptions, very sensible discussions of economic policy, and serious looks at recent history as it would be seen by an economist . . . The authors ruminate more than they analyze' (p. 88) Solow continues:

> the student is not encouraged to make literal use of the apparatus of supply and demand curves. Both books spend time discussing monopolistic elements in real-world markets, but most of the discussion is institutional. Their reflections on the workings of economy are worth reading. They inspire bursts of nostalgia; words like 'civilized' came to mind. (Solow, 1997, p. 89)

Starting in the 1950s, following Samuelson's famous text (Samuelson, 1948), the textbook approach changed. The new style texts placed economics in a scientific framework with the microeconomic presentation organized around supply and demand graphs and a general Walrasian conception of the economy. While the principles-level microeconomic presentations did not present the full optimality presentations, the policy frame that they provided students was one that focused on marginal conditions, and micro policy was discussed in terms of models without significant discussion of the limitations of models. Similarly, its macroeconomics was organized around a Keynesian aggregate expenditures, aggregate production model, in which fiscal policy was needed to keep the economy at full employment, and monetary policy was used to set an optimal interest rate. Samuelson fully recognized the limitations of the models, and some discussion of those limitations show up in addenda in the text and the footnotes. But there is none of the discursive presentation emphasizing how other issues enter into the analysis. Neither is there any broad discussions of limitations of the models such as found in Marshall's *Principles* (1890) or in economic principles textbooks through the 1940s.

Other books followed Samuelson's lead, and that modeling presentation of policy became embedded in economists' thinking. Just how embedded can be seen in Solow's (1997) description of how economists approach problems today. He writes:

> Judicious discussion is no longer the way serious economics is carried out . . . In the 1940s, whole semesters could go by without anyone talking about building or testing a model. Today, if you ask a mainstream economist a question about almost any aspect of economic life, the response will be: suppose we model that situation and see what happens (Solow, 1997, p. 89–90)

8.4   CONCLUSION

The above history demonstrates the changes to the economists' approach to applied economic policy, and to teaching applied economic policy, which occurred in the transition from Classical methodology to neoclassical methodology. In the Classical period and up until the 1940s in the neoclassical period, textbook presentations carefully developed economic policy as only a part of a broader philosophical or social policy; the books were focused on training students to be consumers of economic theory, not producers of economic theory, and the textbook authors saw their role as guiding students in being good consumers of economic reasoning. This meant pointing out the need for context and the limitation of models simultaneously as they taught the models. The narrower neoclassical methodological approach moved directly from economic models to economic policy recommendations. It concentrated on teaching students modeling and understanding the analytics of the model.

These differences are primarily pedagogical differences, and do not necessarily reflect deep changes in economic methodology specialists' beliefs in how economics relates to policy. But, over time, pedagogical decisions have effects, and in economics, they had an enormous effect. They led more and more economists to lose sight of the limitations of models and the need to be humble about what the models are telling us, and what implications can be drawn.

Even if one accepts that economic policy is part of moral philosophy, and that models have to be put in context, an argument can still be made to continue teaching as we do. The issue guiding what economics teaches its students involves practical trade-offs. Consider John Siegfried's consideration (2009) of Stephen Marglin's (2008) call to broaden economic teaching to include much more than the algorithmic knowledge taught in the neoclassical texts. Siegfried agreed with Marglin that teaching students about how models relate to economic policy required much more than what is currently taught, but argued that: 'a persuasive case for a concentrated dose of algorithmic knowledge in economics classrooms can spring from its scarcity elsewhere . . . In the absence of assurance that logical deduction will be emphasized elsewhere in the curriculum, maybe the best use of economics courses is to fill that gap aggressively' (Siegfried, 2009, p. 219).

The difficulty with this argument is that it assumes that students and economists are being trained on the limitations of models elsewhere. But that is not the case. Graduate economic programs provide little discussion of context, and instead concentrate heavily on teaching students modeling techniques. Economic training is geared to creating producers of models, not consumers of models who have the contextual and institutional knowledge, and the incentive to worry, about whether the model is the appropriate model for the purpose. Some economists of course, intuitively or through outside training, incorporate the nuances of applying models to policy problems. But that ability is neither selected for in the admission process, nor is it taught in terms of core content of graduate programs. Those programs emphasize the teaching of modeling techniques, not modeling interpretation. For applied policy, this presents a problem. As Keynes noted in his quotation above, an applied policy economist needs to know both how to model, and how to choose the right model.

The problem with our current approach to teaching models is that it leads to economists who are not trained in the subtleties of applying models to apply models, and to claim the imprimatur of economic science in doing so. Thus, for example, we can see two top macroeconomists, Chari and Kehoe (2006), writing in the AEA's *Journal of Economic Perspectives* that 'recent theoretical advances in macroeconomic theory have found their way into policy' and claiming that:

> The message of examples like these is that discretionary policy making has only costs and no benefits, so that if government policymakers can be made to commit to a policy rule, society should make them do so. (pp. 7–8)

and:

> Macroeconomists can now tell policymakers that to achieve optimal results, they should design institutions that minimize the time inconsistency problem by promoting a commitment to policy rules. (p. 9)

Applied policy, welfare economics, and Mill's half-truths   185

Such hubris about the strong policy implications of highly abstract models whose assumptions do not come close to fitting reality helped lead to the recent financial economic crisis. Such claims of policy certainty flowing directly from models do not sit well with economists trained in the Classical methodology that questions how well the model being used fits the situation being described. For example, Robert Solow, who was trained in the Classical methodology even though he strongly advocates a concentration on modeling, responded to their claims by arguing that their conclusions are totally spurious, and do not deserve to be taken seriously because the dynamic stochastic general equilibrium (DSGE) model that their claims are derived from is so far from the institutional setting of the real-world economy that lessons from the model cannot be directly applied to policy issues.

The primary recommendation following from the arguments in this chapter is that economics policy training could be improved by instituting specific training for applied policy and welfare economics that emphasizes the skills needed to interpret models. It would involve economic history, history of economic thought, real-world institutions, methodology and moral philosophy. This training could exist as a separate track for applied policy economists within economics departments, in public policy programs, in transdisciplinary programs, or in a separate program in political economy as distinct from economic science.

Such training would be much closer to the training that the Classical economists received. The training would involve discussions of technical models, but the goal of the training would be to provide students with a consumer's knowledge of theory and models, rather than with a producer's knowledge of theory and models. The graduates of these applied economics programs, or applied policy tracts, would be seen as the specialists in choosing among models produced by others, and these programs would have their own measures of output quite separate from the measures of output used by current graduate economics programs. Creating a cadre of economic policy specialists could go a long way toward restoring the humility about what claims can be made from our limited models in the face of the enormous complexity of the real-world economy that was expressed in Mill's recognition that analytic models provide at best half-truths.

NOTES

1. Although I call it the Classical method, as I discuss below, its use extended well into what is normally called the neoclassical period.

186   *The Elgar companion to recent economic methodology*

2. See Stephen Medema (2010) for a nice discussion of how Pigou limited the applicability of his models.
3. For a further discussion of Robbins's approach, see David Colander (2009).
4. For a expansion of this issue, see Colander (2011).
5. Specifically, government should adjust resources until a set of marginal conditions are met (Lerner, 1944, p. 96). His rules on income redistribution did not become part of the textbook template. Lerner agreed that we had no basis for making interpersonal welfare comparisons, but argued that because of the uncertainty principle, redistribution was more likely to improve social welfare than hurt it, and thus he supported redistribution, and defined his welfare rules to include redistribution. Later developments switched to a welfare economics focus only on Pareto efficiency.
6. Lerner's early writing played an important role in the socialist calculation debate that was ongoing at the time, and very much concerned the arguments behind the role of the state in the economy. In that debate Lerner advocated market socialism, and argued that socialist planners could give directives to managers to set price at marginal costs, and thereby achieve maximum social welfare.
7. Lerner even extended the analysis to get around interpersonal comparisons of welfare by arguing that while interpersonal comparisons of welfare were impossible, 'probable comparisons' were not, and that redistribution policy should be based on 'probable total satisfaction' (Lerner, 1944, p. 29). Consistent with this view he drew out specific rules for how government could achieve the optimal distribution of income.
8. Ronald Coase's work provides an alternative frame, but few texts are structured around his more Marshallian approach.

REFERENCES

Bergson, Abram (1938), 'A Reformulation of Certain Aspects of Welfare Economics', *Quarterly Journal of Economics*, **52**(2), 310–334.
Bergson, Abram (1954), 'On the Concept of Social Welfare', *Quarterly Journal of Economics*, **68**(2), 233–252.
Chari, V.V. and Patrick J. Kehoe (2006), 'Modern Macroeconomics in Practice: How Theory is Shaping Policy', *Journal of Economic Perspectives*, **20**(4), 3–28.
Colander, David (2009), 'What Was "It" that Robins was Defining?' *Journal of the History of Economic Thought*, **31**(4), 437–448.
Colander, David (2011), 'The Keynesian Method, Complexity, and the Training of Economists', in Arie Arnon, Jimmy Weinblatt and Warren Young (eds), *Perspectives on Keynesian Economics*, Heidelberg, Dordrecht, London and New York: Springer, pp. 183–201.
Colander, David and Casey Rothschild (2010), 'The Sins of the Sons of Samuelson: Vision, Pedagogy and the Zig Zag Windings of Complex Dynamics', *Journal of Economic Behavior and Organization*, **74**(3), 277–290.
Graff, J. de V. (1957), *Theoretical Welfare Economics*, Cambridge: Press Syndicate of the University of Cambridge.
Hicks, John (1939), *Value and Capital*, Oxford, UK and New York, USA: Oxford University Press.
Keynes, John Maynard (1938), Letter to Roy Harrod. 4 July, http://economia.unipv.it/harrod/edition/editionstuff/rfh.346.htm, accessed 15 March 2009.
Keynes, John Neville (1891), *The Scope and Method of Political Economy*, London: Macmillan.
Lerner, Abba (1944), *The Economics of Control*, New York: Macmillan.
Little, Ian Malcom David (1950), *A Critique of Welfare Economics*, Oxford: Clarendon Press.
Marglin, Stephen (2008), *The Dismal Science: How Thinking Like an Economist Undermines Community*, Cambridge, MA: Harvard University Press.

Applied policy, welfare economics, and Mill's half-truths 187

Marshall, Alfred (1890), *Principles of Economics*, London: Macmillan.

Medema, Steven G. (2010), *The Hesitant Hand: Taming Self-Interest in the History of Economic Ideas*, Princeton, NJ: Princeton University Press.

Mill, John Stuart (1838 [1950]), 'Essay on Bentham', in F.R. Leavis (ed.), *Mill on Bentham and Coleridge*, London: Chatto & Windus, pp. 39–98.

Pigou, Arthur Cecil (1920), *The Economics of Welfare London*, London: Macmillan.

Pigou, Arthur Cecil (1935), 'State Action and Laisser-Faire', *Economics in Practice: Six Lectures on Current Issues*, London: Macmillan, pp. 107–128.

Robbins, Lionel (1927), 'Mr Hawtrey on the Scope of Economics', *Economica*, **20**, 172–178.

Robbins, Lionel (1932), *An Essay on The Nature and Significance of Economic Science*, London: Macmillan.

Robbins, Lionel (1981), 'Economics and Political Economy', *American Economic Review*, **70**(2), 1–10.

Samuelson, Paul (1947), *Foundations of Economic Analysis*. Cambridge, MA: Harvard University Press.

Samuelson, Paul (1948), *Economics*, New York: McGraw Hill

Senior, Nassau William (1836), *An Outline of the Science of Political Economy*. London: W. Clowes & Sons; reprinted (1951), New York: Augustus M. Kelley.

Sen, Amartya Kumar (1970), *Collective Choice and Social Welfare*, San Francisco, CA: Holden-Day.

Siegfried, John (2009), 'Really Thinking Like an Economist', in David Colander and KimMarie McGoldrick (eds), *Educating Economists: The Teagle Discussion on Re-evaluating the Undergraduate Economics Major*, Cheltenham, UK and Northampton, MA, USA: Edward Elgar, pp. 215–224.

Solow, Robert Merton (1997), 'How Did Economics Get That Way and What Way Did It Get?' *Daedalus*, **126**, 39–58.

7

Erasmus Journal for Philosophy and Economics,
Volume 6, Issue 2,
Autumn 2013, pp. 1-23.
http://ejpe.org/pdf/6-2-art-1.pdf

A failure to communicate: the fact-value divide and the Putnam-Dasgupta debate

HUEI-CHUN SU
University College London

DAVID COLANDER
Middlebury College

Abstract: This paper considers the debate between economists and philosophers about the role of values in economic analysis by examining the recent debate between Hilary Putnam and Sir Partha Dasgupta. It argues that although there has been a failure to communicate there is much more agreement than it seems. If Dasgupta's work is seen as part of the methodological tradition expounded by John Stuart Mill and John Neville Keynes, economists and philosophers will have a better basis for understanding each other. Unlike the logical-positivist tradition, which treats facts and values as two mutually exclusive concepts, the Mill-Keynes tradition recognizes that facts and values are intertwined. Unlike the Smithian tradition, which blends the study of facts and normative rules, it divides economics into a science that studies "what is" and an art which considers "what ought to be done".

Keywords: methodology, logical positivism, values, positive, normative

JEL Classification: A13, B20, B41

In thinking about the on-going debate between philosophers and economists about the place of values in economics, one cannot help but be reminded of that famous line in the movie *Cool Hand Luke*, "What we've got here is a failure to communicate". Despite attempts to resolve the debate, there seems to be little agreement, with many economists continuing to believe that economics should study and indeed does study facts, not values; many philosophers continuing to

AUTHOR'S NOTE: We would like to thank Partha Dasgupta for helpful comments on an earlier version of this paper. We would also like to thank the anonymous referees and especially the editor Thomas Wells for his careful editing and many suggestions for improvement, many of which we followed. We remain responsible for any errors.

believe that economists are hopelessly confused; and neither side recognizing the other's position as defensible.

A recent flare up of this debate can be seen in the on-going exchange between Hilary Putnam—writing together with Vivian Walsh (2007a; 2007b; 2009; 2012)—and Sir Partha Dasgupta (2005; 2007a; 2009), both representative of the best in their field. The debate between them began in an unusual manner. In his book *An inquiry into well-being and destitution* (1993, 6-7), Dasgupta cited Putnam (1981; 1989) to the effect that an entanglement of facts and values is unavoidable and that that entanglement would influence the way he argued. Based on that citation, and a reading of Dasgupta's work, Putnam saw Dasgupta as an example of how economists can do economic policy analysis right—i.e., by explicitly including ethical judgements in their work.

If Putnam believed that he and Dasgupta were in the same camp, that belief was shattered when, in a 2005 article 'What do economists analyze and why: values or facts?' published in the journal *Economics and Philosophy*, Dasgupta took issue with claims that Putnam had made about how he was including values in his economic analysis. Dasgupta argued that what economists do is analyze facts, and that in professional debates on social policy economists differ primarily on their reading of the facts, not on their values. He further claimed that "Ethics has taken a back seat in modern economics not because contemporary economists are wedded to a 'value-free' enterprise, but because the ethical foundations of the subject were constructed over five decades ago and are now regarded to be a settled matter" (Dasgupta 2005, 221-222). Dasgupta suggested that Putnam was promoting the false impression that modern economics is an "ethical desert".

Dasgupta's paper led to a strong response by Putnam and Walsh in *Economics and Philosophy* (2007a)—to which Dasgupta replied (2007a)—and a longer response in the *Review of Political Economy* (2007b). That ultimately led to a co-edited book (2012), which reprinted their articles together with others by philosophers on their side of the argument. In all these works Putnam and Walsh argue forcefully that Dasgupta has failed to understand Putnam's account of the entanglement of fact and value.

Neither side was persuaded by the other's arguments; despite their exchange in the pages of *Economics and Philosophy* in 2007, both Dasgupta's and Putnam-Walsh's positions remained unchanged. One can see this because Dasgupta published an adapted version of his original

2005 paper in *The Oxford handbook of philosophy of economics* in 2009, under the new title 'Facts and values in modern economics'. Despite the new title the argument remained basically the same as in 2005. The new version made some clarifications in the introductory sections, added a discussion of why Sen's capabilities cannot be seen as primitive ethical notions, and included a short section on estimating poverty. But these changes amplified and clarified his points; they did not change his position. Likewise, Putnam and Walsh did not change their position when revisiting the debate in *The end of value-free economics* (2012) by reprinting their original contributions (2007a; 2007b, 2009). Given the lapse of time, both sides clearly had the chance to amend their published positions if they wanted to. They chose not to. By examining the debate this paper attempts to clarify the issues in dispute and facilitate communication between philosophers such as Putnam and economists such as Dasgupta.

The paper is organized as follows. In Section 1 we review the origins of the debate between Putnam and Dasgupta. In Section 2 we identify two different issues in relation to the debate—the concept of value and the methodology of economics—and argue that these two issues need to be treated separately. We examine the first issue in Section 3 by placing the Putnam-Dasgupta debate in the context of more recent debate about the role of facts and values in the philosophy of science and the philosophy of economics. We examine the second issue in Sections 4 and 5, arguing that the methodology of economics advocated by Dasgupta does indeed belong to a broad classical tradition as Putnam suggested, but to a Mill-Keynes tradition rather than to the Smithian approach presumed by Putnam and Walsh. In Section 6 we conclude by arguing that seeing Dasgupta as a follower of the Mill-Keynes tradition makes it easier to see precisely where Putnam and Dasgupta disagree. Both are convincing within their own context, but outside of that context there is ambiguity and a resulting lack of communication.

1. INTELLECTUAL BACKGROUND TO THE PUTNAM-DASGUPTA DEBATE

To understand the Putnam Dasgupta debate, it is useful to review its origins. In a series of works since the 1980s Putnam has argued against the idea that there is a sharp metaphysical dichotomy between facts and values, and that facts and values are entangled in scientific knowledge (1981; 1990; 1993; 2002; 2003). The main target of Putnam's discussion is logical positivism, which holds that ethical values cannot be legitimate subject-matter of science because they are cognitively meaningless. Putnam's fact-value entanglement arguments are applicable to all sciences, but economics has been of particular interest to him because he believes that logical positivism strongly affected the development of economics in the 1930s, and that its influence still lingers in economics today.

According to Putnam, the logical-positivist movement, combined with several other intellectual currents of the time, shaped economists' idea of economics as a scientific discipline in the twentieth century. Among the results of these influences, Putnam argued, was Lionel Robbins's position requiring a clear-cut distinction between economics and ethics, with ethical judgments having no place in the science of economics (Putnam 2002, 53-54).[1] In Putnam's view, the exclusion of ethics has impoverished economics since then. In particular, the fact-value dichotomy has impoverished the ability of welfare economics to evaluate economic well-being.

Putnam argues that just as economics was embedding a positivist methodology into its vision of itself, philosophy was moving away from logical positivism. As early as 1951 Willard Van Orman Quine launched an attack on the analytic-synthetic dichotomy which, in Putnam's view, eventually collapsed the fact-value dichotomy that lay at the foundation of the logical-positivist approach. In his works Putnam has extended Quine's insights and reinforced the argument against the fact-value dichotomy by exploring the phenomena that he has called the entanglement of fact and value.

The core of Putnam's idea of the entanglement of fact and value is that "the very vocabulary in which we describe human facts [...] frequently fails to be factorable into separate and distinct 'factual' and 'evaluative' components" (Putnam and Walsh 2007b, 185). One of Putnam's own examples can help us understand better what Putnam means by this. According to Putnam, when we say a sentence like 'He is a cruel person', we do not simply 'describe' the person, but also 'evaluate' the person (Putnam 2002, 34-35). It is Putnam's view that when we describe a fact we almost inevitably make an evaluation or

---

[1] While Putman follows the standard way of interpreting Robbins, there is an alternative interpretation that sees Robbins's contribution differently (see Colander 2009). In this alternative view, instead of wanting to keep ethical values out of economics, what Robbins actually wanted to do was to reduce some of the most blatant blending of value judgments and supposedly scientific policy conclusions. We do not discuss such points extensively here since they involve history of thought issues rather than philosophical issues.

value judgment as well. Since making a factual judgment almost inevitably involves value judgments, description and valuation are interdependent and entangled. Note that what Putnam argues against is not the practical *distinction* between facts and values but the metaphysical *dichotomy* or dualism of fact and value (2002, 9-10). The former still considers that fact and value are not the same. Putnam refutes the dichotomy on the ground that the factual and evaluative components in the vocabulary we use are often simultaneously present. While the "cruelty" case may overstate the point, since scientific technical language is generally structured to avoid such obvious entanglements, we fully agree that if one digs deep enough, all descriptive language, and hence all language in science is inevitably value-laden. That is what might be called a base-line metaphysical entanglement that cannot be avoided. But, as a practical matter, one might still want to call a primarily logical proposition, for example, 'Given a utility function with appropriate assumptions, a derived demand curve will be downward sloping', a fact to be distinguished from a relatively more value laden proposition such as, 'Society will be better off if income is redistributed in some fashion'.

One of Putnam's goals is to enrich modern economics by getting economists to recognize not only the negative critique of the fact-value dichotomy but also the positive opportunities of the entanglement of facts and values. Entanglement demonstrates the legitimacy—indeed necessity—of ethical judgments in economic analysis. A major example cited by Putnam of how this opportunity can be taken up by economists is Amartya Sen's capability approach to studying economic well-being.

Several of Dasgupta's works can be seen as practical demonstrations of Putnam's position. His 1993 book *An inquiry into well-being and destitution*, among many other works, shows how economists can and should integrate ethical concerns into their research, and even cites Putnam's work as a justification for this approach. Thus it probably came as some surprise to Putnam that Dasgupta's 2005 article advanced a quite different interpretation of what economists, including Dasgupta himself, were doing. In the resulting exchange both sides seemed to be talking past each other.

2. Tʜᴇ ᴇɴᴛᴀɴɢʟᴇᴍᴇɴᴛ ᴏꜰ ꜰᴀᴄᴛ ᴀɴᴅ ᴠᴀʟᴜᴇ: ᴛʜᴇ ᴅɪꜱᴀɢʀᴇᴇᴍᴇɴᴛ

In a reply jointly written with Walsh, Putnam argues that Dasgupta completely misread his position on the entanglement of facts, theories, and values (Putnam and Walsh 2007a). In response, Dasgupta insists that he understood entanglement perfectly and had no quarrel with it (Dasgupta 2007a).

In examining why they disagree, let us start with an example where their disagreement is evident. In closing his paper, Dasgupta (2005) offers two quotations—from Reutlinger and Pellekaan (1986) and from the World Bank's 1986 *World development report*—to support his central claim that economists have shared ethical values, but differ in their reading of the facts. The same quotations are also used by Putnam and Walsh as evidence that Dasgupta had failed to understand what they meant by the entanglement (Putnam and Walsh 2007b, 185-187).[2] These two quotations are as follows:

> [L]ong run economic growth is often slowed by widespread chronic food insecurity. People who lack energy are ill-equipped to take advantage of opportunities for increasing their productivity and output. That is why policymakers in some countries may want to consider interventions that speed up food security for the groups worst affected without waiting for the general effect of long-run growth (Reutlinger and Pellekaan 1986, 6).

> The best policies for alleviating malnutrition and poverty are those which increase growth and the competitiveness of the economy, for a growing and competitive economy facilitates a more even distribution of human capital and other assets and ensures higher incomes for the poor. Progress in the battle against malnutrition and poverty can be sustained if, and only if, there is satisfactory economic growth (World Bank 1986, 7).

In this case, in saying that economists have shared values, Dasgupta means that the ethical desirability of eliminating destitution is presumed by both sets of authors. He sees the difference in policy recommendations as disagreements concerning the most effective *means* of eliminating destitution that follow from the two parties' differing views of the central causal mechanisms. In contrast, in arguing that the disagreement between the two sets of authors is of an entangled character, Putnam and Walsh mean that the apparent divergence in views regarding the most effective means is actually the result of the authors' different values. In their view, the authors of the *World development report* do not truly share the value of eliminating

---

[2] In fact, the two quotations also appeared in the first chapter of Dasgupta's 1993 book. It is clear that Dasgupta's standpoint did not change over time.

destitution with Reutlinger and Pellekaan: the apparent value agreement is just a disguise for their real unspeakable values (Putnam and Walsh 2007b, 186).

Our claim is that the arguments of both sides can be seen as convincing within their own context while simultaneously being seen as incomplete from the perspective of the other side. Dasgupta is clearly aware that ethical values are often the motivation for economic studies, and hence he agrees that that economics is not value-free. Moreover, he believes, rightly or wrongly, that the ethical values which motivate most economic research are widely shared by economists. There is little doubt that Dasgupta recognizes the entanglement of fact and value at the initial stage of a research project, but he seems to believe that at the later stages of the research, the evaluation of facts will not be entangled with *ethical* values, though he does not deny that other types of values may be involved (Dasgupta 2007a, 471). Putnam disagrees with him on the latter point. For Putnam, it is impossible to make a statement about facts without making an ethical value judgment. He believes that on this point Dasgupta has failed to comprehend the true meaning of his analysis of entanglement and its implications.

Putnam and Walsh argue that the values held by Reutlinger and Pellekaan are different from those of the World Bank, and that this difference in values is at the root of their different reading of the facts. Their sharp critique points out the problem that economists may use so-called 'scientific' theory as cover for ideological beliefs. But can this argument alone defeat Dasgupta's position that economists, even when sharing ends, would still have different views regarding which means would be most effective for achieving them due to their different readings of the facts? And isn't it possible that economists do genuinely agree about some ends, yet still disagree about means due to different understandings of the relevant facts, such as causal mechanisms?

We believe that it is indeed possible, and that as a practical matter good economists, such as Dasgupta, focus their applied work on an analysis of "facts", while recognizing that on a deeper metaphysical level facts and values are intertwined. In developing that applied empirical work, for example in identifying and studying specific causal mechanisms, they will come to different judgments about the facts and their real world significance, but those differing judgments do not mean that they differ about the ultimate goal.

3. Value-free economics?

The debate between Putnam and Dasgupta is just part of a more general debate between philosophers of science. Insight can be gained into their debate by considering that broader philosophical debate, specifically the work of Andrea Scarantino (2009), who divided the relationship between science and values into three types: the 'naïve positivist view', the 'separatist view', and the 'non-separatist view'. The naïve positivist view is that values should not play any role at any stage of the activities of scientific economists and that, if they do, economists have violated the methodological conventions that make economics a science. Neither Putnam nor Dasgupta holds those views. Where they differ is that Dasgupta is more of a separatist, and Putnam is more of a non-separatist.

Following Scarantino (2009), in order to distinguish the separatist and non-separatist views we need to distinguish both between epistemic values and non-epistemic values, and between internal activities and bordering activities. The epistemic/non-epistemic distinction is similar to the distinction made by Mark Blaug between 'methodological values' and 'normative values' (Blaug 1992, 114; 1998, 372). The term 'epistemic value' is used by philosophers of science to refer to those values which govern the meaning and formulation of scientific knowledge. For instance, accuracy, consistency, and simplicity. In contrast, 'non-epistemic value' is used to refer to all other values that may be involved, i.e., values which are not instrumental to the establishment of scientific knowledge. Ethical, political, and socio-cultural values belong to this category. Internal activities are the core activities that economists do—the research that determines what will be considered economic facts (Scarantino 2009, 465-466). They relate to what philosophers call the context of justification. Bordering activities refer to the selection of which economic problems to investigate, or what philosophers call the context of discovery, and to the use made of economic knowledge once acquired.

According to Scarantino, the non-separatist view holds that "both epistemic and non-epistemic values have a legitimate role to play in the 'internal activities' of scientific economists" (2009, 466).[3] Putnam can thus be seen as a non-separatist. For him, it is impossible to exclude

[3] Other scholars who hold this view include Phyllis Rooney (1992), Peter Machamer and Heather Douglas (see Machamer and Douglas 1999; Douglas 2007), and Helen Longino (1990).

values—both epistemic and non-epistemic—from either the internal or the bordering activities of economists.

The separatist view lies in between the naïve positivist view and the non-separatist view. While the naïve positivist view represents the ideal of science as free from all values, the separatist view represents the ideal of science as free only from non-epistemic values because it recognizes the inevitability of epistemic values in scientific activities. Moreover, as Scarantino points out, it is compatible with separatism to see the bordering activities of scientific economics as laden with non-epistemic values. But the legitimate influence of non-epistemic values is restricted to the prior and posterior stages of the pursuit of economic knowledge, such as choosing socially significant problems to work on and interpreting the policy relevance of results.

Using Scarantino's classification, the disagreement between Putnam and Dasgupta about Dasgupta's position can be better understood. Putnam sees Dasgupta as a naïve positivist whereas the view Dasgupta actually holds seems closer to separatism. This understanding of their debate by no means allows us to resolve the ongoing disagreement between non-separatism and separatism. Nevertheless, the removal of an apparent misunderstanding can be a first step to more effective communication between them, since they would at least be in agreement about what it is they are disagreeing about.

Putnam is fully aware of the distinction between epistemic and non-epistemic values. But he does not put much weight on it, because he considers that both types of values are ultimately inseparable (Putnam 2002, 31-33). Indeed, it is likely that non-epistemic values would indirectly influence economists' research by influencing how epistemic values are taken up. But the distinction does help us to clarify that whether economics is value-free is not the key point in the debate between Putnam and Dasgupta: both believe that economists' bordering activities are laden with non-epistemic values and that their internal activities are laden with epistemic values. The real disagreement between them is about whether any part of economic analysis can be free from *ethical* value judgments, or, more precisely, whether economists can avoid making ethical judgments in their internal activities. In our view, Putnam does not respond to this question adequately in his reply to Dasgupta, even if his non-separatist view is the right one.

Several outstanding economists and economic methodologists have advocated a careful study of the impact of values on the scientific activities of economists. For instance, back in the 1930s Gunnar Myrdal (1953 [1930]) argued that economists' personal traits, disciplinary traditions, and the interests and prejudices of the society they lived in would inevitably influence their research through influencing the approach they chose, their explanatory models and theories, the concepts they used, and the procedures they followed in making observations and drawing inferences. In 1973 Myrdal reiterated his argument, emphasizing the importance of studying the sociology and psychology of economists (Myrdal 1973). However, until recently the exploration of these fields remained a "neglected agenda" (see Backhouse 2005). How the formation of economic knowledge is influenced by non-epistemic values acting through epistemic values is indeed an important question. But in addition to pursuing a full account of such issues, there might be some other ways in which economists can improve the quality of economic studies. We argue that Dasgupta believes so and that this is the key message of his 2005 article.

4. DASGUPTA'S MISSED MESSAGE ABOUT ECONOMIC METHODOLOGY

The title of Dasgupta's 2005 paper 'What do economists analyze and why: values or facts?' implies the dichotomy of facts and values rather than their entanglement, as Putnam and Walsh commented. It reinforces the puzzle of why Dasgupta would insist that economists study facts not values if he accepts the entanglement of facts and ethical values, at least to some degree. We believe that Dasgupta had an important message to convey but failed to communicate it clearly, and we suggest that Putnam and Walsh's failure to understand him was partly due to their reading of him as under the influence of the logical-positivist tradition with its demarcation between fact-based science and value-based ethics. Dasgupta's position cannot actually be understood in this logical-positivist tradition.

For Dasgupta, the main challenge for policy analysis in the economics profession at present is not the lack of ethical foundations. The much more pressing issue for economists is to improve their understanding of the factual side of social problems. In our view, Dasgupta's claim that economists share many ethical values is an overstatement, but one that can be justified as a reasonable simplification that explains and justifies why economists try to structure their debates so as to focus on issues where their ethical differences are not in play. The simplification is a useful idealization because it allows Dasgupta to focus on the more important claim that refining our understanding of the factual aspects of a social phenomenon can benefit the policy debate regardless of what one's ethical views are. In our view, this key point in Dasgupta's argument did not receive enough attention from Putnam and Walsh. As an economist, and perhaps especially as a development economist, Dasgupta's main concern is with how to refine our understanding of facts for policy analysis. That is a question about the pragmatic methodology that economists should use. Dasgupta's aim is mainly practical, not theoretical or philosophical. He does not so much downplay the significance of ethics as play up the significance of *operational* solutions that improve policy analysis. As he put it bluntly, "I am a practicing economist, not a philosopher" (Dasgupta 2007a, 370).

Dasgupta is not alone. The goal of improving the reading of facts for practical purposes has a long history in economics. Pursuing this goal does not really distinguish him from other contemporary economists. What makes Dasgupta unusual is his practice of economics, which, as recognized by Putnam and Walsh, distances him from mainstream neo-Walrasian theory and puts him more in line with classical economic theory (Putnam and Walsh 2007b, 195). We also see Dasgupta's approach as in line with the classical tradition. But unlike Putnam, who associated Dasgupta with Adam Smith, we argue that Dasgupta's approach to economic policy analysis is better placed in the Mill-Keynes tradition. Looking through this lens, what Dasgupta is doing is consistent with what he claims he is doing.

5. DASGUPTA AND THE MILL-KEYNES TRADITION OF METHODOLOGY

Putnam and Walsh (2007b, 193-195) quoted extensively from Dasgupta's discussion of destitution to demonstrate that Dasgupta's work belonged to the classical tradition. Using the same passages quoted by Putnam and Walsh, we will provide an alternative reading of Dasgupta.

> [A]ll the equilibria in the timeless economy are Pareto-efficient [...] This means, among other things, that there are no policies open to the government for alleviating the extent of undernourishment other than those that amount to consumption or asset transfers. A common wisdom is that such policies impede the growth of an economy's productive capacity because of their detrimental effect

on saving and investment, incentives, and so forth. But this is only one side of the picture. Our model will stress the other side, which is that a transfer from the well-off to the undernourished can enhance output via the increased productivity of the impoverished (Results 7 and 8). We don't know in advance which is the greater effect, but to ignore the latter yields biased estimates of the effects of redistributive policies. [...]

By developing the economics of malnutrition, I will offer a final justification for the thesis that it is the singular responsibility of the State to be an active participant in the allocation mechanism guiding the production and distribution of positive and negative freedoms. This justification is built on the idea that in a poor economy markets on their own are incapable of empowering all people with the opportunity to convert their potential labour power into actual labour power. As a resource allocation mechanism, markets on their own simply aren't effective. The theory I will develop below also shows how a group of similar poor people can become fragmented over time into distinct classes, facing widely different opportunities. Risk and uncertainty will play no role in this. It is a pristine theory of class formation (Dasgupta 1993, 476-477).

Putnam and Walsh used these passages as evidence of the fact-value entanglement in Dasgupta's work and the concordance between Dasgupta's and Smith's economic writings. But reading Dasgupta through the Mill-Keynes lens gives us what seems a better view of his true intentions. We suggest the similarities of Dasgupta's approach with the Mill-Keynes tradition can be identified from the following two aspects.

a) The knowledge of 'what ought to be' is distinct from, but based on, the knowledge of 'what is'.

Dasgupta's work suggests that he would accept the science-art distinction proposed by John Stuart Mill. On the one hand, science and art are distinct (Mill 1967 [1844], 312). Science, which concerns the knowledge of 'what is', is different in nature from art, which concerns the knowledge of 'what ought to be'. On the other hand, science and art are closely interrelated. Art assigns ends to science; science informs art of the means available for achieving those ends; based on the knowledge provided by science, art decides what ought to be done to achieve the ends (Mill 1974 [1872], 944-945). Note that the science-art distinction is not equivalent to the fact-value dichotomy. A key difference between the two is that while the latter implies that science deals with facts and art deals with values, the former does not.

From the second passage cited above, we can see how Dasgupta intends to base his normative judgment on the knowledge of facts provided by science. The statement that "it is the singular responsibility of the State to be an active participant in the allocation mechanism guiding the production and distribution of positive and negative freedoms" is a normative one. It is clear in Dasgupta's writing that this normative judgment "is built on" the idea that "in a poor economy markets on their own are incapable of empowering all people with the opportunity to convert their potential labour power into actual labour power", which is a reading of fact derived from his scientific economic analysis of malnutrition (Dasgupta 1993, 477). Dasgupta would not deny that his claim that markets are incapable of empowering all people might involve a value judgment, but for him the statement is a positive statement, not a normative one. The statement does not indicate what ought to be done. It alone cannot tell us why the State rather than non-governmental organizations should be the remedy for the failure of markets. It does not even suggest that leaving the markets alone should not be an option, unless we already consider it desirable to try to empower all people to convert their potential labour power into actual labour power and this aim is not trumped by other aims.

b) It is necessary to adopt an interdisciplinary approach to reading facts to remedy the limitations of mainstream models relating to their unrealistic assumptions.

Despite being critical of mainstream economic models, Dasgupta does not deny their contribution. He has issues with them because he believes they present an unrealistic view of the world—because their construction neglects crucial *facts*, such as basic needs and physiological phenomena—and hence they are unable to provide an accurate reading of economic phenomena. For Dasgupta, the mainstream models can be a poor guide to the causal mechanisms involved because of inappropriate assumptions and construction. The ethical values held by economists might be the cause of the problem, but not necessarily. In his 2005 article, Dasgupta shows that as a practicing economist he aims to deal with those cases in which ethical values are *not* the cause of economists' mistaken reading of causality.

In view of the limitations of the standard models, Dasgupta includes scientific knowledge from outside economics in his analysis of policy. In his research, the knowledge provided by disciplines such as physiology, the science of nutrition, ecology, and so on, plays an important role in understanding the factual side of social phenomena.[4]

At the very beginning of chapter 16 of his 1993 book, Dasgupta points out that the standard theory of resource allocation fails to take into account the *fact* that meeting physiological maintenance requirements is a precondition of labour power. The term 'economic disfranchisement' is used by Dasgupta to point out the illusion, suggested by the standard theory, that every labourer is on an equal footing in terms of converting potential labour power into real labour power in the labour market. He therefore attempted to construct a theory that took human physiology into account.

It is true that the ethical values held by Dasgupta may have contributed to his interest in the phenomenon of economic disfranchisement and redistributive policies. Yet it is also true that although concluding that "models that are dissonant with physiological truths are hopelessly incomplete" (1993, 475), Dasgupta does not attack the standard theory from an ethical point of view, but from a factual point of view. From the first passage cited above, we can see that Dasgupta intends to disprove the "common wisdom" by showing that the outcomes derived from the standard model will not come about if the positive effects on productivity of a transfer from the well-off to the undernourished are greater than its negative effects on saving and investment. The approach he took to refute the standard theory is very much 'scientific' in Mill's sense, rather than 'ethical' or 'normative'.

According to Mill, social science is a deductive enterprise, but one which follows the model of the physical sciences, rather than that of geometry. Social science, he wrote,

> infers the law of each effect from the laws of causation on which that effect depends; not, however, from the law merely of one cause, as in the geometrical method; but by considering all the causes which conjunctly influence the effect, and compounding their laws with one another (Mill 1974 [1872], 895).

---

[4] See, for instance, Dasgupta 1990; 1997; 2003; 2007b; 2008; Dasgupta and Ray 1987; Dasgupta and Mäler 2000.

In Mill's view, the complexity of social phenomena does not arise from the number of the laws, but "from the extraordinary number and variety of the data or elements—of the agents which, in obedience to that small number of laws, co-operate towards the effect" (Mill 1974 [1872], 895).

Dasgupta's approach to asset transfer policies is a good example of Mill's deductive method. Dasgupta identifies two main effects of a transfer: decreasing savings and investment on the one hand while increasing the productivity of the impoverished on the other hand. These two tendencies can be seen as co-existent intermediate mechanisms which will have different effects on economic growth. According to the physical 'deductive method', the final result of the transfer policy should be estimated by summing up the individual effects of the co-existent intermediate causes. In contrast, the approach adopted by the standard model is equivalent to the 'geometrical method' because it does not admit the modification of the presumed psychological law (the behaviour of saving and investing will be negatively affected by the transfer) by another law (the improvement in nutrition will increase productivity).

It is worth noting that Mill does not pretend that it is possible to calculate the aggregate result of many co-existent causes with complete precision. In his view, it is beyond human faculties to take into account all the causes which happen to exist in one case (Mill 1974 [1872], 898). But, as a practical science, if economics can provide us with knowledge of tendencies, it gives us a considerable power to "surround [our] society with the greatest possible number of circumstances of which the tendencies are beneficial, and to remove or counteract, as far as practicable, those of which the tendencies are injurious" (Mill 1974 [1872], 898).

From the above discussion, we can see that the scientific aspirations of Dasgupta's economic writings are clearly in line with the approach explicitly stipulated by Mill. This scientific dimension is absent from Smith's work. Indeed, Mill's proposal of the science-art distinction specifically took Smith as a target. In Mill's view, the title and arrangement of Smith's book *An inquiry into the nature and causes of the wealth of nations*, despite being suitable for the purpose of his work, had caused a general misunderstanding of the nature of economics as a science. Smith's approach tended to mix up what makes a nation rich (what is) with what a nation ought to do to increase its wealth (what ought to be done). For Mill, the latter is not an appropriate subject for scientific economics; it should be the subject of political economy as *art* (Mill 1967 [1844], 312). Moreover, according to Smith the object of political economy is firstly to enable the country's people to provide sufficient necessaries and conveniences of life for themselves and secondarily to supply the state with a revenue sufficient for the public service (Smith 1976 [1776], book 5, Introduction). For Mill, the desirability of these objects is determined by art, not by science (Mill 1967 [1844], 312).

Dasgupta is not the only economist whom Putnam and Walsh have held up as a paradigm of Smithian methodology, and not the only one who turns out not to fit that model quite as well as they supposed. Putnam and Walsh have also suggested that Sen's work, and especially his capability approach, is in the Smithian tradition (Putnam 2002, 2003; Putnam and Walsh, 2007b). In terms of Sen's methodology, we do not see it that way—Smith blended normative and positive analysis without separating normative and positive economics in any logical way. Sen does the opposite; he carefully specifies what in his analysis is normative and what is positive, and explains why his normative analysis is much more consistent with most people's normative views than are the implicit normative judgments in standard analysis. This, in our view, puts him in the Mill-Keynes methodological tradition, which evolved from Smith's partly by criticizing Smith for his lack of clarity about the difference between what economics studies and what the ends of economics and economic policy ought to be.

In the first chapter of his book *On ethics and economics* (1987), Sen identifies two origins for economics in ethics and engineering. Sen groups Smith and Mill together in the ethics-related tradition, which is correct in the sense that both Smith and Mill see economics as a branch of moral philosophy (i.e., the ultimate end of economic knowledge is to make life better, and hence ultimately economics cannot be independent from ethics). But we would add an extra distinction to Sen's classification that allows us to distinguish Smith and Mill in terms of their methodology. Whereas Smith blended his normative and positive analysis together, Mill carefully attempted to distinguish art from science. Thus, like Putnam and Walsh, we see Sen as following Smith's (and Mill's) ethical tradition—in the sense of seeing economics as a branch of moral philosophy. But unlike them we see Sen's *methodology* as deriving from the more sophisticated Mill-Keynes tradition rather than Smith's. This is what we mean by saying that Sen belongs to the Mill-Keynes approach, not the Smithian approach.

It is intriguing to note that enriching the nation, the major goal of Smith's political economy, has been implicitly taken over by many modern economists as a value-neutral goal, while equitable distribution, which is less directly addressed by Smith, is considered as value-laden and hence as an illegitimate subject for economics. Mill's distinction between science and art could in effect support Putnam's intention of revealing the biased attitude of some economists towards different ethical values that leads to biased readings of facts.

Dasgupta rarely if ever refers to Mill in his work. However, it is not entirely surprising to find similarities between their methods of doing economics. Daniel Hausman once commented that "[t]he temper and character of modern economics still embodies the Millian vision of the discipline as a separate science" (Hausman 1992, 225). Modern economics may not have developed in quite the way Mill had hoped, but it is fair to say that his analysis of the nature and methodology of economics was indirectly and partially inherited by contemporary economists through the influence of John Neville Keynes and Robbins.

In *The scope and method of political economy* (1917 [1890]), J. N. Keynes took up Mill's distinction between positive science and normative art and further developed it into a tripartite division of economics in accordance with his classification of knowledge According to this classification, a positive science is a body of systematized knowledge concerning what is; normative or regulative science is a body of systematized knowledge relating to the criteria of what ought to be; and an art is a system of rules for the attainment of a given end. Each has its own distinct objectives: for a positive science the objective is to establish uniformities; for a normative science it is to determine ideals; for an art it is to formulate precepts. Accordingly, investigations into economic uniformities, economic ideals, and economic precepts can be categorised respectively as the positive science of political economy, the ethics of political economy, and the art of political economy (see 1917 [1890], 31-36).[5]

In our view, the Millian approach did not end with J. N. Keynes. In particular, we have argued elsewhere (Colander 2009) that Robbins is best interpreted as working within this tradition, and that that sheds

---

[5] For a detailed discussion of Keynes's tripartite division of economics, see Colander 1992.

a quite different light on his message. Specifically, we argue that Robbins (1945 [1932]) advocated not only the importance of separating positive economics from ethics but also a separate, non-scientific branch of economics to deal with issues of values. Robbins noted that the majority of classical economists used the term political economy to cover "a mélange of objective analysis and applications involving value judgments" (1976, 1; 1981, 7). In his 1981 Ely Lecture and in the introduction to his 1976 book *Political economy, past and present*, Robbins suggested that the use of the term 'political economy' should be revived, to maintain a space in economics where ethical values play a central role (1976, 2-3; 1981, 7-8).[6] According to Robbins, this political economy is not part of economic *science*, but it is an integral part of economic studies.

Mill's call for economics as a science separate from art has been largely realized in the economics profession over the past 150 years, but the line of descent from Mill through Keynes and Robbins to today took various turns. Each inflexion caused some changes to the direction of the development of economics, and the final outcome is very different from what Mill would have expected. We do not deny the problems of modern economics that emerged during its formation as a separate discipline. But, with a correct understanding of the Mill-Keynes tradition of methodology, and particularly by recovering the integral role of art in economic studies, the economics profession could do a much better job than it does now to highlight the way values are integrated into economic analysis.[7]

Specifically, we believe that when Dasgupta's arguments are interpreted through the Mill-Keynes lens, rather than a Smithian one, his arguments make much more sense philosophically. They are not deep philosophical arguments but pragmatic arguments about how to move forward in tentatively separating positive truths from normative rules, even while accepting that on a deep level they may not be fully separable. Instead of letting fact-value entanglement lead one to an

---

[6] Robbins uses the term in a narrower sense than Smith: Robbins uses the term to designate only the prescriptive part of economic investigation, whereas Smith's political economy concerned both what we have been calling positive science and normative art.

[7] We have discussed elsewhere how the economics profession can improve by reintroducing the Mill-Keynes methodological tradition (see Colander 1992, 2001, 2013; Su 2012). It involves distinguishing separate methodological approaches for applied policy economics and for the pure science of economics, along the lines suggested by J. N. Keynes.

impasse, one distinguishes those factual judgments and normative judgments that are most separable, accepts that others are not, and gets on with one's analysis.

We are not especially concerned with whether Dasgupta is actually a follower of either Smith or Mill. Our argument is that seeing Dasgupta within the Mill-Keynes tradition helps clarify his methodology. The Mill-Keynes interpretation allows us to understand how Dasgupta considers himself able to integrate ethical considerations into his economic policy analysis without sacrificing the scientific character and objectivity of his economic analysis. In the Mill-Keynes methodological tradition, the scientific branch of economic studies is separated from applied economic policy analysis. The separation is meant to enhance the quality of the latter by improving the understanding of economic phenomena through adopting appropriate scientific methods. Putnam may disagree with the Mill-Keynes methodology, but we believe his criticisms would be better understood by Dasgupta, and other economists, if they took explicit account of the pragmatic art-science foundations of his methodology, and did not reduce them immediately to the fact-value dichotomy associated with the logical-positivist tradition, and which the Mill-Keynes economic tradition did not embrace.

6. Conclusions

The debate between Putnam and Dasgupta was perceived by Putnam to be about whether economics is value-free or not, as indicated by the title of his recent book with Walsh about their side of the debate, *The end of value-free economics*. We have suggested in this paper that this was a misperception. The fact-value divide is problematic, but it is not the key to the Putnam-Dasgupta debate. We have argued that Dasgupta was mistakenly understood by Putnam and Walsh as holding a naïve positivist view, which insists on a dichotomy between fact-based science and value-based ethics and argues that economics should be free from all sorts of values. In our view, the confrontation between Putnam and Dasgupta is actually between a non-separatist view and a separatist view. More specifically, the disagreement between them is about whether it is possible for economists to avoid making ethical value judgments when they try to explain observed economic phenomena in an objective factual way.

The philosophy of science debate between the non-separatist view and the separatist view is on-going. The implications of these two views for scientific activities require more investigation. In particular, if ethical value judgments cannot be avoided even in internal scientific activities—as the non-separatist view claims—then it is important for economists to understand how this entanglement occurs in order to know how to minimize the resulting biases in their research, as much as one can. However, real-world economic problems are pressing and cannot wait for solutions until we have a satisfactory answer to these profound questions. Moreover, even if it is true that economists' reading of facts is inevitably influenced by their personal values, it is not necessarily the case that their different readings of the facts can be solely explained by differences in their *ethical* values. For these reasons, the value of Dasgupta's call for refining the reading of facts should be acknowledged, and the Mill-Keynes tradition rediscovered.

REFERENCES

Backhouse, Roger. 2005. Economists, values and ideology: a neglected agenda. *Revue de Philosophie Économique*, 11: 49-73.
Blaug, Mark. 1992 [1980]. *The methodology of economics: or, how economists explain.* Cambridge: Cambridge University Press.
Blaug, Mark. 1998. The positive-normative distinction. In *The handbook of economic methodology*, eds. John Davis, D. Wade Hands, and Uskali Mäki. Cheltenham (UK): Edward Elgar, 370-374.
Colander, David. 1992. The lost art of economics. *The Journal of Economic Perspectives*, 6 (3): 191-198.
Colander, David. 2001. *The lost art of economics: economics and the economics profession.* Cheltenham (UK): Edward Elgar.
Colander, David. 2009. What was "it" that Robbins was defining? *Journal of the History of Economic Thought*, 31 (4): 437-448.
Colander, David. 2013. The systemic failure of economic methodologists. *Journal of Economic Methodology*, 20 (1): 56-68.
Dasgupta, Partha. 1990. Well-being and the extent of its realization in poor countries. *Economic Journal*, 100 (400): 1-32.
Dasgupta, Partha. 1993. *An inquiry into well-being and destitution.* Oxford: Oxford University Press.
Dasgupta, Partha. 1997. Nutritional status, the capacity for work and poverty traps. *Journal of Econometrics*, 77 (1): 5-37.
Dasgupta, Partha. 2003. Population, poverty, and the natural environment. In *Handbook of environmental and resource economics: environmental degradation and institutional responses*, eds. Karl-Göran Mäler, and Jeffrey R. Vincent. North Holland: Elsevier, 191-248.

Dasgupta, Partha. 2005. What do economists analyze and why: values or facts? *Economics and Philosophy*, 21 (2): 221-278.

Dasgupta, Partha. 2007a. Reply to Putnam and Walsh. *Economics and Philosophy*, 23 (3): 365-372.

Dasgupta, Partha. 2007b. Nature and the economy. *Journal of Applied Ecology*, 44 (3): 475-487.

Dasgupta, Partha. 2008. Nature in economics. *Environment Resource Economics*, 39 (1): 1-7.

Dasgupta, Partha. 2009. Facts and values in modern economics. In *The Oxford handbook of philosophy of economics*, eds. Harold Kincaid, and Don Ross. Oxford: Oxford University Press, 580-640.

Dasgupta, Partha, and Karl-Göran Mäler. 2000. Net national product, wealth, and social well-being. *Environment and Development Economics*, 5 (1): 69-93.

Dasgupta, Partha, and Debraj Ray. 1987. Inequality as a determinant of malnutrition and unemployment: policy. *The Economic Journal*, 97 (385): 177-188.

Douglas, Heather. 2007. Rejecting the ideal of value-free science. In *Value-free science?: ideas and illusions*, eds. Harold Kincaid, John Dupré, and Alison Wylie. Oxford: Oxford University Press, 143-163.

Hausman, Daniel. 1992. *The inexact and separate science of economics*. Cambridge: Cambridge University Press.

Keynes, John Neville. 1917 [1890]. *The scope and method of political economy*. London: Macmillan.

Longino, Helen E. 1990. *Science as social knowledge*. Princeton: Princeton University Press.

Machamer, Peter, and Heather Douglas. 1999. Cognitive and social values. *Science and Education*, 8 (1): 45-54.

Mill, John Stuart. 1967 [1844]. On the definition of political economy; and on the method of investigation proper to it. In *Collected works of John Stuart Mill, vol. IV*, ed. J. M. Robson. Toronto: Toronto University Press, 309-339.

Mill, John Stuart. 1974 [1872]. *A system of logic, ratiocinative and inductive*. In *Collected works of John Stuart Mill, vol. VIII*, ed. J. M. Robson. Toronto: Toronto University Press, 833-952.

Myrdal, Gunnar. 1953 [1930]. *The political element in the development of economic theory*. London: Rutledge and Kegan Paul.

Myrdal, Gunnar. 1973. The need for a sociology and psychology of social science and scientists. In *Against the stream: critical essays on economics*. New York: Pantheon Books, 52-64.

Putnam, Hilary. 1981. *Reason, truth, and history*. Cambridge: Cambridge University Press.

Putnam, Hilary. 1989. Objectivity and the science/ethics distinction. *WIDER Working Paper* 70. World Institute for Development Economics Research, Helsinki, FI.

Putnam, Hilary. 1990. *Realism with a human face*. Cambridge (MA): Harvard University Press.

Putnam, Hilary. 1993. Objectivity and the science-ethics distinction. In *The quality of life*, eds. Martha Nussbaum, and Amartya Sen. Oxford: Clarendon Press, 143-157.

Putnam, Hilary. 2002. *The collapse of the fact/value dichotomy*. Cambridge (MA): Harvard University Press.

Putnam, Hilary. 2003. For ethics and economics without the dichotomies. *Review of Political Economy*, 15 (3): 395-412.

Putnam, Hilary and Vivian Walsh. 2007a. A response to Dasgupta. *Economics and Philosophy*, 23 (3): 359-364.

Putnam, Hilary, and Vivian Walsh. 2007b. Facts, theories, values and destitution in the works of Sir Partha Dasgupta. *Review of Political Economy*, 19 (2): 181-202.

Putnam, Hilary, and Vivian Walsh. 2009. Entanglement throughout economic science: the end of a separate welfare economics. *Review of Political Economy*, 21 (2): 291-297.

Putnam, Hilary, and Vivian Walsh. 2012. *The end of value-free economics*. London: Routledge.

Quine, Willard Van Orman. 1951. Main trends in recent philosophy: two dogmas of empiricism. *Philosophical Review*, 60 (1): 20-43.

Reutlinger, Shlomo, and Jack van Hoist Pellekaan. 1986. *Poverty and hunger: issues and options for food security in developing countries*. Washington: World Bank.

Robbins, Lionel. 1945 [1932]. *An essay on the nature and significance of economic science*. London: Macmillan.

Robbins, Lionel. 1976. *Political economy, past and present: a review of leading theories of economic policy*. London: Macmillan.

Robbins, Lionel. 1981. Economics and political economy. *The American Economic Review*, 71 (2): 1-10

Rooney, Phyllis. 1992. On value in science: is the epistemic/non-epistemic distinction useful? *Proceedings of the Biennial Meeting of the Philosophy of Science Association*, 1: 13-22.

Scarantino, Andrea. 2009. On the role of values in economic science: Robbins and his critics. *Journal of the History Economic Thought*, 31 (4): 449-473.

Sen, Amartya. 1987. *On ethics and economics*. Oxford: Basil Blackwell.

Smith, Adam. 1976 [1776]. *An inquiry into the nature and causes of the wealth of nations*, ed. Edwin Cannan. Chicago: University of Chicago Press.

Su, Huei-chun. 2012. Beyond the positive-normative dichotomy: some remarks on Colander's lost art of economics. *Journal of Economic Methodology*, 19 (4): 375-390.

World Bank. 1986. *World development report*. Oxford: Oxford University Press.

Huei-chun Su is an honorary research associate at the Bentham Project at University College London, UK. She is the author of the book *Economic justice and liberty: the social philosophy in John Stuart Mill's utilitarianism* (Routledge, 2013). Her research interests include history of economic thought, philosophy of social and economic policies, and moral philosophy.
Contact email: <h.su@ucl.ac.uk>

David Colander is College professor at Middlebury College. He has authored, co-authored, or edited over 40 academic books as well as numerous textbooks, and 150 articles on a wide range of topics.

His books have been, or are being, translated into a number of different languages, including Chinese, Bulgarian, Polish, Italian, and Spanish. His most recent book (with Roland Kupers) is *Complexity and the art of public policy: solving society's problems from the bottom up* (Princeton University Press, 2014).
Contact email: <colander@middlebury.edu>

[8]

Framing the Economic Policy Debate

David Colander

Economists' current policy frame, which is organized around the concept of market failure, provides a powerful lens through which to view the world and organize one's thoughts about policy. It is not the only, or most natural, frame through which to view policy. It is a product of history, and it coevolved with the analytic technology of the time. That analytic technology is changing, and as it changes, other policy frames become slightly more likely to be adopted. This article discusses that historical evolution and how changing analytic technology is opening up the possibility for movement away from the market failure policy frame.[1]

Let me be clear from the beginning: my argument is about policy frames, not about current economic theory or mainstream understanding. I am not making an argument that the current theory is wrong or that most economists do not understand or are unfamiliar with the limitations of the current market failure policy frame. One can find many insightful discussions throughout the literature exploring the nuances, caveats, and limitations of the current model. But the discussions seldom make it down to the layperson summaries of economic policy. So the issue is not knowledge or insight of the economics profession. The issue is what might be called the

Correspondence may be addressed to David Colander, 215 Munroe, Interdepartmental Studies, Middlebury College, Middlebury, VT 05753; e-mail: colander@middlebury.edu.
    1. This article summarizes and further develops arguments made in Colander and Kupers 2014.

History of Political Economy 47 (annual suppl.) DOI 10.1215/00182702-3130535

254   David Colander

simplification process—what gets chosen as a standard textbook policy model, which structures laypeople's thinking about what economics has to say about economic and social policy.

Why can we arrive at a policy frame that is limiting even though the underlying economic understanding is not limiting? Because policy frames are not chosen through explicit choice. In current academic institutional structures there is little incentive for economists to reflect on policy frames.[2] Thus the policy frame tends to be selected by historical, institutional, and marketing factors that reflect the needs of economic researchers, teachers, and publishers, not top economists' judgments as to what would be an ideal policy frame from a social perspective. For example, the chosen frame reflects what authors believe the textbook market wants, not their consideration of what they believe students need to learn or of how best to convey deep economic understanding to laypeople.[3]

The article is organized as follows. First, I summarize the current "market failure" policy frame as it is generally presented to policymakers and students. Second, I discuss how that policy frame evolved from a much looser and more inclusive classical policy frame. I conclude with a brief discussion of how recent advancements in analytic and computational technology are increasing the chances for the policy frame to change.

2. I do not discuss the evolution of policy frames here; I have discussed it elsewhere, and my argument is that institutional incentives lead economists to convey a policy frame to laypeople that is nonoptimal. One could argue that a frame is just a frame, and that with appropriate nuances and caveats that one can find in the existing literature, the existing frame, or any well-specified policy frame, can be consistent with the same policies I am advocating be explored. So frames are not necessarily limiting. People familiar with the technical literature surrounding any policy frame should be able to go beyond any specific policy frame and recognize its assumptions and limitations. Thus policy frames are generally considered a pedagogical issue, not a limiting issue for policy. I disagree with that way of seeing policy frames. I see frames as highly limiting. Most laypeople, and many economists, do not have the time and have not explored the technical literature, noting nuances and assumptions of the frame they are using. For that reason, the nuances and caveats necessary to move from the existing policy frame to the one I am advocating, while they were part of the development of ideas, tend to be lost and have not become part of most laypeople's and policymakers' policy frames.

3. An example of this process can be seen in the reviewer pool for economic principles books. This pool is drawn from potential adopters who generally are not cutting-edge economists, deep theorists, or specialists in the area being taught. This group of economists seldom teaches principles and thus, unless one of them decides to write a book, has little to do with the principles course. Those who do write a text quickly learn that the focus groups guiding the edition are not specialists in areas but nonspecialist teachers who are more interested in pedagogy than in nuanced content. They want a better, more teachable, presentation of the existing frame rather than a consideration of broader issues that are not part of the existing frame.

Economists' Current "Market Failure" Policy Frames

The current economic policy frame has two variations—one an activist policy frame, the other a "free market" policy frame. The variant presented in most textbooks is the activist "market failure" policy frame. In this frame, an individual's tastes are given, and the invisible hand of the market is assumed to guide the economy to desirable results. But that guidance is not perfect; for example, externalities and other market failures may exist that the market does not account for. Government policy is needed to correct for these market failures in which private costs do not equate to social costs.[4] The goal of government policy in this policy frame is to make private costs equal to social costs in individual decisions.

The groundwork for the "market failure" frame occurred in the 1930s when multivariate calculus was introduced into economic theory. Multivariate calculus allowed economists to study the theory of optimal allocation in a much more precise manner than they could heuristically or with geometric tools. Although multivariate calculus had been around for a long time, before the 1930s and 1940s mathematical economics was seen simply as a small branch of economics, not as the core. That changed in the 1940s as economics shifted from a Marshallian partial equilibrium "one-thing at a time" approach, in which intuition and judgment guided policy discussion, to a Walrasian general equilibrium approach in which policy discussion was closely connected to theory. Structuring the economic problem within a mathematical control theory framework allowed a much clearer understanding of pure allocative rationing processes and how those processes related to markets. John Hicks's *Value and Capital* (1939) and Paul Samuelson's *Foundations* (1947) changed the way that economic theory was thought about, and laid the groundwork for the market failure policy frame.

The pedagogically focused market failure framework was introduced into economics in Abba Lerner's *Economics of Control* (1944).[5] Paul Samuelson (1948) then took that "economics of control" framework and

---

4. This sense of it as an activist frame can be seen in its introduction into economics. It was introduced by economists such as Abba Lerner and Paul Samuelson who favored an active role for government and was opposed by many of the more laissez-faire economists such as Lionel Robbins, Friedrich Hayek, and Frank Knight. For a discussion of how this came about, see Colander and Freedman 2011.

5. I discuss this history in more detail in Colander 2005 and 2011 and Colander and Kupers 2014.

256   David Colander

put it at the core of his textbook presentation of microeconomic policy. Other texts followed, and, over the years, the market failure policy framework has become so built into the economist's mind-set that few, other than historians of economic thought and heterodox economists, know that other frameworks exist.[6]

This market failure policy frame is built on a theory of costless market success that can be mathematically specified as a multiperson constrained optimization problem with government as an outside controller. It structures the economic policy problem as a LaGrangian constrained optimization problem and in doing so provides important insights into the problem of allocating scarce resources among alternative ends. This framework assumes an institutional structure within which individuals know what they want and have exogenous tastes. They can trade costlessly at equilibrium prices that are somehow determined by the market. Given these assumptions market success can be costlessly achieved through market transactions by individuals voluntarily trading. There are no transactions costs or problems of strategic interaction. Economists' theoretical general equilibrium model demonstrates that the equilibrium achieved after these trades has certain desirable characteristics. The intuitive essence of the policy model is that if people make a voluntary trade, they do so because the trades make them better off. As individuals become better off, society tends to be better off.

While a costless market success model underlies this policy frame, the policy focus of the frame is on market failures. It directs attention to situations in which voluntary trades will not make society better off even though the trades are costless. Much of the policy discussion centers on the possible existence of externalities that occur when there are third parties not explicitly part of the trade who are positively or negatively affected by the trade. When externalities exist, there is a market failure associated with voluntary trade, since all the costs of the trade are not being taken into account by the voluntary traders. In such cases, assumed costless government intervention can bring private costs and social costs into equilibrium, increasing social welfare.

Government's role in this policy frame is not only to internalize externalities. It is also to adjust the income distribution to maximize social welfare. The reason is that private optimization does not necessarily achieve a social optimum; it simply allows improvements from an initial

6. Malcolm Rutherford (this volume) nicely discusses the institutionalist alternative.

position. Whether a social optimum is achieved depends on the distribution at the initial starting point. The market failure policy frame integrates distributional issues into the analysis through the use of a social welfare function that embodies outside-specified normative judgments into the analysis.[7] The government is assumed to know this social welfare function and to have the desire and ability to undertake the appropriate redistributional policies to achieve the optimal social welfare.[8]

Recognition of Limits of the Standard Policy Frame

As I emphasized at the beginning of the article, my focus is on policy frames, not economists' understanding of the issues. The limitations and problems of the market failure policy frame are well known to economists and specialists in public policy. The literature has an extensive discussion of just about any aspect of the policy frame's limitations, and did from early on. As an example of early developers of the frame recognizing its limitations, in this section I briefly consider some of the qualifications included in early seminal work by Abram Bergson (1938) on social welfare functions and Francis Bator (1958) in developing the market failure policy frame. Let me start with Bergson.

In his seminal 1938 article, Bergson carefully distinguished between a social welfare function, W, and an economic welfare function, E. The difference between the two was a set of variables, $r, s, t \ldots$, which were catch-all variables that included all the other elements that affected social welfare. These were allowed to vary in the social welfare function, but were taken as given in the economic welfare function. By distinguishing a *social* welfare function from an *economic* welfare function, he was making the point that any consideration of economic policy needed to be seen as an input into a broader social consideration of policy before it is applied. It could not be applied directly.

By including $r, s, t \ldots$'s in the analysis, market failure is no longer the only way in which the market can fail. There can also be failures of

---

7. Usually the social welfare function that the government is assumed to use is an equality-preferring social welfare function that weights low-income people's utility higher than high-income people's utility. If costless redistribution is assumed, as it generally is, then by redistributing income appropriately, the government can achieve a social optimum.

8. How government accomplishes its task is unspecified. Government is assumed to be an outside controller, which allows the model underlying the framework to be specified as an optimal control theory model.

258   David Colander

market outcomes (Colander 2003). Failures of market outcomes occur
when the market is doing everything it is supposed to in terms of the economic welfare function, but the indirect effects of economic actors on
social welfare through the *r, s, t* . . . 's are overwhelming the direct effects.
In Bergson's approach, any application of the social welfare version of the
market failure policy frame to real-world problems would have to explicitly explore whether these additional elements were important. He writes:

> The symbols r, s, t . . . , denote elements other than the amounts of com-
> modities, the amounts of work of each type, and the amounts of the
> non-labor factors in each of the production units, affecting the welfare
> of the community.
>
> Some of the elements r, s, t . . . , may affect welfare, not only directly,
> but indirectly through their effect on (say) the amounts of X and Y pro-
> duced with any given amount of resources, e.g., the effects of a change
> in the weather. On the other hand, it is conceivable that variations in the
> amounts of commodities, the amounts of work of each type, and the
> amounts of non-labor factors in each of the production units also will
> have a direct and indirect effect on welfare; e.g., a sufficient diminution
> of x_i and y_i may be accompanied by an overturn of the government. But
> for relatively small changes in these variables, other elements in wel-
> fare, I believe, will not be affected. To the degree that this is so a partial
> analysis is feasible.

The market failure policy frame that economists use today does not
distinguish between a social welfare function and an economic welfare
function. Hence, it does not direct students and policymakers to think of
the limitations of focusing their analysis of welfare on material goods
rather than on broader social welfare, as it would have had the distinction
between social and economic welfare been emphasized.[9]

A second example of the early work recognizing the limitations in the
market failure policy frame can be found in Francis Bator's seminal
"Anatomy of Market Failure." Bator (1958, 378–79) writes:

> More important, at this level of discourse—though perhaps it hardly
> need be said—is that statical market efficiency is neither sufficient nor
> necessary for market institutions to be the "preferred" mode of social

9. The distinction between social and economic welfare was lost rather quickly, as Samuelson (1947) did not distinguish Bergson's economic welfare function from a social welfare
function.

organization. Quite apart from institutional considerations, Pareto efficiency as such may not be necessary for bliss. If, e.g., people are sensitive not only to their own jobs but to other people's as well, or more generally, if such things as relative status, power, and the like, matter, the injunction to maximize output, to hug the production-possibility frontier, can hardly be assumed "neutral," and points on the utility frontier may associate with points inside the production frontier. Furthermore, there is nothing preordained about welfare functions which are sensitive only to individual consumer's preferences. As a matter of fact, few people would take such preferences seriously enough to argue against any and all protection of individuals against their own mistakes (though no external effects be involved).

All this is true even when maximization is subject only to technological and resource limitations. Once we admit other side relations, which link input-output variables with "noneconomic" political and organizational values, matters become much more complicated. If markets be ends as well as means, their nonefficiency is hardly sufficient ground for rejection. On the other hand, efficient markets may not do, even though Pareto-efficiency is necessary for bliss. Even with utopian lump-sum redistribution, efficiency of the "invisible hand" does not preclude preference for other efficient modes of organization, if there be any.

In a footnote he adds:

This is too crude a formulation. It is not necessary that markets as such be an "ultimate" value. Political and social (non-output) values relating to the configuration of power, initiative, opportunity, etc., may be so much better served by some form of nonefficient market institutions than by possible alternative modes of more efficient organization as to warrant choice of the former. The analytical point, in all this, is that the outcome of a maximization process and the significance of "efficiency" are as sensitive to the choice of side-conditions as to the welfare-function and that these need be "given" to the economist in the same sense that a welfare function has to be given. (378n4)

Throughout his article, one can find such nuanced discussion of the strengths and weaknesses of the market failure policy frame he is developing. Few texts, including graduate texts such as Mas-Colell, Whinston, and Green 1995, today include such nuanced discussions so that that nuance found in the early specification of the market failure policy frame has not become associated with laypeople's, politicians', and students'

260   David Colander

conceptions of what economics has to say about policy. Given the lack of
discussion of nuance, laypeople are led to see the economic policy frame
as *the* policy frame to use when thinking about economic policy, not as a
useful, but as a limited, policy frame, which needs to be applied carefully
with many addenda, as Bator presented it.

The Stigler-Coase Promarket Policy Frame Variant:
The Market Success Policy Frame

While the above market failure policy frame was being explored and built
into the textbooks, there was a general concern about its use by many
economists who had a promarket orientation. Their concern was that the
market failure policy frame seemed to justify government intervention
because it downplayed many of the reasons that they opposed government
interventions. For example, some opposed government intervention
because of ethical considerations; laissez-faire advocates argued that freedom of choice found in markets was desirable in its own right independent
of whether it maximized economic welfare or not.

   Others such as James Buchanan and Gordon Tullock (1962) argued that
the standard market failure policy frame obscured the public choice problems with government intervention. They argued that politics, not altru-
ism, guided government, and so there should be no presumption that the
government would maximize social welfare even if it could specify it.
Their work led to the development of a concept of government failure that
paralleled the concept of market failure. Government failure occurs when
government does not act in the way assumed by the model. This idea of
government failure has become part of the standard textbook market failure policy frame, and policy is now often presented in a more ideologically neutral setting than previously. It now involves determining the
least-worst option: market failure or government failure.

   These, and other concerns, were all important, but they are adjustments, not alternative frames. The theoretical promarket alternative frame
to the market failure policy frame is not those, but rather what might be
called the Stigler-Coase "market success" policy frame. The difference
between the standard market failure policy frame and the Stigler-Coase
market success policy frame is that the standard "market failure" policy
frame assumes externalities are pervasive in the economy; thus it focuses
on the need for government policy to deal with them. The Stigler-Coase
alternative sees externalities as almost nonexistent because of the private
market's ability to internalize externalities on its own.

The reason externalities are nonexistent is to be found in the assumption of the standard model. If there are no transactions and negotiations costs, as there are not in the formal specification of the market failure model, then why should any externalities exist? Individuals affected by any trade can enter into negotiations with anyone affected to see that their interests are protected. Since trades are assumed to take place only after all negotiations are complete, and there are no negotiations costs, the end result of voluntary activity is that all beneficial voluntary trades are undertaken.[10] Any externalities are internalized by private traders. There is no need for government; given the assumptions of costless negotiations and zero transactions costs, the private market comes to the ideal solution.[11]

**From a Classical Policy Frame to
the Current Policy Frame**

As I have discussed in other papers and books (Colander 2005, 2011; Colander and Friedman 2011; Colander and Kupers 2014), the movement to the current market failure policy frames occurred from the 1930s through the 1960s as economics was moving away from a classical economics methodology, which strictly separated economic theory from economic policy, to a Walrasian neoclassical methodology, which did not. Instead, the Walrasian neoclassical methodology, which underlies the market failure policy frame, blended theory and policy in a formal mathematical model, directly drawing policy results from theoretical models.

I specifically do not call the current policy frames "neoclassical," because doing so makes it seem as if all neoclassical economists would accept them. This is definitely not the case. Many early neoclassical economists, such as Alfred Marshall, Lionel Robbins, and J. M. Keynes, did not use a Walrasian methodology or a mathematical model. Instead, they continued to use a classical methodology that blended the market failure frame into the classical policy frame, making it much more ambiguous as to the policy implications of economic theory. In the classical policy frame, in order to decide policy implications, one had to explore the nuances as well as

10. The social welfare addition is much more difficult to add to this model, but advocates of this market success frame usually take the position that government should have no role in redistribution or any other aspect of social welfare that the economic welfare function does not include.

11. An excellent discussion of how this development occurred can be found in Medema 2011. In Colander and Freedman 2011, we explore the development of these ideas and how they related to policy.

the formal theory. Thus Marshall saw economic theory as an engine of analysis; it was only one of the tools to be used by economists in developing policy. Theory had to be combined with judgment and other insights. Those following a Walrasian neoclassical methodology saw economic theory differently; they saw it as providing direct guidance for policy.

This Walrasian market failure frame of government policy is quite different from the "sophisticated Classical policy frame" found in John Stuart Mill (1848) and some early neoclassical non-Walrasians such as Marshall, Robbins, or even A. C. Pigou. While these non-Walrasians might discuss market failure, that discussion was closely tied to the limitations and nuances of the analysis. The sophisticated classical policy frame presents policy as much more complicated than anything that could be presented in a formal model; it involved numerous noneconomic, philosophical, and normative issues, all of which had to be integrated into the analysis before one could move from theoretical conclusions of models to policy conclusions. Classical economists saw this policy integration as belonging in a different branch of economics than pure theoretical scientific economics.[12] Within this classical policy frame, policy was built on the insights of economic science, but was not based directly on economic science.

The classical justification for laissez-faire was not a theoretical justification that the market was efficient. Laissez-faire was supported by classical economists as a precept, not a theorem. A "precept" is a reasoned judgment based on a consideration of all real-world issues—not just problems highlighted by economic theory. Classical economists' support for laissez-faire was not a theoretical support for an abstract market; it was a practical support for dealing with the problems outside the state because, in their judgment, the state generally could not be relied on to arrive at better solutions. In making that judgment, they incorporated problems of government failure and ethical judgments with economic theory.

Laissez-faire was justified not by science or theory but by appeal to Adam Smith's impartial spectator's judgment. It is a policy position that they felt an educated economist whose ethical judgments reflected the general ethical and moral views of existing society would hold.[13] Laissez-faire held that, while highly imperfect, real-world free markets were the

---

12. J. N. Keynes (1890) called the policy branch of economics "the art of economics." Lionel Robbins (1981) called it "political economy."

13. Classical economists' support for laissez-faire had important ethical elements—classical economists favored individuals having as much freedom as possible. Thus freedom was seen as an end in itself. It was also a means to an end. Freedom allowed individuals to try out new ways of doing things, and generated economic growth.

least-worst option in many cases. But not in all cases. The policy frame came to no noncontextual conclusions; and judgments would have to be continually made—there was no blanket proposition that the market was the best option or that government should or should not intervene in the market.

Why the Classical Policy Frame Was Replaced

The explanation for why the profession moved from the classical policy frame to the market failure policy frame is complicated and deeply integrated with the institutional structure of the profession. My short story goes as follows.[14] In the 1930s economists were discovering how useful multivariate calculus was for thinking about multiple market resource allocation problems. As they did, cutting-edge theorists began moving away from the Marshallian generalized partial equilibrium analysis in which the model's limitations were emphasized, replacing it with a Walrasian general equilibrium approach in which the limitations received less emphasis. Because they were trained in a classical methodological tradition, most initial developers such as Hicks, Samuelson, and Bergson used the market failure policy frame in a nuanced manner. But as their students, and their students' students, moved away from that literary tradition, and as economics became more of a mathematical science, the nuance faded. As a shorthand, economists starting thinking about economic policy as closely connected to the Walrasian model and the market failure policy frame. As that happened, the nuanced classical policy frame gave way to the less-nuanced market failure policy frame.

The classical policy frame was replaced not because economists felt that the classical approach to policy was wrong or because they believed that the market failure frame was a better frame. Instead it was replaced because the market failure policy frame fit better with the mathematical specification of theory that they were developing. Given the analytic technology, it was more teachable; it better fit the evolving pedagogical needs of the economics profession at the time. Specifically, the market failure policy frame nicely fit the technological and analytic developments of the time that were focused on analyzing efficient allocation problems rather than other aspects of economic policy. The policy frame provided elegant simple mathematical models through which these ideas about allocative efficiency could be taught.

14. I develop this explanation more in Colander and Rothschild 2010 and Colander 2011.

264   David Colander

Changing Analytic Technology and the Future of the Market Failure Policy Frame

As I have emphasized above, the "market failure" policy frame is closely tied to the Walrasian general equilibrium model. An implication of that close tie-in is that as analytic technology diverges from the analytics association with Walrasian general equilibrium, the market failure policy frame will come more and more into question. There are some indications that that is happening. Specifically, new work in behavioral economics, encouraged by a blossoming empirical experimentation technology, is allowing economics to explore models in which individuals do not exhibit the strong rationality needed for the Walrasian model. As that happens, new policy proposals such as nudges (Thaler and Sunstein 2008) are developing that do not fit the market failure policy frame. With nudges, economists are suggesting policies to guide individuals in a certain way; policies are not designed to internalize an externality.

Similarly, new analytic technologies are allowing economists to explore multiple equilibria models, in which the policy issues involve a consideration of which basin of attraction the economy will gravitate to and how government policy might influence that gravitation. Such equilibrium selection mechanism problems involve a quite separate set of issues and models that go far beyond single equilibrium Walrasian models. An analysis of tipping points becomes the policy focus, not an analysis of externalities or market failures.

Similarly, new computational technology is allowing economists to explore pattern-matching data models, agent-based models, network models, and epistemic game-theoretical models in which multiple social dimensions can be analyzed simultaneously. Culture and norms no longer need to be taken as given; they can become endogenized and part of the policy discussion.[15] As this new work develops, the evolutionary

15. As an example of how the types of issues considered in pure theory go far beyond the Walrasian framework, consider the following abstract of a recent paper (Hedges et al. 2014): "We introduce a new unified framework for modelling both decision problems and finite games based on quantifiers and selection functions. We show that the canonical utility maximisation is one special case of a quantifier and that our more abstract framework provides several additional degrees of freedom in modelling. In particular, incomplete preferences, non-maximising heuristics, and context-dependent motives can be taken into account when describing an agent's goal. We introduce a suitable generalisation of Nash equilibrium for games in terms of quantifiers and selection functions. Moreover, we introduce a refinement of Nash that captures context-dependency of goals. Modelling in our framework is compositional as the parts of the game are modular and can be easily exchanged. We provide an extended example where we illustrate concepts and highlight the benefits of our alternative modelling approach."

story used to support markets becomes a broader evolutionary story in which, in a single equilibrium model, all we can say about efficiency is that "that which is, is efficient." Government and the market coevolve, undermining any "I Pencil" evolutionary justifications of the market (Read 1958).

None of these analytic and computational approaches fit nicely with the "market failure" policy frame; they go beyond it and raise questions that cannot be easily addressed as market failures. Thus, just as changes in analytic and computational technology encouraged the movement from the classical policy frame to the market failure policy frame, today changes in analytic and computational technology are creating pressures for a change in the existing market failure policy frame to a policy frame broad enough to incorporate these new models and insights. That, at least, is my hypothesis.

References

Bator, Francis. 1958. "The Anatomy of Market Failure." *Quarterly Journal of Economics* 72 (3): 351–79.

Bergson, Abram. 1938. "A Reformulation of Certain Aspects of Welfare Economics." *Quarterly Journal of Economics* 52 (2): 310–34.

Buchanan, James, and Gordon Tullock. 1962. *Calculus of Consent: Logical Foundations of Constitutional Democracy*. Ann Arbor: University of Michigan Press.

Colander, David. 2003. "Integrating Sex and Drugs into the Principles Course." *Journal of Economic Education* 34 (1): 82–91.

———. 2005. "From Muddling through to the Economics of Control: Views of Applied Policy from J. N. Keynes to Abba Lerner." In *The Role of Government in the History of Economic Thought*, edited by Steven G. Medema and Peter Boettke. *History of Political Economy* 37 (supplement): 277–91.

———. 2011. "Applied Policy, Welfare Economics, and Mill's Half-Truths." In *The Elgar Companion to Recent Economic Methodology*, edited by John Davis and Wade Hands, 173–86. Cheltenham: Edward Elgar.

Colander, David, and Craig Freedman. 2011. "The Chicago Counter-revolution and the Loss of the Classical Liberal Tradition." Working paper, Middlebury College.

Colander, David, and Roland Kupers. 2014. *Complexity and the Art of Public Policy: Solving Society's Problems from the Bottom Up*. Princeton, N.J.: Princeton University Press.

Colander, David, and Casey Rothschild. 2010. "The Sins of the Sons of Samuelson: Vision, Pedagogy, and the Zig Zag Windings of Complex Dynamics." *Journal of Economic Behavior and Organization* 74 (3): 277–90.

Hedges, Jules, Paulo Oliva, Evguenia Winschel, Viktor Winschel, and Philipp Zahn. 2014. "A Higher-Order Framework for Decision Problems and Games." arxiv.org /abs/1409.7411.

266   David Colander

Hicks, John. 1939. *Value and Capital: An Inquiry into Some Fundamental Principles of Economic Theory.* Oxford: Clarendon Press.

Keynes, J. N. 1890. *The Scope and Method of Political Economy.* London: Macmillan.

Lerner, Abba. 1944. *The Economics of Control: Principles of Welfare Economics.* New York: Macmillan.

Mas-Colell, Andreu, Michael Whinston, and Jerry Green. 1995. *Microeconomic Theory.* New York: Oxford University Press.

Medema, Steven. 2011. *The Hesitant Hand: Taming the Self-Interest in the History of Ideas.* Princeton, N.J.: Princeton University Press.

Mill, John Stuart. 1848. *Principles of Political Economy.* London: Longmans, Green.

Read, Leonard. 1958. "I Pencil: My Family Tree as Told to Leonard E. Read." www.econlib.org/library/Essays/rdPncl1.html.

Robbins, Lionel. 1981. "Economics and Political Economy." *American Economic Review* 71 (May): 1–10.

Samuelson, Paul. 1947. *Foundations of Economic Analysis.* Cambridge, Mass.: Harvard University Press.

———. 1948. *Economics.* New York: McGraw-Hill.

Thaler, Richard, and Cass Sunstein. 2008. *Nudge.* New Haven, Conn.: Yale University Press.

15

Complexity Economics and Workaday Economic Policy

David Colander

Abstract

Much of what filters down to standard economists about complexity economics are summaries of abstract analysis that are generally seen as having little direct impact on the workaday policy analysis that most economists do. This chapter argues that complexity theory has significant implications for workaday economic policy. Even if economists do not accept that the complexity *scientific theory* of the economy is ready for prime time, the complexity vision, which pictures an economy as a complex evolving system undergoing continual evolutionary change, has direct relevance for their workaday applied policy. The reason is that good applied policy is not applied science but rather more like engineering. This chapter explains why applied policy should not be viewed as applied science and explores some implications and examples of how using a complexity frame for economic policy changes workaday applied economic policy analysis.

Specifically, it is argued that complexity policy opens up economics to a wide range of policies that go beyond the standard allocation policies that economists tend to focus on in the standard policy approach, and supplements them with a set of policies designed to influence the ecostructure within which individuals operate. This adds what might be called formation policy to allocation policy. Formation policy does not see the market and government as opposites, but rather views them as coevolving institutions. Formation policy is designed to influence that coevolution. An example of how complexity policy differs from standard policy can be seen in distribution policy. The standard approach to distribution policy tends to focus on redistributive taxes such as progressive income and wealth taxes. The complexity policy approach to distribution focuses more on modifying the length and nature of evolving property rights as embedded in patent and copyright law.

Introduction

For those of us working in complexity economics, it is an exciting time, and we sometimes wonder why all economists are unable to see complexity's potential and usefulness. Why doesn't everyone join us and jump on the complexity bandwagon? One reason is that much of what filters down to standard economists from complexity economics are summaries of abstract analysis—critiques of Walrasian general equilibrium theory, discussions of butterfly effects, sensitive dependence on initial conditions, and stories of "living economies in a computer"—narratives which, while interesting, are generally seen as having little direct impact on the workaday policy analysis that most economists do.

The reality is that workaday economics is done with little reference to abstract theory, new analytic techniques, or advanced computational technology. You don't teach general equilibrium to beginning or even intermediate students; you're lucky if they follow supply and demand. You don't base your policy analysis on general equilibrium theory; you develop a simple model, collect data, process that data, and come to a conclusion. Abstract theory, whether complex or not, has little direct relevance to workaday economics.

Despite its lack of direct relevance, most economists are interested in complexity economics. But they are interested in it as a consumption good—a throwback to the abstract thinking done in graduate school during late night bull sessions when they asked the big questions—not as a production good that affects their applied policy research. The general sense of standard economists is that when it comes to their applied policy analysis, complexity economics has little to add, other than that the economy is complex, something they already knew.

My goal in this chapter is to challenge that view, and to explain why complexity has enormous implications for how workaday applied policy economics is done.[1] The argument can be summarized as follows: Complexity economics involves both a *complexity scientific theory* of the economy and a *complexity vision* of the economy. Most economists are willing to accept that the vision of the economy as a complex evolving system undergoing continual evolutionary change is interesting; it resonates with their intuition. But economists are generally far less likely to accept that a complexity scientific theory of the economy is ready for prime time. For them, complexity economics has not cleared the scientific bar. Because standard economists see good applied policy as applied science, it follows that, for them, complexity economics has little relevance for their workaday applied policy.

Here I argue that that view of "applied policy as applied science" is wrong. The centrally important creative and design part of applied policy is not dependent on the reigning scientific paradigm because it is not applied science. If done in a reasonable way, it has little concern with what the scientific paradigm is.

This "applied policy is not applied science" approach is well understood, and followed, in the engineering profession. It is not understood, or followed, in economics. A change in that view would have significant implications for

---

[1] It also has significant implications for how economics is taught, but that involves a different set of issues than those I will discuss here.

workaday economics, making workaday applied policy analysis much more open to complexity and evolutionary policy insights. It would mean that economic policy work would not be limited by what we scientifically know; it would be based on any information or idea that might be useful in fashioning a solution to the policy problem under consideration. So even if one holds that complexity science is still in the formative stages, and that complexity analytic tools and models are not ready for prime time, complexity economics can still have important implications for how workaday applied economic policy is done.

First, I address complexity science and vision, and their relation to economists' current policy frame. Second, I discuss why applied policy should not be seen as applied science, but rather as engineering, and how adopting an engineering methodology makes the complexity vision important for workaday policy analysis. Finally, I explore some implications and examples of how using a complexity frame for economic policy changes workaday applied economic policy analysis.

Complexity Science and Complexity Vision

Policy is often thought of as applied science. What is meant by a scientific theory is generally ambiguous and much in debate; however, in economics, economic science is usually interpreted as work that has developed out of existing Walrasian general equilibrium theory. Complexity science challenges that Walrasian general equilibrium (WGE) theory as the core scientific theory. As Wilson et al. stated in their overview paper for this Forum, complexity economics challenges (a) the equilibrium focus of the WGE theory (namely, complexity economics would model economic systems as "complexly adaptive and frequently out of equilibrium," not as a system in equilibrium), and (b) the unrealistic treatment of preferences and rationality in WGE theory (complexity theory views preferences and tastes as endogenous, and rationality as being far more complicated than WGE theory does). They argue that making these changes involves a paradigmatic shift in economics.

The problem for complexity economics supporters is that the large majority of economists are not ready for a paradigmatic shift in economics, not because they love general equilibrium theory but because they have learned to live with it. General equilibrium theory serves as a background policy frame, providing the theoretical basis for cost-benefit analysis, guidance for whether and how to internalize externalities as well as how to conduct tax and subsidization policy.[2] In fact, it indirectly underlies almost all of economists' thinking about

---

[2] Policy following from behavioral economics, such as nudges, is the exception. Because it is an exception, it has been slow to be accepted by standard economists as anything other than a tangential addendum to standard economic policy.

policy. It has been extraordinarily useful in structuring thinking about policy; it has met a usefulness criterion.

Despite its indirect importance, WGE theory has little direct relevance to workaday economic policy. The standard economist's actual workaday applied policy economics makes almost no direct reference to WGE theory, social welfare functions, or welfare theorems. That theory is too abstract to use directly when thinking about policy. For most economists, WGE theory is something they learned in graduate school and has since receded to the deep recesses of their minds. While it lurks in the background, it is not what they are thinking of when they do applied policy. Because WGE theory is not seen as directly relevant for applied policy analysis, complexity economists' challenge to WGE theory is seen as having little relevance to them. They do applied policy analysis, and the musings of economic theoreticians worried about abstract complexity issues is seen as having little direct impact on what they do.

For most standard economists, even those sympathetic to complexity ideas, complexity economics does not yet meet the standards of scientific understanding. It involves conjectures and speculation about the economy that, while interesting, are scientifically unproven and thus remain in the speculative branch of economics. For most standard economists, complexity economics is not yet ready to replace WGE theory, which, while limited and hobbled by untenable assumptions, is at least logically correct, and has been demonstrably useful in providing a guide for policy.

I am not a scientific methodologist and am not qualified to render a meaningful opinion on whether using WGE theory as economists' core scientific model is appropriate or not. My leanings are that it is not, but I accept, by design, that formal scientific general theories embody unrealistic assumptions. Scientific theories are developed to provide abstract understanding, not policy guidance; unrealistic assumptions are the cost of the clarity needed for truth. Thus, I can accept that keeping WGE as the scientific theory might follow from scientific methodology, which places an enormous burden of proof on a new theory. Paradigmatic changes in science do not, and should not, come lightly; scientific methodology is designed to counter people's proclivity to be fast pattern completers—and see things that are not there. Scientific methodology involves what I call a set of slow pattern completing rules. That conservative methodology is designed to ensure that science is based on the most likely true knowledge.

The above issues are debatable, but for purposes of this article, I will accept that the arguments for keeping WGE as economists' scientific theory are tenable. For most economists, that is the end of the story. For them, complexity is not ready to become the new paradigm in economics: it has few implications for applied policy since applied policy is applied science. This is the step that I want to challenge here. I argue that applied policy should not be seen as applied science, and that even though much applied policy is done with little thought of formal scientific methodology and general equilibrium theory, both limit indirectly what economists do in their applied policy. If applied policy is more explicitly seen as engineering, the debate about what economists' scientific theory is becomes almost irrelevant to how applied policy analysis is conducted. That allows complexity to influence economists' policy analysis in ways that it currently does not.

Applied Economics Is Not Applied Science

If applied economics should not follow a scientific methodology, what methodology should it follow? My answer is that applied economics should follow *an engineering methodology* (this idea is further developed in Colander 2015). Engineers do not see engineering as applied science. Engineers use science and, where appropriate, use scientific methodology. However, engineers differ from scientists in that they allow and encourage analysis to be based on intuition, guesses, gut feelings, and a whole variety of elements which they do not claim meet scientific muster. The reason why is that good engineering is a creative endeavor. It is not a formal scientific endeavor. Its goal is to solve problems—to discover solutions that work in the real world, not to find capital T (or even small t) truth. If a solution that works in the real world does not work in the existing scientific theory, so be it.

Billy Vaughn Koen (2003) defines the engineering method as "the strategy for causing the best change in a poorly understood or uncertain situation within the available resources." Alternatively, he defines it as the use of the best available engineering heuristics to solve problems. Those definitions serve as useful statements of the method appropriate for workaday applied economic policy. Koen emphasizes that since no part of knowledge is infallible, appropriate heuristics include all theories, models, and any other aid (e.g., intuition, experience, expert knowledge) that may usefully lead to a solution. In this engineering method, nothing is off the table. By explicitly calling the models and other aids that an engineer uses to arrive at a conclusion *heuristics*, Koen calls attention to any model's problems and encourages a methodological approach that is open to all evidence and arguments. Engineering, and hence applied policy, has a different threshold of importance than science. Science searches for truth; whereas engineering, if applied to economic problems, searches for answers to policy questions.

Translated into economics, this means that WGE theory is simply one of many heuristics that might be useful in tackling the wide range of policy issues that economics considers. Its usefulness in applied policy can only be ascertained by considering how its usefulness compares to the other heuristics, such as a complexity policy frame's usefulness for the particular problem at hand. An applied policy economist following an engineering methodology would be continually trying alternative heuristics to see which is most useful for a particular set of problems; this person would be far less tied to the standard WGE policy frame than standard economists are.[3]

Koen emphasizes that the appropriate heuristics will be constantly changing, and discussion of them will be part of what every engineer does. Thus, while abstract methodology is not much discussed by engineers, practical methodology is constantly discussed. It is integrated into what engineers do, so all engineers are simultaneously engineers and methodologists. Put another way, methodology is an important part of engineering, but it is a narrowly applied micro-methodology of best practices for particular areas, with a very loose general methodology that can probably best be described as an *educated common sense* methodology. Koen calls it a "universal method." The particular branch of engineering, and the particular problem the engineers are trying to solve, will determine how important the scientific heuristic is and how important other heuristics are. There is no one overriding engineering heuristic. Engineering heuristics make no attempt to be value free. Engineering recognizes that values are an integral part of policy analysis and, instead of trying to be value free, is concerned with making the values in the analysis clear, so outsiders can decide whether they agree with them or not.

Thinking of applied economic policy as engineering, not science, opens up new avenues of policy considerations that allow complexity insights to enter the policy discussion long before the science of complexity is ready for prime time. It encourages economic discourse about policy to include much more daydreaming, speculation, and playing around with ideas. Specifically, using an engineering methodology for applied policy, the assumptions that currently guide much of the policy analysis done by economists—exogenous tastes, no interdependent utility functions, no contagion, no evolutionary institutions, and extreme rationality—would not be limiting on policy analysis. They were only used because they led to tractable scientific models: all have their roots in WGE theory not in their usefulness for policy, but their usefulness in finding the truth.

Using an engineering methodology, the standard assumptions would no longer hold the power over applied policy that they currently do. The WGE heuristic would likely be replaced by a variety of heuristics that are more consistent with observed empirical reality for policy purposes, even as one kept WGE as one's scientific theory. Using the complexity vision to think about policy allows applied policy analysts to modify scientific assumptions for their policy heuristics, and to explore policy issues that are outside the standard ones economists examine. Eliminating these arbitrary assumptions would change

---

[3]   Extreme care must be used in actually applying heuristic insights into policy, and ensuring that moral issues are integrated into the analysis, which is one of the reasons the welfare economics followed the path that it did: it wanted to avoid addressing issues of morality and value judgments. However, as Hume long ago noted, policy inherently involves morality and value judgments. To pretend they are not there is not a viable option.

policy analysis enormously. It would open up a wide range of policies to exploration by economists using different models.

Let me be clear: my argument is not that the complexity vision would overthrow existing theory and applied policy. Where the existing models work better than the new models as a guide for policy, the existing models will continue to be used. But what works best—what is the best current state-of-the-art heuristic—can only be known by comparison of the usefulness of the various models. This comparison is not happening now.

Implications of the Complexity for Policy

If the engineering approach to applied policy were followed, the complexity frame for policy would be one of the alternative frames that would be explored. In Colander and Kupers (2014), I explored some of the ways in which thinking about policy would change using a complexity frame:

1. We don't understand the complex evolving economy, and probably can never understand it fully. Complex systems are not amenable to control, and we should give up the ambition to control the economic system.
2. While we cannot control the economy, we can influence it in a myriad of ways; the standard policy model rules out many of these avenues; influence comes about not just through incentives within the existing institutional structure. A key focus of policy within the complexity policy frame involves positively influencing the evolution of institutions. It involves issues of formation as well as allocation.
3. The economy and the government are coevolving complex systems that cannot be considered separately. There aren't separate market and government solutions to problems. Solutions can be more bottom-up or more top-down, but both require some type of either explicit or implicit government policy to bring them about, even if that policy is to do nothing. The market is not the opposite of the government; successful market economies are testimonies of the success of previous government policies.
4. The success of bottom-up policy depends on the ecostructure within which people operate and the normative codes that they follow. Thus ecostructure and norms policy are central to complexity policy.
5. There is no general complexity policy; complexity policy is contextual and consists of a set of tools, not a set of rules, to help the policy maker come to reasonable conclusions.
6. Government is an evolving institution and can evolve in different ways. Complexity policy includes policies that affect government, and the role of government will change with the problems and the current

state of government. There can be no noncontextual general policy recommendations.

7. Complex systems often experience path dependencies, nonlinearities, and lock-ins. Methods need to be designed to determine when these have occurred, and policies reflecting these dynamics need to be designed to influence the economy's evolution.

8. Policies can be achieved with bottom-up or top-down methods of influence. Top-down policies should not be seen as a one-time policy, but as a policy process that evolves as institutions evolve. Bottom-up policies allow endogenous evolution as institutions involve.

How these issues relate to policy involves a multifaceted set of considerations that can only be touched on here. In the following discussion, I give a sense of how they can affect workaday applied policy economics.

Ecostructure and Activist Laissez-Faire Policy

A major difference between the complexity frame and the standard WGE control policy frame is that the complexity frame does not view the market and the government as polar opposites; it sees them as having coevolved and as highly interdependent. This means that complexity policy analysis cannot use a market solution as a reference point for policy analysis because the market would not exist without government. In the complexity policy frame, "efficiency" is not a general goal within the model; policy goals have to be specified by the policy analyst. Efficiency has meaning only in relation to those outside specified goals.

What in the WGE policy frame are seen as market failures are, in the complexity frame, seen as ecostructure failures: they involve a failure in the formation of institutions. Policies on how to address these failures effectively might entail either more or less direct government involvement. Complexity theory does not tell you which. Put another way, instead of a market versus government policy dichotomy, the complexity policy frame has a bottom-up versus top-down policy dichotomy, and the choice between them is based not on theory but rather on judgments, such as a judgment on how similar policies have worked elsewhere in similar circumstances. In the complexity policy frame there is no definitive theoretical argument for or against a policy; instead, a researcher uses history and context-specific model heuristics as guides.

Bottom-up policy is the complexity equivalent to laissez-faire policy. But bottom-up policy is quite different from laissez-faire as is often interpreted. Within the complexity frame, laissez-faire is a government policy of encouraging bottom-up solutions to problems; it is not an absence of government policy.[4] Bottom-up policy has government actively encouraging individuals to

---

[4]   As discussed elsewhere (Colander 2009), sophisticated Classical economists saw policy in this way, and is what Lionel Robbins meant when he said that "laissez-faire is the state."

solve their own problems, and providing an ecostructure that will help them do so. It tries to maintain fairness, but otherwise stays out of the way. Top-down policy is designed to solve the problem using existing government institutions. Bottom-up policy tends to be slower than top-down policy, but it also tends to be more robust since it utilizes individuals' local knowledge which is unavailable to government policy makers.

In the complexity frame, there is no necessary correlation between one's concern about social problems and one's view of the efficacy of top-down or bottom-up solutions. For example, one can be enormously socially concerned but still be a strong bottom-up policy supporter if one's assessment is that government top-down policies to address social problems have serious negative side effects. Elinor Ostrom provided guidance for thinking about bottom-up policy within the context of common pool resources. Her work and the sophisticated interpretations of Ronald Coase (Medema 2011) can be seen as early pioneering efforts within the complexity policy frame.

Developing the Ecostructure to Achieve Social Goals

One way to demonstrate how using a complexity frame changes workaday applied policy work is to discuss how it has changed my applied policy work. In my current research, I am part of a large group working on developing an ecostructure that will encourage bottom-up solutions to social problems. This research involves understanding the nature of what we call "for-benefit" enterprises, which are market-oriented enterprises run to achieve social goals, not private goals (Colander 2012). There is enormous interest and support for the development of these institutions, primarily from politicians, lawyers, and businesspeople. I am one of the few economists working on the project.

My interest came about from talking to some successful socially concerned entrepreneurs who had earned sufficient income to fulfill all their material needs and wants before they were 30, and who were thus turning to philanthropy. After exploring existing nonprofits, they became disillusioned with their effectiveness and were looking for a better way to achieve their social goals. This led them to explore whether they could set up private enterprises devoted to solving the social problem of their interest. Instead of just giving money, they wanted to "invest" and manage the enterprise whose bottom line would be their social goal. Interest in the topic led to a movement to create a fourth sector of the economy—one that would have many of the governance structures of private enterprises, but would have social, not private profit, goals. My contribution to the project has been in (a) exploring what standard economic theory has, and in the past has had, to say about profit maximization (they are different); (b) explaining economists' approach to integrating normative views into their analysis of the way the market works, and (c) exploring how the type of institution they would like to set up differs from other related institutions, such as L3Cs, B-corps, triple bottom-line companies, and social businesses.

The project has me working with lawyers, businesspeople, and policy wonks on specific policy questions. The research has far less focus on general solutions than my previous standard applied policy research.[5] Even though the project does not focus on general solutions, it has led me to think about them and work on a paper that contrasts a "pure for-(social)-benefit enterprise" with its pure polar opposite—a "for-profit" enterprise of standard theory, with most real-world firms falling somewhere between the two extremes.

The project is very much applied policy work, but it is quite different from the applied policy work done in standard economics. It is suggestive of how applied policy work would change if economists adopt a complexity policy frame. It has been much more collaborative and transdisciplinary than my other research. It involves much more thinking outside the standard model and significant study of past economists' writing, as I try to come to grips with how economists' current policy heuristics evolved. The focus is on finding practical solutions to specific problems and issues. The research might lead to a "general solution" but the flow is from *specific to general* solution, not from *general to specific* solution as it is with most current "standard" economic work.

Policy Based on Replicator Dynamics

Having described how my research agenda changed when I switched to a complexity policy frame, I will discuss another way in which complexity will likely change workaday applied policy economics. Complexity economics gives researchers a new method of simplification along with new analytical and computational tools that free economists from relying on developing a specific analytically solvable model. Instead of building an equilibrium model, economists can develop and explore an evolutionary model within which research only has to specify the replicator dynamics, not the full equilibrium system.

Supplementing the standard policy frame with the complexity policy frame makes applied policy economists far less dependent on being able to specify the equations in the model, allowing them to base their policy analysis on more than the equilibrium properties of the model. In the complexity frame, instead of picturing the economy as a set of interdependent equations moving toward equilibrium, as is done in the standard policy frame, researchers can picture existing reality as the result of replicator dynamics that evolve over time. They can then create agent-based models to analyze those replicator dynamics and explore alternative policies designed to influence those replicator dynamics within these agent-based models.[6] Agent-based models allow researchers to

---

[5]   In the month preceding this Forum, I attended two conferences related to this "for-benefit" topic: one in Washington sponsored by the Fed and the Urban Institute; another at Harvard sponsored by INET and Harvard. Both were highly interdisciplinary and involved issues normally considered outside the purview of economists.

[6]   Important developmental work is being done in expanding and developing agent-based model-

explore and base policy thinking on nonlinear dynamic models in which complex realities emerge and evolve. This means that tractable unique equilibrium models no longer need to be assumed; in fact, the very concept of equilibrium can be replaced by a new concept, basins of attraction, which opens up the formal study of equilibrium selection mechanisms. As these replicator dynamics complexity models are explored, new possibilities for policy will emerge.

The change is similar to one that is occurring in medicine, where standard medicine conceives of health policy as fighting germs, viruses, and bacteria. This approach is being currently supplemented by two alternative approaches. One is an evolutionary approach in which individuals are seen as ecosystems for billions of organisms which coevolve with individuals. Within this frame, a person's health is dependent on how that entire ecosystem works. The second is a genetic approach in which an individual's genetic code plays a central role in his or her health. In genetic medicine, a minute change in the genetic code can have enormous effects on the health of an individual. In both approaches, germs only capture part of the story. Just as the development of genetic and evolutionary theory have opened up entirely new branches of health policy, so too can the complexity frame open up entirely new branches of applied economic policy.

A Norms Policy

Once one thinks of the economic system in terms of its replicator dynamics, one is led naturally to a new type of economic policy for applied policy economists to explore: norms policy (a policy designed to achieve desired ends by influencing the tastes and norms of individuals). The reason one is led to norms policy is that in the complexity frame, norms are endogenous, so they naturally become part of the policy discussion (see, e.g., Fehr and Fischbacher 2004).

Accepting that norms are endogenous has significant implications for workaday applied policy analysis. For example, economists' current control policy frame directs researchers to think of policy in terms of government passing a law, a tax, or some other control measure to achieve the desired result. But that need not be the case. Once one uses a complexity model that has endogenous norms, mores, and culture-determining behavior, one is presented with a possible alternative for role government, not as a controller or law maker but as an influencer of norms. Roland Kupers and I argue that one of the most important roles for government is to provide a moral compass for society (Colander and Kupers 2014). If government fails to provide this, it will likely fail in everything. Once it has provided that moral compass, it can consider policies

---

ing relevant for policy. For example, George Mason University has developed a Computational Public Policy Laboratory under the direction of Rob Axtell, and Josh Epstein (2013) has recently expanded the nature of agents to include neurological foundations, allowing additional exploration of behavioral issues with agent-based models.

designed to influence the norms in society positively. Behavioral economic "nudges" are beginning to explore this policy space, but the implications of endogenous norms and tastes go far beyond nudging.

Another example involves adding a new set of policy tools—influence tools—to its policy arsenal. Influence tools guide individuals toward "positive" norms. They might involve measures to legislate a new type of "government guidances"; that is, laws that are not enforced through power, but through social pressure—something like a fatwa in Islamic religion. These set of guidances might be called legislated mores; they are what people, through government, have decided are positive rules of behavior. Violating a more would not be punishable in the way a misdemeanor or a felony is; it would not lead to a fine or imprisonment. It might, however, lead to public disapproval and serve as a basis for deciding whether a person behaved appropriately in insurance and private tort claims.

Many of the gray areas of current policy, where individual rights seem to conflict with what society considers good practices, could be addressed using such government-specified mores. Examples where such mores, rather than laws, might be useful include activities such as wearing a seatbelt, using drugs, and certain sexual behaviors. Actions that are now criminalized could be decriminalized but simultaneously discouraged. How effective would such mores be? That is an empirical issue which applied policy economists would need to explore, using the broader complexity frame, in their analysis of how effective alternative methods are in discouraging behaviors which people (through government) have decided to inhibit.

An Alternative Complexity Policy Approach to Achieving a More Desirable Income Distribution

Let us now consider how an economist's policy approach to a specific problem—income distribution—might change if a complexity frame was adopted. Economists' current applied policy heuristic deals with income distribution as a *re*distribution problem. By that I mean that it takes marginal productivities as given and asks: How can one develop redistributive taxes that bring about a more desirable income distribution?

The complexity frames suggests an alternative approach. Rather than trying to *change the income distribution given marginal productivities*, one might consider policies that change tastes, norms, and institutionally determined marginal productivities using the complexity approach. Policy could be designed to structure the property rights and institutions so that the marginal productivities of individuals are more equal, thereby making the distribution of income more equal without resorting to redistributive taxation. Here are some examples of policies that could be examined to achieve such goals:[7]

---

[7] This discussion is based on Colander (2014). The ideas here are not tied to taking a complexity

1. Property rights could be more limited in duration. Patent and copyright laws could be designed for shorter periods, so that benefits could be passed on more quickly to the broader public. This could include: (a) significantly limiting intellectual property rights; (b) encouraging institutions that favor open source software and material; and (c) issuing 100-year leases on land, instead of perpetuity property rights, so that land would revert to social wealth and be re-leased when the lease comes due.
2. Competition could be more strongly supported by limiting government-based monopolies: (a) Regulatory structures of institutions could allow for narrower specialists, so that the rents created are spread more widely and more competition is created. (b) Open certification that does not require specific high-priced formal training programs but rather "open-to-anyone" certification exams could be instituted. (c) At-risk students could be provided with a "bottom-up" educational option, in which they would receive the money that would have gone into educating them, if they learn the material on their own.
3. Individuals' social, not materialistic, proclivities could be encouraged: (a) Society could advocate and support a stronger tradition of social responsibility of the rich, so that achieving social goals becomes a favored luxury good. Andrew Carnegie's *gospel of wealth* could be built into the fabric of society. (b) Institutions could be designed to encourage social benefit, rather than private benefit entrepreneurship. (c) Materialism embedded in the GDP goals could be countered by replacing GDP with other measures of social success, such as Sen's Capabilities Index.

Conclusion

For most economists, complexity economics has little effect on their workaday applied policy economics. However, complexity economics has the potential to make an enormous difference in applied policy workaday economics by leading economists to a different way of framing policy—one that sees their work not as applied science, but as engineering.

Creative design engineering involves asking big questions that go beyond those that we can address in science. Examples include: What happens to effective policy if tastes are endogenous? How would an economy function with a different set of property rights? How might we change laws to make "for-benefit" institutions more prevalent? What institutional setup might lead to what society would see as a fairer distribution of income? An engineering approach

---

view, but taking such a view is much more likely to lead economists to make such policies a central focus of their research. For a nice discussion of problems with existing policy toward property rights, see Boldrin and Levine (2010) as well as Doctorow (2014).

allows us to explore different answers to these big questions by changing them into real-world policy questions, which can then be answered with existing computational and analytic technology.

Economists have failed society because they have not done this. By allowing their policy discussion to be guided, without explicit consideration, by the WGE policy frame, economists have stopped asking the big questions that might have been intractable when the WGE frame was first adopted, but which are no longer intractable. Economic policy has not kept up with analytic and computational technology. They have missed asking obvious policy questions. The exploration of policy within a broader complexity frame will open up new avenues for economic policy analysis.

PART III

METHODOLOGY FOR MACROECONOMICS

[10]

THE MACROFOUNDATIONS OF MICRO

David C. Colander
Middlebury College

In the opening chapter of his pathbreaking textbook, Paul Samuelson reproduced a picture from N. R. Hanson's *Patterns of Discovery* [1961].[1] From one perspective, it looked like a picture of antelopes; from another perspective, it looked like a picture of birds. The point of the example was that the same reality can look fundamentally different depending on one's perspective and that revolutions in a discipline occur through these changes in perspective.

Perspective is fundamental to understanding theories, because, ultimately, any theory is built on a vision — a way of putting reality together. That vision guides one in choosing assumptions and in interpreting results. Vision allows one to make the leap of faith necessary to believe that one's "theory" is more than a jumble of meaningless tautological equations. It was Keynes's vision that made Keynesian economics "spread like a disease among South Sea Islanders" [Samuelson, 1964], and it was Lucas's vision that made New Classical economics spread like the flu virus in a university. (In both cases economists over fifty were immune.)

This paper argues that such a change in perspective is currently underway in macro and that the new emerging perspective can be called a "macrofoundations of micro" perspective. This new perspective changes the nature of the macroeconomic debate and provides a theoretical foundation for a Keynesian macroeconomic revival, in which the Classical model is seen as a special case of the more general Keynesian model, rather than the way things are currently — the Keynesian model being seen as a special case of the Classical model, in which nominal wage inflexibility is assumed.

This perspective is arrived at by carrying Lucas's critique of macro models to its logical conclusion. Not only does policy change the structural characteristics of the model, so do individuals' expectations; without making *ad hoc* assumptions, it is impossible to distinguish structural and non-structural changes.

The first Keynesian revolution set off by the publication of *The General Theory* initially involved such a change in perspective, and it is not surprising that Samuelson's book, which translated the Keynesian revolution into a textbook model that students could follow, should have included the bird/antelope picture. The change in perspective that the first Keynesian revolution brought about completely separated macro from micro. They were different approaches: macroeconomics looked at the aggregate economy from one perspective, micro from another. The new macro perspective allowed one to talk about interrelationships among aggregates without specifying the underlying individual choice theoretic framework, while the micro perspective retained the traditional individual choice theoretic perspective in which individuals maximized utility over the entire set of choices.[2]

Eastern Economic Journal, Vol. 19, No. 4, Fall 1993

THE NEOKEYNESIAN EVOLUTION AND THE MICROFOUNDATIONS OF MACRO

This dual perspective was problematic, since most individuals agreed that micro and macro are related and should be unified. Much work in what came to be called neoKeynesian economics involved relating the macro analysis to microeconomic choice theoretic notions. That work began a shift in perspective away from a macro- and toward a micro-perspective, a shift in perspective that would ultimately lead to the New Classical revolution. The reason is that the neoKeynesian integration of micro and macro was done from a micro perspective. As the work became known, a slow and subtle change from a macro- to a micro-perspective took place in researchers' minds. The evolving neoKeynesian perspective differed from the old Keynesian perspective, and as the evolution proceeded, those antelopes kept looking more and more like birds.

The neoKeynesian work was not the only work being done that focused on microfoundations. As the neoKeynesian developments were occurring, simultaneously much work in micro was relating individual choice to aggregate general equilibrium results over infinite horizons. These two sets of work started to come together in the late 1960s and early 1970s as the microfoundations-of-macro literature developed. That microfoundations-of-macro work attempted to connect macro results with microfoundations directly, in a much more fundamental way than previous neoKeynesian attempts. The basic premise of the microfoundations-of-macro literature was that if an aggregate model were to assume any individual behavior, such as is implied by wage or price inflexibility, that behavior had to come out of a microeconomic choice theoretic framework. This work extended the shift in perspective that the neoKeynesian evolution had begun; the picture was looking more like birds all the time. All those old Keynesians who insisted that they kept seeing antelopes were having illusions (money or otherwise).

This microfoundations-of-macro work was soon incorporated with work on rational expectations that originated with Muth [1961], but that did not become well known until it was picked up by Robert Lucas [1972] and other New Classical macroeconomists. What New Classical macroeconomics did was to bring macro expectations into the microeconomic choice theoretic framework and complete the change in perspective. In a New Classical perspective there was no question that the picture was one of birds. From an analytic viewpoint, the result was impressive because the rational expectations assumption allowed a broader integration of microeconomic individual choice theory with macro than had hitherto existed.

That combination was fruitful in the sense that it generated significant research by both Classicals and Keynesians. New Classicals, such as Robert Lucas [1975] and Thomas Sargent and Neil Wallace [1976] showed that, assuming competitive markets and a unique equilibrium, the macroeconomic problem disappeared when individuals had rational expectations.

This New Classical work led to Keynesian responses that offered a number of justifications for the Keynesian approach. Elsewhere, I have divided those responses into two categories: New Keynesian and New neoKeynesian [Colander, 1992a;

1992b]. The New neoKeynesian response, which includes the work of economists such as Gregory Mankiw and David Romer [1990], took a micro perspective and attempted to explain why individuals would rationally choose to override the Walrasian market. This New neoKeynesian work showed that with fixed money contracts, menu costs, or various types of imperfect information, Keynesian results could be coaxed out of the traditional microeconomic choice theoretic foundations.

This was not an easy thing to do; since this work was using a micro perspective, it was the equivalent of convincing people that Classical birds were really Keynesian antelopes, even though they looked, felt, and chirped like birds. If the people you were convincing were nearsighted enough, and wanted to believe, they could be convinced, but, from a micro perspective, with clear eyesight, a New neoKeynesian antelope looks like what it is, a Classical bird in antelope clothing.

A key element of this New neoKeynesian work is the representative agent approach. New neoKeynesian formal analysis is done at the partial equilibrium level, and then the results are intuitively extended to the aggregate economy using a representative agent analogy. No explicit consideration is given to the problems of that aggregate extension of the partial equilibrium analysis, and the resulting analysis is meshed into a unique-equilibrium Walrasian framework.

I classify that coaxing of Keynesian results out of a traditional choice theoretic framework as New neoKeynesian rather than simply New Keynesian to separate that work from another set of work that makes a much more substantive shift in response to the New Classical challenge. This work involves a fundamental change in perspective, and from that new perspective, the macro picture is clearly one of antelopes, and one can see birds in it only by the reverse mental gymnastics used by the New neoKeynesians.

This work starts from the premise that one cannot analyze the aggregate using a representative agent analogy because any analysis that does not deal with those interdependencies is conceptually flawed.

THE IMPORTANCE OF INTERDEPENDENCIES AND MULTIPLE EQUILIBRIA

This New Keynesian work changes the perspective by giving up the unique-equilibrium Walrasian competitive framework and replacing it with a multiple equilibrium framework in which disequilibrium adjustment paths can affect equilibrium outcomes and there is no unique connection between individual decisions and equilibrium outcomes. All decisions are conceived as fully interdependent with other decisions.

Any resulting formal macroeconomic model that follows from this vision is hopelessly complex from an analytic standpoint, but the problems it describes are intuitively obvious. Depending on the nature of the interdependencies assumed among individual decision makers, any aggregate outcome is possible. The resulting equilibria are sometimes called sunspot equilibria — because an equilibrium can be caused by seemingly irrelevant aspects of the economy; in other models they are called path-dependent equilibria, because the equilibria arrived at are dependent on the disequilibrium adjustment paths that led to those equilibria. But the key element of these models is that almost any result is possible, depending on where one begins.

The existing formal New Keynesian models and discussion are embryonic. No New Keynesian claims that their models are any more than suggestive of the dynamic interdependencies that exist. What distinguishes them is their unwillingness to make the leap of faith that allows them to brush aside the problems of interdependencies and to assume a unique aggregate equilibrium.

Giving up that micro framework changes the perspective and the nature of the questions asked. From this multiple-equilibrium perspective the New neoKeynesian response, which tries to justify the Keynesian view within a unique-equilibrium framework, is viewed as a slight modification to Classical economics. It is tangential to the main Keynesian analysis since from a multiple-equilibria macro perspective there is no need to justify fixed nominal wages and prices as a reason for output fluctuation. An output fluctuation is simply a movement from one equilibrium to another and is to be expected. It does not need explanation. What needs explanation is why the real-world aggregate economy is as stable as it is — why output does not fluctuate more than it does.

The stability of output in the real world economy is often used as implicit justification for the unique-equilibrium assumption. New Keynesians do not accept that; they believe the stability is caused by conventions and institutional constraints on individual behavior and that to understand the general stability and periods of instability in the economy requires a far more complicated analysis than can be captured in a model assuming a unique aggregate equilibrium.

Work on this new analytic approach, for the most part, has been highly theoretical and abstract; some of it, such as Michael Woodford [1986; 1990] begins in a game theoretic context and analytically shows that multiple equilibria are a likely outcome. Other work [Rosser, 1991] has considered systems with nonlinear dynamics in which sudden shifts from one path to another can occur. Still other work [Diamond, 1982; Howitt, 1985] has considered the macroeconomy from a search theoretic framework and has argued that even with full price flexibility, additional market trading has positive externalities and therefore can change the aggregate equilibrium. These New Keynesian economists have shown in these highly abstract analyses that multiple equilibria are the norm and that unless one rules out interdependencies by assumption, no unique equilibrium exists.

The absence of a unique equilibrium poses serious questions for the New Classical resolution to the macro/micro integration, since many alternative choices may be individually rational, each consistent with a different aggregate equilibrium. Even using all information available to them through the market, individuals, acting alone, will have no way of knowing which equilibrium to expect. One arrives at a unique equilibrium only by making strong *ad hoc* assumptions. From a New Keynesian perspective, it is Classical, not Keynesian, economics that is guilty of "adhocery".

THE MACROFOUNDATIONS OF MICRO   451

From the New Keynesian multiple-equilibria perspective, talking about a microfoundation of macro, independent of institutional context, is meaningless. In specific, traditional individual choice theory, in which aggregate results correspond to non-contextually determined representative agent decisions, is irrelevant to the microfoundations to macro. The New Keynesian perspective maintains that before there is any hope of undertaking meaningful micro analysis, *one must first determine the macro context within which that micro decision is made.* It is that macro context that lets individuals choose among likely multiple equilibria and makes the choice theoretic foundation contextually relevant. In doing so, however, the macro context imposes institutional constraints on individual decision makers, and these constraints must be considered in deriving any microfoundations to macro. Thus establishing appropriate macrofoundations of micro must logically be done before one establishes any microfoundations of macro, and any micro analysis independent of a macrofoundation is irrelevant game-playing.[3]

Now one could argue that Walrasian perfectly competitive markets provide an appropriate macrofoundation. Elsewhere I have argued that they do not for three reasons. The first is that they are institutionally unstable [Colander, forthcoming], by which I mean that some individuals will have an incentive to monopolize and change the perfectly competitive institutions to monopolistic ones and that at the margin no one will have an incentive to oppose them. Thus, Walrasian markets do not meet the minimum logical requirement of local stability. Any institutional structure used as a macrofoundation should be, at least locally, stable.

The second reason is that the traditional Walrasian general equilibrium structure requires more rationality than individuals have. It requires them to make billions of rational calculations every moment of every day. As Leijonhufvud [1993] nicely points out, doing so is the equivalent of assuming that because a person can jump off the ground — can make a contextual rational decision — that the person can fly like a bird — make noncontextual rational decisions. It is far more reasonable to picture individuals, like ourselves, with limited brainpower, able to exhibit some rationality, but relying on inertia and rules of thumb to make many decisions. If individuals are rational, their rationality is a bounded rationality within an institutional and expectational context. The macrofoundations of micro must specify that context.

The third reason is related to the second and concerns the absence of money in the Walrasian general equilibrium system. Money is a social convention that makes the aggregate economy operate more efficiently. It affects the coordination of the entire system and reduces the number of calculations an individual must make. Money has *no role* if individuals are super-rational and there is a perfectly competitive system. But it does have a role in our real-world economy and hence in any real-world relevant macrofoundations of micro. But money enters the economy not as a component of individual utility, or even aggregate production, functions; instead, it is part of the macrofoundational structure of the economic system and must be modeled as such.[4] Questions about money illusion and whether there is a dichotomy between the real and nominal sectors are non-questions since, in the macro institutional structure, the real and nominal decisions are so entwined that illusion and reality blend into one. Thus, in the macrofoundations-of-micro literature, the entire attempt to integrate money into the Walrasian general equilibrium system is a needless waste of time. It must be integrated in the macrofoundations of micro, and its integration is incompatible with a Walrasian general equilibrium system.

The analytic basis of this macrofoundations-of-micro approach goes back to Herbert Simon's work on bounded rationality [1959]. Simon argues that deciding over an entire range of possible choices exceeds the processing capacity of economic decision making units. Because it does, the decision making process has meaning only with a macro context. There is no one-to-one mapping between aggregate results and individual decisions. Put another way, the aggregate economy acquires a life of its own.

This view of the aggregate economy suggested by the macrofoundations-of-micro approach is, in many ways, Austrian, since the information processing achieved by the economic system is not directly related to the information processing of individuals. Many Austrians, however, make an additional normative assumption that the existing institutional structure should be seen within a broader evolutionary context that makes the existing institutional structure efficient, or at least beyond the society's ability to improve upon it. In Simon's approach, that assumption is inappropriate. All one can say is that the existing institutional structure exists. That difference is important because it opens up the possibility of studying alternative institutional structures and potentially finding a preferable one.

Ironically, it was a project extending Simon's research program examining how to integrate process into microeconomic analysis, in which Muth [1961] was a participant, that led to rational expectations. Struggling with the problem, Muth proposed to cut the Gordian Knot and eliminate process entirely [Simon, 1978; 1979]. Forget process: assume in the model expectations consistent with the equilibrium of that model. He called those model-consistent expectations "rational expectations." The New Keynesian macrofoundations-of-micro approach is a reversion back to Simon's work. It assumes that process is fundamentally important and that Muth's solution presumed far too much information processing capability of individuals.

In the macrofoundations-of-micro perspective one cannot escape process, and one cannot meaningfully relate noncontextual individual choice theory with macro analysis until one has first determined the relevant macro context within which a micro decision is made. Thus, whereas the microfoundations-of-macro work forged an integration of micro and macro from a unique Walrasian general equilibrium perspective, the New Keynesian macrofoundations-of-micro perspective is attempting to forge an integration from a macro perspective and to devise a micro perspective to fit into macro, rather than the other way around.

HOW CAN ONE DETERMINE AN APPROPRIATE MACROFOUNDATION?

To say that before one starts developing a microfoundation to macro one needs a macrofoundation to micro is not to argue that what we currently view as Keynesian macrofoundations is the right approach. The mechanistic multiplier and the modified IS/LM model are naïve and misleading. They involve as much a denial of the importance of institutional structure as does the microfoundations literature.

THE MACROFOUNDATIONS OF MICRO   453

Exactly how to go about determining an appropriate analytic macrofoundation for micro is not clear. The work of Barkley Rosser [1991], Michael Woodford [1986, 1990], Andrei Schleifer [1986], John Bryant [1983], and others, which elsewhere I have classified as New Keynesian, is attempting to arrive at an analytic solution to the problem. While these researchers have been successful in demonstrating analytically the possibility of multiple equilibria and in showing how, once one takes seriously the possibility of non-linear dynamics, jumps from one equilibrium to another can occur, they have not been very successful in providing much assistance in determining a meaningful macrofoundation. The main value of their analytic work has been to demonstrate the need for, and the difficulty of determining, a macrofoundation.

I suspect that if an analytic approach is going to provide a macrofoundation of micro, a multi-step analytic approach must replace the one-step analytic approach currently being used. The first step would be what might be called a "deductive institutional approach" in which one analyzes the rational choice of economic institutions along the lines suggested by Buchanan's constitutional analysis [Colander, forthcoming]. Those deductively-derived institutions then become the macrofoundation for microeconomic theorizing. This means that the constraints those institutions impose on individuals must be built into the micro theorizing. Thus New Keynesian economics might have a representative agent but it would be a fundamentally different representative agent than used by New neoKeynesians or New Classicals. In its conception the macrofoundations representative-agent would incorporate macro-institutional constraints on its behavior. More likely, it will have a number of representative agents interacting along the lines described by Allan Kirman [1992].

An analytic approach is not the only way to arrive at a macrofoundation. Two alternative approaches are a simulation approach and the institutional approach. Axel Leijonhufvud is a strong advocate of the simulation approach, and he is involved with the Center for Computation Economics at U. C. L. A., where most work along this line is taking place. In "Towards a Not-Too-Rational Macroeconomics" Leijonhufvud [1993] makes arguments similar to those in this paper about the unsatisfactory nature of the unique-equilibrium Walrasian approach and the failure of analytic methods of arriving at what I call the macrofoundations of micro. He then argues that in other sciences when analytic solutions are not forthcoming, scientists use computer simulations to arrive at a solution, and that it would make sense for macroeconomists to do likewise. In Leijonhufvud's approach, the macrofoundations of micro would be determined by simulation. Micro decisions would be analyzed contingent on the simulation-determined institutional structure.

Another approach to macrofoundations is what I call the institutional or Post Keynesian approach. In this approach, as opposed to computer simulation, one uses the real-world economy to simulate the reduced-form relationships. Since these aggregate real-world individual decisions are made contingent on the existing institutional structure, empirical observation is the only way to determine the macro-constrained micro choice. The work on wage contours and price ratchets falls within this framework. (A modification of this approach is to supplement empirical observation with institutionally-constrained micro-analytics in which the perceived reality determines the institutional constraints, but one still conducts analytic choice theoretic exercises within that observationally-determined environment.)

THE MACROFOUNDATIONS OF MICRO AND THE CANONICAL MODEL

Once one views the macroeconomic problem through the macrofoundation-of-micro perspective, many of the issues that had previously been in debate are simply non-issues. Price inflexibility does not need a unique-equilibrium Walrasian microfoundation; the search for reasons for price inflexibility as a justification for fluctuations in aggregate output are irrelevant exercises, at least at this stage of inquiry. Menu cost analysis and implicit contract theorizing become, perhaps, fun analytic exercises, but unnecessary for establishing a basis for Keynesian macroeconomics.

Since these issues become so clear in the macrofoundations-of-micro perspective, I have been perplexed to explain why they have received so little attention in the literature. Keynes made it quite clear that he believed that his was the general theory and the Classical theory was the special case, assuming full employment. From a macro perspective, Keynes is correct; from a micro perspective it is the Classical theory that is the general theory and the neoKeynesian model that is the special case, the Classical model modified by fixed wages and prices.

I have come to the conclusion that one of the prime reasons why Keynesian, or macro, insights have been lost is that a unique Walrasian general-equilibrium perspective has been embedded in the canonical aggregate model used by both neoKeynesians and Classicals. The micro perspective inherent in that model directed all formal analysis to a micro perspective.

Specifically, the canonical model's use of an aggregate production function that assumes a one-to-one mapping between inputs and aggregate output eliminated the possibility of multiple equilibria, and the assumption of a linear dynamics eliminates the possibility both of sudden jumps from one equilibrium to another and of path dependency. Since all previous attempts to provide a microfoundation for macro have been based on that unique-equilibrium aggregate production function with linear dynamics, it is not surprising that any time a microfoundation was formalized, the logical outcome was a micro perspective. Formal modeling of the macrofoundations-of-micro perspective must start with the proposition that the standard aggregate production function is inconsistent with multiple aggregate-equilibria and hence with a perspective that identical inputs of capital and labor can be associated with different levels of output. Garretsen [1991] and van Ees [1991] make arguments along these lines.

To incorporate the macro perspective into the model, one must specify an aggregate production function that can have different properties than the individual firm production function. It must be a function that has no one marginal productivity of inputs, but, instead, has many, depending on at which of the multiple equilibria the economy arrives. In the macrofoundations-of-micro perspective, the individual decisions can only be specified, given one of those macro equilibria.

A MORE LIMITED REALM FOR THEORY

To point out that this alternative macrofoundations perspective exists is only a very limited first step in the analysis. It is also the easiest one. It disparages much of the existing work without replacing it and suggests that the understanding of macro questions lies in taking seriously the complexity of those questions, not assuming away complexity for analytic convenience. It is a step that, once taken, is nihilistic: much existing macro theory and even the possibility of doing tractable macro theory is obliterated.

It is, I suspect, these nihilistic implications of the macrofoundations approach that have led macro theorists to avoid them. If the macro economy is almost infinitely complex, any tractable model will at best be suggestive. At best, what we might hope to achieve from macro theorizing are suggestive results of directional implications of observed shocks. Global normative statements fall by the wayside and are replaced by statements about potential tendencies to deviate from a dynamic path.

The macro perspective will also fundamentally change the way we do macroeconometrics. Macroeconometric models built up from micro relationships specified independently of institutional context will also fall by the wayside and will be replaced with models with far fewer theoretically-imposed structural limitations on the models. Robert Basmann's [1972] and Christopher Sims's [1980] attacks on macroeconometrics fit in nicely with the macrofoundations-of-micro perspective. Once one accepts that macro theory can lead to almost any result, forecasters will have to turn elsewhere — to pure statisticians who can extract maximum information from statistics independent of theory.

CONCLUSION

The fact that the perspective one takes determines the conclusion one arrives at is not surprising. What is surprising is that the importance of perspective has been so little discussed in the literature. Recent developments in the macrofoundations of micro bring the debate back to a debate about perspective and for that reason are a welcome advance — one likely to bring significant gains to our understanding of the aggregate economy, or at least to our understanding of what we do not know about that macro economy. Ultimately, any research program will be based on a leap of faith. Developing meaningful dialogue about faith is difficult; justifying faith with analytics is impossible. Ultimately, any researcher must answer the question: What simplifications will my faith allow me to make in the name of analytic tractability? Those simplifications define the perspective, and are what ultimately will differentiate macro models.

The change in perspective that an alternative leap of faith involves is not only for macro. Ironically, the changes will be more major for micro than for macro, since from a macro perspective much of what we currently teach as micro is out if its macro context and hence inappropriate. Exactly where the macrofoundations of micro might lead is unclear. Changes in perspectives are the most difficult to predict and — who knows? — maybe when the work is complete, Hanson's picture described at the beginning of this article will be of neither birds nor antelopes. Some economist may well pull a rabbit out of it.

NOTES

I would like to thank Robert Clower, Kenneth Koford, Paul Samuelson, Paul Davidson, Kevin Hoover, Barkley Rosser, Christöf Ruhl and the editor of this *Journal* for helpful comments on early drafts of this paper.

1. The earliest edition to which I had access, the 6th edition, had this diagram in it. I do not know whether it was in earlier editions.
2. There are, of course, different branches of microeconomics, and, as discussed in Landreth and Colander [1994], it was the Neo-Walrasian tradition that dominated the profession. Thus, when I refer to a micro perspective, I refer to the new Neo-Walrasian perspective. This Neo-Walrasian perspective saw macro issues from a micro perspective. The Marshallian tradition was somewhat different; it did not accept that one could build up from individual to general. The Marshallian approach was not followed up, except for the work of Post Keynesians, Leijonhufvud and Clower. The macrofoundation of micro approach follows in this Marshallian tradition, and could be called Marshallian Macro.
3. The term macrofoundations, I suspect, has been around for a long time. Tracing the term is a paper in itself. Axel Leijonhufvud remembered using it in Leijonhufvud [1981]. I was told that Roman Frydman and Edmund Phelps [1983] used the term and that Hyman Minsky had an unpublished paper from the 1970s with that title; Minsky remembered it, but doubted he could find it and told me that he used the term in a slightly different context. I was also told by Christof Ruhle that a German economist, Karl Zinn, wrote a paper with that title for a *Festschrift* in 1988, but that it has not been translated into English. I suspect the term has been used many more times because it is such an obvious counterpoint to the microfoundations of macro, and hence to the New Classical call for microfoundations. While he does not use the term explicitly, Bruce Littleboy [1990], in work that relates fundamentalist Keynesian ideas with Clower and Leijonhufvud's ideas, discusses many of the important issues raised here.
4. In a recent paper, Clower and Howitt [1993] extend Clower's earlier arguments and discuss the issue of the use of money in the economy, arguing that it must be analyzed as part of the structure of the economy, not as another good.

REFERENCES

Basmann, R. L. The Brookings Quarterly Econometric Model: Science of Number Mysticism? and Argument and Evidence in the Brookings-S. S. R. C. Philosophy of Econometrics, respectively, Chapters 1 and 3, in *Problems and Issues in Current Econometric Practice,* edited by K. Brunner. Columbus, Ohio: College of Administrative Science, Ohio State University, 1972.

Bryant, J. A Simple Rational-Expectations Keynes-Type Model. *Quarterly Journal of Economics,* August 1983, 525-28.

Clower, R. and Howitt, P. Money, Markets and Coase. Unpublished manuscript, 24 February 1993.

Colander, D. The New, the Neo and the New neo. *Methodus,* June 1992a.

_____. Is New Keynesian Economics New? Unpublished manuscript, 1992b.

_____. New Keynesian Economics in Perspective. *Eastern Economic Journal,* Fall 1992.

_____. Economists, Institutions and Change, in *Advances in Austrian Economics,* edited by Mario Rizzo. Greenwich, CT: JAI Press, forthcoming.

THE MACROFOUNDATIONS OF MICRO   **457**

Diamond, P. A. Aggregate Demand Management in Search Equilibrium. *Journal of Political Economy,* October 1982, 88-94.

Frydman, R. and Phelps, E. *Individual Forecasting and Aggregate Outcomes: "Rational Expectations" Examined.* Cambridge: Cambridge University Press, 1983.

Garretsen, H. *Keynes, Coordination and Beyond.* U. K.: Edward Elgar, 1991.

Hanson, N. R. *Patterns of Discovery.* New York: Cambridge University Press, 1961.

Howitt, P. Transaction Costs and the Theory of Unemployment. *American Economic Review,* March 1985, 88-100.

Kirman, A. Whom or What Does the Representative Individual Represent? *Journal of Economic Perspectives,* Spring 1992.

Landreth, H. and Colander, D. *History of Economic Thought,* 3rd ed. Boston: Houghton Mifflin, 1994.

Leijonhufvud, A. *On Keynesian Economics and the Economics of Keynes.* New York: Oxford University Press, 1968.

_____. *Information and Coordination: Essays in Macroeconomic Theory.* New York: Oxford University Press, 1981.

_____. Towards a Not-Too-Rational Macroeconomics. *Southern Economic Journal,* July 1993, 1-13.

Lerner, A. and Colander, D. *MAP: A Market Anti Inflation Plan.* New York: Harcourt Brace Jovanovich, 1981.

Littleboy, B. *On Interpreting Keynes: A Study in Reconciliation.* London: Routledge, 1990.

Lucas, R. Expectations and the Neutrality of Money. *Journal of Economic Theory,* April 1972, 1103-24.

_____. An Equilibrium Model of Business Cycles. *Journal of Economic Theory,* December 1975, 1113-44.

Mankiw, G. and Romer, D. *New Keynesian Economics.* Boston: MIT Press, 1990.

Muth, J. Rational Expectations and the Theory of Price Movements. *Econometrica,* 29, 1961, 315-35.

Phelps, E. *Microfoundations of Macroeconomics.* New York: Norton, 1969.

Rosser, B. *From Catastrophe to Chaos: A General Theory of Economic Discontinuities.* Boston: Kluwer Academic Publishers, 1991.

Samuelson, P. *Economics.* New York: McGraw Hill, 1961.

_____. The *General Theory* in 1936, in *Keynes's General Theory,* edited by R. Lekachman. New York: St. Martin's Press, 1964.

Sargent, T. and Wallace, N. Rational Expectations and the Theory of Economic Policy. *Journal of Monetary Economics,* April 1976, 169-83.

Schleifer, A. Implementation Cycles. *Journal of Political Economy,* 94, 1986, 1163-90.

Shackle, G. L. S. *Keynesian Kaleidics.* Edinburgh: Edinburgh University Press, 1974.

Simon, H. *Models of Man.* New York: Wiley, 1959.

_____. On How to Decide What to Do. *Bell Journal of Economics,* Autumn 1978, 494-507.

_____. Rational Decision Making in Business Organizations. *American Economic Review.* 1979, 493-513.

Sims, C. A. Macroeconomics and Reality. *Econometrica,* January 1980, 1-48.

van Ees, H. *Macroeconomic Fluctuations and Individual Behavior.* U.K.: Edward Elgar, 1991.

Woodford, M. Stationary Sunspot Equilibria in a Finance Constrained Economy. *Journal of Economic Theory.* October 1986, 128-37.

_____. Self-Fulfilling Expectation and Fluctuation in Aggregate Demand, in *New Keynesian Economics,* edited by G. Mankiw and D. Romer. Boston: MIT Press, 1990.

[11]

Int'l. Journal of Political Economy, vol. 33, no. 2, Summer 2003, pp. 17–35.
ISSN 0891–1916 / 2005 $9.50 + 0.00.

DAVID COLANDER

Post Walrasian Macro Policy and the Economics of Muddling Through

Post Walrasian economics is the future of economics (including what Setterfield [2003] defined as political economy), or at least I'd like to think so. Actually, I started using the term a while ago and hoped that it would catch on, but it didn't to any great extent. But I believe it should, and in this paper, I expand on my earlier discussion of Post Walrasian macroeconomic policy (Colander and van Ess 1996). I divide the paper into three parts. First, I define what I mean by Post Walrasian macroeconomics. Second, I discuss some of the theoretical differences between Post Walrasian and Walrasian macro theorizing as they relate to policy. Finally, I discuss how an acceptance of Post Walrasian economics might change the focus of macro policy discussions.

Definition and Terminology

I'm a historian of recent economic thought, which means I try to make what's happening in the profession understandable to people outside the profession. That's not an easy task, because often, even those of us inside the profession do not know what is happening. Classifications are important to historians of thought, because they

David Colander is Christian A. Johnson Distinguished Professor of Economics at Middlebury College.

provide the framework through which we tell students the story of the development of economics.

Back in the 1960s, when I learned macroeconomics, it was presented by historians of recent economic thought as a debate between fairly well-specified and distinguishable schools of macroeconomists—Keynesians, neoclassicals, monetarists, and radicals. Those distinctions broke down in the 1970s and 1980s, when the issues that had seemed to separate those groups evolved into other issues, or were simply dropped unresolved, as the profession moved on to new debates. This evolution led to a variety of new classifications—new classical, neo-Keynesian, new Keynesian, post-Keynesian (with various hyphens and capitalizations)—and by the 1980s, the classification situation could best be described as classification anarchy. By the 1990s, the debates in macroeconomics had further evolved, and even the new terms were no longer useful for capturing the differences among various economists on issues of macro policy. The pedagogical reaction to that anarchy was to downplay differences among schools in the texts, and to present macroeconomics as a unified approach.[1] In the texts, there were no longer Keynesians, monetarists, or classicals; there were simply macroeconomists.

The tendency to downplay differences among macroeconomists was amplified, because at the same time the debates in macro were evolving, the profession itself was evolving, causing the term "neoclassical" to lose much of its relevance as a descriptor of modern economics (Colander 2000a). The economics that has emerged in the twenty-first century is significantly different from the economics described as neoclassical in the history of thought texts. Modern economics has loosened its connection to the holy trinity—rationality, equilibrium, and greed—and moved toward a much more comprehensive trinity, which might be described as cognitive awareness, purposeful behavior, and sustainability. This broader trinity allows for a much broader range of models than did the old trinity, and the acceptance of this new trinity eventually will change the way economics is done.[2]

The degree to which the old trinity is violated varies among economists, but what I mean by this evolution is that top graduate schools no longer automatically shun individuals who do not maintain a belief in the old trinity. Thus, we see work in behavioral economics, nonlinear dynamics, evolutionary game theory, statistical pattern analysis (econophysics), and experimental economics as acceptable elements of conventional economics. Examples abound: Peter Howitt is at Brown; Buz Brock is at the University of Wisconsin; Mat Rabin is at Berkeley; David Laibson is at Harvard; Xavier Gabaix is at MIT; the list could be significantly expanded.

The change is ongoing, but undergraduate students have little sense of the change, because it has not yet shown up, other than in the ubiquitous boxes that students don't read, in standard undergraduate texts. In my view, however, good conventional economists are open to issues framed in this broader trinity, and cutting-edge work in economics is usually tied in some way to these changes. (Of course, I define a "good economist" as an economist who is open to at least thinking about these issues.)

As I struggled with the problems of relating the debates that I felt still existed in macroeconomic policy to students, I found myself developing finer classifications—for example, comparing the new Keynesian economics with the new neo-Keynesian economics. As I reflected upon these distinctions, I came to the conclusion that the Keynesian-based comparisons at this point were beyond the grasp of any nonspecialist, and thus were not especially helpful as classifiers (Colander 1998). This led me to give up on the old classifications and move to a new, Walrasian/Post Walrasian classification that was not burdened by the historical baggage of the earlier classifications.

Others, such as Bowles and Gintis (1993) and Stiglitz (1993), did much the same thing (although we used the terminology somewhat differently), and "Post Walrasian" became part of the vocabulary of those economists who have a proclivity toward classifications. However, while it is part of the vocabulary, it has hardly caught on; I would say it is emerging, but not yet emergent, which means that its use has not gone beyond the occasional mention in the journals. But I am hopeful that it will catch on, because I see it as a useful term to help students and outsiders understand recent developments in the debates in macroeconomics and macro policy.

Now that I've given the context, let me turn to what I mean by Post Walrasian economics. In Colander (1996), I specified three characteristics of Post Walrasian economics. Those three characteristics were as follows:

1. Multiple equilibria and complexity

2. Bounded rationality

3. Institutions and non-price-coordinating mechanisms

These are all aspects of the movement away from the holy trinity and toward the broader and looser foundational requirements of theorizing. None of these are characteristics of Post Walrasian economics alone, and, in fact, most are aspects that heterodox economists have been pushing for years. What has changed in the past decade is that mainstream economics is beginning to embrace them and include research based on them as part of the conventional research program. The Post Walrasian classification encompasses both mainstream and nonmainstream economists.

What hasn't followed from conventional economics is a significant discussion of the *policy implications* of this expanded research program. Instead, in an effort to tie policy to theory, the conventional discussion of policy almost inevitably remains in reference to a Walrasian model.[3] Thus, much of the Post Walrasian policy discussion has primarily been within the heterodox community, because its members have been willing to follow up on the policy implications of the broader holy trinity.[4]

I suspect that the reason why conventional economics has tied its policy approach to the Walrasian model is that once one moves to the broader trinity, models can be devised to support a wide range of policy interventions, and theory becomes far less useful. Put bluntly, in terms of drawing out policy conclusions from the theory, giving up the holy trinity means that almost anything goes, and that formal theory can no longer be used as a direct guide for policy. When you have models with multiple equilibria, path dependency, nonlinear dynamics, endogenous tastes, institutional restrictions, and hysteresis, there are so many degrees of freedom that theory presents little in the way of restrictions on policy. With that many degrees of freedom, a sufficiently capable modeler can devise a theoretical model to support any policy. What this means is that if one accepts the broader trinity, theory must acquire a different purpose; its use must change from theory guiding policy to theory and models aiding one's intuition.

Theoretical Differences and Policy

To see the policy differences between the Walrasian and Post Walrasian approaches, it is helpful to consider their underlying visions. Walrasian economics has, as its underlying vision, the standard Walrasian general equilibrium model of the economy. It focuses on a unique equilibrium model where market failures are characterized as deviations from optimality. Its research strategy is to develop that model from its microfoundations and analyze what a rational individual would do if he or she had full information about the economy. Put another way, Walrasian economics is the study of how infinitely rational individuals operate in a rich information environment.

Post Walrasian economics has a different underlying vision. It sees the economy as too complicated to have a meaningful microfoundation. It sees individuals as bright, but not bright enough to exhibit full rationality. Full intertemporal rationality is impossible to even contemplate, because agents are seen as changing and evolving. For example, the agent as a child is only tangentially related to the same agent as a retiree; the experiences of growing up shape the rationality of the adult.[5]

On the macro level, the result of agent interaction in such a complex environment should be chaos, but that chaos is prevented by the development of institutions and codes of ethics that limit agents' actions. Thus, rather than destabilizing the economy, preventing the achievement of full equilibrium, as is the case in the Walrasian vision, institutions and bounded rationality become ways in which the economy is stabilized. The central question for Post Walrasians is not: Why does the economy exhibit instability and fluctuations? It is: Why does it exhibit as little instability as it does? The Post Walrasian answer is that bounded rationality and institutions limit individuals' actions to a subset that maintains aggregate stability. In such a complex environment, institutions naturally become a central element in the study of the economy, and the rationality assumptions used in any model are institution specific. Thus, in contrast to Walrasian economics, Post Walrasian economics is the study of how reasonably bright individuals operate in an information-poor environment.[6]

From Control to Muddling

In relating theory to policy, this change in focus requires a change in the way we think about welfare economics and applied policy. Conventional welfare economics follows what might be called an economics of control approach. It assumes that policy makers know the underlying outcome-generating functions of the economy, and that the policy goal is to optimize a social welfare function subject to constraints. Not only are agents assumed to be infinitely bright and operating with rich information sets, but so, too, are policy makers. Conventional welfare economics is the analysis of how infinitely bright policy makers operate within rich information sets.

The Keynesian economics I learned (which is more appropriately called neo-Keynesian) also used an economics of control approach, following a functional finance view in which macro policy makers operated in an information-rich environment. Abba Lerner (1944) presented both micro and macro policy approaches in his *The Economics of Control,* which played a key role in establishing the textbook foundations for economic policy analysis. The basis for policy in the two branches of economics was not parallel. In micro, both agents and policy makers were assumed to operate in rich information environments and to have infinite computing capabilities. However, in macro, that was not the case. Macro welfare analysis—functional finance—differed from micro welfare analysis, because it assumed that agents operated in an information-poor environment and had limited computing capabilities, but that policy makers operated in a rich information environment and had infinite computing capabilities.

As the microeconomic foundations of macroeconomics were explored, and the two approaches were integrated, the neo-Keynesian policy analysis, which was based on Lerner's functional finance welfare approach, was attacked by new classical economists on consistency grounds. New classical economists argued that if policy makers had full information, rational individuals should also be assumed to have full information available to them. And if agents have that information, then many of the benefits of Keynesian policies are eliminated; in fact, most of the Keynesian problems of stabilization and equilibrium at undesirable unemployment levels would not exist.[7] Fluctuations are simply reflections of shifts in intertemporal choices, or irreducible noise in a stochastic system, and unemployment is simply the result of intertemporal inconsistencies combined with institutional rigidities. This lack of consistency between agent and policy-maker assumptions played an important role in the movement away from Keynesian economics and the development of the modern dynamic stochastic intertemporal equilibrium approach to macro.[8]

Model consistency between agents' information sets and policy-makers' information sets seems logically desirable; if policy makers have access to that information, then why shouldn't the agents in the model also have access to it, at least at a cost? So, modern Walrasian macro is defensible on these consistency grounds. The Post Walrasian argument is that there is another way to achieve the consistency. Rather than assume that individuals and policy makers have full rationality and rich information sets, as conventional Walrasian macro does, the Post Walrasian approach is to start from the other direction—to assume both policy makers and agents are operating within an information-poor environment, and, while bright, are not infinitely bright. In the Post Walrasian vision, no universally agreed-upon model of the economy is available. Not only are agents muddling, using rules of thumb, and lacking a firm foundation for what they are doing, so too are economic policy makers and economists. In the muddling-through vision, economic policy becomes far less grand; it becomes the search for rules of thumb that work temporarily in a specific institutional environment. As institutions evolve, these rules of thumb also evolve.

Muddling through is a pragmatic exploration of policy that is used when one does not have the correct model, or when one does not know a method of determining the correct model.

This difference in view has significant implications for how we think of economists' role in policy and in how we relate theory to policy. In Post Walrasian economics, there is no hope for finding an optimal policy; instead, all we try to do is to help policy makers make slightly better choices than they otherwise would have.

I see Post Walrasian policy work operating on two fronts. One of these fronts is what can be called a research and development front; it explores alternative institutional environments that might improve the operation of the economy. An example of theoretical research that serves as a foundation for such applied policy is Mundell's optimal currency work (Mundell 1961) that explored the nature of currency systems that were not tied to nations' borders. Another is Abba Lerner's and my work on market-based incomes policies (Lerner and Colander 1980) that explored the nature of price controls and the aggregate constraint that unit of account stability places on the steady-state equilibrium of a system. Such speculative work is about the implications of different institutional arrangements. It is broad and suggestive and is designed to get people thinking about issues in different ways than they previously have.

The second front of Post Walrasian policy is much more specific. It accepts the existing institutions and considers how those existing institutional arrangements might be improved. Whereas the research and development work is broad and general, this work is specialized and often technical. The researcher begins from specific problems and then chooses a model incorporating general insights that seem to fit. The problems define the research topic, not the model and data availability as, in general, is currently the case.[9]

Much economic policy work in microeconomics follows what I am calling this Post Walrasian methodology. It is little tied to abstract Walrasian theory, is not dependent on hyperrationality, and is institution specific. It was central to Milton Friedman's approach (see Hirsch and de Marchi 1990) and is the approach that "reduced form" labor economists currently use. These reduced-form economists have a loose general theoretical conception of theory, but most of their work is statistical in nature and does not depend on formal general equilibrium theory. It is pragmatic and ad hoc: Do charter schools improve educational outcomes? Does the minimum wage increase unemployment significantly?

"Structuralist" labor economists have attacked that reduced-form approach as incorrect, as it has no formal welfare foundation. But in the Post Walrasian view, that attack is meaningless, because no formal welfare foundation for policy exists. The relevance of Post Walrasian applied policy work depends not upon formal welfare analysis but upon the strength of the arguments it makes—what McCloskey (1998) called its rhetoric, but which might better be called heuristic argumentation based on educated commonsense and technical knowledge.

Early Keynesian's and monetarist's applied policy work used this reduced-form applied-policy approach, but then in debates, Keynesians started structuring their models in a Walrasian framework and adding a general equilibrium foundation to their analysis, where individuals were assumed to have infinite computing powers. Tobin's work in expanding the asset analysis in the Keynesian model is an example (Tobin 1980). As that happened, Keynesian economics evolved into neo-Keynesian analysis. However, in their policy analysis, these Keynesian economists kept the functional finance welfare foundations. New classicals attacked that work as lacking a full microfoundation, and reduced-form Keynesianism has since faded in importance.

In its place, new classical and new Keynesian macroeconomics has made Walrasian macro theory an extension of micro theory. Today, younger conventional macroeconomic theorists use a stochastic intertemporal equilibrium vision of the macro economy. In today's conventional applied macro, specific policy proposals are pulled from highly abstract models that assume individual optimization in a full information environment. An example is Chari and Kehoe's analysis of a primal approach to fiscal policy focusing on optimal taxation (Chari and Kehoe 1999). This work tries to shed light on how monetary and fiscal policy should be set over the long run and over the business cycle by integrating the optimal taxation literature into a Walrasian general equilibrium model. Chari and Kehoe (1999: 1673) arrive at four policy propositions, including the need to have capital taxes going to zero after the first period and the interest rate ultimately going to zero.

That is not the type of policy work that is seen as useful in the Post Walrasian vision. In Post Walrasian theory, models are not representations of reality but are aids in thinking about real problems. The policy implication from one model will not be sufficient to draw any real-world policy conclusions; instead, it will be tied with historical understanding and results from other models, and by a heuristic approach that provides one with an initial view of what the problem is and whether the analytic models are providing useful insights. Schelling (2003) has called this approach "vicarious problem solving," in which agents are assumed to "operate in a purposeful manner, aware of their values and alert to their opportunities" (v). Using this approach, the researcher figures out what an agent might do by imagining him- or herself in the person's position, as best he understands that position, and deciding what that person will likely do given that person's aims, values, objectives, and constraints. This vicarious problem-solving approach places limits on the formal analytic models we use. It tells us whether the model's results make sense.

Assumptions of formal models are chosen to match the best representation of the existing reality that one can vicariously get, and the results of the formal model are matched or calibrated to real-world data. That is where the new work in developing the new foundational assumptions of economics comes in. In developing one's theory, one uses information gathered from experiments, the insights of behavioral economists, and even surveys (such as Bewley's [1999] work on wage rigidities). When analytic theory fails, one turns to whatever sources of guidance work. Where one can, one develops agent-based models in which the rationality of agents is evolved from system sustainability conditions rather than assumed. And when theory fails, one falls back on the statistical analysis of data, such as vector autoregression analysis loosely guided by theory.[10]

Applying Unfinished Theory to Policy

The distinction between Walrasian and Post Walrasian economics can be overdone. Modern Walrasian economics has gone beyond the standard approach, and there are few economists left who are still limiting their research to the strict Walrasian program. Thus, the relevant contrast for Post Walrasians is with what might be called the extended Walrasian program. This extended Walrasian program loosens the strict Walrasian assumptions in a number of ways. For example, it loosens the information and rationality requirements and includes an analysis of bounded rationality. Sargent's (1993) work can be interpreted along these lines. It also no longer accepts the need for a unique equilibrium and, thus, includes multiple equilibria, which, in turn, make the specification of rationality more complicated and necessitate a meta-analysis involving equilibrium selection mechanisms.

The extended Walrasian program also allows conventions and institutions to be embedded in multiple stages in the optimization process that lead to temporary rules or limits on agent's behavior in the form of institutions. The macro branch of the new institutional economics and evolutionary game theory could fit within this extended Walrasian program. Optimization still occurs, but it is a multiple optimization process that is done in reference to multiple variables changing at different speeds. These emerging, extended Walrasian research programs are far from their Walrasian origins, and, in my view, eventually, the Post Walrasian/Walrasian distinction will itself become untenable as the two approaches converge. But that is years away.

Where the Post Walrasian approach differs from the Walrasian approach is in how to apply theory to policy in the interim. The Walrasian approach to developing the model is to modify one assumption at a time. The difficulty for policy analysis with this "remove one assumption at a time" approach is that the assumptions are interdependent. If assumptions are interdependent, the policy results of models that have modified the assumptions are suspect. For this reason, when applying models to policy, mainstream economists generally take a conservative approach to policy analysis and tie their policy discussion to the developed formal Walrasian model, not to the extended Walrasian model. Most conventional macro policy work and discussion, such as work on inflation targeting, monetary independence, optimal fiscal policy, and growth policy, have followed a conservative connection between theory and policy, connecting policy to the Walrasian models we know and not to the new, untested, extended Walrasian models that have not yet been significantly explored.

The Post Walrasian approach agrees that the results of models in which assumptions are adjusted one assumption at a time are suspect and are not especially useful for policy guidance. But, in most cases, the full-information, full-rationality model is also not useful. In Post Walrasian theory, one is attempting to develop models in which assumptions are adjusted equally on the margin so that the nature of interrelationships is maintained. This is, of course, not easy to do, because each of the deviations from the core assumptions makes the modeling more complicated, and the addition of all of them—institutions, bounded rationality, and multiple equilibria—makes the analytic modeling process from microfoundations integrating all of them impossible.

It is this conservative approach to relating theory and policy that, in my view, today differentiates heterodox and conventional economists. The conventional approach of basing policy on developed theory has given macro policy a highly conservative cast, and has prevented conventional economists from exploring a variety of policy issues. It has been left to nonmainstream economists and the occasional conventional economist, such as Joseph Stiglitz, to push the policy envelope. Thus, I would argue that much of this unconventional work on policy fits nicely under the Post Walrasian heading, and it is in policy where heterodox economists play the most important role.

Rather than starting with a general formal vision of the model, Post Walrasian policy analysis starts with a specific policy problem and attempts to model an economy in which the assumptions match the observed characteristics in the economy. Instead of having a single, well-specified formal model, it has a variety of well-specified formal models, as well as a variety of informal modeling techniques. It uses a combination of these to add insight into policy problems. Eventually, this approach will be systematized, and in a book I am currently working on with Buz Brock, we are attempting to do so in what we call the economics of muddling through.[11]

In our approach, the first step in any policy analysis is to place it into a category of models. Is it a Walrasian general equilibrium-type problem, in which case computable general equilibrium models may provide some insight? Is it a nonlinear-type problem, in which case statistical mechanics models may be helpful? Is heterogeneity likely to be important, in which case agent-based models may be necessary to provide some guidance as to how the events will transpire? Is the problem likely one of multiple equilibria, where the equilibrium selection mechanism will likely become the focal point of the analysis? Is the problem too complicated for formal analytic specification? If so, then will straight data analysis, such as vector autoregression and cointegration, provide useful insights? As I see it, the Post Walrasian economists will come to a problem with a set of statistical and analytical tools to solve problems that policy makers have. How does one tell which approach works—through a study of the data and history of the problem. In the muddling through approach, economists are closer to engineers, who study particular problems using a variety of models, than they are to scientists.

I sometimes like to picture the difference between the Walrasian and Post Walrasian approaches to theory and policy by reference to the building of medieval cathedrals. These cathedrals were built following a Post Walrasian approach. The builders did not rely on scientific laws to guide the building but relied instead on accumulated rules of thumb of what worked and what did not. The building proceeded by trial and error. Different methods of construction would be pushed to the limit until a cathedral caved in somewhere, and then the rules of thumb would change. As the stored knowledge increased, the cathedrals became more grandiose, even without a specific understanding of the laws underlying them. That understanding came much later. Post Walrasian policy follows that same approach. It is conducting policy without a full knowledge of the general laws of the economy, if there are any. What you can find, at best, are general rules of thumb for how things have worked in the past, and possibly some exploitable patterns. Walrasian economics follows a different approach to policy; it is a search for the underlying architectural plans of the economy.

A Change in Goals

Another significant change that I believe occurs when one takes a muddling-through approach to policy rather than an economics-of-control approach involves the goals of policy. For a variety of reasons, Walrasian economic policy has focused on efficiency—interpreted as maximum output regardless of the distribution of that output—as the goal of policy.[12] This is, in part, due to the assumption of a unique equilibrium and stability of the system and, in part, due to the evolution of policy analysis, where economists attempted to remain value-free in their analyses.

Because Post Walrasian work relies less on analytical models and more on simulations and on reduced form, heuristic, and agent-based models that are better equipped to handle disaggregation and heterogeneous agents, it can better consider issues of distribution. Thus, equity and the total output/distribution trade-off will become a more important element in policy analysis than it is currently.

The need to include equity in policy analysis has often been remarked upon. But, other societal goals are also likely to get more focus. System resilience is one of these goals. In multiple equilibria models, questions of shifts from one equilibrium to another become central to the analysis, and the stability of that equilibrium becomes a policy issue. An important policy question that economics currently does not shed much light on is: Will the institutional structure be sufficiently resilient to withstand the shocks that hit it? If it is not, the economy might well shift to a completely new equilibrium as the institutional structure changes.[13] Specifically, if one can rank equilibria, the resilience of the system to shocks becomes an important policy issue. Increasing the resiliency of the economy at a good equilibrium becomes an important policy goal to complement distribution and total output goals.

There is a strong case to be made for a negative trade-off between resiliency and maximizing total output, because maximizing total output often involves using a single "most efficient"
method of production. Using a single method of production tends
not to be resilient, and if some problem develops with that method,
it can cause a sudden shift to another equilibrium. A policy may
be efficient, in the sense of achieving maximum output, but that
equilibrium may not be resilient, and one may well decide that a
less efficient output with more resiliency is better.

A third change in goals that Post Walrasian economics will likely
include involves determining policy-invariant normative goals of
society, thereby integrating normative goals directly into the policy
analysis. As behavioral economics deals with meta-utility functions and individual irrationalities, these can be built into policy.
And as the new agent-based models give us insight into such issues, we can expect the policy goals that are integrated in the models
to become more complicated.

Conclusion

Let me conclude with some general observations about some changes
in thinking about specific macro policy that I believe will occur
with an adoption of a Post Walrasian approach. One is that aggregate demand will be looked at again as a determinant of growth,
because in path-dependent and multiple equilibrium models, it can
significantly change the equilibrium. Growth analysis will not solely
focus on supply-side issues; aggregate demand and supply will be
interrelated and will be analyzed as interdependent (Colander 1999;
Setterfield 1999). In monetary policy, I would see more of a focus
on income policies as a way of lowering steady-state unemployment. These policies have a potential role in models where aggregate equilibrium does not necessarily require micro equilibrium,
and the price adjustment process exhibits asymmetries.

The argument for these policies will be dependent on models
and data analysis, but those models will not tell us if the policies
are good or if they should be implemented; they will simply provide food for thought and reflection—an input into the broader

social decision process, not the decision process itself. The motto of neoclassical economics was "there's no such thing as a free lunch." The economics of control changed that to a motto where free dinners were available to economic controllers through the science of economics. The motto of muddling through goes back to "there's no such thing as a free lunch," but adds the proviso that once in a while, you can snitch a sandwich, and policy analysis is designed to snitch a few.

Notes

1. Textbooks lag the profession by a decade at least, and while the intermediate texts present a unified approach, the approach they present is not consistent with the intertemporal equilibrium framework of modern theoretical macroeconomics. Instead, they present an older IS/LM framework based on the demand for and supply of money and savings/investment equilibriums. More recent work, such as that found in the *Handbook of Macroeconomics* (Taylor and Woodford 1999) provides a dynamic stochastic intertemporal equilibrium foundation for the new integration (McCallum and Nelson 1999) and will likely be working its way into the intermediate texts in the next few years. See Colander (2004).

2. With that evolution, not only did the term "neoclassical" lose its relevance, but also, the term "heterodox" did as well, because heterodox had generally been defined in opposition to a neoclassical orthodoxy. As the orthodoxy evolved and broadened, what heterodox economists–including political economists, analytical, and otherwise–were in opposition to became hazier, and in the 2000s, it is no longer possible to easily distinguish orthodox from heterodox economics in terms of content. These ideas are discussed at length in Colander, Holt, and Rosser (2004).

3. This is true in both micro- and macroeconomics. In this paper, I concentrate on macro policy issues.

4. Occasionally, a conventional economist explores policy outside the standard model. An example is Stiglitz's (2002) recent work.

5. In such an environment, policy not only affects agents' actions, it also affects agents' underlying utility functions, so that a social welfare specification of optimal policy based on agents' utility functions is impossible unless one works with agents' policy-invariant utility functions. Work in the foundations of behavioral economics and meta-utility analysis is beginning to explore this issue.

6. I see the early Keynesian economics as a movement toward this Post Walrasian vision, although it was quickly derailed into a Walrasian framework.

7. An example of the implications of this approach for policy can be seen in Robert Lucas's recent Presidential Address to the American Economic Association (Lucas 2003), in which he argued that stabilization produces little welfare gain, and that the policy focus of macro should be on growth.

8. The reason for the downfall of Keynesian economics is debatable, and my

argument does not depend on it. Post-Keynesians question whether Keynesian economics truly made that assumption, and they argue that it is neo-Keynesian economics, not the true Keynesian economics, that has fallen. Paul Davidson's attempt to focus Keynesian economics on the nonergodicity of the system is consistent with the argument I am making. As I discussed in Colander (2003), the functional finance approach to macro policy remained the policy-makers' approach. It
also remained the approach to policy presented in the undergraduate texts because
of the lags involved in translating theory into policy-relevant models, and because
both the policy makers and the texts had to deal with real-world policy issues.

9. I recently interviewed Harvard students and asked the difference between
sociology and economics. They said that in sociology the important problems
define the research agenda, whereas in economics the available models and data
sources define the research agenda. Post Walrasian economics expands the number of basic models and increases the range of acceptable data, and follows an
approach closer to the sociological approach, but at a more technical level.

10. In part, the Post Walrasian approach is simply a return to the earlier macro
approach, which proceeds to policy proposals from loosely formulated theories
and statistical analysis without the burden of having a firm noncontextual formal
microfoundation for theory—in muddling through, one cannot have a firm foundation for theory. Examples of the modern reduced-form approach include Ray
Fair's and John and Wendy Cornwall's work (Cornwall and Cornwall 2001; Fair
2001a, 2001b).

11. See Colander (2003) for a preliminary discussion of the issues.

12. The addition of other goals of policy highlights a terminological shortcut that
economists have made when discussing policy. That shortcut is talking about efficiency as a goal of policy. Efficiency, in and of itself, cannot be a goal of society.
Efficiency is achieving some outside determined goal as cheaply as possible. Economists have taken to using efficiency as shorthand for referring to the goal of achieving
the highest level of market output. This works as shorthand if redistribution is free, or
not of concern, and the activities have no influence on other measures and goals, and
that the demands are homothetic so that redistribution would not change the measure
of aggregate output. But as soon as other goals are included, the term "efficiency" is
most appropriately used as a method incorporating all goals. Thus, what is usually
called efficiency should be called maximizing total output.

13. In Colander (2000b), I argued that deflation—downward flexibility of the
price level—would have such effects and cannot be considered an acceptable
adjustment mechanism. This, I believe, was the early Keynesian view of price
level flexibility, and much early Keynesian applied policy analysis was concerned
with maintenance of the system.

References

Bewley, T.F. 1999. *Why Wages Don't Fall.* Cambridge: Harvard University Press.
Bowles, S., and H. Gintis. 1993. "Post Walrasian and Post Marxian Econom-
    ics." In *Markets and Democracy: Participation, Accountability and
    Efficiency,* ed. S. Bowles, H. Gintis, and B. Gustafsson, pp. 1–10. Cam-
    bridge: Cambridge University Press.

Chari, V.V., and P. Kehoe. 1999. "Optimal Monetary and Fiscal Policy." In *Handbook of Macroeconomics*, ed. J. Taylor and M. Woodford, pp. 1671–1745. Amsterdam: North-Holland.

———. 2003. "Muddling Through and Policy Analysis." *New Zealand Economic Papers* 7 (December).

Colander, D. 1998. "Beyond New Keynesian Economics: Post Walrasian Economics." In *New Keynesian Economics/Post Keynesian Alternative*, ed. R. Rotheim. Aldershot, UK: Edward Elgar.

———. 1999. "A Post Walrasian Explanation of Wage and Price Inflexibility and a Keynesian Unemployment Equilibrium System." In *Growth, Employment and Inflation, Essays in Honour of John Cornwall*, ed. M. Setterfield, pp. 211–25. London: Macmillan.

———. 2000a. "The Death of Neoclassical Economics." *Journal of the History of Economic Thought* 22, no. 2 (June): 127–43.

———. 2000b. "Post Walrasian Macroeconomics and IS/LM Analysis." In *IS-LM and Modern Macroeconomics*, eds. W. Young and B.Z. Zilberfarb. Boston and London: Kluwer.

———. 2003. "Functional Finance, New Classical Economics, and Great Great Grandsons." In *Reinventing Functional Finance*, eds. E. Nell and M. Forstater, pp. 35–51. Aldershot, UK: Edward Elgar.

———. 2004. "The Strange Persistence of IS/LM." *History of Political Economy* 36, no. 4 (Supplement, December): 305–22.

Colander, D., ed. 1996. *Beyond Micro Foundations: Post Walrasian Macroeconomics.* Cambridge: Cambridge University Press.

Colander, D., and H. van Ess. 1996. "Post Walrasian Macroeconomic Policy." In *Beyond Micro Foundations: Post Walrasian Macroeconomics*, ed. D. Colander, pp. 207–20. Cambridge: Cambridge University Press.

Colander, D., R. Holt, and B. Rosser. Forthcoming. *The Changing Face of Economics.* Ann Arbor: University of Michigan Press.

Cornwall, J., and W. Cornwall. 2001. *Capitalist Development in the 20th Century.* Cambridge: Cambridge University Press.

Fair, R.C. 2001a. "Is There Empirical Support for the 'Modern' View of Macroeconomics?" Discussion Paper 1300, Yale Cowles Foundation, New Haven.

———. 2001b. "Bootstrapping Macroeconometric Models." Discussion Paper 1345, Yale Cowles Foundation, New Haven.

Hirsch, A., and N. de Marchi. 1990. *Milton Friedman: Economics in Theory and Practice.* New York: Harvester Wheatsheaf.

Lerner, A. 1944. *The Economics of Control.* London: Macmillan.

Lerner, A., and D. Colander. 1980. *MAP: A Market Anti Inflation Plan.* San Diego: Harcourt Brace.

Lucas, R. 2003. "Macroeconomic Priorities." *American Economic Review* 93, no. 1: 1–14.

McCallum, B., and E. Nelson. 1999. "An Optimizing IS-LM Specification for Monetary Policy and Business Cycle Analysis." *Journal of Money, Credit and Banking* 31 (August): 296–316.

McCloskey, D. 1998. *The Rhetoric of Economics.* 2d ed. Madison: University of Wisconsin Press.

Mundell, R.A. 1961. "A Theory of Optimal Currency Areas." *American Economic Review* 51 (November): 509–17.

Sargent, T.J. 1993. *Bounded Rationality in Macroeconomics.* Oxford: Clarendon Press.

Schelling, T. 2003. "Foreword." In *Collective Choice: Essays in Honor of Mancur Olson*, ed. J. Heckelman and D. Coates, pp. iii–iv. Berlin: Springer.

Setterfield, M. 2003. "What is Analytical Political Economy?" The Symposium on Post Walrasian Economics, Marcoeconomic Policy, and the Future of Analytical Political Economy, Trinity College, Hartford, Connecticut, May 2–4.

Setterfield, M., ed. 1999. *Growth, Employment and Inflation: Essays in Honour of John Cornwall.* London: Macmillan.

Stiglitz, J.E. 2002. *Globalization and Its Discontents.* New York and London: W.W. Norton.

———. 1993. "Post Walrasian and Post Marxian Economics." *Journal of Economic Perspectives* 7, no. 1: 109–14.

Taylor, J., and M. Woodford. 1999. *Handbook of Macroeconomics.* Amsterdam: North-Holland.

Tobin, J. 1980. *Asset Accumulation and Economic Activity.* Oxford: Basil Blackwell.

[12]

David Colander

HOW ECONOMISTS GOT IT WRONG:
A NUANCED ACCOUNT

ABSTRACT: *In the wake of the financial crisis of 2008, many economists have blamed economics for having failed to warn us. Paul Krugman, for example, in a well-known* New York Times Magazine *article, suggests that Classical economists were blinded by the beauty of mathematics, and that Keynesian economics is the path of the future. This paper argues that the evolution of economic thinking is much more nuanced than Krugman portrays it, and that instead of embracing what has become known as Keynesian economics, macroeconomists should rather re-embrace the broader Classical economic tradition, of which Keynes was an important part.*

Paul Krugman has become the voice of economists for many politicians and laypeople. Thus, when he wrote an article entitled "How Did Economists Get It So Wrong?" (Krugman 2009), it was widely interpreted as the definitive word on the subject. Krugman is a wonderful writer, and some parts of the story he tells are dead on. But other parts are misleading from the standpoint of either the historian of economic thought or of a student of economics as it is currently practiced, and as it was practiced in the run-up to the financial crisis.

The overriding problem with Krugman's story is that it's too black and white. There are good guys—the Keynesian gang—and bad guys— the Chicago gang; the bad guys drove the good guys out of town in the

David Colander, colander@middlebury.edu, Department of Economics, Middlebury College, Middlebury, VT 06753, is the author, *inter alia*, of *The Making of an Economist, Redux* (Princeton, 2007).

Critical Review 23(1–2): 1–27   ISSN 0891-3811 print, 1933-8007 online
© 2011 Critical Review Foundation   DOI: 10.1080/08913811.2011.574468

1980s, but they got their comeuppance in the crisis, so now after the financial crisis the good guys can return to their rightful predominance.

The true story is nowhere so clear-cut; it is a story of shades of gray, not of black and white. It's a story that is full of nuances—a story in which it is hard to tell the good guys from the bad guys.[1] It is a story in which the nuanced understanding of past economists was lost, resulting in excessive claims for the field's scientific understanding of the macroeconomy. The main body of academic economists pretended, and some of them actually believed, that they understood a complex system that they did not (and still do not) understand. Therefore they failed to express their ideas and arguments with the appropriate humility. The real story involves a systemic problem with almost all groups of economists, which led to their unwillingness to accept the commonsense reality that the economy is complex—far too complex to fully understand with the analytical tools that have been, and currently are, available.

Systemic Pressures against "Modeling" Complexity

Earlier economists, both Keynesian and Classical, recognized the complexity of the real-world economy. This recognition led them either to avoid using formal models or else to limit the implications they drew from formal models. They derived only highly tentative policy precepts from their models, which they applied with educated common-sense judgment. They called this policy application *art*, not science, because they recognized that formal models do not provide a substitute for judgment, but only, at best, an aid to it. As analytic tools have improved, the ways in which models can assist judgment have increased, but we are still far from having a meaningful model of the macro-economic economy that sheds definitive light on how it works. This means that judgment remains essential.

The systemic problem with contemporary economics involves incentives gone wrong, in two ways. The first problem is that when academic economists write for other academic economists, common sense seems too "common," as in ordinary or unprofessional; so even those who have it learn to hide it. Commonsensical insights are too obvious; they don't lead to journal articles, which are the means by which academic economists advance. The second problem is that when writing for popular audiences, black-and-white stories (like Krugman's) sell. These stories necessarily obscure nuances and give a misleading interpretation of what is actually going on. While Krugman is not the only nor even the worst sinner, his recent argument about where the profession went wrong demonstrates the problem vividly. In the remainder of this paper, I will consider three specific parts of his story where his unshaded narrative gets in the way of real understanding.

Krugman's Attack on Classical Economics

The first misleading part of Krugman's story involves the hatchet job he does on Classical economics, which he equates with Chicago-school economics.

Traditionally, Classical economics meant economics in the tradition of Adam Smith and John Stuart Mill, which dominated English-language economics for more than a century. Starting in about 1870, it was gradually replaced over a period of seventy years by what came to be called Neoclassical economics. Neoclassical economics was highly heterogeneous, and had many divergent strains. Some of its strains incorporated Classical insights and methods; others didn't. Keynes worked in the Marshallian strain that remained firmly in the Classical tradition, but the later followers of Keynes (often called Neo-Keynesians) moved away from that Classical tradition. What came to be called New Classical economics was a reaction to Neo-Keynesian ideas, and has little connection to this Classical tradition.

Krugman lumps all of these types of economics together. For example, he tells the reader that Neoclassical economists "elaborated on the concepts of their 'classical' predecessors," and that the Classical policy view was to "have faith in the market system." Even recognizing the need to simplify for a general audience, this is so far from the real story that if any of my history-of-thought students wrote it, they would fail the course. The more nuanced story is that Classical economics was fundamentally different from Neoclassical economics, which in turn was fundamentally different from New Classical economics.

Classical economics used a very different methodological approach than either of its two successors—an approach that was part of a larger philosophical tradition that had its origins in the Scottish Enlightenment. *Classical economists accepted that the economy was a complex system.* True, this implied that the economy couldn't be controlled: Efforts to control the complex economic system would always produce unintended consequences. But this didn't mean that Classical economists advised that we should "trust the market." It meant only that they often thought that alternatives to a very imperfect market might be worse.

Thus, contrary to Krugman, Classical economists, far from being clueless about financial crises, had a sophisticated grasp of how they could occur. The two best-known works of Classical macro/monetary economics—Henry Thornton's *Paper Credit* (1802) and Walter Bagehot's *Lombard Street* (1877)—show a deep understanding of financial policy issues and of how to deal with crises that they felt were *inevitable*. Contemporary economists who actually read Thornton or Bagehot would gain a much better understanding of the recent financial crisis than they got from their core graduate macro course.

Contrary to what Krugman writes, Classical economists did not argue for the market on efficiency grounds; rather they argued for it on philosophical, practical, and common-sense grounds. They saw the market as the least-worst alternative for achieving important goals. Those goals included much more than material welfare, which the Classicals saw as only a part of society's welfare (and a declining part at that). The broader goals included basic freedoms and a fulfilling life. Material welfare contributed to these goals, but was not the end goal. Amartya Sen's work on capabilities (Sen 1985) is a continuation of these broader Classical themes—themes that have been lost by a large majority of the modern economics profession.

Contrary to what Krugman asserts, most Classical economists did not claim that they had the answers to what government should do about policy, and they carefully couched scientific argument and modeling results as merely some among the many considerations to take into account when making public policy. Nassau Senior (1836, 2–3), one of the first economists to spell out the Classical method, wrote that

> An economist's conclusions, whatever be their generality and their truth, do not authorize him in adding a single syllable of advice. That privilege belongs to the writer or statesman who has considered all the causes which may promote or impede the general welfare of those whom he addresses, not to the theorist who has considered only one, though among the most important of those causes. The business of a Political Economist is neither to recommend nor to dissuade, but to state general principles, which it is fatal to neglect, but neither advisable, nor perhaps practicable, to use as the sole, or even the principal, guides in the actual conduct of affairs.

Contrary to what Krugman implies, moreover, Classical economists did not have a one-dimensional view of policy. They did not believe that the market was perfect or that government involvement was always unjustified. Steven Medema's *The Hesitant Hand* (Medema 2009) and Denis O'Brien's *The Classical Economists Revisited* (O'Brien 2004) provide accessible displays of the enormous range of Classical economists' policy views. Some, in fact (including John Stuart Mill), supported variants of socialism, even as they maintained a general laissez-faire philosophy.

But what about that philosophy? For the best Classical economists, laissez faire was not a rigid proscription of all government involvement in the economy. Instead, it was a warning to think five or six times before one advocates a policy that had to be implemented by government.[2] Laissez faire was not a theoretically derived precept, a purported product of scientific work; Classical economists explicitly disavowed any scientific foundation for their laissez-faire policy prescriptions, which they arrived at using a combination of their theories and their educated common sense—based, in turn, on their study of history and their understanding of how government actually worked. On this foundation they developed a belief that policy interventions often had unintended and undesirable consequences. When the political controller is himself controlled by political intrigue, not by genuine concern for the welfare of society, it makes sense to limit the controller's control.

To prevent themselves from overstating the relevance of their arguments from science for policy, Classical methodologists, such as J. N. Keynes (John Maynard's father) (1891), argued that it was necessary to maintain two branches of economics: the pure science, which dealt with theoretical and scientific issues; and the art, which dealt with policy issues. The two branches had fundamentally different methodologies and fundamentally different outputs.[3] The outputs of the pure science of economics were theorems and facts—neither of which, as Senior noted in the passage quoted above, had direct relevance for policy. Only in this pure science of economics was the methodology explicitly mathematical; mathematics forces researchers to be precise and careful and to at least get the logic of the argument right.

In mathematical modeling, one develops theorems. But if a logical theorem is to be accepted as relevant for policy—what classical economists called a policy precept—it would have to be shown to be empirically relevant to the case at hand. Classical economists didn't have the tools or data to test their theorems empirically, which is why the best of them were very modest about claiming that theorems were relevant for policy.[4]

In contrast, the *art* of economics, which sometimes went under the name of "political economy," had a much broader domain and a much looser methodology.[5] To do political economy one needed a knowledge of history, philosophy, and ethics. In arriving at a policy conclusion, the political economist had to integrate his knowledge with economic insights derived from theories and an educated common sense. Classical economists, such as John Stuart Mill, were dismissive of abstract theory and models as a guide for policy. They saw models as presenting, at best, half-truths (Mill 1838). As J. N. Keynes (1891, 83) put it, "the art of political economy will have vaguely defined limits and be largely non-economic in character."[6]

From Classical to Neoclassical

The evolution of economics from these broad Classical themes to a narrower set of what came to be called Neoclassical themes started in the late 1800s and continued well into the twentieth century. It happened as the study of economics moved to the university. As that happened, the study of the economy changed from being a sidelight, which people did in addition to their real jobs, to being the full-time activity of professional economists. Economists no longer actually took part in the activities they were describing; instead, they spent their working hours teaching, writing, and thinking about economics. As that happened, the *metis* that comes from daily contact with an economic system faded from economists' writing. This institutional change in the structure of the discipline fundamentally altered economists' background knowledge of the economy, as well as their incentives about what to study and how to express their ideas.

Instead of primarily writing for the broad lay public and emphasizing common sense, as earlier Classical economists had done, economists began to write more for other economists; they became more explicitly mathematical, more interested in theory per se, and less interested in real-world issues. The field of economics accordingly narrowed, and the philosophical, historical, and institutional knowledge that was so central to Classical economists' analysis of policy began to be lost.[7] As publications became an increasingly important metric for advancement and success, economists began to see themselves more as scientists and less as artists who brought a wide range of understanding to the table. Thus, the study of economics became more focused on the pure science of economics. It became more technical and mathematical. This institutional change led to the movement from Classical to Neoclassical economics.

A similar institutional change in the natural sciences led to scientific advances. Unfortunately, economics—and social science generally—did not see such progress. I suspect that this is because the social sciences involve a greater degree of complexity than do the natural sciences. The basic units in social science, which economists call agents, are strategic, unlike the basic units of the natural sciences. Economics can be thought of as an unruly physics, where strategic atoms foil any efforts to understand or control them.[8]

Strategic agents complicate formal modeling enormously; they make it impossible to have a perfect model since they increase the calculations one would have to make in order to solve the model beyond the number that the fastest conceivable computer could process in a finite amount of time. Even to begin formally modeling such a complex system required a whole new branch of mathematics, game theory, which was invented only in the 1940s by John von Neumann and Oscar Morgenstern (1944). The formal study of economics as a complex system only began in the 1980s with an innovative seminar at the Santa Fe Institute. Formally studying complex systems requires rigorous training in the cutting edge of mathematics and statistics along with a highly creative mind. Inevitably, complex systems exhibit path dependence, nested systems, multiple speed variables, sensitive dependence on initial conditions, and other non-linear dynamical properties. This means that at any moment, right when you thought you had a firm result, all hell could break loose.

Different Branches of Neoclassical Economics

Economists in the late 1880s and early 1900s did not have the technical expertise, the analytical tools, or the computing power to start dealing with these problems, so they (quite reasonably) simplified and studied problems that their analytical techniques *could* deal with. There were many ways to simplify, and what is called Neoclassical economics was actually a multitude of competing approaches. At various times from the

1870s to the 1970s, when Neoclassical economics was most prevalent, a variety of different Neoclassical approaches dominated the English-speaking world at various times.[9]

One branch—the Marshallian branch, named after Keynes's mentor, Cambridge economist Alfred Marshall—did not lose its Classical roots; it is best seen as part of the broader Classical tradition. It was the dominant "Neoclassical" approach in English-speaking countries from the 1890s until the 1930s or 40s. Marshallian economics saw economics as a set of tools, not as a completed theory.[10]

A second Neoclassical branch—the Walrasian branch, named after French economist, Leon Walras—deviated more significantly from Classical economics; it saw economic theory as providing a unified model of the economy, even to the exclusion of reality. This is the branch of that, Krugman rightly complains, got lost in the beauty of the mathematics.

If Walrasian Neoclassical economists had kept in mind that their model was so far from reality that little of practical relevance could be gained from it, it would have been a useful model. Economists using the Walrasian model helped clear up many logical confusions in the Marshallian branch of Neoclassical economics. But many Walrasian Neoclassical economists made a fatal mistake that Classical economists had avoided and had strongly warned against: They drew policy conclusions directly from their models and theory. They gave up the strict separation of science and art that Classical economists had maintained, discarding the insight that economic theory was far too simple to shed much light on policy issues in a system as complex as the economy.[11]

However fair Krugman's criticisms of modern Walrasian Neoclassical economics might be, it is unfair to apply those criticisms to Classical economics generally. The larger Classical tradition is definitely not guilty of being blinded by the beauty of mathematics, nor of defending the proposition that we should "have faith in the market."

Is Keynesian Economics the Future of Macroeconomics?

Krugman also misses some important nuances in his discussion of Keynesian economics. Krugman presents Keynesian economics as the correct path forward; the future of economics involves a return to

Keynes. He writes that "Keynesian economics remains the best frame-work we have for making sense of recessions and depressions."

Before one can say whether or not Krugman is right, one must define Keynesian economics. That isn't easy. Keynesian economics means many different things to many different people. The majority of differences of opinion about whether or not we should follow the Keynesian path reflect different conceptions of what the Keynesian path is, more than they reflect differences of opinion of the path that macroeconomics should follow. As with Krugman's blanket criticism of Classical economics, the issue of whether we should follow the Keynesian path is nowhere near as black and white as Krugman presents it. There are so many different possible meanings of Keynesian economics that suggest-ing that we should follow it obfuscates more than it clarifies.

Keynes wrote the *General Theory* in 1936, when economics was shifting from the broad-based Classical approach toward the narrower, Walrasian Neoclassicism, which emphasized comparative static mathe-matical models of multi-market equilibria. Keynes was not part of this Walrasian transformation. He was an economist of the Marshallian variety, meaning that he eschewed mathematics. (Marshall [1906] is famous for arguing that economists should use mathematics only as a guide to their own reasoning, and should burn the mathematics before presenting their ideas.) Marshall's brand of Neoclassical economics saw economic theory as providing a set of tools that economists could use to solve the small microeconomic issues that he felt economists could have something concrete to say about. He did not attempt to use economic theory as a foundation for large macro ideas, because he did not think the theory was up to the task. Thus, he avoided the theoretical analysis of such issues as the aggregate efficiency of markets or the total level of employment. He stayed with what he called a partial equilibrium or one-thing-at-a-time approach, which involved looking at issues that his supply-and-demand framework could shed some light on.

Although Keynes was a student of Marshall, he had little interest in the narrow themes with which Marshall's analysis was concerned. (Keynes's colleague, Gerald Shove, is reported to have remarked that Keynes "never spent the half hour necessary to learn price theory," by which he meant Marshallian microeconomics). However, while Keynes was not interested in Marshall's narrow themes, he maintained a Marshallian approach to thinking about the economy, and he did not see models as providing policy answers. Thus, he wrote that "the theory of economics . . . is a method rather than a doctrine, an apparatus of the mind, a technique of thinking which helps its possessor to draw correct conclusions" (Keynes 1921, v).

A second difference between Keynes and Marshall is that Keynes was active in policy debates, and was highly skilled at it. Keynes was also quite willing to make use of rhetorical arguments to support a policy position that he believed was correct. He did not object to his followers blending theory and policy (which Classical methodologists had warned against) as long as they favored his currently preferred policy views. Thus, he was willing to allow his theory to be used as justification for a policy even when the theory wasn't up to the task. This gave him an advantage over other Classical economists and accounts for some of the success of his theory.

Another major reason for Keynes's success was marketing. He audaciously called his work *The General Theory*, but it was at best a rough sketch of a theory, which was more vision than model. Keynes's sly implication of a theoretical revolution on par with Einstein's was, in many ways, as modern New Classical economist Robert Lucas (2004) said, "just so much hot air."

The limitations of Keynes's work were recognized early on. Contrary to what Krugman implies, the *General Theory* was not widely hailed by economists. Most economists saw Keynes's book as severely flawed. For example, reviews by Jacob Viner (1936) and Roy Harrod (1937) were supportive but critical. Keynes's colleague, Dennis Robertson, who specialized in macroeconomic issues, was dismissive. Chicago economist Frank Knight's comments were more than critical; he wrote that the things in the *General Theory* that were new weren't true, and that the things in it that were true weren't new. Even Alvin Hansen (1936), who later became the face of Keynesian economics in the United States, gave *The General Theory* what can at best be described as a lukewarm review.

How did such a flawed book lead to major revolution in economic thinking? The answer is a combination of the right place and the right time,[12] marketing skills, and the ability of the "Keynesian" classification to morph into whatever fit with the major changes that were taking place in the profession at the time. These included the change from Marshallian to Walrasian Neoclassicism, the introduction of econometrics, the movement to a more policy-activist sensibility, and the introduction of simple graphical models as central pedagogical devices.

The General Theory's primary success and largest initial influence were, moreover, among graduate students and younger economists who had less training in Classical economic thought, and who were not familiar with cutting-edge developments that were going on in Classical macro (Colander and Landreth 1996). They found in Keynes what beginning students often search for—seemingly easy answers to difficult questions. They were interested in policy, not fine points of theory or methodology. Faced with the Depression, they wanted a theory that told them that they should do what common sense told them they should do—get the government to undertake policies to end the crisis. What was called the Keynesian revolution was a surface revolution about policy sensibilities not a theoretical revolution. It was not a revolution in scientific understanding.

Paradoxically, the success of Keynesian economics depended on abandoning some of its most important insights, its Classical methodological roots, and the subtle understanding of policy that flowed from those roots. Nowadays, following the *General Theory's* protean reception among younger economists, *General Theory* is often associated with the use of expansionary monetary and fiscal policy. But in the 1930s many Classical economists supported such policies as well, and Keynes's support of these policies predated the *General Theory*. Classical economists could support such expansionary policies in the 1930s, even though theoretically those policies didn't fit their model, because they recognized that they *had* no adequate model of the aggregate economy, and that they would have to deal with the crisis using educated common sense and their knowledge of history. As one of the strongest opponents of government intervention, William Hutt (1979, 45), later reflected, "Once the persistent ignoring of 'Classical' precepts has precipitated chaos and insurmountable political obstacles obviously block the way to noninflationary recovery, only a pedant would oppose inflation." Similarly, Keynes' method of choosing the model appropriate for the situation does not lend itself to proposing a blanket answer to any policy question. Keynes took a much more nuanced view of policy than the usual understanding "Keynesian economics" would indicate, as shown by his reaction when one of his young followers, Abba Lerner, argued in favor of a deficit at a Federal Reserve seminar that the both attended. Keynes took him to task for supporting deficit spending (Colander 1984).

It is important to demystify Keynes's ideas because if we are to truly understand Keynesian economics, we have to also understand that Keynes was writing as part of the Classical/Marshallian tradition, which did not view theoretical models as leading to direct policy implications. That Keynesian methodological nuance, rooted in the Classical distinction between economic science and policy art, was lost by his followers, and Keynes did not vigorously object to this loss. By the 1950s, Keynesian economics was equated with the use of fiscal policy to steer the economy, and Keynesian models were seen as providing a justification for the use of activist monetary and fiscal policy; yet in *The General Theory*, there is almost no mention of fiscal policy at all.

Given this history, there is a natural confusion about what Keynesian policy is. One could never predict what policy position Keynes would take on a new issue, and he would change his views often.[13] This is because the policies he supported were only tangentially tied to his models and, as his father had argued, were based largely on non-economic grounds.[14] I have no idea whether or not Keynes would have supported the 2008 stimulus package (but whatever position he took, he would have defended it persuasively).

Keynes's Distortion of Economic History

Another reason for the success of Keynes's economics was his rhetorical skill, and Krugman has similar skills. Krugman follows in Keynes's footsteps by using those skills to oversimplify his opponents' arguments. In *The General Theory* Keynes distorted the history of economics as much or more than Krugman does. By skipping over the intricacies of Classical economics, Keynes helped perpetuate the belief that Classical economists were clueless about depressions, recessions, and unemployment (a canard that Krugman happily repeats). For example, in *The General Theory*, Keynes uses Classical economists' belief in Say's Law (that supply creates its own demand) to argue that Classical economists did not believe that general unemployment could exist. Thus he created a false contrast between Classical economics and his "theory," which could explain general unemployment. Consider what Say himself wrote, though:

> In the first place my attention is fixed by the inquiry, so important to the present interests of society: What is the cause of the general glut of all the

markets in the world, to which merchandise is incessantly carried to be sold at a loss? What is the reason that in the interior of every state, notwithstanding a desire of action adapted to all the developments of industry, there exists universally a difficulty of finding lucrative employments? And when the cause of this chronic disease is found, by what means is it to be remedied? On these questions depend the tranquility and happiness of nations. (Say 1821, 2)

In truth, Classical economists did study how coordination failures in markets could lead to depressions, and they attempted to analyze what happened when one industry affected another, which in turn affected others, creating a feedback loop. They recognized that such feedbacks could lead the aggregate economy astray, but they also recognized that they didn't have the formal analytic tools to capture these feedbacks in a meaningful way. So they did not pretend to have a formal theory of the aggregate economy. They did, however, offer insights into broad general relationships, such as the quantity theory of money and Say's Law, which seemed to hold true, and which would help people avoid fallacious reasoning.[15]

The Neo-Keynesian Diversion

The insertion of "Keynesian" models into a Walrasian framework came to be called the Neoclassical/Neo-Keynesian synthesis. This synthesis consisted of multiple equations describing actions of actors in different markets—the labor market, the goods market, and the money market—but included no dynamics. In these models researchers would "solve" the model for an equilibrium, and then explore how changes in what they called exogenous variables would lead to a new equilibrium. They then compared the old and new equilibria to find the effect of policy changes.[16] This procedure served as a foundation for how macroeconomists were taught about the macroeconomy from the 1950s until the 1980s, and it still remains in most undergraduate macroeconomic textbooks today.

The primary advantages of the Neo-Keynesian/Neoclassical synthesis were that it seemed to fit the economy in a loose way, and that it was useful for structuring thoughts for pedagogical purposes. But it has serious limitations both for thinking about policy and for thinking about what was really going on in the macroeconomy, other than for general guidance.

One problem was that to make the models tractable, Neo-Keynesian/ Neoclassical models simply ignored the strategic behavior of agents, which is that aspect of economics that makes the formal study of economics so difficult. It pictured the macroeconomy as a system that could be described by mechanical laws that did not take into account that their agents were strategic, and that their strategic actions would undermine any knowable mechanical law as soon as you attempted to undertake policy based on those laws.[17] A second problem was that the synthesis had no analysis of the underlying complex dynamics; it could not specify how a variable in the model changed. They simply assumed that somehow the system smoothly moved to a new equilibrium, unaffected by the dynamics of getting there. The adoption of these simple models led economists to shift from thinking of dynamics too complex to be modeled as the cause of an economic depression to positing instead a comparative static explanation for a depression—wages that did not adjust.[18]

These Neo-Keynesian models were operationalized with econometrics, a newly developing field of economics, making macroeconomics one of the hottest fields of study. Econometric models made the models seem impressive to lay people. Direct policy conclusions were drawn from these macroeconometric models—"Here is how much fiscal policy we will need, here is how much monetary policy we will need." Classical economists, of course, had approached modeling very differently, as had Keynes—who opposed macroeconometrics and who, in his review of work by an early developer of macroeconometrics (Keynes 1939), Jan Tinbergen, challenged the basic premise of econometrics, arguing that "the method is one neither of discovery nor criticism."[19] This makes it hard to see how the macroeconometric path followed by Neo-Keynesian economists through the 1970s can be reasonably described as Keynesian.

Why did Neo-Keynesian economics develop as it did? It was not because researchers consciously decided that econometrics would shed the most light on macroeconomics (Colander 2006 and 2009). Instead, it was an unintended consequence of individual macroeconomic researchers following their own self-interest, combined with academic incentives to eschew common sense. It was a systemic failure of the economics profession—a failure that persists today.

I present this history to demonstrate the ambiguity in the term *Keynesian*. In many ways, what became known as Keynesian was the antithesis of Keynes. The entire Neo-Keynesian, neo-Walrasian approach was quite outside the British Classical tradition of which Keynes was a part. This is not to say that the model that developed had no relationship to Keynes's arguments. It was in accord with an important aspect of Keynes's ideas, specifically the recognition that macroeconomic laws could be fundamentally different from microeconomic laws. This observation, which is a central identifying feature of complex systems, could have led to a major change in the Classical theoretical vision, and thereby made a major theoretical contribution to economic understanding. Unfortunately, the vision was lost as policy and theory became hopelessly intertwined.

In order to develop a formal Keynesian model with a distinct macroeconomics and without complex dynamics, economists had to assume that macroeconomic laws were definite, knowable, and unchanging. In principle such laws could be derived from microeconomic relationships, although Keynesian economists admitted it was not quite clear how to do so.[20] The assumption of knowable and unchanging laws was very un-Keynesian, and it certainly violated the basic Classical premise that an economic system with strategic agents was too complex to derive knowable and unchanging laws. This assumption also obscured important elements of the policy debate.

In summary, Neo-Keynesian and Neoclassical economists replaced a messy, imprecise, and modeling-resistant Classical explanation of why a depression might occur—an explanation that suggested that the problem lay somewhere in the dynamics of the system and were closely tied with financial issues—with a precise model stating that the problem lay in the fact that "exogenous variables" were not at the right level, and that we could model how those exogenous variables affected the economy through mechanical multipliers of aggregate consumption levels embedded in a comparative static multi-market equilibrium model.

I am not arguing that the mechanistic models had no purpose. As long as they weren't taken too seriously and were used judiciously, many of these mechanistic models were extremely useful as a rough guide to policy issues. Moreover, as computational power and data availability advanced the models became more useful. They provided the rough and ready guides for thinking about policy that policy makers needed. To the extent that the Neo-Keynesian/Neoclassical models were presented as

rough engineering models that were useful in thinking about policy—
which is how many practitioners saw and used them—they were a useful
advance. But to the degree that they were presented as scientific models,
and as the only tool one needed—as something that could be used
blindly—they had a negative effect on the practice of economics. This
façade of scientific precision created the illusion that Neo-Keynesians
had the answers to macroeconomic policy, that activist monetary and
fiscal policy could steer the wheel of the economy, and that anybody
who opposed such policies was a fool who wanted to drive the economy
without a steering wheel. Using the models in this way served only a
rhetorical function and stifled good policy discussion.

The Rise of New Classical Economics

Starting in the 1960s and for the next fifty years, economists began to
discover that Classical economists were not quite the numbskulls that
Keynes had made them out to be, and that Neo-Keynesian theories—
which young economists, in their quick embrace of a clear theory, had
accepted as truth—were far too simple even to come close to a
meaningful model of the macroeconomy. The black-and-white approach to understanding the economy, which Keynes had used to his
rhetorical advantage, now boomeranged on Keynesian economics.
Instead of recognizing that there were important and complementary
truths in both Neo-Keynesian and Classical insights, Keynesian
economics itself fell victim to the black/white division. The result was
that Keynes and the Neo-Keynesians were treated as outrageously by
many later critics as Keynes had treated Classical economists.

I agree with Krugman that the simplistic criticisms of Keynesian
economics that one hears among some macroeconomists today are
misplaced. But that does not mean that these modern macroeconomists
are stupid or that the policy views of the critics of "Keynesianism" don't
warrant serious consideration.

The reason Neo-Keynesian economics was replaced by "New
Classical" Chicago economics in the 1980s was that the Neo-Keynesian
model had serious logical problems. New Classical economics, in the
tradition of Robert Lucas and Thomas Sargent, made an important
contribution to macroeconomics by highlighting these problems. They
pointed out that strategic behavior on the part of economic agents would

undermine basic Neo-Keynesian "laws" and undermine its mechanistic policy prescriptions. In doing so they brought back important Classical insights.

However, they made two mistakes. The first, relatively minor, mistake was that they claimed to be arguing against *Keynesian* economics and policies, not Neo-Keynesianism. The much more serious mistake is the same one that Keynes himself made: They both allowed less-careful followers to draw policy implications from their models of the economy, when they should have pointed out that no such model can be used as a direct guide to policy because the macroeconomy is too complicated to be formally modeled in a satisfactory way. The New Classical economists made their model tractable but unrealistic by essentially assuming away all coordination problems; hence, like the Neo-Keynesian models, New Classical models contain no analysis of how complex dynamics might feed back and (conceivably) cause a structural breakdown in the entire economy. New Classical economists get around the problem of agents' strategic behavior by creating models that eliminate the need for strategy. It's tidy, but it's not especially helpful in guiding our macroeconomy.[21]

Putting Keynes's Contribution into Perspective

I provide this history of macroeconomics not to undermine Keynes's contribution but to put it in perspective. His contribution involved vision more than it did substance, and that vision was extraordinary. He went beyond earlier Classical economists who worried about coordination failures and small feedback effects; he recognized that, combined, these feedback effects could paralyze the economy, recovering only with government action. He was the first well-known Classical economist to point out that, in the aggregate, there are just too many coordination problems to expect that the market will always provide the proper coordination.

What Keynes did not provide was a formal macroeconomic theory to explain how those coordination problems in a complex system could lead to an economic depression. He also did not explain why, generally, the economy worked reasonably well, even when on the face of it, a system as complex as the economy should result in chaos.[22] Until economists explain in a formal theory why the economy works, there is no hope of meaningfully explaining why it sometimes stops working.

So as a scientific theory of macroeconomics, Keynesian economics failed, and that failure led what was called Keynesian economics to fade away.

What does this history mean for Krugman's argument? It means that regardless of how much respect one has for Keynes (obviously I am a strong admirer), one has to recognize that he did not solve either the theoretical or policy conundrum of macroeconomics. To do that would have required untying the Gordian Knot of complex systems; Keynes simply cut it, and then convinced a group of students to accept the cut rope as if it were an unknotted rope, and to believe that what came to be known as Keynesian economics was scientifically correct. That led macroeconomic theory down a blind alley that blended policy and theory: What were called Keynesian theories always seemed to lead to policy activism; and what were called Classical theories always seemed to lead to no government involvement. That did not reflect the subtle views of Classical economists or of Keynes. It muddled serious discussion of both theory and policy.

Mathematics Is Not the Problem

Krugman's discussion of mathematics and economics misses another important subtlety. He writes:

> The economics profession went astray because economists, as a group, mistook beauty, clad in impressive-looking mathematics, for truth. Until the Great Depression, most economists clung to a vision of capitalism as a perfect or nearly perfect system. . . . Unfortunately, this mathematicized and sanitized vision of the economy led most economists to ignore all the things that can go wrong.

The problem with Krugman's argument about mathematics is twofold.

First, it suggests that Classical economists supported the market because of some mathematical model. As should be clear from what I have said thus far, that is not true. Classical economists, and the Marshallian branch of Neoclassical economists (of which later "free-market" economists such as Milton Friedman were an offshoot), fought against the mathematicization of economics in order to keep the deeper philosophical insights of Classical economics in the forefront of their analysis. It was in fact Keynes's followers who led macroeconomics down the mathematical path; they developed simple mathematical "scientific" macro models and derived policy conclusions from them. Instead of models being engines of discovery and analysis, as they were for Marshall, they became pseudoscientific justifications for the policy a given economist supported.[23]

The second problem with Krugman's argument is that it casts mathematical models as the villains. But the problem with macroeconomics is not, and never was, the mathematical models. The true cutting-edge mathematical economists are pushing new frontiers, and have been doing so for decades. They deserve praise, not contempt (Colander, Holt, and Rosser 2004). The future of the science of economics is mathematics—mathematical models that will likely be much more complicated than the current models.

Mathematical models can be extremely useful. But if they are used without understanding their enormous limitations, it can create the false impression that the models themselves are problematic, not the way they are used.[24] They can give pseudoscientific support to policies that stifle debate about their merits.

A unified scientific model of the macroeconomy—which takes into account its full complexity—does not exist. But scientific study does not depend on having a unified model. All it requires is a critical approach, a focus on understanding for the sake of understanding, and a commitment to reporting the results with the modesty that our lack of understanding demands. Lionel Robbins (1927, 176) made this quite clear in his essay on the appropriate method for economists to follow:

> What precision economists can claim at this stage is largely a sham precision. In the present state of knowledge, the man who can claim for economic science much exactitude is a quack. The problems of human motive we have to analyze with the "vast amorphous phantoms" of psychology at their back are nebulous enough in all conscience. It is not because we believe that our science is exact that we wish to exclude ethics from our analysis, but because we wish to confine our investigations to a subject about which positive statement of any kind is conceivable.

As Robbins makes clear, mathematical models should be used only with great prudence. The macroeconomic models that Keynes's followers developed were unsupportable on purely scientific grounds. Those models, however, could have (and should have) been used as back-of the envelope guides to thinking about very complicated issues.

20   *Critical Review Vol. 23, Nos. 1–2*

Had they been presented as such, and had applied macroeconomists focused their energies on dealing with the nuances of policy (which is where the true differences lay), the history of macro would have been quite different.

Despite the current problems in economics, progress is being made and perhaps a future historian of economic thought will look back and see the most recent development in macroeconomics in a positive light. She will explain the "New Classical/Real Business cycle interlude" as the inevitable result of the macro pseudoscience inherent in the "Walrasian Neoclassical/Neo-Keynesian interlude," which had become dominant in the 1960s and 70s. Maybe this future historian will also point out that eventually, macroeconomics returned to its Classical roots, but modernized them to take into account enormous advances in analytic and computational power that changed the way empirical data could be integrated with the mathematics of complex systems involving interacting strategic agents. She will describe a highly mathematical science of macroeconomics—one of beautiful and elegant models—that a small group of complex system theorists developed. She will point out that macroeconomic practitioners keep the insights of these models in the back of their minds to frame their thinking about the macro economy, but that they use a wide variety of less elegant, but more useful engineering models combined with educated common sense and judgment for specific policy guidance.

The Systemic Failure of the Economics Profession

Why does that not describe contemporary macroeconomics? The reason is systemic. Professional economists have been unwilling to admit that the economy is far too complex to be captured by any unified model. In private discussions among ourselves we recognize this complexity, but we don't add the appropriate warning labels to our models when they are discussed in public. There, we pretend we understand more than we do.

I suspect the reason we do so is that only recently have analytic and computational tools been developed that might begin to allow even ultra-mathematicians to say something useful. I have predicted that ultimately this work will lead to a new Post Walrasian macroeconomics (Colander 2006) that is neither Keynesian nor Classical but is simply macroeconomics. But the fact is that most of us are not good enough mathematicians to make a real contribution to the analysis of complex systems, and after you've said that the economy is complex, unless you *are* an ultra-mathematician, there's not much more to say in terms of pure science.

However, if we give up the pretense of full scientific understanding, we free the majority of economists to return to the branch of economics that Classical economists saw as the most important one for policy making—the applied branch of economics, its "art." This art of economics is the applied policy branch of economics. This is where most academic economists can make contributions—as long as we possess common sense, an ability to understand (but not necessarily to produce) high theory, a knowledge of institutions, and a knowledge of history. The systemic failure in economics manifests itself in policy economists who don't even realize that these qualities are important, and who instead engage in black-and-white polemics such as Krugman's. What would best further understanding is an economics profession trained to recognize and highlight the shades of gray that inevitably exist in policy issues. This would lead to a wider recognition that policy actions have both costs and benefits.

For example, expansionary monetary and fiscal policy may help expand the economy temporarily, but it will likely stop the larger necessary structural changes from taking place. When Chicago econo-mists point this out, they are making a valid point. They deserve better than Krugman's claim that the recommendations of Chicago economists "are the product of a Dark Age of macroeconomics in which hard-won knowledge has been forgotten." Similarly, what is called the Keynesian position deserves better than to be described as reflecting "schlock economics" that are "based on discredited fairy tales." We deserve better from tenured professors of economics at major universities.

For economics to progress, we need to change the structure of the profession. We need more economists trained in the subtlety of policy issues and institutional realities. We need far fewer economists trained as producers of macroeconomic theory (but those few who are trained as macroeconomic theorists need much stronger training in advanced mathematics and statistics) and far more trained to consume it. Applied macroeconomists need to know how macroeconomic and financial institutions really work, and they need to know the history of economic ideas and of the economy itself. It follows, then, that the solution for the macroeconomics profession isn't, as Krugman suggests, merely to re-embrace Keynes. Instead, the solution is to re-embrace the Classical tradition, in which Keynes was an important participant.

NOTES

1. I use guys, because almost all the participants in the debate have been male; female economists have tended to be more attuned to shades of grey.
2. Even Keynes recognized this. In his "The End of Laissez Faire" (Keynes 1926), he points out that the best Classical economists did not support a blanket laissez-faire approach. However, their subtle policy views did not get translated into textbooks. So eventually "the dogma" of laissez faire "got hold of the educational machine. . . . The political philosophy, which the seventeenth and eighteenth centuries had forged in order to throw down kings and prelates, had been made milk for babes, and had literally entered the nursery." As evidence that laissez faire was not a fundamental theorem of Classical economics, Keynes cites the comment of a leading Classical methodologist, John Elliot Cairnes (1870), that "the maxim of laissez-faire has no scientific basis whatever, but is at best a mere handy rule of practice."
3. The need to separate out the two was reiterated by J. M. Keynes's contemporary, Lionel Robbins (1932 and 1981), whose work supposedly serves as the foundation for modern methodology in economics.
4. Classical economists came in many different varieties. David Ricardo was probably the most important outlier of the position I am equating with the Classical tradition; his attempt to merge theory and policy without empirical evidence acquired the name the Ricardian vice. The best expression of Classical theory is found in the writings of John Stuart Mill. The Millian tradition was carried on by later Neoclassical economists such as Alfred Marshall and Lionel Robbins. These economists were extremely careful about drawing policy inferences from scientific theory. They may have had strong policy views, but they made it clear that these views were not views derived from the science of economics.
5. The term *science* can be interpreted in many ways. Following J. N. Keynes, I am interpreting it narrowly, and it might be called pure science. Later economic writers distinguished between light-bearing science—pure science undertaken for the sole purpose of understanding—and fruit-bearing science (applied or engineering science), whose primary purpose was policy application. Applied science involved creating policy-relevant models and then applying those models with judgment—as a rough guide. The models were not meant to provide definitive results.
6. J. M Keynes (1938) continued in the Classical tradition, and did not see any particular model as the correct one:

> Economics is a science of thinking in terms of models joined to the art of choosing models which are relevant to the contemporary world. It is compelled to be this, because, unlike the typical natural science, the material to which it is applied is, in too many respects, not homogeneous through time. The object of a model is to segregate the semi-permanent or relatively constant factors from those that are transitory or fluctuating so as to develop a logical way of thinking about the latter, and of understanding the time sequences to which they give rise 'in particular cases. Good economists are scarce because the gift for using 'vigilant observation' to choose good models, although it does not require a highly specialized intellectual technique, appears to be a very rare one.

7. The process of change took decades. An economist's working lifespan is about 40 years, so on average, their work reflects training they received decades earlier. Thus, even today, the economics training of most economists of Robert Solow's or Paul Samuelson's vintage reflects the approach to Neoclassical economics that had not lost touch with the Classical approach.

8. The fact that social science's basic units are people also gives social science an alternative approach to understanding—intuition and empathy with the unit of study. A physicist can't feel what it is like to be an atom. An economist can feel what it is like to be a person (at least sometimes). For Classical economists, this alternative approach was central to their analysis. As Neolassical economics evolved and became more mathematical, however, the "intuition approach" was abandoned as economists strove for precision. Only now, with the development of behavioral economics, are intuition and empathy returning to modern economics, grounded in game theory and experiments.

9. The group of economists who are described as Neoclassical are so varied that the term's usefulness can be questioned (Colander 2000) Along with the competition within the Neoclassical school, two non-Neoclassical groups, Historical and Institutionalist economists, carried through the Classical view that a knowledge of history and institutions was important; they argued against an overreliance on formal theory. These groups remained important through the 1950s.

10. Marshall retained the Classical vision of economics as a complex system, and in his *Principles* (1890) he carefully warned readers about the limitations of his models. Unfortunately, the Marshallian sensibility as expressed in *Principles* did not survive and later textbooks dropped the Marshallian addenda, focusing solely on teaching the technical aspects of supply and demand analysis. Economists' conception of economic policy switched from broad Classical conceptions of a "fulfilling life" to a single, narrow goal—efficiency, which they interpreted to mean producing the most goods at the least cost.

11. The issues are of course more complicated, and there were differences in views even among the subgroup of "Walrasian" economists. Thus, any blanket criticism of even this subgroup is inappropriate; many who worked in the Walrasian framework fully recognized its limitations. For example, it was general-equilibrium theorists Gerard Debreu (1974), R. Mantel (1974), and Hugo Sonnenschein (1972 and 1973) who formally showed that the Walrasian

attempt to build macroeconomics on microfoundations was doomed. Another of the developers of general-equilibrium theory, Kenneth Arrow, led the way in establishing the Santa Fe Institute's economics program, which has pioneered the most likely future of macroeconomic theorizing by focusing on complexity.

12. The recession of 1937 was important in the success of *The General Theory* in the U.S. From 1933 to 1936, the U.S. economy had experienced strong growth, and advocates of alternative policies were losing adherents. With the recession of 1937, that changed, and many more economists were open to the proposition that a revolution in economic thinking was necessary.

13. It is reported, perhaps apocryphally, that when he was challenged on his tendency to change his views, he retorted: "When the facts change, I change my mind. What do you do?"

14. At one point Alvin Hansen (quoted in Colander and Landreth 1996) recalls Abba Lerner asking Keynes: "Mr. Keynes, why don't we forget all this business of fiscal policy, public debt and all those kinds, and have some printing presses?" Keynes replied, "It's the art of statesmanship to tell lies, but they have to be plausible lies."

15. For further discussion of these issues, see my essay on the history of macroeconomics in Colander 2006.

16. In these models, the primary difference between the Neo-Keynesian and Neoclassical versions was the assumption of fixed wages in the Keynesian model, which would allow an unemployment equilibrium to exist, and flexible wages in the Neoclassical model, which would not allow unemployment. This made the primary difference between Neo-Keynesian economics and Neoclassical economics the assumption of fixed wages, even though Keynes had emphasized in *The General Theory* that that was not the primary difference.

17. Pure general-equilibrium theorists—including many of the best mathematical economists—long ago abandoned any simplistic notion of the usefulness of the Walrasian model. They use the model not for policy purposes, but to understand the structural issues involved in thinking about the complex system that is our economy.

18. In Colander 1988 and 2006 I have suggested that this happened because the comparative static models fit the replicator dynamics of the academic profession, which had begun focusing on publication. Exploring these models allowed young economists to get published and to advance without having a deep knowledge of past ideas that had previously been expected of them.

19. This criticism has to be seen in the context of someone writing in 1939, with its highly limited computing power and data.

20. When I asked Paul Samuelson (quoted in Colander and Landreth 1996, 160) about this, he said that "we always assumed that the Keynesian under-employment equilibrium floated on a substructure of administered prices and imperfect competition. I stopped thinking about what was meant by rigid wages and whether you could get the real wage down; I knew it was a good working principle."

21. The rational-expectations assumption that allowed this tidiness came from a project to integrate process and learning into economics as part of the early work on artificial intelligence (Colander and Guthrie 1979).

22. Economists still haven't fully explained this in an intuitively satisfying way, and only complex-system theorists are even trying to do so with their analysis of emergent properties.

23. Krugman is very much a part of that "simple model" tradition: He made his reputation by creating simple mathematical models that came to policy conclusions that non-mathematical economists had long been arguing for. So, unless he had a change of heart, for him to be arguing against mathematics seems disingenuous at best.

24. Many of the economists who developed the Walrasian general-equilibrium model, such as Kenneth Arrow and Frank Hahn, did not use it to directly guide policy, but instead to clear up their understanding of the logic of the model. As Hahn (1981) said back in the 1970s, the general-equilibrium model was worth exploring, but was not as useful as general-equilibrium theorists had hoped. So they moved on—precisely what you would expect scientists to do.

REFERENCES

Bagehot, Walter. 1877. *Lombard Street: A Description of the Money Market*. New York: Scribner, Armstrong and Co.

Cairnes, J. E. 1870. "Introductory Lecture on Political Economy and Laissez Faire." University College London. (As cited by Keynes 1926)

Colander, David. 1984. "Was Keynes a Keynesian or a Lernerian?" *Journal of Economic Literature* 22(4): 1572–75.

Colander, David. 1988. "The Evolution of Keynesian Economics." In *Keynes and Public Policy after 50 Years*, ed. Omar Hamouda and John Smithin. Cheltenham, U.K.: Edward Elgar.

Colander, David. 2000. "The Death of Neoclassical Economics." *Journal of the History of Economic Thought* 22(2): 127–43.

Colander, David, ed. 2006. *Post Walrasian Macroeconomics: Beyond the DSGE Model*. Cambridge: Cambridge University Press.

Colander, David. 2009. "Economists, Incentives, Judgment, and the European CVAR Approach to Macroeconometrics." *Economics Ejournal* 3.

Colander, David, and Robert Guthrie. 1980. "Great Expectations: What the Dickens Do Rational Expectations Mean?" *Journal of Post Keynesian Economics* 3.

Colander, David, and Harry Landreth, eds. 1996. *The Coming of Keynes to America*. Cheltenham, U.K.: Edward Elgar.

Colander, David, Ric Holt, and Barkley Rosser. 2004. *The Changing Face of Economics*. Ann Arbor: University of Michigan Press.

Colander, David, et al. 2009. "The Financial Crisis and the Systemic Failure of the Economics Profession." *Critical Review* 21(2–3): 249–67.

Debreu, Gerard. 1974. "Excess Demand Functions." *Journal of Mathematical Economics* 1: 15–21.

Hahn, Frank. 1981. "General Equilibrium Theory." In *The Crisis in Economic Theory*, ed. Daniel Bell and Irving Kristol. New York: Basic Books.

Hansen, Alvin. 1936. "Mr. Keynes on Underemployment Equilibrium." *Journal of Political Economy* (October): 667–86.

Harrod. Roy. 1937. "Mr. Keynes and Traditional Theory." *Econometrica*.

Hutt, William. 1979. *The Keynesian Episode: A Reassessment*. Indianapolis, Ind.: Liberty Press.

Jonnson, Per. 1995. "On the Economics of Say and Keynes' Interpretation of Say's Law." *Eastern Economic Journal* 21 (Spring): 147–55.

Keynes, J. M. 1921. "Introduction to Cambridge Economic Handbooks." In *Money*, ed. D. H. Robertson. Cambridge: Cambridge University Press.

Keynes, J. M. 1926. "The End of Laissez Faire." In *Essays in Persuasion*. London: Hogarth Press.

Keynes, J. M. 1936. *The General Theory of Employment, Interest and Money*. New York: Harcourt Brace.

Keynes, J. M. 1938. Letter to Roy Harrod. 4 July. In idem, *Collected Works*, vol. 14. http://economia.unipv.it/harrod/edition/editionstuff/rfh.346.htm

Keynes, J. M. 1939. "Comment." *Economic Journal* 44: 558–56.

Keynes, J. N. 1891. *The Scope and Method of Political Economy*. London: Macmillan.

Kirman, Alan. Forthcoming. *Complexity and Macroeconomics*. London: Routledge.

Krugman, Paul. 2009. "How Did Economists Get It So Wrong?" *The New York Times Magazine*, 6 September.

Leijonhufvud, A. 1976. *Keynesian Economics and the Economics of Keynes*. Oxford: Oxford University Press.

Lucas, Robert. 2004. "My Keynesian Education." *History of Political Economy* 36: 12–24

Mantel, R. 1974. "On the Characterization of Aggregate Excess Demand." *Journal of Economic Theory* 7: 348–53.

Marshall, Alfred. 1890. *Principles of Economics*. London: Macmillan.

Marshall, Alfred. 1906. Letter to Arthur Lyon Bowley, February. In *The Correspondence of Alfred Marshall Economist*, vol. 3, ed. John Whitaker. Cambridge: Cambridge University Press.

Medema, Steven. 2009. *Adam Smith's Lost Legacy: The Hesitant Hand*. Princeton: Princeton University Press.

Mill, John Stuart. [1838] 1950. "Essay on Bentham in Mill on Bentham and Coleridge." In *Mill on Bentham and Coleridge*, ed. F. R. Leavis. London: Chatto and Windus Publishers.

O'Brien, Denis. 2004. *The Classical Economists Revisited*. Princeton: Princeton University Press.

Pigou, A. C. 1933. *Theory of Unemployment*. London: Macmillan.

Robbins, Lionel. 1927. "Mr. Hawtry on the Scope of Economics." *Economica* 7: 172–78.

Robbins, Lionel. 1932. *An Essay on the Nature and Significance of Economic Science*. London: Macmillan.

Robbins, Lionel. 1981. "Economics and Political Economy." *American Economic Review* (May): 1–10.

Say, Jean Baptiste. [1821] 1967. *Letters to Mister Malthus*, trans. John Richter. London: Sherwood, Neoly, and Jones.

Sen, Amartya. 1985. *Commodities and Capabilities*. Oxford: Oxford University Press.

Senior, Nassau William. [1836] 1951. *An Outline of the Science of Political Economy*. New York: Augustus M. Kelly.

Sonnenschein, H. 1972. "Market Excess Demand Functions." *Econometrica* 40: 549–63.

Sonnenschein, H. 1973. "Do Walras' Identity and Continuity Characterize the Class of Community Excess Demand Functions?" *Journal of Economic Theory* 6: 345–54.

Thornton, Henry, ed. 1802. *An Inquiry into the Nature and Effects of the Paper Credit of Great Britain*. London: Kessinger Publishing.

Viner, Jacob. 1936. "Mr. Keynes and the Causes of Unemployment." *Quarterly Journal of Economics* 51(1): 147–67.

Von Neumann, John, and Oskar Morgenstern. 1944. *Theory of Games and Economic Behavior*. Princeton: Princeton University Press.

Waldrop, Mitchell. 1992. *Complexity: The Emerging Science at the Edge of Order and Chaos*. New York: Simon and Schuster.

[13]

Vol. 3, 2009-9 | April 2, 2009 | http://www.economics-ejournal.org/economics/journalarticles/2009-9

Economists, Incentives, Judgment, and the European CVAR Approach to Macroeconometrics

David Colander

Middlebury College

Abstract

This paper argues that the DSGE approach to macroeconometrics is the dominant approach because it meets the institutional needs of the replicator dynamics of the profession, not because it is necessarily the best way to do macroeconometrics. It further argues that this "DSGE theory-first" approach is inconsistent with the historical approach that economists have advocated in the past and that the alternative European CVAR approach is much more consistent with economist's historically used methodology, correctly understood. However, because the European CVAR approach requires explicit researcher judgment, it does not do well in the replicator dynamics of the profession. The paper concludes with the suggestion that there should be an increase in dialog between the two approaches.

Special issue "Using Econometrics for Assessing Economic Models"

JEL: C10. A1

Keywords: Methodology; macroeconometrics; general to specific; DSGE; VAR; judgment; incentives

Correspondence
David Colander, Department of Economics Middlebury College, Middlebury, Vermont, 05753, USA; email: colander@middlebury.edu

I would like to thank Peter Kennedy, Katarina Juselius, Lawrence Boland, Kevin Hoover, Casey Rothschild, Aris Spanos, and Thomas Mayer for important suggestions on earlier versions of this paper. I have definitely not taken all their advice so only I am responsible for the arguments here.

Economics: The Open-Access, Open-Assessment E-Journal   1

1   Introduction

> To tell an economist that he chooses that type of work and that viewpoint which will maximize what his income is, he will hotly say, a studied insult. Such market-oriented behavior will be characterized not with our customary phrases such as consumer sovereignty, but in terms as harsh as "intellectual prostitution". To adapt one's views to one's audience is hardly to be distinguished from the falsification of evidence and other disreputable behavior (George Stigler 1982: 60).

In this opinion paper I ask a simple question: Why has the European General-to-Specific Approach to Empirical Macro (Hendry 1995; Johansen 1996; Juselius 2006) had only limited success in the competition for ideas for doing applied macroeconomic policy in the U.S.? As an illustration of the General-to-Specific approach I shall discuss the cointegrated vector auto regression (CVAR) approach, primarily developed in Europe and used by many of the contributors of this special issue, and compare it to the Dynamic Stochastic General Equilibrium (DSGE) approach, primarily developed in the U.S. where it is considered the correct approach to doing macroeconometrics.

The initial reaction to this question by most U.S. economists likely will be: "What approach is he talking about? We haven't heard of the CVAR approach; it must be a minor approach by some out-of-the-mainstream economists." Given the lack of familiarity of many economists with this approach, I will discuss in Section 2 what I mean by the European CVAR approach, why I call it European, and how it differs from the DSGE approach. In Section 3, I shall discuss some hypotheses explaining why the European CVAR approach is not winning out in the competition of ideas and methods and relate these to the notion of a representative researcher and the invisible hand of truth. In Section 4, I take a historical look at the evolution of macroeconomic theory and how that evolution is related to incentives; I argue that there is little historical foundation for the pre-eminence of theory approach as interpreted by DSGE advocates, and in fact, there is historical evidence suggesting that their approach is an approach that earlier economists would have strongly condemned. In Section 5, I characterize the policy implications of the two approaches and discuss the role of theory and judgment in the CVAR versus the DSGE approach. In Section 6, I combine the arguments in the above sections, and argue that given the current replicator dynamics of the academic economics profession, there is a bias against methods, such as the European CVAR method, that explicitly require the use of researcher intuition and judgment in the analysis.

2   The European CVAR and the U.S. DSGE Approach to Econometrics

There are two ways of thinking about the macroeconomy. The first, which I call the Walrasian approach, sees the macro economy as a system that we can best understand through the lens of formal micro-founded theory, based in carefully specified micro foundations. Most recently, it is an approach associated with the DSGE model. It is the dominant approach taught in U.S. graduate schools and held by U.S. macro economists. It is a formal theory-first approach. As Campos et al. (2005: 1) point out this approach "insists on a complete theoretical model of the phenomena of interest prior to data analyses."

The alternative approach, which I see the European CVAR approach as consistent with, sees the macro economy as more complex than that and does not see a rigid microeconomicly grounded theory as especially helpful in shedding light on most macroeconomic problems. This approach, which elsewhere I have called the Post Walrasian approach (Colander 2006), has also been nicely described by Campos, Eriksson and Hendry. It sees the economy as "a complicated, dynamic, nonlinear, simultaneous, high-dimensional, and evolving entity [in which] "social systems alter over time; laws change and technological innovations occur." (Campos et al. 2005: 1) This alternative approach can be found in small pockets throughout the world, but tends to be more prevalent in Europe, which until recently did not buy into the DSGE approach anywhere near as completely as did the U.S.

There tends to be a similar divide between the U.S. and Europe in macroeconometrics. The DSGE theory-first approach to macroeconometrics tends to dominate in the U.S. while in Europe there has been, until recently, a more eclectic approach, and it is within these eclectic approaches that one finds the CVAR approach.

2.1   Methodology of the Two Approaches

The two approaches to macroeconometrics differ significantly in their underlying methodology. The Walrasian approach, which underlies the predominant dynamic stochastic general equilibrium (DSGE) approach in macroeconomics, concentrates on carefully developing the theoretical model first. Advocates argue that one must first specify the theoretical model before one can even have a hope of adequately grasping the complex empirical reality. If one does not develop, and stay true to, such a carefully specified theoretical model, one will likely be fooled by spurious empirical relationships. This means that a DSGE researcher sees all macroeconomic issues through a DSGE lens. To keep the formal model tractable, this DSGE approach generally requires the researcher to disregard the institutional environment and complex dynamics as possible explanations for why what we observe differs from what theory predicts.

The DSGE approach requires that only a fully pre-specified theoretical model can be brought to the data. It is a "theory-first" methodology, where "theory first" means a carefully specified and fully developed formal theory which may deviate significantly from the characteristics of the economy that intuitively might be important. Only after having fully developed the underlying microeconomic theory in a highly simplified model do advocates of the DSGE approach bring their model to the data. When they do bring it to the data, they generally use calibrated values for some parameters of the model and Bayesian estimation methods to reconcile the information in the data with the theory model. While this DSGE approach allows for some flexibility by representing part of the empirical dynamics with a simple VAR it usually does so

Economics: The Open-Access, Open-Assessment E-Journal 3

without using the VAR to check for misspecification such as parameter non-constancy. (Parameters are assumed to be constant.)

What I am calling the European CVAR approach uses a quite different methodology. Because it sees the outcomes of the economy as data points from a complex system, where by complex I mean a system that involves so many interactions and potential non-linearities that intuitively, one could not hope to fully specify a formal model of the system, the European CVAR approach gives smaller weight to any specific formal theory, and instead uses a broad heuristic theoretical understanding of the economy, which is guided by, but not necessarily dominated by, a formal theory.[1] Thus, for example, the European CVAR approach would address the recent crisis within a system of equations where economic behavior is allowed to persistently deviate from long-run economic equilibrium states. It would provide information on which other variables react on these persistent movements away, and where in the system the adjustment takes place. Rather than assuming one correct theory it would be open to theoretical explanations that are consistent with agents who drive prices away from long-run attractors for significant periods of time.

The European CVAR approach does not deny rationality and equilibrium as the foundation of hard core theory; it simply questions the usefulness of an oversimplified theoretical model that, to anyone other than a true believer, intuitively does not correspond to a model that would reasonably explain economic behavior as it manifests itself in observed economic data.[2]

Given the concern about knowledge that can be deduced from formal theory that CVAR advocates have, it is not surprising that the CVAR approach gives more emphasis to data analysis. Advocates of this approach use a carefully constructed econometric methodology designed to extract as much information as one can from the data. (My focus in this paper is the cointegrated vector autoregressive (CVAR) approach advocated by Søren Johansen and Katarina Juselius (Johansen and Juselius 2006; Juselius 2006), but the approach is also related to the related general-to-specific approach advocated by David Hendry (Hendry 2000, 2009). (I see both of these approaches are consistent with the broad archeological approach methodologically advocated by Kevin Hoover (Hoover 2006; Hoover et al. 2008)).

These approaches all share the feature that they view economic reality as a dynamic system of pushing forces, which give rise to stochastic trends, and pulling forces, which give rise to long-run relations (Hoover et al. 2008). Thus, in this European CVAR approach the formal theory of a static economy is adapted to a more heuristic theory that incorporates the researcher's judgment about the effects of institutions, and dynamics on the theoretical results into one's theoretical intuition of what the formal theory is telling one. The European CVAR macroeconometric approach is designed to allow the *complexity* of the economic reality to speak as freely as possible through the lens of the *institutional environment*. The data analysis blends with the theoretical analysis to produce a vision of reality that is not necessarily correct, but is the best that can be arrived at given such a complex system as the macroeconomy.

---

[1] I have discussed these issues further in Colander (1996, 2006).

[2] When considering the simplicity of the underlying theory assumptions relative to the complexity of the economy typical of many DSGE models, it may not come as a big surprise that they have been essentially silent about explaining many observed events in particular the more recent ones.

2.2   The Importance of Judgment in the European CVAR Approach

The important aspect of the European CVAR approach for my argument in this article is that it explicitly requires the researcher to use judgment about the applicability of theoretical, institutional and empirical information to arrive at a conclusion from the analysis. The analysis is as much art as it is science. It is an approach that has a long history in economics and I would argue is consistent with the Marshallian/Keynesian approach that J.M. Keynes summarized as follows:

> Economics is a science of thinking in terms of models joined to the art of choosing models which are relevant to the contemporary world. It is compelled to be this, because, unlike the typical natural science, the material to which it is applied is, in too many respects, not homogeneous through time. The object of a model is to segregate the semi-permanent or relatively constant factors from those which are transitory or fluctuating so as to develop a logical way of thinking about the latter, and of understanding the time sequences to which they give rise in particular cases. Good economists are scarce because the gift for using "vigilant observation" to choose good models, although it does not require a highly specialized intellectual technique, appears to be a very rare one (Keynes 1938).

I associate the CVAR approach to macroeconometrics with Europe because its use is more prevalent in Europe than in the U.S.[3] But, even in Europe, the CVAR approach is not necessarily winning in the competition with the DSGE models. Instead, it is becoming increasingly accepted by macroeconomists, in particular in Central Banks, that the appropriate approach to empirical macro policy analysis is the "theory-first" DSGE model approach. In particular in the U.S., but also widely in Europe, the DSGE theory-first approach is in fact becoming the only allowable way to do macroeconometrics. Chari et al. (2009) summarize this generally accepted methodological view when they write "an aphorism among macroeconomists today is that if you have a coherent story to propose, you can do it in a suitably elaborate DSGE model." Even Michael Woodford's more balanced consideration of the state of macroeconomics (Woodford 2009) does not cite any of the European work as belonging in the new synthesis in macro. For the majority of top U.S. macroeconomists, it is as if the European method does not exist.

3   Some Hypotheses about Why the European CVAR Approach Is Not Winning Out

Economists unfamiliar with the European CVAR approach to macroeconometrics will likely assume that the reason why this approach is losing out and is not mentioned or

---

[3] Thus, whereas in my interviews with U.S. graduate students, (Colander 2007) almost none had heard of the CVAR and Hendry approaches, in my interview with European graduate students (Colander 2010) many more were familiar with it. European and U.S. economics are, of course, intertwined, and there are advocates of both positions in both places. For example, Hoover is a Duke. However, he was trained in England, and as I will discuss below the approach to macroeconometrics that I am referring to is much more prevalent in Europe that in the U.S. Thus, I feel it is appropriate to call it the European approach to econometrics.

discussed in papers on modern macroeconomics is that it is not as good as the DSGE approach. The implicit assumption of most economists is that the cream rises to the top. Since the DSGE approach has risen to the top, it must be the cream. This view would follow from the following implicit assumption about the idea and method selection process in economics which many economists probably would find plausible: Ideas and methods compete, and while the competition is messy, the better ideas and methods (those more likely to represent the truth in an uncertain world) tend to win out in a sufficiently short time to make it reasonable to assume that prevailing ideas and methods are the best ideas and methods.[4] One could say there is what might be called an invisible hand of truth that guides the competition toward the truth. This paper challenges that assumption. It argues:

1. When one uses an economist's lens to analyze the selection mechanism of methods and ideas as it has developed in economics, there is a likely bias in this selection mechanism, so one would not necessarily expect that the best ideas and methods would rise to the top.
2. Based on casual observation, that bias is likely to favor the DSGE theory-first approach over the European CVAR approach.

The specific aspect of the European CVAR approach that I see biasing the choice against it is its explicit reliance on researcher judgment as part of the analysis. My argument is that any method requiring judgment does not do well in the replicator dynamics of the current U.S. economics profession and increasingly in the European economics profession. By that I mean that, other things equal, research methods that explicitly emphasize the need for explicit judgment lead to fewer publication than do research methods that rely on firm rules and avoid discussions of judgment, or make them implicit in shared assumptions and conventions, such as the acceptance of a formal theory, or a statistical test for significance. The fewer publications reduce the probability of advancement for researchers using that methodology, and thus over time, tends to work against its use.

The bias against judgment is inherent in a blind peer review system. Such systems gravitate toward methodologies that incorporate conventions and implicit judgments that make researcher judgment less important in deciding whether the paper is publishable or not. My suspicion is that the DSGE approach became more prevalent in the U.S. compared to Europe because the U.S. has emphasized a blind journal article peer review system of advancement whereas, until recently Europe had a more eclectic review system that was less phobic about judgment.[5]

3.1   The Representative Researcher and the Invisible Hand of Truth

The essence of my first argument is that, given the existing academic institutions in economics, the dynamic "truth" force pushing for the best idea and method to win out is

---

[4] Challenging that assumption has been an ongoing theme of my research starting with Colander (1991). Elsewhere (Colander 2010) I have called this view the "representative researcher" view of the competition of ideas. In the representative researcher view of methodology the ideas that win out are those ideas that a representative researcher would choose.

[5] These ideas are discussed in more depth in Rosser et al. (2010) and Colander (2010)

relatively weak in comparison to other specific institutional forces that have little to do with the truth of the idea or the usefulness of a method in arriving at the truth. Instead of institutional incentives directing researchers to choose the "best method"—the method that a representative researcher is assumed to chose—these institutional forces direct researchers toward "institutionally consistent" methods of analysis that offer the best advancement potential within the existing institutional structure. My point is that institutionally consistent methods are not necessarily the methods that are most likely to lead to the truth. While the "appropriateness of the approach or idea" (its contribution toward seeing the truth) clearly plays a role in that process, many other forces do as well, which means that the intricacies of the institutional structure of the economics profession become central to the understanding of economists' choice of ideas and methods.[6]

For example, in an institutional structure that requires a certain type of peer review for advancement, some research methods and ideas are more likely to be amenable to that peer-review process than others. My argument is that those "institutionally consistent" ideas and methods are likely to be favored by the profession over others that do not fit so well in the existing particular type of peer review system. That, I argue, may well be the case with the European CVAR method.

The institutional feedback on theory and method choice described above has not previously been considered by economic methodologists because they tend to think of the competition of ideas as occurring within a *representative researcher's* mind.[7] So, unless that representative researcher is ideological or stupid (which few, outside heterodox economists, believe is the case), the representative researcher can be assumed to choose the idea and method that best captures the truth. This leads economists to the implicit conclusion that the "best" methods and ideas win out.

My conclusion is different and follows from my alternative way of thinking about the economics profession.[8] As George Stigler (1982) in the introductory quotation suggested might be the case, I see economists as motivated by self-interest and incentives. Specifically, I see the economics profession as a complex system in which many models and methods are competing. That competition takes place in a very specific institutional environment, and over time the incentives in that environment feeds back on the choices researchers make about models and method. Thus, the current emphasis on economists accumulating quality-weighted journal article publications plays a major role in determining the models and methods that the profession adopts.

My hypothesis is that in the current academic economics institutional environment of "publish or perish" (in the right journals) there are very few incentives for top young

---

[6] That is why I have directed much of my work toward understanding those institutional structures.

[7] In doing so, they fall subject to the same fallacy of composition that I believe DSGE modelers fall into; they attribute rationality to the system results that would only likely exist if the system were a single individual.

[8] As will be obvious to readers familiar with methodological work, the approach I use has connections to the work of Thomas Kuhn and Imre Lakatos. Since discussing it would involve a long discussion, and I have briefly discussed this work elsewhere (Landreth and Colander 2001), I will not discuss it here, other than to say that my approach differs from their in that I am describing a complexity field of science (Colander 2000) rather than a standard field of science. I ague that in such complexity fields of study, where less guidance comes from empirical work, much more focus has to be given to professional advancement incentives in the choice of assumptions and methodologies than they do in the standard natural sciences.

economists to reflect on the overall economic research process, but there are strong incentives for them to focus on narrow technical issues. The reason is that there are few publishing outlets for broad reflective pieces that would count in the advancement and promotion criteria.[9] It follows that, other things equal, those researchers who think about such issues are much less likely to advance in the field of economics. [10]

Because there are few incentives within the profession to be reflective on the overall rationality of profession's methods and ideas, few economist are reflective. Most are concerned with narrower issues—issues that lead them to success within the existing institutional structure. Because few economists are focused on taking a broad reflective approach, the composite view of all researchers is a composite of views of economists who have few incentives to think deeply about the issues. Hence, there is no justification for assuming that the composite of economists' views will reflect the view of a reflective representative researcher. It follows that the "representative researcher" approach is not the way to think about how the profession arrives at its methods or ideas. If one accepts my complex system view of the profession, such a composite "representative researcher searching for the truth" view of the profession's views is incorrect.

4   Incentives and the Evolution of Macroeconomic Theory

Elsewhere, (Colander 2006) I have applied this view to the history of macroeconomic theory. In that work I have argued that the path that the Keynesian revolution followed can be best understood within this institutional incentive approach to the competition of ideas. I argued that Keynes had a vague vision of the macroeconomy as a complex system with multiple basins of attraction and complex dynamics. He sensed that such a system could get into trouble and could end up at an undesirable equilibrium. Unfortunately, the mathematics to deal formally with such issues was not fully developed at the time, and most economists were not even close to having the technical expertise needed to formally frame the issue in such a vision.

So while Keynes's initial idea was visionary, it was not an idea that could survive within the then existing institutional framework that advanced economists on the basis of their writings. This worked against highly mathematical economists of the time, such as Richard Strotz (Strotz et al. 1953) and Richard Goodwin (1947), who were developing that complexity vision formally. The problem was that most economists of the time felt uncomfortable dealing with the complex mathematics needed to formally deal with the complexity vision of the macroeconomy that Strotz and Goodwin were putting forward. Their work was beyond the level of many of the economists at the

---

[9] This obviously differs by institution. For example, at a liberal arts colleges, such as where I am at, there is a stronger incentive to do such reflective work, and work that involves judgment, since a wider range of scholarly output is considered than is the case at most universities. But even at institutions that include a wider range of scholarly output in their advancement criteria, there are few outlets for such reflective research that would move a young economist up in the profession.

[10] Elsewhere (Colander 2009a) I have distinguished a "consumer's knowledge" of theory from a "producer's knowledge" of theory, arguing that to use a theory in policy one needs a "consumer's knowledge" but that students are only taught to be producers, and that there are outlets only for producers, not consumers.

time. It also worked against heuristic economists, such as G.L.S. Shackle (1955) or Hyman Minsky (1986) whose work focused on developing an intuitive understanding of macroeconomics within that complexity vision. Their heuristic work reflected an educated "consumer's understanding" of the complexity approach, but did not offer a clear path forward to advance it. Neither of these approaches did well in the competition of ideas in the post Keynesian period.

In the representative researcher view, the failure of these approaches must have been because they were flawed, and not as good as the ideas or methods that won out. In my complex systems view of the economics profession, the explanation may have been (and I suspect it was) that these methods and ideas did not offer a research path for students that would allow them to survive and advance in the then-existing replicator dynamics of the profession.

The problem for the students of the highly mathematical economists of the time was that such mathematical research was incomprehensible to most economists. Only few researchers were on the forefront of both mathematics and economics. While these highly mathematical economists were seen as brilliant, they were far ahead of their times, and their students did not do well in the replicator dynamics of the time. The reason was that most of the "peers" doing the reviews of the research did not have the mathematical sophistication to see the contributions of these students as adding significantly to our understanding.[11] Thus, these mathematical economists generated few highly successful students to carry on their complexity views, and the latter faded away. The problem for the students of the heuristic economists was somewhat different. Once their professors had pointed out that the economy is complex, nonergodic, and fundamentally subject to uncertainty, there was not much more to say. This meant that the students did not do well in the replicator dynamics of the profession because they simply repeated the insights of their professors.

The result of these failures was that, instead of becoming a complexity revolution, the "Keynesian revolution" was quickly translated into a rather mundane set of ideas that were more amenable to the peer review replicator dynamics of the time. Keynesian economics, which could have been the beginning of a complexity revolution in economics, evolved into NeoKeynesian economics, which modeled the economy as a unique equilibrium, comparative static, multi-market equilibrium system, in which the only problem was institutional rigidities. The current mainstream of modern US macroeconomics argues as if NeoKeynesian economic theory is the only alternative to the DSGE modeling approach. This is far from the case. In my view, the serious alternative to the DSGE model is the complex systems model of macroeconomics (Colander et al. 2008) and the European macroeconometric approach is best seen as the empirical branch of that complex systems approach.

4.1   Macroeconometrics, Incentives, and the Complex Systems Approach

In other papers and books, (Colander 2006) I have discussed in more depth my complex systems view of the evolution of macroeconomic theory. In this paper, my interest is in on a very small sub-issue of my larger story—the profession's choice of

---

[11] For a discussion of some of the problems of peer review in economics, see Shepherd (1995)

macroeconometric method and its lack of interest in the European approach to macroeconometrics. My argument here is not that the European approach to macroeconometrics is necessarily better than the theory-first DSGE approach. My goal is simply to argue that, when one considers the incentives within the profession that guide model and method choice, that there are strong reasons to believe that, given current incentives, the profession would choose the theory-first DSGE approach not because it is inherently better in some broader sense, but because it better fits the institutional incentive structure of academic economics.[12]

Aris Spanos (this issue) nicely discusses the issues in debate between the general to specific approach (which is a part of what I am calling the European CVAR approach, and the prevalence of theory approach, which I am calling the theory-first DSGE approach to macroeconometrics. He presents the debate as one in which there are reasonable arguments on both sides. In taking this moderate view, he stands in marked contrast to Robert Solow's condemnation of the DSGE modeling approach (Solow 2008). Solow, who represents what might be called the recent Neoclassical NeoKeynesian tradition in macroeconomics, sees the DSGE approach as essentially a "rhetorical swindle" that the "macro community has perpetrated on itself, and its students" (Solow 2007: 235). The CVAR approach, while not sharing Solow's support of the more traditional macroeconomic models, agrees with Solow in that assessment not because the DSGE model is logically incorrect, but because it does not pass the judgment test; it is simply beyond belief that with all the assumptions the DSGE model must make to arrive at a formal model, that that model sheds much light on the type of short run problems that the macro economy often experiences. It simply does not meet the "common sense" test, so unless there are other arguments for using it, it is not an approach to policy that anyone other than someone who has been taught that it is the only correct theory would use as the sole approach for thinking about macroeconomic policy.

Within the "representative researcher" view of the economics profession, Solow's comment has no foundation; he is arguing that the ideas and methods that have won out within the profession are not the best, and are highly flawed. Within my complex system view of the profession, Solow's remark may well make sense; he is arguing that the replicator dynamics in the profession have produced economists who may be good at succeeding within the current academic institutions, but that, in his judgment, those academic institutions are flawed because those institutions have allowed a method that makes little intuitive sense to become a required method for all macroeconomists.[13] The argument of this paper supports Solow's more uncompromising view of the theory-first DSGE approach. While there are certainly arguments for both sides, as Spanos argues, there is, in my view, far less support for the current theory-first DSGE approach than the DSGE modelers have assumed.

---

[12] As an example of the failure of the European approach, consider that when, in my recent study of graduate economic education in the U.S. I asked graduate students at six top university programs about cointegrated vector auto regression, or the general the specific approach to macroeconometrics few students had heard about it.

[13] I discuss these issues further in Colander (2009b).

4.2   The Lack of Historical Foundations of the "Theory-First" Approach

One of the arguments that supporters of the DSGE modeling approach use, and that Spanos accepts, is that the theory-first approach is simply carrying on a tradition that has long existed in economics; thus, historically there is some justification for such an approach. I will argue below that this is an incorrect assessment of the history of economics.

Specifically, I argue that those economists who took a strong interest in methodology, such as Nassau Senior (1836), J. N. Keynes (1891) or Lionel Robbins (1932), would not agree with the theory-first DSGE methodology. While it is true that Senior, Keynes and Robbins downplayed empirical work, their arguments in support of theory and against empirical work have to be understood in context. At the time Keynes and Robbins were writing, empirical work was rudimentary; the lack of data, statistical tools, and computing power made it almost impossible to derive any sound knowledge from data analysis. Their downplaying of empirical work at the time implies nothing about their views about the role of data or empirical work today. For example, after discussing the problems with empirical work Robbins writes: "Fortunately there is reason to suppose that in the future the alliance between the economy theorist and the statistician will be even closer than it has been in the past." (Robbins 1930: 21). Thus, all that one can surmise from the lack of support of empirical work of earlier economists is that *given the empirical techniques of the time*, they felt that they could not rely on empirical work to answer questions. So, the *historical connection argument* that economists have taken a "prevalence of theory" over an empirically based approach cannot be seen as providing historical support for the current "prevalence of theory" approach. Methodology is, and should be, dependent on technology; when technology changes, methods should change as well.

4.3   What Earlier Economists Meant by "Theory" was not what DSGE Advocates Mean by "Theory"

A second reason why methodological practices of earlier economists cannot be used as historical justification for the current "DSGE theory-first" approach over the European approach is that for earlier economists "theory" meant something quite different than does "theory" for modern macroeconomists. Specifically, earlier economists distinguished between economic science and political economy.[14] For them, theory in economic science meant something different than theory in political economy.

Nassau Senior, who focused his work on identifying and organizing basic principles in a scientific framework (Schumpeter calls him the first "pure theorist" in economics.) wrote the following:

> (The economist's) premises consist of a very few general propositions, the result of observation, or consciousness, and scarcely requiring proof, or even formal statement, which almost every man, as soon as he hears them, admits as familiar to

---

[14] The discussion here is a summary about which I have written about at length. Since much of modern economics' approach relates to Robbins, who in turn based his approach on the Classical methodological approach, I will concentrate on his approach.

his thoughts, or at least as included in his previous knowledge: and his inferences are nearly as general, and, if he has reasoned correctly, as certain, as his premises.

But his conclusions, whatever be their generality and their truth, do not authorize him in adding a single syllable of advice. That privilege belongs to the writer or statesman who has considered all the causes which may promote or impede the general welfare of those whom he addresses, not to the theorist who has considered only one, though among the most important of those causes. The business of a Political Economist is neither to recommend nor to dissuade, but to state general principles, which it is fatal to neglect, but neither advisable, nor perhaps practicable, to use as the sole, or even the principle, guides in the actual conduct of affairs (Senior 1836: 2–3).

For Senior, economic science was a branch of logic. In the science of economics one did theory, which meant drawing theorems from almost self-evident principles. Economic theory was not meant to directly guide policy, which he saw a much more complicated issue. To move from the theorems of the science of economics to policy required common sense judgment and institutional knowledge which economic theorists did not necessarily possess. The method was further developed by Keynes (1891) in his famous summary of economist's methodology. Like Senior, Keynes saw the science of economics as a relatively narrow branch of economics. In this science of economics, theory meant something very similar what to the DSGE modelers have in mind. Their scientific theory was a highly formal set of propositions that consisted of primarily deductive reasoning based on first principles. It consisted of this because, given the empirical tools of the time, deductive reasoning was the only branch of economics that could potentially rise to the level of scientific knowledge.[15] *For Keynes and for many Classical and early neoclassical economists, however, that scientific theory had little relevance to policy analysis;* it was only one tool among many to be used by a political economist. Lionel Robbins was quite clear about this. In his review of Hawtrey (Robbins, 1927), a review that included many of the ideas that would later become embodied in his famous 1932 essay, Robbins stated clearly what he thought about using scientific theory to derive precise policy conclusions. He writes:

> What precision economists can claim at this stage is largely a sham precision. In the present state of knowledge, the man who can claim for economic science much exactitude is a quack (Robbins 1927: 176).

For both Keynes and Robbins, policy discussions did not belong in the science of economics; they belonged in political economy or in what Keynes called the art of economics. Theory in political economy was a much broader theory than the formal theory of science. It consisted of an understanding of the formal scientific theory, but also an understanding of the limitations of that theory, accepted value judgments of society, as well as knowledge of the institutions of the times. *Political economy theory*

---

[15] Alfred Marshall (1890) downplayed the distinction between political economy and economic science, and started using the term science in a broader sense, but he also argued strongly *against* any use of formal deductive models as part of the analysis. For Marshall, all of economics was what earlier classical economists had called political economy (Colander 2009b).

was a common sense theory that captured the educated common sense of economists of the time. It was a theory that involved, and had to involve, value judgments.

Robbins made the need to separate the science of economic from political economy clear in his Ely Lecture. He writes:

> My suggestion here, as in the Introduction to my *Political Economy: Past and Present,* is that its (political economy) use should be revived as now covering that part of our sphere of interest which essentially involves judgments of value. Political Economy, thus conceived, is quite unashamedly concerned with the assumptions of policy and the results flowing from them. I may say that this is not (*repeat not*) a recent habit of mine. In the Preface to my *Economic Planning and International Order,* published in 1937, I describe it as "essentially an essay in what may be called Political economy as distinct from Economics in the stricter sense of the word. It depends upon the technical apparatus of analytical Economics; but it applies this apparatus to the examination of schemes for the realization of aims whose formulation lies outside Economics; and it does not abstain from appeal to the probabilities of political practice when such an appeal has seemed relevant (Robbins 1981: 8).

For Robbins, the theory of economic science was simply the "technical apparatus" of the theory of political economy. But that theory of political economy went far beyond that technical apparatus, and included a much wider range of argumentation and understanding.

This history sheds a quite different interpretation to the historical antecedents to the theory-first DSGE approach. It is not similar to the approach that Classical economists used. When Classical economists stated that policy was based on theory, they did not mean it was based on a single scientific theory (that was simply a "technical apparatus") as is done by DSGE advocates. Instead, policy was based on a broader sense of theory that included judgments of relevance of the technical apparatus to the problem at hand. What Robbins never would have done is to directly draw policy conclusions from a theoretical model without considering the appropriateness of the theory to the problem at hand. Yet this is precisely what the "theory-first" DSGE model advocates seem to claim: if we do not ground our models in formal theory, we will know nothing.[16] The problem is that when we do ground our policy thinking in formal theory that is not relevant to the problems at hard, we can end up thinking we know something that we don't, which in many ways is worse than knowing that we do not know something.

When one combines these two historical insights about earlier economist's method, arguments, it is clear that rather than being a continuation of economist's method, the "theory-first" DSGE model approach is a significant deviation from earlier economist's method. In fact, I would argue that the European approach to macroeconometrics is much closer to the spirit of the classical approach to policy analysis. No doubt, the European approach differs from the earlier approach in that it gives more focus to empirical data. But that can be explained by the change in empirical technology. Today, much more in the way of data is available; much more in the way of statistical tools are available and much more in the way of computing power is available. These advances have opened up a new way to doing macroeconomic theory and of developing policy-

---

[16] The problem with that reasoning was pointed out by Kevin Hoover (2006).

useful macroeconomic theory. This means that today, it may be possible to discover patterns in the data in ways that are fundamentally different than existed in Keynes' and Robbins' time, and only a Luddite would not want to take advantage of those.

5   Characterizing the Debate in Macroeconometrics

With that historical background, let me reconsider the debate between the DSGE theory-first approach and the European approach to macroeconometrics. As my discussion of the history of economics makes clear, the approach being used by the majority of macroeconomists should be called the "preeminence of the DSGE theory" approach, not the "preeminence of theory" approach that characterized Classical economics. The modern DSGE methodology is not an approach that elevates *theory* above empirical work, but instead is an approach that elevates one particular way of using theory -the DSGE modeling approach- above all other ways. The theory-first DSGE approach is best seen as a highly limiting way of doing macroeconometrics, and macroeconomic policy. It is an approach that Senior, Keynes and Robbins would have strongly opposed.

To see the misuse of theory in policy analysis that can occur by users of the theory-first DSGE approach, consider V.V. Chari and Patrick Kehoe's (2006) discussion of policy relevance of the DSGE model. They write:

> The message of examples like these is that discretionary policy making has only costs and no benefits, so that if government policymakers can be made to commit to a policy rule, society should make them do so (Chari and Kehoe 2006: 7–8).

and:

> Macroeconomists can now tell policymakers that to achieve optimal results, they should design institutions that minimize the time inconsistency problem by promoting a commitment to policy rules. However, to what particular policies should policymakers commit themselves? For many macroeconomists considering this question, quantitative general equilibrium models have become the workhorse model, and they turn out to offer surprisingly sharp answers (Chari and Kehoe 2006: 9).

For Robbins, such statements are ones only a quack would make.

5.1   The Role of Theory in the European CVAR Approach

As I understand it, the European CVAR approach to macroeconomics is not anti-theoretical in the broad political economy sense. It is a blend of broad theory disciplined by careful data analysis. The idea is to uncover empirical regularities in the data that can be given a broad interpretation given the underlying theory models. That's why Hoover calls it an archeological approach: carefully excavated results are used to guide theorists as to what theories to use. This, of course, does not exclude the possibility that the empirical results might be masking the true relationships and that her or his intuition tells the economist to disregard the highly imperfect data. Therefore, before making judgment about policy, the European approach requires the economist to carefully consider the relationship between the best available theory and the best available data. *The key to the European approach to macroeconometrics is bringing the data to the theory, and bringing the theory to the data.* To do that is an art that requires researcher judgment, so researcher judgment is integral to the European method. In some ways it is a "wisdom of crowds of specialists" approach, where specialists compare analyses and interpretations, argue about differences in interpretation, and come to a conclusion.

Let me reiterate. The European CVAR approach does not put data ahead of political economy theory; it simply uses data in sorting through the many alternatives that a broad political economy theory may lead to. Thus, the European CVAR approach is totally compatible with what could be called a "prevalence of theory" approach in the political economy context. If one cannot gain any reliable information from the data, then one would have to rely on broad political economy theory combined with a good understanding of institutions. This would be in the tradition of Henry Thornton or Walter Bagehot—a tradition carried on by modern economists such as Charles Goodhart and Perry Mehrling. Their work is theory-first in the European tradition.

Using the European CVAR approach, one takes an agnostic approach to the value of the data and theory analysis. The empirical model analysis may be highly informative, in which case it would be used to provide guidance to policy, or it may be of limited value, in which case one accepts that one has to rely on one's intuition and knowledge of institutions to guide policy. If that's the best we can do, so be it. However, it seems plausible that an empirical methodology that allows the data to speak as freely as possibly about underlying empirical mechanisms is more likely to be able to discriminate between these two cases than a methodology that forces one particular view on the data. Because of limitations of our data and our theories, economic policy will always be based on judgment to some extent. To pretend we know the theory is not sufficient for claiming a "scientific" foundation of our policy.

5.2   Why the CVAR Approach Might Seem Anti-DSGE

The European approach to macroeconometrics is not inherently anti-DSGE theory. However, it may seem to be anti-DSGE theory for two reasons. The first is that the DSGE model, contrary to the European CVAR, does not specifically allow for intuitive judgment to be part of the analysis. It requires researchers to use a model of the macroeconomy that, in its current state of development, does not include a significant number of heterogeneous agents, the possibility of complex dynamics, multiple equilibria, and structural breaks. For most non macroeconomic specialists, it strains credibility that no intuitive judgment is needed to make the DSGE model applicable. But the DSGE theory-first approach does not allow such judgment. Somehow, in spite of the large amount of uncertainty that will naturally be associated with such a model, it is supposed to shed significant light on a macroeconomy that includes all those omitted elements and guide us as to how to set fiscal and monetary policy. Were that the case, it would truly be a miracle.

The above argument does not deny that useful theories may well be counterintuitive, nor that the implausibility of the DSGE model alone is not sufficient reason to abandon it. If it could be shown that the DSGE model fits that data better than alternatives, that intuitive implausibility of the DSGE model could be overridden by the empirical results.

This leads to the second reason why the European approach seems anti-DSGE. When European researchers put the DSGE model to careful empirical tests, they have found that the DSGE model does not meet these data criteria either.

An example of its failure can be seen by considering a recent paper by Peter Ireland (2004) that purported to take the DSGE model to the data. In his study, Ireland started with the assumption that a simple real business cycle model can explain the US experience in the post–Second World War period. He made his theoretical model more "flexible" by imbedding it in a DSGE model framework in which total factor productivity was assumed to be a stochastic near unit root trend driving the other variables. The paper was impressive, and was high-level cutting edge work to almost all economists who do not specialize in time series econometrics, such as myself, and the large majority of economists, including many DSGE macro theorists. It was published in a good journal.

To test the difference between the European CVAR approach and the theory-first DSGE model approach to macroeconometrics, I asked Johansen and Juselius to consider Ireland's paper for a conference I was organizing. Specifically, I asked them to highlight the difference between the two approaches. I had expected the normal nuanced differences, but that is not what I got; what I got was a blistering critique of the Ireland paper. These can be found in Johansen (2006) and Juselius and Franchi (2007).[17]

For European macroeconometrics advocates, Ireland's paper has two serious problems. The first is that it fails to meet some minimum statistical assumptions. As discussed by Spanos, its failure to meet these is not in debate between DSGE modelers or European macroeconomists modelers. The problem is that Ireland made assumptions about empirical relationships in the data that, if one were not fully committed to the view that the theory is right independent of the data, should have been tested, and if he had tested them, the assumptions would have been seen to be false. But he did not test them.[18] If he was committed to the view that the theory was right independent of the data, then why even bother bringing the model to the data. It would seem more reasonable for him to just state that the model is right, and skip bringing it to the data. That may be the correct way; the information to be gleaned from the data is highly questionable; my point is simply that if you are going to bring a model to the data, then it should be done in a meaningful way.

Juselius and Franchi carried the analysis of Ireland's paper further; they show that when the correct specification tests were done in the Ireland model, essentially all of Ireland's results are rejected! Moreover, when the model is reformulated based on the European approach, the conclusions are reversed! Despite Juselius and Franchi's negative findings, the DSGE model is not necessarily wrong, and some other theory right. All their findings mean is that Ireland's paper, which seemed to be providing empirical support for the DSGE model, did not provide that support. If one believes that the DSGE model is the model economists should use, the justification must lie in one's

---

[17] While Ireland's work is chosen as an example, it should be seen as representative, and other papers could have been chosen to represent the U.S. theory comes first approach.

[18] The failure of Ireland's paper to meet the statistical assumptions should have meant that the paper never should have made it through the peer review process, and the fact that is did should raise serious concerns about that peer review process. When, at my suggestion, in private correspondence, Johansen raised these issues with Ireland, Ireland seemed unconcerned about them.

intuition that the DSGE model is the correct model, not in the knowledge that the DSGE model fits the data.

The question macroeconomic empirical researchers have to ask is whether Ireland's paper is an anomaly, or whether it is an example of the disregard for the data that the "DSGE model first" approach encourages. I am not enough of an econometrician to make a conclusive judgment on this issue, but the sense that I get from my interviews with economists, and from my studies of U.S. graduate economic education (Colander 2007) is that Ireland's cavalier approach to empirically testing the model is representative of the more general "DSGE model first" macro approach to data analysis that most U.S. graduate students are taught, and that they consequently practice.

6   The Bias against Methods Based on Intuition and Judgment in the Economics Profession

Let me now combine the two arguments of the paper—the bias in the replicator dynamics of the economic academic institutions, and the lack of success of the European CVAR approach. My claim is that it is likely that the success of the DSGE model approach as compared to the European approach is in large part due to a bias in the replicator dynamics of the profession against methods such as the CVAR approach the explicitly requires researcher judgment. The problem is that the European approach requires macroeconomists to explicitly base their arguments on intuition and judgment, both about the data, the institutions and the theory. Such judgments are difficult to assess, and almost impossible to assess in blind peer review journals. Who does the analysis matters. This means that papers using the European CVAR approach do not have a ready outlet in journals and thus the method does not do well in the replicator dynamics of the profession.

The bias in the current replicator dynamics of the economics profession against analysis which emphasizes the need for explicit judgment is in my view a key explanation for the success of the theory-first DSGE-model approach and the lack of success of the European approach. The DSGE theory-first approach allows one to proceed as if one needs no intuition and judgment. It revels in the counter intuitiveness of the theory, seeing counter intuitiveness as strength rather than a weakness, and thus allows all sorts of models that do not pass a minimum intuitive smell test. And then it does not require researchers to bring the model to the data in a reasonable way.

I suspect that Ireland did not test whether the basic underlying assumptions in his model were true because the publishing incentive system he faced, and his commitment to "theory comes first" macroeconomics, did not guide him to do so. Instead, it guided him to get a published paper. He was successful; the paper was published and widely cited because it used high-level econometric techniques, and because it brought a "DSGE model to the data." In the current academic economics incentive structure, publishing has almost become an end in itself, and there is little cost associated with a mistake or taking a less than careful approach.[19]

---

[19] Now I am certainly not claiming that all U.S. macroeconometrics involves sloppiness, or that it is only macroeconometrics that involves sloppiness. What I am suggesting is that the incentive system in academic economics encourages researchers to hide judgment. This sloppiness has been pointed out by a

It is that same focus on publishing that biases the economics profession against the European method of econometrics. The problem is that the European approach does not offer an unambiguous alternative model to replace the "theory-first DSGE model" with. It is a method, not a model. Thus, it requires one to be a specialist in both statistics, in the history of institutions and in macroeconomic theory. It does not allow a separation between the three. Moreover, to choose among alternative theories, a researcher using the European approach must make numerous substantive judgments about the appropriateness of the assumptions. Those substantive judgments must be made on the basis on intuition, one's understanding of theory, and one's understanding of institutions.[20]

The importance of judgment in the European approach can be seen in the following comment from Søren Johansen (Johansen and Juselius 2010). In it he stated:

> So there is now something called the Johansen Procedure, and it is completely misleading to believe it can as such be applied to data that are fractionally integrated or heteroscedastic, or whatever. The Johansen procedure consists of checking the assumptions and then once you know the model is reasonably OK, you go and apply it. It is not just pressing the J button – that is certainly completely inappropriate - but this is unfortunately how it has often been used. It may look like you are doing sophisticated econometric work, but what you are doing is probably close to worthless. My contribution to cointegration analysis was simply to analyze the maximum likelihood estimator and the likelihood ratio test in the Gaussian model. But before you use maximum likelihood, you have to be sure that you have the right model, otherwise the estimator and test do not have the optimal properties you think they have.

> Most econometrics is still taught as methods - almost like cookbooks where you have receipts for method 1, method 2, and method 3. That's not the way Katarina [Juselius] and I approach the data. We first choose the method that fits the circumstances. It needs a lot more careful thinking than is usually associated with writing an applied paper in econometrics. Of course, this has nothing to do with cointegration, but it has everything to do with carefully applying statistical methods to data. With modern computers, it is getting easier to do, but it is also getting easier to do wrongly.

The DSGE model allows separation of theory from empirical work. That reduces the judgment researchers must make: Accept that the DSGE model is the right one, and get on with one's work. That allows individuals to specialize—some can specialize in theory—even though intuitively one might have a hard time justifying that further work on the theoretical model is helping us understand the problems we face in the economy.

---

number of researchers, including Edward Leamer (1983), Lawrence Summers (1991), Deirdre McCloskey (McCloskey and Ziliak 1996), William Dewald (Dewald et al. 1986), and Peter Swan (2006) among others. The assessment that was held by many economists was that the informational content of many aspects of empirical research in macro was close to zero (Cooley and Leroy 1981). Despite the concerns expressed about the informational content of the econometric studies, thousands of such studies were published in the U.S.

[20] It is these substantive judgments that Classical economists saw as part of the "theory" when talking about political economy. Political economy theory was the technical apparatus of scientific theory modified by educated common sense and institutional knowledge.

It doesn't require one to be simultaneously a theorist, a macro econometrician, and a institutionally knowledgeable practitioner to publish. Judgments are still there, but they are implicit; they are hidden in the consensus about method and model, which makes them undebatable, even though they should be at the center of the debate.

The correct use of the European CVAR approach is much more demanding than just pushing the J-button. It requires a researcher to be a simultaneous expert in theory, macroeconometrics and institutions, and to use her or his judgment in coming to a conclusion. It eschews cookbook methods. This makes it difficult to publish in the economic professional environment that guides researchers to use cookbook methods that have come to be accepted because they can be blindly refereed. The true Johansen method requires researcher judgment and thus is not easily amenable to advancement systems that are highly dependent on blind referring processes. That is my judgment of why it is not the generally accepted method, and why it will have a difficult time becoming the generally accepted method unless the institutions change.

7   Conclusion

Let me conclude by summarizing my answer the question I posed at the beginning: Why has the European approach to macroeconometrics had only limited success in the competition for ideas? My answer is that a likely reason is that it is not as compatible with the replicator dynamics of the academic economics profession as is the DSGE-model first approach.

I certainly am not claiming that I have proven my argument. The arguments in this paper are laced with judgments and intuition based on informal, not formal, evidence. Ultimately, such judgments play an important role on all economists' arguments. My hope with this paper is not to prove anything, but rather to stimulate discussion and debate among those who have a deeper understanding of the various approaches than I do. Ideally that debate would lead each side to spell out their judgments and intuitions. In my view, such a debate would add much more to our understanding of the macroeconomy and do more to further macroeconomic thought than would another 100 papers extending the DSGE model or 100 papers applying the cointegrated VAR model to a data set.

References

Campos, J., N. Eriksson, and D. Hendry (2005). General to Specific Modeling: An Overview and Selected Bibliography. International Finance Discussion Papers 838. Board of Governors of the Federal Reserve System.

Chari, V.V., and P. Kehoe (2006). Modern Macroeconomics in Practice: How Theory Is Shaping Policy. *Journal of Economic Perspectives* 20(4): 3–28.

Chari, V.V., P Kehoe, and E. McGrattan (2009). New Keynesian Models: Not Yet Useful for Policy Analysis. *Macroeconomics* 1 (1): 242–266.

Colander, D. (1991). *Why Aren't Economists as Important as Garbagemen?* Armonk, New York: Shape Publishers.

Colander, D. (1996). *Beyond Micro Foundations.* Cambridge: Cambridge University Press.

Colander, D. (2000). *The Complexity Vision and the Teaching of Economics.* Cheltenham: Edward Elgar.

Colander, D. (2006). *Post Walrasian Macroeconomics: Beyond the DSGE Model.* Cambridge: University Press Cambridge.

Colander, D. (2007). *The Making of an Economist Redux.* Princeton, NJ: Princeton University Press.

Colander, D. (2009a). How Did Macro Theory Get So Far off Track, and What Can Heterodox Macroeconomists Do to Get It Back on Track? Forthcoming in E. Hein, T. Niechoj, and E. Stockhammer (eds.), *Macroeconomic Policies on Shaky Foundations - Whither Mainstream Economics?* Marburg: Metropolis.

Colander, D. (2009b). What Was It That Robins Was Defining? *Journal of the History of Economic Thought* (forthcoming).

Colander, D. (2010). *The Making of a European Economist.* Cheltenham: Edward Elgar (forthcoming).

Colander, D., P. Howitt, A. Kirman, A. Leijonhufvud, and P. Mehrling (2008). Beyond DSGE Models: Toward an Empirically Based Macroeconomics. *American Economic Review* 98(2): 236–240.

Cooley, T., and S. Leroy (1981). Identification and Estimation of Money Demand. *American Economic Review* 71:825–204.

Dewald, W., J. Tursby, and R., Anderson (1986). Replication in Empirical Economics: The Journal of Money, Credit and Banking Project. *American Economic Review* 76: 587–603.

Goodwin. R. (1947). Dynamic Coupling with Especial Reference to Markets Having Production Lags. *Econometrica* 15: 181–204.

Hendry, D. (1995). *Dynamic Econometrics.* Oxford: Oxford University Press.

Hendry, D. (2000). *Econometrics: Alchemy or Science?* 2nd ed. Oxford: Blackwell.

Hendry, D. (2009). The Methodology of Empirical Econometric Modelling: Applied Econometrics through the Looking-Glass. Forthcoming in *The Handbook of Empirical Econometrics*, Palgrave.

Hoover, K. (2006). The Past as Future: The Marshallian Approach to Post-Walrasian Econometrics. In D. Colander (ed.), *Post Walrasian Macroeconomics: Beyond the Dynamic Stochastic General Equilibrium Model.* Cambridge: Cambridge University Press.

Hoover, K., S. Johansen, and K. Juselius (2008). Allowing the Data to Speak Freely: The Macroeconometrics of Cointegrated Vector Autoregression. *American Economic Review.* 98: 251–255.

Ireland, P. (2004). A Method for Taking Models to the Data. *Journal of Economic Dynamics and Control* 28 (6): 1205–1226.

Johansen, S. (1996). *Likelihood-Based Inference in Cointegrated Vector Auto-Regressive Models.* Oxford: Oxford University Press.

Johansen, S. (2006). Confronting the Economic Model with the Data. In D. Colander (ed.), *Post Walrasian Macroeconomics: Beyond the Dynamic Stochastic General Equilibrium Model.* Cambridge: Cambridge University Press.

Johansen, S., and K. Juselius (2006). Extracting Information from the Data: A European View on Empirical Macro. In D. Colander (ed.), *Post Walrasian Macroeconomics: Beyond the Dynamic Stochastic General Equilibrium Model.* Cambridge: Cambridge University Press.

Johansen, S., and K. Juselius (2009). Interview. Forthcoming. in B. Rosser, R. Holt and D. Colander (eds.), *The Changing Face of European Economics.* Cheltenham: Edward Elgar.

Juselius, K. (2006). *The Cointegrated VAR Model: Econometric Methodology and Empirical Applications.* Oxford: Oxford University Press.

Juselius, K., and M. Franchi (2007). Taking a DSGE Model to the Data Meaningfully. *Economics—The Open Access, Open Assessment E-Journal.* Vol. 1, 2007-4. http://www.economics-ejournal.org/economics/journalarticles/2007-4.

Landreth, H., and D. Colander (2001). *History of Economic Thought.* Boston: Houghton Mifflin.

Leamer, E. (1983). Let's Take the Con out of Econometrics. *American Economic Review* 73 (1): 31–43.

Keynes, J. N. (1891). *The Scope and Method of Political Economy.* London: Macmillan.

Keynes, J.M. (1938). Letter to Roy Harrod. 4, July. http://economia.unipv.it/harrod/edition/editionstuff/rfh.346.htm (Accessed 3-15-09)

McCloskey, D.N., and S. Ziliak (1996). The Standard Error of Regression. *Journal of Economic Literature* 34: 97–114.

Minsky, H.P. (1986). *Stabilizing an Unstable Economy.* New Haven: Yale University Press.

Robbins, L. (1927). Mr. Hawtrey on the Scope of Economics. *Economica* 7: 172–178.

Robbins, L. (1930). The Present Position of Economic Science. *Economica* 10: 14–24.

Robbins, L. (1932). *An Essay on the Nature and Significance of Economic Science.* London: Macmillan.

Robbins, L. (1981). Economics and Political Economy. *American Economic Review* 71 (2): 1–10.

Rosser, B., R. Holt, and D. Colander (2010). *European Economics at a Crossroads.* Cheltenham: Edward Elgar Publishers. Forthcoming.

Senior, N. (1836 [1938]). *An Outline of the Science of Political Economy.* New York: AM Kelley.

Shackle, G.L.S. (1955). *Uncertainty in Economics and Other Reflections.* Cambridge: Cambridge University Press.

Shepherd, G. (1995). *Leading Economists Ponder the Publication Process.* Arizona: Thomas Horton and Daughters.

Solow, R. (2007). Comment on Colander's Survey. In D. Colander (ed.), *The Making of an Economist Redux.* Princeton, NJ: Princeton University Press.

Solow, R. (2008). The State of Macroeconomics. *Journal of Economic Perspectives* 22 (1): 243–249.

Spanos, A. (2009). The Pre-Eminence of Theory" versus the CVAR Perspective in Macro-econometric Modeling." *Economics–The Open-Access, Open-Assessment E-Journal,* Vol. 3, 2009-10. http://www.economics-ejournal.org/economics/journalarticles/2009-10.

Stigler, G. (1982). Do Economists Matter. In G. Stigler (ed.), *The Economist as Preacher.* Oxford: Basil Blackwell.

Strotz, R. H., J.C. McAnulty, and J. B. Naines, Jr. (1953). Goodwin's Nonlinear Theory of the Business Cycle: An Electro-Analog Solution. *Econometrica* 21: 390–411.

Summers, L. (1991). The Scientific Illusion in Empirical Macroeconomics. *Scandinavian Journal of Economics* 93(2): 129–148.

Swann, P. (2006). *Putting Econometrics in Its Place.* Cheltenham: Edward Elgar.

Woodford, M. (2009). Convergence in Macroeconomics: Elements of the New Synthesis. *Macroeconomics* 1: 267–279.

[14]

American Economic Review: Papers & Proceedings 2008, 98:2, 236–240
http://www.aeaweb.org/articles.php?doi=10.1257/aer.98.2.236

COMPLEXITY AND DYNAMICS IN MACROECONOMICS: ALTERNATIVES TO THE DSGE MODELS[†]

Beyond DSGE Models:
Toward an Empirically Based Macroeconomics

By DAVID COLANDER, PETER HOWITT, ALAN KIRMAN, AXEL LEIJONHUFVUD,
AND PERRY MEHRLING*

Maybe there is in human nature a deep-seated perverse pleasure in adopting and defending a wholly counterintuitive doctrine that leaves the uninitiated peasant wondering what planet he or she is on.
—Robert Solow[1]

There has, for some time, been a strong under-current of opposition to modern macroeconomic models which, in their latest incarnation, have coalesced around dynamic stochastic general equilibrium models. Critics ask: how can models that assume away any agent coordination problems shed much light on macro phenomena that are intrinsically involved with such problems? They argue that what makes macroeconomics a separate field of study is the complex properties of aggregate behavior that emerge from the interaction among agents. Since in a complex system aggregate behavior cannot be deduced from an analysis of individuals alone, representative agent models fail to address the most basic questions of macroeconomics.

† *Discussants:* Stephen Turnovsky, University of Washington; Duncan Foley, New School University.

* Colander: Middlebury College, Middlebury, VT 05753 (e-mail: colander@middlebury.edu); Howitt: Brown University, Providence, RI 02912 (e-mail: Peter_Howitt@brown.edu); Kirman: GREQAM, 2 Rue de la Charité, 13002 Marseille, France (e-mail: kirman@ehess.cnrs-mrs.fr); Leijonhufvud: UCLA and University of Trento, via Belenzani, 12 I-38100 Trento, Italy (e-mail: axel@ucla.edu); Mehrling: Barnard College, 3009 Broadway, New York, NY 10027 (e-mail: pgm10@columbia.edu).

[1] Robert Solow (2006, 236) made this statement as he reflected on how the macro model had gone so far astray. He further states that (flaws in the previous model) "would not explain why the macro community bought so incontinently into an alternative model that seems to lack all credibility...."

To many young economists who are unfamiliar with the history of macro, the thought of doing macro without representative agent micro foundations is almost heretical. How can one hope to say anything formally about the macro economy without "sound microfoundations"? To do so, they have been taught, would be ad hoc. In truth, however, nothing could be more ad hoc than the standard microfoundations; as economists such as Pareto, Hicks, and Koopmans have made clear, the assumptions we make about individuals in microeconomics are based on introspection, not on any mass of coherent empirical evidence or even on any intuitive plausibility criteria. The only justification of the hyper-rational, self-interested agent typically used in standard macro models was that it was consistent with the characterization used in micro theorizing. And even that justification is now disappearing with the rise of behavioral economics.

To make the needed break from the past, macroeconomists must acknowledge that micro foundations are a choice variable of theorists. The appropriate choice cannot be determined a priori; it needs to be made in reference to empirical data and educated common sense in a way that will lead to useful macro models. The current standard approach in macro does not do that; instead it clings to the rational, self-interested agent microfoundations. Then, as discussed in Alan Kirman (1992), to avoid the Sonnenschein-Mantel-Debreu aggregation problem—namely the problem that the aggregation of individual behaviors does not generally inherit the nice properties of those agent behaviors—it makes the additional ad hoc representative individual assumption.

A more reasonable approach to macro theory would recognize that the behavior of the

VOL. 98 NO. 2   BEYOND DSGE MODELS: TOWARD AN EMPIRICALLY BASED MACROECONOMICS   237

aggregate need not correspond to the behavior of the components, and that it generally cannot be derived from a consideration of the latter alone. *Any meaningful model of the macro economy must analyze not only the characteristics of the individuals but also the structure of their interactions.* Such a view is commonplace in other disciplines, from biology to physics and sociology. They recognize that the aggregate behavior of systems of particles, molecules, neurons, and social insects cannot be deduced from the characteristics of a "representative" of the population. The same is true for economic systems; the fallacy of composition exists, and must be dealt with (Howitt 2006).

The arguments above have been stated many times before. Why then are we hopeful that restating them is worthwhile? The reason for our optimism is that the tools and technology necessary to build complex models are being assembled and increasingly applied by the economics profession. These new tools, which are being adapted from disciplines as varied as physics, biology, computer science, and psychology, allow the profession to move beyond DSGE models to more comprehensive, and potentially more meaningful, models. The other papers in this session provide an introduction to some of these approaches, tools, and models that are further developed in Colander (2006). In this paper we put the new models and techniques into perspective.

To understand why we are convinced that this is the right way to move forward in macro, it is helpful to briefly review the history of the field. Up until the 1940s or 1950s, macroeconomics proceeded without a formal theory. Macroeconomic policy was based on a loose and largely empirical understanding of the macro economy. The field advanced through trial and error, as economists learned from the experience of the past, in the same way that stonemasons learned from the past as they developed methods to build cathedrals long before they understood the formal scientific principles that determine whether or not their constructions would fall down. Similarly, economists used simple, informal macro models, such as the quantity theory and the Keynesian Cross, that captured elements of the macro economy and provided guidance for policy, all in advance of the necessary formal scientific principles. Economic theory had not moved into its axiomatic and mathematical

phase at that time, so the idea of a macroeconomic model based on axioms concerning individual behavior was not even envisaged.

While we are sympathetic to this engineering approach for policy purposes, and will argue that there is a modern-day equivalent to this earlier approach that economists can benefit from using today, the approach is justifiable only if its limitations are kept in mind. As an engineering model, it is about solving immediate problems and it does not provide a deep scientific understanding of the way in which the macro economy functions, nor is it intended to do so. This has not always been recognized. With the development of macro econometric models in the 1950s, many of the Keynesian models were presented as having formal underpinnings of microeconomic theory and thus as providing a formal model of the macro economy. Specifically, IS/LM type models were too often presented as being "scientific" in this sense, rather than as the ad hoc engineering models that they were. Selective micro foundations were integrated into sectors of the models that give them the illusory appearance of being based on the axiomatic approach of General Equilibrium theory. This led to the economics of Keynes becoming separated from Keynesian economics.

The exaggerated claims for the macro models of the 1960s led to a justifiable reaction by macroeconomists wanting to "do the science of macro right," which meant bringing it up to the standards of rigor imposed by the General Equilibrium tradition. Thus, in the 1970s the formal modeling of macro in this spirit began, including work on the micro foundations of macroeconomics, construction of an explicit New Classical macroeconomic model, and the rational expectations approach. All of this work rightfully challenged the rigor of the previous work. The aim was to build a general equilibrium model of the macro economy based on explicit and fully formulated micro foundations.

Given the difficulties inherent in such an approach, researchers started with a simple analytically tractable macro model, which they hoped would be a stepping stone toward a more sensible macro model grounded in microfoundations. The problem is that the simple model was not susceptible to generalization, so the profession languished on the first step; and rational expectations representative agent models mysteriously became the only allowable modeling method.

Moreover, such models were directly applied to policy even though they had little or no relevance. The result was the situation that Solow refers to in the beginning of this paper.

The reason researchers clung to the rational expectations representative agent models for so long is not that they did not recognize their problems, but because of the analytical difficulties involved in moving beyond these models. Dropping the standard assumptions about agent rationality would complicate the already complicated models, and abandoning the ad hoc representative agent assumption would leave them face to face with the difficulties raised by Sonnenschein, Mantel, and Debreu. While the standard DSGE representative models may look daunting, it is the mathematical sophistication of the analysis, and not the models themselves, which are difficult. Conceptually, their technical difficulty pales in comparison to models with more realistic specifications: heterogeneous agents, statistical dynamics, multiple equilibria (or no equilibria), and endogenous learning. Yet, it is precisely such models that are needed if we are to start to capture the relevant intricacies of the macro economy.

Building more realistic models along these lines involves enormous work with little immediate payoff; one must either move beyond the extremely restrictive class of economic models to far more complicated analytic macro models, or one must replace the analytic modeling approach with virtual modeling. Happily, both changes are occurring; researchers are beginning to move on to models that attempt to deal with heterogeneous interacting agents, potential emergent macro properties, and behaviorally more varied and more realistic opportunistic agents. The papers in this session describe some of these new approaches.

One important characteristic of this new work is that it is uninterested in full agent model equilibria. As biologist Stuart Kaufman has remarked, "An organism in equilibrium is dead." Instead, the new work looks for *system equilibria*, in which agent disequilibria offset each other so that the aggregate system is unchanging, even though none of the components of the individual agents in the model is in equilibrium. Aggregate systems in equilibrium have lots going on inside them, and the goal of this new work is to relate the micro dynamics with the macro equilibrium. This places the models in the realm of statistical

mechanics, and opens up a new range of tools, such as cluster analysis and ultrametrics, which can be used to explore them (Masanao Aoki and Hiroshi Yoshikawa, 2006). It even offers the possibility of jettisoning all micro foundations, and, using dimensional analysis, analyzing the aggregate economy with zero-rationality agents, as the econophysics literature is doing (Doyne Farmer et al. 2006)

All this work is both statistically and mathematically technical. The simple truth is that formal macro theorizing that extends beyond where we currently are can no longer be done by the general macro economic theorist without specialized knowledge of various branches of mathematics and statistics, in the same way that theoretical physics cannot be done by engineers or applied physicists alone. With the increase in technical sophistication of the tools now available, scientific economics is at the stage where it must give up the notion that a generalist macroeconomic scientist can do it all—policy, theory, and empirical work.

The way that macroeconomic theorists have kept ahead of the game until now has been to concentrate on a very specific part of mathematics applicable to the set of restricted models that they use. That approach does not work. If we are to develop newer, more encompassing macroeconomic theories, modern macroeconomists must expand their modeling repertoire, using all available analytic techniques and computational methods.

I. ACE Modeling

Because the analytic macro models discussed above are so technically difficult, it is not clear which, if any, will provide a meaningful advance. However, because of the increase in computing power over the past decade, there is another approach that cuts the Gordian analytic knot and uses agent based computational economic (ACE) models to analyze the macro economy. In ACE models, researchers create virtual worlds that can be used as test beds to study macroeconomic phenomena. The ACE modeling method is described in the LeBaron/Tesfatsion paper (2008).

The advantage of the ACE approach for macroeconomics in particular is that it removes the tractability limitations that so limit analytic macroeconomics. ACE modeling allows researchers to choose a form of microeconomics appropriate for the issues at hand, including breadth of agent types, number of agents of each type, and nested hierarchical arrangements of agents. It also allows researchers to consider the interactions among agents simultaneously with agent decisions, and to study the dynamic macro interplay among agents. Researchers can relatively easily develop ACE models with large numbers of heterogeneous agents, and no equilibrium conditions have to be imposed. Multiple equilibria can be considered, since equilibrium is a potential outcome rather than an imposed requirement. Stability and robustness analysis can be done simultaneously with analysis of solutions.

II. The Engineering Approach: Taking the Models to Policy

We are a long way from analytic and ACE models being intuitively satisfying. For example, in a truly satisfying ACE model, the agents will have access to ACE modeling results, making the modeling process itself endogenous to the model. That was the problem that John Muth attempted to sidestep with his assumption of rational expectations. But process endogeneity cannot be sidestepped; endogenous process systems continually unfold in ways that likely can never be fully understood from a vantage point within the system. Because of the inherent complexity of the problem, even the new advanced analytic and ACE macro models described above should be seen as stepping stones on the path to a deeper model of macro sometime in the future. At present, they are still far too simple to bring directly to policy; they are, at best, suggestive. Thus, researchers must be careful about drawing anything other than suggestive inferences about macro policy from the models. Ad hoc models, as all scientific macro models are at this point, provide ad hoc policy advice; they can do no better.

If all scientific macro models are still ad hoc, how should one undertake macro policy today? Our answer is that policy economists need to go back to the engineering approach that economists used up until the 1940s and 1950s. That engineering approach does not search for scientific understanding; it searches for models that shed light on the problems at hand. Because of the statistical and computational advances that

have been made in the past half century, the modern macro engineering approach will not be limited to the heuristic and ad hoc econometric models that they used, but instead can use sophisticated statistical models to complement our understanding. It is time to return to an engineering approach to macro policy that has long existed in econometrics, and accept that one can, and should, search for relationships among macroeconomic variables without worrying about the behavioral foundations of those relations.

The use of vector auto-regression (VAR) models which posit linear relations among various macro time series is one way to do this. These models do away with the restrictive assumptions of causal models such as DSGE, and thus are a good starting point for a modern engineering macro model. Such an approach is now widely used to make forecasts and to guide macro policy. Today, in particular, for short-term forecasts and analysis, researchers are more and more turning away from formal theoretical models of any type and are using VAR models.

That approach makes practical sense, but as all researchers know, statistical models alone do not provide answers; one's theory influences one's interpretation of the statistical models. The question is: how do we integrate the statistical results with our theories? One approach being suggested is to use DSGE models as Bayesian priors for the analysis. (Marco Del Negro and Frank Schorfheider 2004). We find that approach unsatisfying. A more reasonable approach is to assume the "true" macro model is unknown, and to entertain multiple candidate theories.

The Hoover/Johansen/Juselius paper (2008) offers an alternative, attractive approach that switches the role of theory and statistical analysis. Instead of letting theory guide data, they let the data guide both policy and theory choice. The central tools in this approach are cointegrated vector auto-regressive (CVAR) statistical models, and general-to-specific statistical modeling. These tools allow the researcher to take an archeological approach to the data—relying on the statistical tools to guide the policymaker in finding the stable statistical relations among variables in the past.

This modern engineering approach requires continuous interaction between the researcher and the data. Cointegration does not lead to clear-cut answers; to make decisions about the grey areas, the researcher must have a good sense of the strengths and weaknesses of the various theories. Results will vary according to the decisions he or she makes, and thus the results are researcher specific. To make reasonable decisions, the researcher cannot hold just one theory. Doing so will all too often simply lead the researcher to confirm whatever theory he holds (see Johansen 2006). In short, the modern macro engineering researcher cannot be a technician who applies technical tools to data, but rather must be a craftsman who integrates the best computer-aided statistical analysis possible with the best general theoretical and institutional knowledge, allowing him or her to interpret the data.

III. Conclusion

Einstein once said that models should be as simple as possible but not more so. If the macro economy is a complex system, which we think it is, existing macro models are "more so" by far. They need to be treated as such. We need to acknowledge that our current representative agent DSGE models are as ad hoc as earlier macro models. There is no exclusive right to describe a model as "rigorous." This does not mean that work in analytical macro theory should come to a halt. But it should move on to models that take agent interaction seriously, with the hope that maybe, sometime in the future, they might shed some direct light on macro policy, rather than just provide suggestive inferences. In the meantime, the best approach to macro policy is to come back to earth and to adopt an engineering approach in which macro econometricians see themselves as builders, not architects.

REFERENCES

Aoki, Masanao, and Hiroshi Yoshikawa. 2006. *A Reconstruction of Macro: A Perspective from Statistical Physics and Combinatorial Stochastic Processes.* Cambridge: Cambridge University Press.

Colander, David, ed. 2006. *Post Walrasian Macro: Beyond the DSGE Model.* Cambridge: Cambridge University Press.

Del Negro, Marco, and Frank Schorfheide. 2004. "Priors from General Equilibrium Models for VARs." *International Economic Review,* 45(2): 643–73.

Farmer, Doyne, Laxslo Gillemot, Giulia Iori, Suprya Krishnamurthy, Eric Smith, and Marcus Daniels. 1988. "A Random Order Placement Model of Price Formation in the Continuous Double Auction." In *The Economy as an Evolving Complex System III,* ed. Larry Blume and Steven Durlauf, 175–206. Oxford: Oxford University Press.

Hoover, Kevin D., Søren Johansen, and Katarina Juselius. 2008. "Allowing the Data to Speak Freely: The Macroeconometrics of the Cointegrated Vector Autoregression." *American Economic Review,* 98(2): 251–55.

Howitt, Peter. 2006. "Coordination Issues in Long-Run Growth." In *Handbook of Computational Economics, Vol II: Agent-Based Computational Economics,* ed. Leigh Tesfatsion and Kenneth Judd, 1605–24. Amsterdam: North Holland.

Johansen, Søren. 2006. "Confronting the Economic Model with the Data." In *Post Walrasian Macro:Beyond the DSGE Model,* ed. David Colander, 287–300. Cambridge: Cambridge University Press.

Kirman, Alan. 1992. "Whom or What Does the Representative Individual Represent?" *The Journal of Economic Perspectives,* 6(2): 117–36.

LeBaron, Blake, and Leigh Tesfatsion. 2008. "Modeling Macroeconomies as Open-Ended Dynamic Systems of Interaction Agents" *American Economic Review,* 98(2): 246–50.

Solow, Robert. 2006. "Reflections on the Survey." In *The Making of an Economist Redux,* ed. David Colander, 234–38. Princeton, NJ: Princeton University Press.

PART IV

PRAGMATIC METHODS FOR DOING ECONOMICS AS A PROFESSION

[15]

Written Testimony of David Colander
Submitted to the Congress of the United States, House Science and Technology Committee
July 20th, 2010

Mr. Chairman and members of the committee: I thank you for the opportunity to testify. My name is David Colander. I am the Christian A. Johnson Distinguished Professor of Economics at Middlebury College. I have written or edited over forty books, including a top-selling principles of economics textbook, and 150 articles on various aspects of economics. I was invited to speak because I am an economist watcher who has written extensively on the economics profession and its foibles, and specifically, how those foibles played a role in economists' failure to adequately warn society about the recent financial crisis. I have been asked to expand on a couple of proposals I made for NSF in a hearing a year and a half ago.

Introduction

I'm known in the economics profession as the Economics Court Jester because I am the person who says what everyone knows, but which everyone in polite company knows better than to say. As the court jester, I see it as appropriate to start my testimony with a variation of a well-known joke. It begins with a Congressman walking home late at night; he notices an economist searching under a lamppost for his keys. Recognizing that the economist is a potential voter, he stops to help. After searching a while without luck he asks the economist where he lost his keys. The economist points far off into the dark abyss. The Congressman asks, incredulously, "Then why the heck are you searching here?" To which the economist responds—"This is where the light is."

Critics of economists like this joke because it nicely captures economic theorists' tendency to be, what critics consider, overly mathematical and technical in their research. Searching where the light is (letting available analytic technology guide one's technical research), on the surface, is clearly a stupid strategy; the obvious place to search is where you lost the keys.

That, in my view, is the wrong lesson to take from this joke. I would argue that for pure scientific economic research, the "searching where the light is" strategy is far from stupid. The reason is that the subject matter of social science is highly complex— arguably far more complex than the subject matter of most natural sciences. It is as if the social science policy keys are lost in the equivalent of almost total darkness, and you have no idea where in the darkness you lost them. In such a situation, where else but in the light can you reasonably search in a scientific way?

What is stupid, however, is if the scientist thinks he is going to find the keys under the lamppost. Searching where the light is only makes good sense if the goal of the search is *not to find the keys,* but rather to understand the topography of the illuminated land, and how that lighted topography relates to the topography in the dark where the keys are lost. In the long run, such knowledge is extraordinarily helpful in the practical search for the keys out in the dark, but it is only helpful where the topography that the

David Colander—Written Testimony, July 20th, 2010

people find when they search in the dark matches the topography of the lighted area being studied.

What I'm arguing is that it is most useful to think of the search for the social science policy keys as a two-part search, each of which requires a quite different set of skills and knowledge set. Pure scientific research—the type of research the NSF is currently designed to support—ideally involves searches of the entire illuminated domain, even those regions only dimly lit. It should also involve building new lamps and lampposts to expand the topography that one can formally search. This is pure research; it is highly technical; it incorporates the latest advances in mathematical and statistical technology. Put simply, it is rocket (social) science that is concerned with understanding for the sake of understanding. Trying to draw direct practical policy conclusions from models developed in this theoretical search is generally a distraction to scientific searchers.

The policy search is a search in the dark, where one thinks one has lost the keys. This policy search requires a practical sense of real-world institutions, a comprehensive knowledge of past literature, familiarity with history, and a well-tuned sense of nuance. While this search requires a knowledge of what the cutting edge scientific research is telling researchers about illuminated topography, the knowledge required is a consumer's knowledge of that research, not a producer's knowledge.

How Economists Failed Society

In my testimony last year, I argued that the economics profession failed society in the recent financial crisis in two ways. First, it failed society because it over-researched a particular version of the dynamic stochastic general equilibrium (DSGE) model that happened to have a tractable formal solution, whereas more realistic models that incorporated purposeful forward looking agents were formally unsolvable. That tractable DSGE model attracted macro economists as a light attracts moths. Almost all mainstream macroeconomic researchers were searching the same lighted area. While the initial idea was neat, and an advance, much of the later research was essentially dotting i's and crossing t's of that original DSGE macro model. What that meant was that macroeconomists were not imaginatively exploring the multitude of complex models that could have, and should have, been explored. Far too small a topography of the illuminated area was studied, and far too little focus was given to whether the topography of the model matched the topography of the real world problems.

What macroeconomic scientific researchers more appropriately could have been working on is a multiple set of models that incorporated purposeful forward looking agents. This would have included models with multiple equilibria, high level agent interdependence, varying degrees of information processing capacity, true uncertainty rather than risk, and non-linear dynamics, all of which seem intuitively central in macroeconomic issues, and which we have the analytical tools to begin dealing with.[1] Combined, these models would have revealed that complex models are just that—

---

[1] I have called this research into more complex economic models, Post Walrasian macroeconomics, and have spelled out what is involved in Colander, 1996, 2006.)

2

David Colander—Written Testimony, July 20th, 2010

complex, and just about anything could happen in the macro-economy. This knowledge that just about anything could happen in various models would have warned society to be prepared for possible crises, and suggested that society should develop a strategy and triage policies to deal with possible crises. In other words, it would have revealed that, at best, the DSGE models were of only limited direct policy relevance, since by changing the assumptions of the model slightly, one would change the policy recommendation of the model. The economics profession didn't warn society about the limitations of its DSGE models.

The second way in which the economics profession failed society was by letting policy makers believe, and sometimes assuring policy makers, that the topography of the real-world matched the topography of the highly simplified DSGE models, even though it was obvious to anyone with a modicum of institutional knowledge and educated common sense that the topography of the DSGE model and the topography of the real-world macro economy generally were no way near a close match. Telling policy makers that existing DSGE models could guide policy makers in their search in the dark was equivalent to telling someone that studying tic-tac toe models can guide him or her in playing 20th dimensional chess. Too strong reliance by policy makers on DSGE models and reasoning led those policy makers searching out there in the dark to think that they could crawl in the dark without concern, only to discover there was a cliff there that they fell off, pulling the US economy with it.

Economists aren't stupid, and the macro economists working on DSGE models are among the brightest. What then accounts for these really bright people continuing working on simple versions of the DSGE model, and implying to policy makers that these simple versions were useful policy models? The answer goes back to the lamppost joke. If the economist had answered honestly, he would have explained that he was searching for the keys in one place under the lamppost because that is where the research money was. In order to get funding, he or she had to appear to be looking for the keys in his or her research. Funders of economic research wanted policy answers from the models, not wild abstract research that concluded with the statement that their model has little to no direct implications for policy.

Classical economists, and followers of Classical economic methodology, which included economists up through Lionel Robbins (See Colander, 2009), maintained a strict separation between pure scientific research, which was designed to be as objective as possible, and which developed theorems and facts, and applied policy research, which involved integrating the models developed in science to real world issues.² That separation helped keep economists in their role as scientific economists out of policy.

---

² Nassau Senior, the first Classical economist to write on method put the argument starkly. He writes. "(the economist's) conclusions, whatever be their generality and their truth, do not authorize him in adding a single syllable of advice. That privilege belongs to the writer or statesman who has considered all the causes which may promote or impede the general welfare of those whom he addresses, not to the theorist who has considered only one, though among the most important of those causes. The business of a Political Economist is neither to recommend nor to dissuade, but to state general principles, which it is fatal to

David Colander—Written Testimony, July 20th, 2010

It did not prevent them from talking about, or taking positions on, policy. It simply required them to make it clear that, when they did so, they were not speaking with the certitude of economic science, but rather in their role as an economic statesman. The reason this distinction is important is that being a good scientist does not necessarily make one a good statesman. Being an economic statesman requires a different set of skills than being an economic scientist. An economic statesman needs a well-tuned educated common sense. He or she should be able to subject the results of models to a "sensibility test" that relates the topography illuminated by the model to the topography of the real world. Some scientific researchers made good statesmen; they had the expertise and training to be great policy statesmen as well as great scientists. John Maynard Keynes, Frederick Hayek, and Paul Samuelson come to mind. Others did not; Abba Lerner and Gerard Debreu come to mind.[3]

The need to separate out policy from scientific research in social science is due to the complexity of economic policy problems. Once one allows for all the complexities of interaction of forward looking purposeful agents and the paucity of data to choose among models, it is impossible to avoid judgments when relating models to policy. Unfortunately, what Lionel Robbins said in the 1920s remains true today, "What precision economists can claim at this stage is largely a sham precision. In the present state of knowledge, the man who can claim for economic science much exactitude is a quack." (Robbins, 1927, 176)

Why Economists Failed Society

One of J.M. Keynes's most famous quotes, which economists like to repeat, highlights the power of academic economists. He writes, "the ideas of economists and political philosophers, both when they are right and when they are wrong, are more powerful than is commonly understood. Indeed, the world is ruled by little else. Practical men, who believe themselves to be quite exempt from any intellectual influences, are usually the slaves of some defunct economist. Madmen in authority, who hear voices in the air, are distilling their frenzy from some academic scribbler of a few years back." (Keynes, 1936: 135) What this quotation misses is the circularity of the idea generating process. The ideas of economists and political philosophers do not appear out of nowhere. Ideas that succeed are those that develop in the then existing institutional structure. The reality is that academic economists, who believe themselves quite exempt from any practical influence, are in fact guided by an incentive structure created by some now defunct politicians and administrators.

---

neglect, but neither advisable, nor perhaps practicable, to use as the sole, or even the principle, guides in the actual conduct of affairs." (Senior 1836: 2-3)
[3] Gerard Debreu is a great economic scientist who is clear about his work having no direct policy relevance; he did not try to play the role of policy statesman. Abba Lerner was less clear about keeping the two roles separate. This lead Keynes to remark about Lerner "He is very learned and has an acute and subtle mind. But it is not easy to get him to take a broad view of a problem and he is apt to lack judgment and intuition, so that, if there is any fault in his logic, there is nothing to prevent it from leading him to preposterous conclusions." (Keynes, 1935: 113) There are also economists whom I consider great statesmen, but not great scientists. Herbert Stein and Charles Goodhart come to mind.

4

David Colander—Written Testimony, July 20th, 2010

Bringing the issue home to this committee, what I am saying is that you will become the defunct politicians and administrators of the future. Your role in guiding research is pivotal in the future of science and society. So, when economists fail, it means that your predecessors have failed. What I mean by this is that when, over drinks, I have pushed macroeconomic researchers on why they focused on the DSGE model, and why they implied, or at least allowed others to believe, that it had policy relevance beyond what could reasonably be given to it, they responded that that was what they believed the National Science Foundation, and other research support providers, wanted.

That view of what funding agencies wanted fits my sense of the macroeconomic research funding environment of the last thirty years. During that time the NSF and other research funding institutions strongly supported DSGE research, and were far less likely to fund alternative macroeconomic research. The process became self-fulfilling, and ultimately, all macro researchers knew that to get funding you needed to accept the DSGE modeling approach, and draw policy conclusions from that DSGE model in your research. Ultimately, successful researchers follow the money and provide what funders want, even if those funders want the impossible. If you told funders it is impossible, you did not stay in the research game.

One would think that competition in ideas would lead to the stronger ideas winning out. Unfortunately, because the macroeconomy is so complex, macro theory is, of necessity, highly speculative, and it is almost impossible to tell a priori what the strongest ideas are. The macro economics profession is just too small and too oligopolistic to have workable competition among supporters of a wide variety of ideas and alternative models. Most top researchers are located at a small number of interrelated and inbred schools. This highly oligopolistic nature of the scientific economics profession tends to reinforce one approach rather than foster an environment in which a variety of approaches can flourish. When scientific models are judged by their current policy relevance, if a model seems temporarily to be matching what policy makers are finding in the dark, it can become built in and its premature adoption as "the model" can preclude the study of other models. That is what happened with what economists called the "great moderation" and the premature acceptance of the DSGE model.

Most researchers; if pushed, fully recognize the limitations of formal models for policy.[4] But more and more macroeconomists are willing to draw strong policy conclusions from their DSGE model, and hold them regardless of what the empirical evidence and common sense might tell them. Some of the most outspoken advocates of this approach are Vandarajan Chari, Patrick Kehoe and Ellen McGrattan. They admit that the DSGE model does not fit the data, but state that a model neither "can nor should fit most aspects of the data" (Chari, Kehoe and McGratten, 2009, pg 243). Despite their agreement that their model does not fit the data, they are willing to draw strong policy

---

[4] For example, Robert Lucas one of the originators of the DSGE modeling approach, in some of his writings, was quite explicit about its policy limitations long before the crisis. He writes "there's a residue of things they (DSGE models) don't let us think about. They don't let us think about the U.S. experience in the 1930's or about financial crises and their real consequences in Asian and Latin America; they don't let us think very well about Japan in the 1990's." (Lucas, 2004) Even earlier (Klamer, 1983) Lucas stated that if he were appointed to the Council of Economic Advisors, he would resign.

5

David Colander—Written Testimony, July 20th, 2010

implications from it. For example, they write "discretionary policy making has only costs and no benefits, so that if government policymakers can be made to commit to a policy rule, society should make them do so." (Chari and Kehoe, 2006; pg 7, 8)

While they slightly qualify this strong conclusion slightly later on, and agree that unforeseen events should allow breaking of the rule, they provide no method of deciding what qualifies as an unforeseen event, nor do they explain how the possibility of unforeseen events might have affected the agent's decisions in their DSGE model, and hence affected the conclusions of their model. Specifying how agents react to unexpected events in uncertain environments where true uncertainty, not just risk, exists is hard. It requires what Robert Shiller and George Akerlof call an animal spirits model; the DSGE model does not deal with animal spirits.

Let's say that the US had followed their policy advice against any discretionary policy, and had set a specific monetary policy rule that had not taken into account the possibility of financial collapse. That fixed rule could have totally tied the hands of the Fed, and the US economy today would likely be in a depression.

Relating this discussion back to the initial searching in the light metaphor, the really difficult problem is not developing models; they really difficult policy problem is relating models to real world events.[5] The DSGE model is most appropriate for a relatively smooth terrain. When the terrain out in the dark where policy actually is done is full of mountains and cliffs, relying on DSGE model to guide policy, even if that DSGE model has been massaged to make it seem to fit the terrain, can lead us off a cliff, as it did in the recent crisis. My point is a simply one: Models can, and should, be used in policy, but they should be used with judgment and common sense.

DSGE supporter's primary argument for using the DSGE model over all other models is based on their model having what they call micro foundations. As we discuss in Colander, et al. (2008) *what they call micro foundations are totally ad hoc micro foundations.* As almost all scientists, expect macroeconomic scientists, fully recognize, when dealing with complex systems such as the economy, macro behavior cannot be derived from a consideration of the behavior of the components taken in isolation. Interaction matters, and unless one has a model that captures the full range of agent interaction, with full inter-agent feedbacks, one does not have an acceptable micro foundation to a macro model. Economists are now working on gaining insight into such interactive micro foundations using computer generated agent-based models. These agent based models can come to quite different conclusions about policy than DSGE models,

---

[5] Keynes recognized this. He wrote (1938) "Economics is a science of thinking in terms of models joined to the art of choosing models which are relevant to the contemporary world. It is compelled to be this, because, unlike the typical natural science, the material to which it is applied is, in too many respects, not homogeneous through time. The object of a model is to segregate the semi-permanent or relatively constant factors from those which are transitory or fluctuating so as to develop a logical way of thinking about the latter, and of understanding the time sequences to which they give rise in particular cases. Good economists are scarce because the gift for using "vigilant observation" to choose good models, although it does not require a highly specialized intellectual technique, appears to be a very rare one."

David Colander—Written Testimony, July 20th, 2010

which calls into question any policy conclusion coming from DSGE models that do not account for agent interaction.

If one gives up the purely aesthetic micro foundations argument for DSGE models, the conclusion one arrives at is that none of the DSGE models are ready to be used directly in policy making. The reality is that given the complexity of the economy and lack of formal statistical evidence leading us to conclude that any particular model is definitely best on empirical grounds, policy must remain a matter of judgment about which reasonable economists may disagree.

How the Economics Profession Can Do Better.

I believe the reason why the macroeconomics profession has arrived in the situation it has reflects serious structural problems in the economics profession and in the incentives that researchers face. The current incentives facing young economic researchers lead them to both focus on abstract models that downplay the complexity of the economy while overemphasizing the direct policy implications of their abstract models.

The reason I am testifying today is that I believe the NSF can take the lead in changing this current institutional incentive structure by implementing two structural changes in the NSF program funding economics. These structural changes would provide economists with more appropriate incentives, and I will end my testimony by outlining those proposals.

Include a wider range of peers in peer review

The first structural change is a proposal to make diversity of the reviewer pool an explicit goal of the reviewing process of NSF grants to the social sciences. This would involve consciously including what are often called heterodox and other dissenting economists as part of the peer reviewer pool as well as including reviewers outside of economics. Along with economists on these reviewer panels for economic proposals one might include physicists, mathematicians, statisticians, and individuals with business and governmental real world experience. Such a broader peer review process would likely encourage research on a much wider range of models, promote more creative work, and provide a common sense feedback from real world researchers about whether the topography of the models matches the topography of the real world the models are designed to illuminate.

Increase the number of researchers trained to interpret models

The second structural change is a proposal to increase the number of researchers explicitly trained in interpreting and relating models to the real world. This can be done by explicitly providing research grants to interpret, rather than develop, models. In a sense, what I am suggesting is an applied science division of the National Science Foundation's social science component. This division would fund work on the appropriateness of models being developed for the real world.

7

David Colander—Written Testimony, July 20th, 2010

This applied science division would see applied research as true "applied research" not as "econometric research." It would not be highly technical and would involve a quite different set of skills than currently required by the standard scientific research. It would require researchers who had a solid consumer's knowledge of economic theory and econometrics, but not necessarily a producer's knowledge. In addition, it would require a knowledge of institutions, methodology, previous literature, and a sensibility about how the system works—a sensibility that would likely have been gained from discussions with real-world practitioners, or better yet, from having actually worked in the area.

The skills involved in interpreting models are skills that currently are not taught in graduate economics programs, but they are the skills that underlie judgment and common sense. By providing NSF grants for this interpretative work, the NSF would encourage the development of a group of economists who specialize in interpreting models and applying models to the real world. The development of such a group would go a long way towards placing the necessary warning labels on models, making it less likely that fiascos, such as the recent financial crisis would happen again.

Bibliography

Chari, V.V., and P. Kehoe, 2006. Modern macroeconomics in practice: How theory is shaping policy. *Journal of Economic Perspectives* 20(4), 3-28.

Chari, V.V., P Kehoe and E. McGrattan, 2009. "New Keynesian Models: Not Yet Useful for Policy Analysis" *Macroeconomics,* (AEA) vol 1. No. 1

Colander, David, 1996. (ed.) *Beyond Microfoundations: Post Walrasian Economics*, Cambridge, UK. Cambridge University Press.

Colander, David, 2006. (ed.) *Post Walrasian Macroeconomics: Beyond the Dynamic Stochastic General Equilibrium Model*, Cambridge, UK. Cambridge University Press.

Colander, David, 2009. "What was 'It' that Robbins was Defining?" *Journal of the History of Economic Thought*, December. Vol. 31:4, 437-448.

David Colander, Peter Howitt, Alan Kirman, Axel Leijonhufvud, and Perry Mehrling, 2008. "Beyond DSGE Models: Toward an Empirically Based Macroeconomics" *American Economic Review,* 98:2, 236–24.

Keynes, John Maynard, 1935. Letter to Lionel Robbins 1st May, 1935. Reprinted in Colander, David and Harry Landreth, 1997. *The Coming of Keynesianism to America*, Cheltenham, England. Edward Elgar.

Keynes, John Maynard, 1936. *The General Theory of Employment, Interest and Money,* London. Macmillan.

8

David Colander—Written Testimony, July 20th, 2010

Keynes, J.M., (1938). Letter to Roy Harrod. 4, July.
   http://economia.unipv.it/harrod/edition/editionstuff/rfh.346.htm

Klamer, Arjo, 1984. *Conversations with Economists: New Classical Economists and
   Opponents Speak Out on the Current Controversy in Macroeconomics*, Lanham,
   Maryland. Rowman and Littlefield Publishers.

Lucas, Robert, 2004. "My Keynesian Education" in M. De Vroey and K. Hoover (eds.)
   *The IS'LM Model: Its rise, Fall and Strange Persistence, Annual Supplement to Vol.
   36 of History of Political Economy,* Durham, NC, Duke University Press

Robbins, Lionel, 1927. "Mr. Hawtrey on the Scope of Economics" *Economica.* Vol. 7,
   172-178.

Senior, Nassau William, 1836. (1951). *An Outline of the Science of Political Economy*,
   New York. Augustus M. Kelly.

Solow, Robert, 2008. "The state of macroeconomics" *Journal of Economic Perspectives*
   22(1), 243-249.

9

16

2 Moving beyond the rhetoric of pluralism

Suggestions for an "inside-the-mainstream" heterodoxy

David Colander

Introduction

Most observers would agree that a healthy field of study needs diversity and a vibrant and open market for ideas. Thus, it would seem that calls for pluralism in economics, such as have been made by self-described heterodox economists, would be welcomed by the mainstream economics profession. They haven't been; the calls have been essentially ignored by the mainstream, leading some heterodox economists to argue that the mainstream of economics is unpluralistic, closed-minded, and ideologically biased. In turn, heterodox calls for pluralism are seen by many in the mainstream as simply calls for the mainstream to listen to the heterodox economist's particular point of view, and not as true calls for pluralism.

Because it fails to achieve the desired ends, I find the rhetoric of pluralism unhelpful. Heterodox calls for pluralism do not increase openness or foster communication between heterodox and mainstream economists because such calls suggest that mainstream economists somehow do not favor openness to alternative views, and that the reason why mainstream economists are not open to heterodox ideas is because mainstream economists are closed-minded. Seeing the mainstream's rejection of their ideas as due to the mainstream's closed-mindedness may make heterodox economists feel better, but it is not a way to open up dialog between mainstream and heterodoxy. Some mainstream economists may indeed be closed-minded, just as some heterodox economists are. But that's life. Other mainstream economists are open-minded, and, in my view, it is toward those open-minded economists that heterodox economists should be directing their arguments. It is time for heterodox groups to move beyond the rhetoric of pluralism.

One can debate endlessly whether the mainstream of the profession is pluralistic. In some ways it is, and in other ways it isn't. For heterodox groups to dwell on ways in which the profession is unpluralistic doesn't gain them anything in terms of furthering their views with those mainstream economists who are open to change. While I agree with heterodox critics that mainstream economics has entrenched views, and has developed structures to protect those views, I do not see this as unusual or something unique to the field of economics. It is simply how the real world works. The heterodox groups with which I am familiar have as entrenched views as does the mainstream, and oftentimes the institutional protections are stronger within heterodox groups than they are within mainstream groups. So, in my view, it makes little sense to rail against such structures that naturally develop within any ongoing system.

In this chapter I advocate an alternative strategy – what might be called an "inside-the-mainstream" heterodoxy. As opposed to emphasizing the non-pluralistic aspects of the mainstream, this strategy emphasizes opening up dialog with that part of the mainstream that is open to change. As we discuss in Colander *et al.* (2004) this part of the mainstream is much larger than is often portrayed by heterodox economists. Mainstream economics is not neoclassical and cannot usefully be seen as a monolithic group with a single "orthodox" view. Instead it is a complex adaptive system of many competing views – views often as diverse as those held by heterodox economists. The mainstream is characterized by multiple layers of distinctions and gray areas of understanding about scope, method, and interpretation of results. At any one time, one view in the mainstream may be dominant, but that dominance does not necessarily reflect an entrenched orthodoxy, and it is not necessarily the view of all in the mainstream; it simply represents the way the intellectual forces play out at this particular time. Because of the multifacetedness of the mainstream, it is not *beliefs* that separate mainstream from heterodoxy; it is *attitude* and willingness to compete within a given set of rules and institutional structures. Mainstream economists are willing to compete within those rules; heterodox economists aren't.

Because mainstream economists are limited by implicit and explicit institutional norms and rules, their beliefs, their research, and their teaching, all may differ (Colander 2005a). For example, just because one works on general equilibrium models does not mean that one accepts that general equilibrium is an acceptable description of the economy. Similarly, just because one works on game theory does not mean that one believes most people are perfectly rational. Research and beliefs can differ. Mainstream researchers' decisions about the subject matter they will study, the methods they use, and what they teach are part of a complicated set of practical, strategic decisions that do not necessarily reflect their deep views about how the economy works or what are interesting questions.

Because the mainstream has highly restrictive limitations on method and scope, for them, many ideas and issues are outside the purview of economics. But in the best of the mainstream economists, underneath any seeming orthodoxy is often an openness to ideas and a desire to see economics progress and consider these difficult issues. But to be open to any one else's ideas about such questions, these open-minded mainstream economists must be convinced that the person raising the questions understands the reasoning that led mainstream economics to avoid that question and to follow a more traditional mainstream approach.

In my view too many heterodox economists begin with the premise that mainstream economists don't understand the problems and limitations with

38   *D. Colander*

"orthodox" mainstream arguments, and that it is the heterodox economist's job to point them out. That approach stops dialog. Such heterodox economists have little chance of communicating with open-minded mainstream economists since, almost by definition, that heterodox critic has not recognized the deep understanding of the issues that these open-minded mainstream economist have, or at least think they have. Communication fails, natural allies are kept apart, and entrenched views are reinforced rather than attacked.

The alternative strategy for heterodox economists that I support is a strategy built on opening lines of communication. It does not emphasize distinctions between heterodoxy and mainstream but rather deemphasizes them. It attempts to establish lines of communication among all economists. I suggest that young heterodox-leaning future economists will be more effective critics if they follow this alternative strategy.

Why a change in heterodox approach is needed

Mainstream economics would benefit from much more interaction with heterodox economists. That isn't happening. Heterodox economics is losing ground, and their ideas are not getting a hearing from the mainstream profession. In fact, heterodox economics is not only losing ground, it is not even holding its own; it is being squeezed out of the university academy, as deans and other decision makers respond to pressure from mainstream economists to support mainstream economics, not heterodox economics. The case of Notre Dame is but the most recent case, and now the squeeze on heterodox views is moving to Europe as well. This is leading to a loss in diversity in the profession, which I see as bad for economics.

In trying to understand what can be done about this squeeze, it is important to think about it from an administrator's perspective. Few administrators are in a position to make judgments about what economic ideas are best, so he or she naturally turns to a ranking or to outside experts for guidance. Numerous published rankings have developed, which all come to quite similar results because they all reflect the same natural science ranking system, which is a system that determines rankings on quality-weighted journal article publications and citations, in an attempt to determine importance and influence.

I fully agree with heterodox economists that the existing ranking approach that has developed in economics is far from optimal and is in many ways perverse. It deemphasizes subjective valuation of ideas. It encourages fads. It directs research away from major ideas that will improve society and directs research toward clever, but relatively unimportant, publishable articles. It gives no value to books and little or no value to traditional publishing outlets for heterodox economists. It also gives no value to the many other contributions economists make, such as teaching and policy advising. It leads researchers to focus their research output on a selected set of journal article publications, even though efficient scholarly communication on many issues would take place through Internet discussion and postings.

Unfortunately, the system is what it is, and I am not sure how it can be changed without the development of an alternative ranking system. (That's why I think that developing alternative ranking systems that administrators would find both acceptable and compelling, as achieving the ends that they want to achieve, should be a front burner research issue for heterodox economics groups). But despite any unfairness, even if the current ranking system is unfair, it is a system that heterodox economists will have to live with and operate within.

One reason why no better ranking system has developed is that it is extremely difficult to independently judge the "best" research in a field where empirical data are generally insufficient to guide researchers in choosing the "best" idea. What is "best" will be, to some degree, internally defined within the profession and will have some degree of arbitrariness to it. The context within which the idea is expressed, and by whom it is expressed, will both contribute to its being considered a "good" idea. A second reason why is that, for all its faults, the current ranking system has a number of advantages. First, it is transparent. All economists, heterodox and orthodox, know what it is and how it is calculated, and can choose to play by it or not. Second, it is a ranking system that is not directly tied to any particular ideology. The higher you score on the "rankings" the more desirable you are to economics departments. To most departments it matters less what you have to say and matters more that you have said it in the right journals. The ideology is there, as it inevitably will be in any research, but it is indirect, not direct.[1]

Most mainstream journal editors would gladly create controversy and do not see themselves as promoting any specific orthodoxy, although implicitly I agree they often do. They are open to new ideas if those ideas are expressed in the right form. That means that the ideas are embedded in a formal model or are buttressed by rigorous statistical analysis (even if that analysis requires the use of poor proxies for what one is trying to measure), and/or are pushing the envelope on a statistical or analytical technique. As I discuss in Colander (2007), graduate economics students at top schools do not feel limited by any orthodoxy in what issues they look at, and the directions that the top mainstream economists convey to their graduate students are to "tell me something I don't already know," not to "tell me something that fits an orthodox mold."[2]

I'm not saying that the mainstream is openly looking to modern heterodox economics for ideas. Telling anyone "something they don't already know" is difficult, and telling extremely bright economists who have succeeded in the profession, and who are being given the accolades of the profession, "something they don't already know" is very hard indeed. But I am saying that the best of the mainstream are open to new ideas and will work hard to see that new ideas get nurtured, as long as those ideas fit their view of science and of what "good economics" are.[3]

It is that openness to competing ideas that has led to the recent turmoil within mainstream economics. Today mainstream economics should not be thought of as a static entity, but rather as a complex adaptive system in which a variety of ideas and approaches compete. Within the mainstream, broadly defined, we have econophysicists developing models of zero-rationality agents, behavioral economists developing models of non-rational choice, and complexity economists arguing that the stochastic dynamic general equilibrium model is almost useless in providing insight into the macro economy. We also have experimental economists changing the way economics is done and evolutionary game theorists changing the overall frame of vision of economics. The mainstream profession is abuzz with competing ideas and approaches. While almost none of these new ideas and approaches are core mainstream, they are acceptable to the mainstream, despite the fact that they are "heterodox" ideas in reference to the orthodox neoclassical thought, which is what most heterodox economists have in mind when they talk about orthodoxy.

In my use of the term "mainstream" I include all these ideas, and more. While many mainstream economists consider these new ideas stupid, and many of the closed-minded ones, of which I agree there are many, will not even consider them, the best of that mainstream will. What I am arguing is that heterodox economists should promote a dialog with this "best of the mainstream" group, and that there is an environment at the edge of the mainstream where heterodoxy can exist and possibly even prosper.

Two paths for heterodoxy

If the mainstream is open to heterodox ideas, at least on the edge of the mainstream, what accounts for the difficulty that most self-defined heterodox economists face? I see two reasons. The first is that all ideas face enormous competition in the economics profession; it is not easy getting one's ideas heard. The top graduate schools recruit very bright students and train them in how to write papers with the right combination of technique and content that will get them a job, get them published, and get them tenure. They create graduates who will succeed in the existing environment. Heterodox programs have not done that; they have tended to see themselves as outside of the mainstream. Heterodox graduate programs generally have trained students in their particular heterodox tradition and have not given significant training in the latest developments in mainstream economics, in advanced analytical or empirical techniques, or in how to write an article that will advance them in a mainstream-controlled environment.

That would be fine if these heterodox students were being sent out into an environment that valued that heterodox tradition, but all too often these heterodox students are sent out into an environment controlled by the mainstream that is hostile to the heterodox tradition and to the way in which they were trained. All too often these heterodox students aren't being equipped with the tools necessary to survive in that environment outside of some protected heterodox niches, which are becoming smaller generation by generation. Regardless of how bright these heterodox economists are, in competition with the mainstream-trained young economists who have been primed to survive in the existing environment, most of the young heterodox economists naturally lose out. The reality is that effective "inside-the-mainstream" heterodoxy requires not only solid technical skills, but rather superior technical skills. The only ones who are allowed to break the rules are those who have demonstrated a full command of them.

A related reason why young heterodox economists have such a hard time is that while the mainstream is open to ideas, it is not open to the form that those ideas take. Mainstream economics is a highly restricted conversation, with a strong commitment to limiting the conversation to those ideas that fit into a formal mathematical model and which allow econometric consideration. To enter the mainstream conversation, models and econometrics have to be blended in just the right way to convince the mainstream profession that the author has something to add.

This limitation of form of expression leads mainstream economists to work on only those sets of ideas that their tools can shed some light on. Other issues are not worked on, not because they are not considered important, but because the mainstream economists believe that they cannot say anything about them in a way that can enter the economics conversation. Mainstream graduate students recognize that the conventions that have developed in economics are highly limiting. As one graduate student noted in discussions with me, sociologists look at important issues that they can't say anything about, while economists look at unimportant issues that they can say something about.

Heterodox economists rail against these conventions, and they violate them; they choose to talk about what they consider important issues, even if they don't have the tools to do it in a manner that fits the mainstream conventions. That unwillingness to accept mainstream conventions about form is in large part what separates out what might be called an "inside-the-mainstream" heterodox economist from an "outside-the-mainstream" heterodox economist. In my view, it is primarily heterodox economists' unwillingness to accept the mainstream conventions about form, less than the particular ideas or ideology that they hold, that is the distinguishing characteristic of the "outside-the-mainstream" heterodox economics.

I am not criticizing heterodox economists for not accepting mainstream conventions; I am simply pointing out that in doing so they are essentially shutting themselves out of the mainstream conversation and making it very difficult for them, and more importantly for their students, to succeed in an environment controlled by the mainstream.[4]

Despite my concerns, my preferred form of communication is much closer to the heterodox approach than it is to the mainstream economic approach. Thus, I am highly sympathetic to the heterodox complaints about form. I agree that just because the available tools can't handle an issue does not mean that the issue should not be considered by economists. I also agree that somehow the profession should be broad enough to include multiple frames of communication, so that when the tools become available, there is a framework of economic thought to tie together with those tools. The question is how best to bring that about.

Here is where I differ from most heterodox economists. Even though I share

42   *D. Colander*

many of the concerns of self-described heterodox economists, I work hard to carry on a dialog with the mainstream and to put the heterodox concerns in a way that the mainstream will hear and will consider. I admit; I seldom succeed, but at least they will talk to me.[5] My approach is different from that of many self-described heterodox economists. They carry on their own conversation and seldom enter into the mainstream conversation. In the long run, I suspect that for most heterodox groups, it is a losing strategy – a strategy that will result in heterodox traditions being further squeezed from the profession. Hence, I suggest that heterodox groups consider an alternative "inside-the-mainstream" strategy. Specifically, my suggested approach is that some heterodox economists consider seeing themselves within this environment, rather than seeing themselves as existing solely in the heterodox environment. Essentially, I am suggesting a Fattah-type approach to the mainstream rather than a Hammas-type approach. This "inside-the-mainstream" approach would engage the mainstream as much as possible and be more open to accepting mainstream conventions about form than most heterodox economists are willing to do.

I don't expect many of those who are established in the heterodox movement to choose this approach. The wounds of the battles are too raw. And it is true that they are providing an important service; there are benefits to the profession from an "outside-the-mainstream" heterodoxy that points out its foibles and creates an alternative – benefits that do not exist for an "inside-the-mainstream" heterodoxy, who are always close to being co-opted. But being an "outside-the-mainstream" heterodox economist is a tough life, especially for young heterodox economists. I present these ideas in the hope that some of the younger heterodox economists will consider it as an alternative.

Below, I list some suggestions for those in the heterodox community who are interested in exploring this approach or in opening a dialog with the mainstream and becoming part of the "inside-the-mainstream" heterodoxy.[6]

Suggestions for an "inside-the-mainstream" heterodoxy

Criticize the best of the profession, not the worst

As I have discussed above, the economics profession has much diversity of thought and play of ideas. Heterodox criticisms of a mainstream orthodoxy that do not take that diversity into account are unlikely to be heard. Criticisms that see the profession as a complex adaptive system are much more likely to be heard. Whenever I hear a heterodox economist criticizing the "neoclassical orthodoxy," I can only feel that they are speaking to the converted and will not have any chance of entering into a conversation with the mainstream.

Concentrate on areas where you can make a difference

As I have argued in Colander (2005a), principles textbooks are full of neoclassical ideas and often are not consistent with much of the latest thinking in the profession. One of the reasons textbooks are inconsistent with the best thinking in the profession is that the mainstream does not focus on teaching or pedagogy. This lack of concern about teaching by the mainstream leaves an opening for "inside-the-mainstream" heterodox economists. By addressing their arguments to the narrow issue of what economists teach in their textbooks and not to the issue of economists' research, heterodox economists are on much firmer ground and can get a better hearing from mainstream journals.

See the heterodox conversation as an incubator for ideas

I am sympathetic to those heterodox economists who want to stay out of the mainstream debate. Ideas need nurturing, and the environment for ideas within mainstream economics is unfriendly. Its requirement that ideas be formally modeled make it hard for novel ideas to develop. Heterodox economics communities provide an incubator environment within which ideas can germinate and sprout. They develop their own institutional structure which provides institutional validation of their ideas and support mechanisms which allow the ideas to thrive within its limited environment. They are wonderful idea incubators, which allow people to have more friendly critics around who treat their ideas more gently than they would be treated in mainstream economics. This gentle treatment gives the ideas a chance to germinate and perhaps even to sprout. Thus, the "outside-the-mainstream" heterodox community plays an important role.

Prepare your ideas to leave the incubator

Ideas cannot remain in the incubator forever, and for the heterodox communities to serve the function of incubator, they must transfer the idea, developed in heterodoxy, up to the mainstream. All too often, what happens with ideas developed in heterodox economics is that they remain in their incubator and do not cross-pollinate with mainstream ideas. Both heterodox and mainstream economics are worse off for it. Thus, for the most part, the new ideas that have entered the mainstream in recent years, even though they parallel ideas heterodox economists have pushed for years, did not enter through heterodoxy, and the mainstream work almost never cites heterodox work.

For example, until recently the analytic and computational tools to consider uncertainty were not developed, and Post Keynesian economists who emphasized uncertainty fell outside-the-mainstream conversation. With the development of complexity tools in mathematics, today the ideas of Post Keynesians are being integrated without any reference to Post Keynesians. Similarly with Institutional Economics' concern with socioeconomic aspects and institutional feedback on individuals. Before the development of evolutionary game theory, such concerns could not be integrated into mainstream theory; today they can be, and are. But it is being done with almost no reference to Institutionalists who kept these ideas alive as mainstream economics completely ignored them.

To make the transfer from the heterodox incubator to the mainstream, the ideas must be developed in a formal model and buttressed by technical empirical work. This transfer is difficult; often, the reason the mainstream has shied away from the complicated issues that heterodox economists see as important is highly likely to have been that mainstream economists thought the issues were intractable given the existing tools, not because the mainstream did not believe such issues were important. What this means is that for the heterodox ideas to enter the mainstream, the tools must change. They can only be dealt with formally by bringing more sophisticated mathematics and statistics to bear on the issue than the mainstream is currently using.

See mathematicians and technical economists as your allies, not your nemesis

Mainstream economics is a formal modeling field; it is not going to change. It has chosen the issues it has because the tools it has available could be used to shed light on those issues. Advanced mathematicians can bring in new ideas because they have new ways of looking at issues that mainstream economists know were important, but shied away from because they didn't have the techniques to handle them. Thus, there is a natural symbiosis of heterodox economics with advanced applied mathematical economics and statistics. That symbiosis has not been developed, in part because heterodox economists have been anti-math. In my view heterodox economists should be precisely the opposite – they should welcome higher and higher levels of mathematical and statistical formalization into economics because that is what will allow the formal consideration of the issues they want considered.

Most heterodox economists don't have the skills to do that formal mathematical work, and I am not arguing that they should develop them. But I am arguing that "inside-the-mainstream" heterodox economics should have a working knowledge of what is going on in high-level mathematics and statistics, with an eye to see if new analytic techniques may be able to address some of the issues they believe should be addressed. Where there are, the "inside-the-mainstream" heterodox economists should be exploring possibilities for joint work with ultra mathematicians and ultra statisticians, who do have the skills and the interest in ideas. There is a natural connection between these two groups.

Become involved in mainstream organizations

Organizations such as the American Economic Association and European Economic Association are generally controlled in theory by the members, but in practice they are controlled by a small group of mainstream economists. Few people vote in elections, and the nominating committees keep the control in the hands of a small group of elite graduate school economists. Whereas individual departments and economists don't have to be pluralistic, these organizations must at least appear to be. "Inside-the-mainstream" heterodox economists would become involved in these organizations; they would vote in them and, if they have enough support, would influence the profession through their role in these organizations. I see heterodox economists volunteering to serve on committees and coming up with suggestions for new programs to "broaden" the education and training of economists that could get support in the broader mainstream community.

Worry less about methodology

Many heterodox economists focus on methodological issues. For an "inside-the-mainstream" heterodox economist, that is a mistake. Unless he or she is a philosopher specializing in methodology, just about everything to be said about methodology has been said. To think that anyone but a specialist is going to have much to add on methodology is similar to a neophyte thinking he can do better than an index fund in investing.

Instead of complaining or discussing methodological problems, an "inside-the-mainstream" heterodox economist would be working on specific institutional problems that both underlie and affect methodology, such as creating an alternative ranking system. If the current ranking system does not put heterodox research in an appropriate light, he or she would develop a research agenda designed to create an alternative ranking system that does, and explain why it is a better system. There are many foibles with the current ranking systems, especially as a ranking system for economists who are primarily teachers of economics or are involved in "hands-on" applied policy. Heterodox interests fit much better into what undergraduate teaching needs, and were a separate "teaching-oriented" research ranking system developed, heterodox economics would come out much better in the rankings.

Don't dwell on unfairness

If there is to be a dialog, it has to originate from heterodox economists. The mainstream has the power and has little incentive to give it up, and for the most part is totally unaware of a heterodoxy even existing.[7] Heterodox economists today find themselves in precarious positions and are being squeezed out institutionally both in the United States and in Europe. Is it fair that most of the effort toward communication will have to be on the heterodox economist's side? Absolutely not. But so what? Regardless of how unfair the profession is to you, it does not help to feel sorry for yourself.

I fully agree, heterodox economics are discriminated against and ill-treated. But complaining about it will not change the situation when the other side has the power. So, I see no other option than to live with it. If you define your role in a way that allows you to succeed within the institutions that exist, you have more of a chance of changing the institutions than you do if you are marginalized. Toward that end, I do not see it as especially helpful to distinguish oneself as a heterodox economist, and not just as an economist who has certain beliefs. To differentiate oneself as heterodox places one in opposition to an orthodoxy that the mainstream doesn't believe exists, and thereby reduces the possibility of communication with the very people who I believe heterodox economists should be communicating with.

Conclusion

I do not expect my suggestions to be well received by the heterodox community, just as my ideas are generally not well received in the mainstream community. I offer them in the hope of establishing better lines of communication between mainstream and heterodox economists. I am not arguing that all, or even most, established heterodox economists should become "inside-the-mainstream" heterodox economists. Most established heterodox economists have found a comfortable institutional niche for themselves, which allows them to expound their ideas to a friendly group of fellow economists and students. They can do quite well as an "outside-the-mainstream" heterodox economist.

The reason I wrote this chapter is that the trend I see occurring in the profession is one in which the heterodox community is increasingly marginalized. It is becoming harder and harder for heterodox students to exist in the "outside-the-mainstream" heterodox niches. In my view, the heterodox niche that currently exists may not be a sustainable niche within the economics profession. In any case heterodox students should expect that the niche will come under increasing competitive pressures from the mainstream. Unless the heterodox program expands within the economic profession, or otherwise grows through interdisciplinary programs which establish themselves outside of economists' normal niches (as feminist economics has done), heterodox students will generally have a harder time than their professors, and their students' students will have an even harder time existing in that niche.

In my view a dynamic profession is a blend of many different ideas, all competing to be heard. Currently self-described heterodox ideas are not being heard. The "inside-the-mainstream" heterodoxy approach suggested in this chapter offers a way for young heterodox economics to exist in the mainstream environment and for heterodox ideas to become blended in with mainstream ideas. It is a heterodoxy that is continually changing and multifaceted. It is opportunistic and concentrates on those niches where heterodox ideas can flourish. The theoretical part of this heterodoxy would likely integrate with researchers from physics, math, and statistics programs that allow heterodox economists to push the frontier of techniques as well as ideas. The non-technical part of this heterodoxy would concentrate on teaching undergraduate economics and would provide an undergraduate teaching of economics that is much broader than that which is currently taught. Improving that teaching would be a major contribution to both the profession and the society.

Moving beyond the rhetoric of pluralism   47

Notes

1 I discuss my view of how ideology enters mainstream economics in Colander (2005b).
2 There is, of course, no shortage of closed-minded mainstream economists, just as there is no shortage of closed-minded heterodox economists. In my considerations of mainstream and heterodox economists, I am talking about the best of both groups.
3 For example, Ken Arrow played a critical role in guiding and nurturing the Santa Fe complexity work, and in supporting Brian Arthur's attempt to broaden economics, even though he was associated with the general equilibrium theory that it was meant to replace.
4 Were mainstream economists to accept this broader form of communication, new methods of deciding what is good or not, including new rankings, would have to develop. I suspect that these alternative rankings and methods of choosing among ideas would likely be *as* discriminatory to heterodox ideas and to heterodox economists, *or more so*, than the current ones. In any case, the economics profession would be a far different profession than it is now. But I am not sure that it would be a better profession. From the vantage point of a supporter of heterodox ideas, a commitment to form over content in limiting the conversation has much to be said for it because it makes it less likely that ideology will limit the conversation.
5 My tendency to try to promote dialog between different groups has made me the only white male Anglo Saxon protestant token that I know of. When heterodox economists are looking for a token mainstream economist to talk to they often invite me. When mainstream economists are looking for a token heterodox economist to invite, they often invite me.
6 The suggestions here are an expansion of the argument developed in Colander (2003) and Colander, Holt, and Rosser (2007).
7 I initially entitled this chapter "What does mainstream economics think of heterodox economics?" I changed it because my honest answer to that question was that they don't think about it. For the most part, the mainstream is unaware of the existence of an "outside-the-mainstream" heterodoxy.

References

Colander, D. (2003) "Post Walrasian Macroeconomics and Heterodoxy: Thinking Outside the Heterodox Box," *International Journal of Political Economy*, 33(2): 68–81.
—— (2005a) "What Economists Teach and What Economists Do," *Journal of Economic Education*, 36(3): 249–260.
—— (2005b) "Economics as an Ideologically Challenged Science," *Revue de Philosophie Economique*, 1: 3–24.
—— (2007) *The Making of an Economist Redux*, Princeton, NJ: Princeton University Press.
Colander, D., Holt, R.P.F., and Rosser, Jr., B. (2004). *The Changing Face of Economics: Conversations with Cutting Edge Economists*, Ann Arbor: University of Michigan Press.
—— (2007). "Live and Dead Issues in the Methodology of Economics," *Journal of Post Keynesian Economics*, 30 (2): 303–312.

17

CHAPTER 36

CREATING HUMBLE ECONOMISTS

A Code of Ethics for Economists

DAVID COLANDER

INTRODUCTION

FROM the movie *Inside Job*, one gets the sense that economists are ethically challenged because they take payments for writing papers that say what the funders of their research want them to say. The sense conveyed by the movie is that economists are for sale. In my view, that is far from the case; economists are not for-hire any more than a similar group of academic experts, and probably significantly less than many, because by academic standards, economists tend to be well paid. The money given to economists by groups that support the policy positions they are espousing, either in the form of honoraria for a talk, payment as a director or consultant to the company, or funding for research, is seldom the reason economists are supporting their policy positions. The causal link generally goes the other way around. Thus, though I support reasonable, minimally invasive measures that increase transparency of funding, I see such measures as having little effect on the ethical failings of the economics profession. Economists will espouse the positions they espouse whether or not the funding takes place. If academic economists were primarily interested in the money, they could earn significantly more income by leaving academia and entering business or finance. Money, or biased support of research, in my view, is not the most serious ethical issue facing the economics profession. The ethical problem of economists is deeper.

The more serious ethical problem of economics has little to do with the funding of economic research on either the right or the left. It has to do with lack of humility. By this I mean that we economists have a tendency to convey more scientific certainty in our policy positions than the theory and evidence objectively would allow. Too many economists are willing to make seemingly definitive scientific statements about policy based on models, that they know, or should know, are highly imperfect. It was that tendency that I (Colander et al., 2009) criticized the profession for in the recent crisis. Back in 1927, Lionel Robbins (Robbins, 1927) argued that "what precision economists can claim at this stage is largely a sham precision. In the present state of knowledge, the man who can claim for economic science much exactitude is a quack." (176). Despite the advances economic science has made, that remains true today. Yet, all too often economists allow lay people and policymakers to believe that our policy suggestions have far more scientific foundation than a neutral objective observer would give them.

Good economists recognize our tendency to do this, but too often allow other individuals and other economists to convey their findings and policy views in ways that make those views seem far more scientifically grounded than they are. This tendency is exacerbated by an ethical failing in the reporting profession, which, when looking for a good story, will gravitate to economists who most overstate the conclusions of policy. A newspaper article concluding with "This finding is at best suggestive, and goes far beyond what one can say with scientific certainty" does not endear a reporter to his or her editor. Thus, not only are economists as a group not humble enough, but what lay people are presented as economists' policy recommendations also are often the policy recommendations of the least humble economist. In summary, my argument is that lack of humility in conveying the limitations of their results is the most serious ethical problem facing economists; it played a much larger role in causing the recent financial crisis than did the type of payments highlighted by *Inside Job*. Thus, any new code of ethics for economists should deal with that humility problem.

APPLIED SCIENCE VS. ENGINEERING

How does one go about creating humble economist? I don't have a complete answer to that, but one step toward doing so would involve a change in the self-image of applied economists. Currently applied economists see themselves as applied scientists. My argument in this chapter is that that needs to change. Applied economists should see themselves as engineers, not as applied scientists, as Howard Wolowitzes, rather than Sheldon Coopers or even Leonard Hofstadters. That change in self-image would be an important step toward creating a more humble economics profession and would bring about major changes in their method, which would contribute toward creating a more ethical economics profession.

I suspect that to many economists my argument that most economists should see themselves as engineers, not applied scientists, will seem strange. Isn't engineering just applied science? My answer is no, it isn't; if anything science is applied engineering. Engineering and applied science can be distinguished by their primary goals and methods.

The primary goal of science is finding the truth—understanding for the sake of understanding. Science's methods are consistent with that goal, and those methods have evolved into relatively formal prescriptions about methods that guide and limit scientists in their work. Back of the envelop calculations, value judgments, guestimates, heuristic models, rough generalizations from case studies, commonsense observation, and fudge factors are not the methods to establish scientific truths. The scientific method requires rigorous analysis and precise conventions to counter individuals' tendency toward fast pattern completion. A set of conventions about how to do empirical analysis; how to develop models; the appropriate level of statistical significance of empirical work such as appropriate t values; and the appropriate structure of experiments such as randomized, double blind, placebo-controlled experiments, become part of its method.

Doing good science is costly and time consuming, but the amount of time or effort it takes to resolve an issue is not deemed a legitimate consideration in establishing a scientific result. A scientific truth is timeless, and if your goal is true understanding, then anything less than the methodological gold standard is not good enough to establish the truth. Applied science involves the translation of scientific findings to solve real-world problems and, in principle, it holds itself up to the same standards as does science because the primary goal is scientific understanding. Applied science has science and the scientific method at its core.

Engineering is different than science. The primary goal of engineers is solving a specific problem with available resources, and an engineering solution can be judged only relative to its cost. Whereas the scientific method does not allow shortcuts to save time and money, the engineering method does. Engineering is by nature applied, and it need not have a scientific core, or general formal methodological prescriptions based on the scientific methods. Billy Vaughn Koen (2003), who has written what appears to be the current standard methodological treatise for engineering, defines the engineering method as "The strategy for causing the best change in a poorly understood or uncertain situation within the available resources" (7). He describes an engineer as an individual who solves problems using engineering heuristics. He argues that an engineer makes no pretense of having found the truth, or having found the "correct" model.[1] An engineer focuses on finding solutions that work, and uses whatever methods he or she finds best leads to finding a solution to the particular problem he or she is trying to solve. In the engineering field, there are no rigid prescriptions guiding method.

Engineering uses science when appropriate, but where science does not have an answer to a part of the question that is needed to come to a policy recommendation, an engineer finds the best answer he or she can, and uses that. An engineering method might involve back of the envelop calculations, input from other specialties, guestimates, and individual judgment—whatever is needed to provide the best answer an engineer can provide to the problem he or she is trying to solve. In providing an engineer's recommendation, an engineer follows the "weakest link principle"—and presents

---

[1]   Koen argues that the engineering method, which he calls a universal method, predates the scientific method, and that the scientific method is simply an application of the engineering method when the research goal is to find the truth rather than to solve a particular problem.

his or her recommendation with no more certainty than he or she has in the weakest link of the analysis needed to arrive at a solution.

This difference in focus between applied science and engineering means that the engineering method can differ significantly from the applied science method. If a rule of thumb seems to work in similar cases, it will be incorporated even though it has no scientific foundation. If arriving at a policy recommendation involves making value judgments, the engineering method makes what it believes are reasonable value judgments. There is no need to shy away from them. If the data don't exist that meet appropriate levels of statistical significance, or if it doesn't seem cost effective to collect and analyze the data to that level of precision, the engineer uses the best data he or she can to arrive at the solution he or she believes appropriate.

I am not arguing that engineering uses an "anything goes" methodology. Acceptable heuristics, which is what engineers call methodology, develop endogenously within the engineering profession about which approaches are acceptable and which aren't. These state-of-the-art methods change over time (which is why "state of the art" is an important concept in any engineering methodology) and are developed by the engineering specialists in a particular field. Acceptable heuristics can differ in different branches of engineering, and there is no overarching methodogical requirement, other than "what seems to work."

I am fully aware of the ambiguity of the term "science," and I agree that, in principle, it makes no difference whether someone calls him- or herself an applied scientist or an engineer —it is just a name. But, as I hope I have made clear in the preceding text, the method that an applied researcher uses matters a lot, both in how an applied researchers goes about his or her research and in how he or she presents research findings. To the degree that self-classification affects method, it makes a big difference.

My argument is that most economists (and most applied natural scientists as well) are actually engineers, who, in practice often go about their research (and should go about their research) using an engineering method. The problem I see is that they don't use it enough, and they don't make it clear to others that they are using an engineering method, not a scientific method. Their self-classification as applied scientists leads them to contort their methodological approach to attempt to make it seem to fit a scientific method, and to present their research findings and conclusions as scientific truths, not as rough and ready engineering insights that can be useful in looking at particular problems. Seeing oneself as a scientist undermines the humility the actual practice of applied economics warrants.

Presenting findings as scientific findings give those findings an aura of validity that goes beyond the method used. An example of what I mean can be seen in econometric findings, which are often presented as having met scientific standards, when in fact the findings are often engineering guestimates based on reasonable proxies. Because even the reasonable proxies are often highly imperfect, the empirical results should be seen as highly questionable regardless of the statistical precision of the analysis. To present results as meeting a 95 percent confidence interval can lead nonspecialists to have more confidence in the results than is warranted. Applied economists data mine and choose models based on analytic tractability, not appropriateness to the process. That all makes sense, but to present results of work that uses these reasonable ad hoc engineering methods as scientific results, and not as engineering results, does not.

My argument is that most applied economics involves many of the same pragmatic methods as does engineering. But we economists tend to be less open about our actual methods because they seem to violate scientific methodology. We think of applied economics as applied science, which places scientific models and scientific facts at the center of our analysis. For example, we justify a Dynamic Stochastic General Equilibrium (DSGE) modeling strategy because it is more "scientific" than other modeling strategies even though it is forcing our macro models into a form that intuitively doesn't fit the macro reality. With sufficient gyrations, DSGE models can be made to fit, but from an engineering standpoint it is unclear what one has gained from the analytic contortions necessary to do so, and the loss of not using models that can better capture the likely problems faced by a macroeconomy likely overwhelm any gains from having a broad formal model. The situation is similar with standard macro models.

An engineer's approach to modeling such a complex system as the macro economy would likely focus much more on statistical models and methods of pulling patterns out of the data. It would explore a wide variety of formal models to gain analytic insight, and then would integrate the many variety of models with the statistical models to interpret the patterns. That would involve a fundamentally different way of doing macro and of thinking about macro problems. The situation is similar with micro models. Economists focus much of their applied micro policy discussion on Pareto optimal solutions even though we know that all actual policies will violate Pareto optimality. We can contort our micro policy models designed to provide Pareto optimal solutions to provide insight into non-Pareto optimal solutions, but, generally, that contortion comes at a cost. It means that we spend less time discussing other models that better fit non-Pareto optimal solutions. They lead us away from "reasonable person solutions" that more closely reflect society's value judgments. An engineering applied microeconomics would likely have an entire branch devoted to measuring society's value judgments and integrating those judgments into applied policy instruments. Our scientific applied micro leaves the topic almost totally undiscussed.

My interest in this chapter is not in how economists' research methods and applied economics would change if economists saw themselves as engineers; it is in how economists' view of themselves and presentations of their findings would change if they saw themselves as engineers. My argument is that economists who see themselves as engineers would be much more humble in their presentation of results than are economists who see themselves as applied scientists. Because the engineering method is by nature pragmatic and often scientifically unjustified, and makes no claim to being the truth, an "economic engineer" would tend to be more modest about his or her work. Accepting that economists are engineers, not applied scientists, would take economic policy out of the realm of science and put it in the realm of engineering or art, where uncertainty reigns, and where the need for judgments is explicitly acknowledged. Debates in economic policy would move outside of economics, and the role that economic models play would change.

Applied economists as engineers would not claim scientific status for our policy pronouncements, and heuristics would develop to compare various policy pronouncements of different economists. Those heuristics would recognize that the judgments underlying policy pronouncements are subject to legitimate debate, and that debate about nuance would tend to make our policy pronouncements more humble.

A Code of Ethics for Economists

My goal in this chapter is not to make the argument for economists seeing themselves as engineers; I have dealt with that in another paper (Colander, 2011). My goal here is to explain how seeing ourselves as engineers, not applied scientists, would help us arrive at a code of ethics for economists. My hypothesis is the following: If it is true that economics is essentially engineering, then a code of ethics for engineers should nicely translate into a code of ethics for economists. I believe it does so. To demonstrate that, I went to the National Society of Professional Engineers and found their code of ethics. (http://www.nspe.org/Ethics/CodeofEthics/index.html). I then did a global change of the word "engineer" to "economist," and arrived at the following code, which I believe would make a good first effort at a code of ethics for the economics profession.

CODE OF ETHICS FOR ECONOMISTS (ADAPTED FROM THE CODE OF ETHICS FOR ENGINEERS)

Preamble

Economics is an important and learned profession. As members of this profession, economists are expected to exhibit the highest standards of honesty and integrity. Economics has a direct and vital impact on the quality of life for all people. Accordingly, the services provided by economists require honesty, impartiality, fairness, and equity, and must be dedicated to the protection of the public health, safety, and welfare. Economists must perform under a standard of professional behavior that requires adherence to the highest principles of ethical conduct.

I. Fundamental Canons

Economists, in the fulfillment of their professional duties, shall:

1. Hold paramount the safety, health, and welfare of the public.
2. Perform services only in areas of their competence.
3. Issue public statements only in an objective and truthful manner.

4. Act for each employer or client as faithful agents or trustees.
5. Avoid deceptive acts.
6. Conduct themselves honorably, responsibly, ethically, and lawfully so as to enhance the honor, reputation, and usefulness of the profession.

II. Rules of Practice

1. Economists shall hold paramount the safety, health, and welfare of the public.
   a. If economists' judgment is overruled under circumstances that endanger life or property, they shall notify their employer or client and such other authority as may be appropriate.
   b. Economists shall approve only those economics documents that are in conformity with applicable standards.
   c. Economists shall not reveal facts, data, or information without the prior consent of the client or employer except as authorized or required by law or this Code.
   d. Economists shall not permit the use of their name or associate in business ventures with any person or firm that they believe is engaged in fraudulent or dishonest enterprise.
   e. Economists shall not aid or abet the unlawful practice of economics by a person or firm.
   f. Economists having knowledge of any alleged violation of this Code shall report thereon to appropriate professional bodies and, when relevant, also to public authorities, and cooperate with the proper authorities in furnishing such information or assistance as may be required.
2. Economists shall perform services only in the areas of their competence.
   a. Economists shall undertake assignments only when qualified by education or experience in the specific technical fields involved.
   b. Economists shall not affix their signatures to any plans or documents dealing with subject matter in which they lack competence, nor to any plan or document not prepared under their direction and control.
   c. Economists may accept assignments and assume responsibility for coordination of an entire project and sign and seal the economics documents for the entire project, provided that each technical segment is signed and sealed only by the qualified Economists who prepared the segment.
3. Economists shall issue public statements only in an objective and truthful manner.
   a. Economists shall be objective and truthful in professional reports, statements, or testimony. They shall include all relevant and pertinent information in such reports, statements, or testimony, which should bear the date indicating when it was current.
   b. Economists may express publicly technical opinions that are founded upon knowledge of the facts and competence in the subject matter.

c. Economists shall issue no statements, criticisms, or arguments on technical matters that are inspired or paid for by interested parties, unless they have prefaced their comments by explicitly identifying the interested parties on whose behalf they are speaking, and by revealing the existence of any interest the economists may have in the matters.

4. Economists shall act for each employer or client as faithful agents or trustees.

   a. Economists shall disclose all known or potential conflicts of interest that could influence or appear to influence their judgment or the quality of their services.

   b. Economists shall not accept compensation, financial or otherwise, from more than one party for services on the same project, or for services pertaining to the same project, unless the circumstances are fully disclosed and agreed to by all interested parties.

   c. Economists shall not solicit or accept financial or other valuable consideration, directly or indirectly, from outside agents in connection with the work for which they are responsible.

   d. Economists in public service as members, advisors, or employees of a governmental or quasi-governmental body or department shall not participate in decisions with respect to services solicited or provided by them or their organizations in private or public economics practice.

   e. Economists shall not solicit or accept a contract from a governmental body on which a principal or officer of their organization serves as a member.

5. Economists shall avoid deceptive acts.

   a. Economists shall not falsify their qualifications or permit misrepresentation of their or their associates' qualifications. They shall not misrepresent or exaggerate their responsibility in or for the subject matter of prior assignments. Brochures or other presentations incident to the solicitation of employment shall not misrepresent pertinent facts concerning employers, employees, associates, joint venturers, or past accomplishments.

   b. Economists shall not offer, give, solicit, or receive, either directly or indirectly, any contribution to influence the award of a contract by public authority, or which may be reasonably construed by the public as having the effect or intent of influencing the awarding of a contract. They shall not offer any gift or other valuable consideration in order to secure work. They shall not pay a commission, percentage, or brokerage fee in order to secure work, except to a bona fide employee or bona fide established commercial or marketing agencies retained by them.

III. Professional Obligations

1. Economists shall be guided in all their relations by the highest standards of honesty and integrity.

   a. Economists shall acknowledge their errors and shall not distort or alter the facts.

   b. Economists shall advise their clients or employers when they believe a project will not be successful.

   c. Economists shall not accept outside employment to the detriment of their regular work or interest. Before accepting any outside economics employment, they will notify their employers.

   d. Economists shall not attempt to attract an economist from another employer by false or misleading pretenses.

   e. Economists shall not promote their own interest at the expense of the dignity and integrity of the profession.

2. Economists shall at all times strive to serve the public interest.

   a. Economists are encouraged to participate in civic affairs; career guidance for youths; and work for the advancement of the safety, health, and well-being of their community.

   b. Economists shall not complete, sign, or seal plans and/or specifications that are not in conformity with applicable economics standards. If the client or employer insists on such unprofessional conduct, they shall notify the proper authorities and withdraw from further service on the project.

   c. Economists are encouraged to extend public knowledge and appreciation of economics and its achievements.

   d. Economists are encouraged to adhere to the principles of sustainable development in order to protect the environment for future generations.

3. Economists shall avoid all conduct or practice that deceives the public.

   a. Economists shall avoid the use of statements containing a material misrepresentation of fact or omitting a material fact.

   b. Consistent with the foregoing, economists may advertise for recruitment of personnel.

   c. Consistent with the foregoing, economists may prepare articles for the lay or technical press, but such articles shall not imply credit to the author for work performed by others.

4. Economists shall not disclose, without consent, confidential information concerning the business affairs or technical processes of any present or former client or employer, or public body on which they serve.

   a. Economists shall not, without the consent of all interested parties, promote or arrange for new employment or practice in connection with a specific project for which the economist has gained particular and specialized knowledge.

   b. Economists shall not, without the consent of all interested parties, participate in or represent an adversary interest in connection with a specific project or proceeding in which the economist has gained particular specialized knowledge on behalf of a former client or employer.

5. Economists shall not be influenced in their professional duties by conflicting interests.

   a. Economists shall not accept financial or other considerations, including free economic designs, from material or equipment suppliers for specifying their product.

    b. Economists shall not accept commissions or allowances, directly or indirectly, from contractors or other parties dealing with clients or employers of the economist in connection with work for which the economist is responsible.

6. Economists shall not attempt to obtain employment or advancement or professional engagements by untruthfully criticizing other economists, or by other improper or questionable methods.

    a. Economists shall not request, propose, or accept a commission on a contingent basis under circumstances in which their judgment may be compromised.

    b. Economists in salaried positions shall accept part-time economics work only to the extent consistent with policies of the employer and in accordance with ethical considerations.

    c. Economists shall not, without consent, use equipment, supplies, laboratory, or office facilities of an employer to carry on outside private practice.

7. Economists shall not attempt to injure, maliciously or falsely, directly or indirectly, the professional reputation, prospects, practice, or employment of other economists. Economists who believe others are guilty of unethical or illegal practice shall present such information to the proper authority for action.

    a. Economists in private practice shall not review the work of another economist for the same client, except with the knowledge of such economist, or unless the connection of such economist with the work has been terminated.

    b. Economists in governmental, industrial, or educational employ are entitled to review and evaluate the work of other economists when so required by their employment duties.

    c. Economists in sales or industrial employ are entitled to make economics comparisons of represented products with products of other suppliers.

8. Economists shall accept personal responsibility for their professional activities, provided, however, that Economists may seek indemnification for services arising out of their practice for other than gross negligence, where the economist's interests cannot otherwise be protected.

    a. Economists shall conform with state registration laws in the practice of economics.

    b. Economists shall not use association with a noneconomist, a corporation, or partnership as a "cloak" for unethical acts.

9. Economists shall give credit for economics work to those to whom credit is due, and will recognize the proprietary interests of others.

    a. Economists shall, whenever possible, name the person or persons who may be individually responsible for designs, inventions, writings, or other accomplishments.

    b. Economists using designs supplied by a client recognize that the designs remain the property of the client and may not be duplicated by the economist for others without express permission.

   c. Economists, before undertaking work for others in connection with which the economist may make improvements, plans, designs, inventions, or other records that may justify copyrights or patents, should enter into a positive agreement regarding ownership.

   d. Economists' designs, data, records, and notes referring exclusively to an employer's work are the employer's property. The employer should indemnify the economist for use of the information for any purpose other than the original purpose.

   e. Economists shall continue their professional development throughout their careers and should keep current in their specialty fields by engaging in professional practice, participating in continuing education courses, reading in the technical literature, and attending professional meetings and seminars.

DISCUSSION

In adapting the code, I specifically only changed the terms "engineer" and "economist," and made no other changes. What was amazing to me is how little I saw that seemed inappropriate to me. In fact there was only one statement in the entire code that I found objectionable, and that was Statement 7-a.[2] This is in stark contrast to other codes of ethics that I explored for other groups such as lawyers or for subgroups of economists who have developed explicit codes. I even have more differences with George DeMartino's short "Economist's Oath" than I do with this engineer's code of ethics. For example, I would question DeMartino's paragraph in his Oath about "exposing oppression" and "giving voice to the needs and aspirations of the dispossessed," and his statement in favor of pluralism (DeMartino, 2011: 232).

It is not that I necessarily disagree with ethical sentiments behind these statements, but I have a serious problem with their ambiguity and the way in which they may be interpreted. For example, what if one believes that other's theoretical perspective is totally wrong? Then I would believe that one has a responsibility to point that out, and not be pluralistic. Similarly, how are we to say what "oppression" is, or what a "self-serving argument of the privileged" is? (DeMartino, 2011: 232). In my view, any oath or code of ethics should avoid such references to terms that are subject to ambiguous interpretation as much as possible.

---

[2] The statement is "Engineers in private practice shall not review the work of another engineer for the same client, except with the knowledge of such engineer, or unless the connection of such engineer with the work has been terminated." That statement provided more protection than I would believe is appropriate. But I see this as inappropriate for both economists and engineering. There should, in my view, be a general presumption that others will review and criticize one's work and no requirement that the person be informed that that is happening.

What was amazing to me is how well the engineer's code of ethics comported with my implicit code. This consistency of code exists even though the engineering profession operates quite differently than the economics profession in that engineering is generally private sector based, and economics more academic or public sector based. But the sentiments conveyed were consistent with the methodology I see as appropriate for applied economists.

Let me now turn to the question: Would adopting a variation of an engineering code of ethics make a difference? In practice, I suspect not, simply because I don't see codes of ethics as significantly affecting behavior. But were economists to accept that they were engineers, not scientists, and change their methodology and presentation of research results accordingly, it would make a major difference. To demonstrate the differences it would make, in the following I suggest some places where I believe economists would be required to change what they do to meet this ethical code.

- Rule II 1a (If economists' judgment is overruled under circumstances that endanger life or property, they shall notify their employer or client and such other authority as may be appropriate.) should have led the economists developing financial derivative models to warn the public. (It was this ethical failing that we highlighted in Colander et al., 2009.)
- Rule II 2a (Economists shall undertake assignments only when qualified by education or experience in the specific technical fields involved.) should have stopped many economists from making pronouncements about policy as economists, rather than making pronouncements as private individuals, which they are free to do.
- Rule II 2b (Economists shall not affix their signatures to any plans or documents dealing with subject matter in which they lack competence, nor to any plan or document not prepared under their direction and control.) should stop economists from advocating policy solutions outside of their specific area of expertise.
- Rule II 3a (Economists shall be objective and truthful in professional reports, statements, or testimony. They shall include all relevant and pertinent information in such reports, statements, or testimony, which should bear the date indicating when it was current.) should lead economists to emphasize more than they do how much economic theory changes over time, and does not reflect scientific truth, but rather engineering truth.
- Rule II 3c (Economists shall issue no statements, criticisms, or arguments on technical matters that are inspired or paid for by interested parties, unless they have prefaced their comments by explicitly identifying the interested parties on whose behalf they are speaking, and by revealing the existence of any interest the economists may have in the matters.) would catch the funding issues that *Inside Job* highlighted.
- Rule II 4a (Economists shall disclose all known or potential conflicts of interest that could influence or appear to influence their judgment or the quality of their

services.) goes beyond Rule 3c and places a restriction on broader conflicts of interests that often are more important than financial ones.

- Rule III 1b (Economists shall advise their clients or employers when they believe a project will not be successful.) is another important rule that would affect many economic consulting jobs, where it seems all too often economists come up with conclusions that fit the client wants to hear—conclusions that are sometimes referred to as "stadium project" conclusions because in studies these projects tend to have much bigger positive impacts than they have in practice.
- Rule III 6 (Economists shall not attempt to obtain employment or advancement or professional engagements by untruthfully criticizing other economists, or by other improper or questionable methods.) would call into question certain comments by some economists about other economists' proposals.

I could go on, but these examples should make my point. Adoption of a variation of the Engineer's Code of Ethics would have a much broader reach than would DeMartino's Economist's Oath, or would a code designed to deal with the ethical problems highlighted by *Inside Job*. Perhaps the aspect I find most appealing about the engineering code of ethics is that it expresses a humility about one's goals. It makes no sweeping claims about goals, but rather focuses on the economic engineer's individual actions. In my view such an individual action-oriented code creates a professional ethic that is stronger than a more inclusive oath or code that deals with moral judgments such as "opposing oppression" and "giving voice to the needs and aspirations of the dispossessed."

By being limited about the nature of the code, we can be more humble. In a well-known passage, Keynes wrote that "If economists could manage to get themselves thought of as humble, competent people on a level with dentists, that would be splendid." I never quite understood Keynes' dentist allusion, but I would suggest if we could replace "dentist" in the quotation with "engineer," that would indeed be splendid.

REFERENCES

Colander, David. 2013. "The Systemic Failure of Economic Methodologists." *Journal of Economic Methodology* 20(1), 56–68.

Colander, David, Alan Kirman, Michael Goldberg, Brigitte Sloth, Katarina Juselius, Armin Haas, and Thomas Lux. 2009. "The Financial Crisis and the Systemic Failure of the Economics Profession." *Critical Review* 21(2–3), 249–267.

DeMartino, George. 2011. *The Economist's Oath*. Oxford: Oxford University Press.

Koen, Billy Vaughn. 2003. *Discussion of the Method*. Oxford: Oxford University Press.

Robbins, Lionel. 1927. "Mr. Hawtrey on the Scope of Economics." *Economica* 172–178.

Annotated bibliography of Colander's methodological work

[1]   1979, 'Realistic and Analytic Syntheses of Macro and Micro Economics' (with Kenneth Koford), *Journal of Economic Issues*, **13** (3), 707–32.
      This article argues that there are two different types of syntheses that we should be striving for in macro: one is a full analytic synthesis; it is scientific and formal, and is what economists currently focus on. The other is realistic and informal and is designed to be a useful heuristic when actually using the models to guide policy.

[2]   1983, 'Guiding the Invisible Hand' (with Abba Lerner), *International Journal of Transport Economics*, **10** (1–2), 25–34.
      This article distinguishes Lerner's approach to policy from Hayek's approach. It argues that planning is always necessary; the policy question concerns the nature of the planning, not whether there should be planning by government.

[3]   1987, 'Why Economists Aren't as Important as Garbagemen', *Journal of Economic and Monetary Affairs*, July, reprinted in David Colander (1991), *Why Aren't Economists as Important as Garbagemen? Essays on the State of Economics*, Armonk, New York: Sharpe Publishing, pp. 19–29 (Chapter 1 of this volume).

[4]   1987, 'The Making of an Economist' (with Arjo Klamer), *Journal of Economic Perspectives*, **1** (2), 95–111.
      This article reports the results of a survey of graduate economics students at top graduate programs in the US. It documents that little emphasis is giving to students having a knowledge of institutions or a knowledge of economic literature. The study was the impetus for the COGEE Report done by the American Economic Association on the nature of graduate education.

[5]   1990, *The Making of an Economist* (with Arjo Klamer), Boulder and London: Westview.
      This book expands on the article of the same name and includes interviews with graduate students at top schools along with a discussion of the implications of the findings.

[6]   1991, *Why Aren't Economists as Important as Garbagemen? Essays on the State of Economics*. Armonk, New York: Sharpe Publishers.
      This book collects eleven essays of Colander's on the state of economics and economics profession, including Chapter 2 presented in this volume. These essays are pioneering work in using an economic approach to analyse economists' behavior. They provide an intriguing and insightful sociological investigation of economics profession. It is Colander's view that knowing the forces behind economists' behavior (for example, selection of research agenda and methods) can help design institutions (including the promotion policy of the profession) that provide desirable incentives for economists to adopt the methodology appropriate for different types of economic studies.

[7]   1992, 'The Lost Art of Economics', *Journal of Economic Perspectives*, **6** (3), 191–8 (Chapter 3 of this volume).

[8]   1993, 'The Macrofoundations of Micro', *Eastern Economic Journal*, **19** (4), 447–57, reprinted in D. Colander (ed.), *Beyond Microfoundations: Post Walraisan Macroeconomics*, 1996, Cambridge: Cambridge University Press, pp. 57–68 (Chapter 10 of this volume).

[9]   1994, 'The Art of Economics by the Numbers', in Roger Backhouse (ed.), *New Directions in Economic Methodology*, London and New York: Routledge, pp. 35–49, reprinted in Colander (ed.), *The Lost Art of Economics*, 2001, pp. 47–61.

This article first argues that it is necessary to divide economics into three branches (that is, positive economics, normative economics and art of economics) and that it is essential to apply different methodology appropriate for each branch. It then provides six common sense methodological rules for the art of economics: (1) do not violate the law of significant digits; (2) be objective; use the reasonable person criterion to judge policy; (3) use the best economic theory available; (4) take in all dimensions of the problem; (5) use whatever empirical work sheds light on the issue at hand; and (6) do not be falsely scientific; present only empirical tests that are convincing to you. Despite considering that most economists will not be interested in formal methodology, this chapter suggests that it is possible for such a work to make changes to the practice of applied policy work done by academic economists. It argues that the discussion of methodology will filter into textbooks and eventually have an impact on tenure criteria and editorial policy of journals, even though that will be a slow process.

[10]   1994, 'Vision, Judgment, and Disagreement among Economists', *Journal of Economic Methodology*, **1** (1), 43–56, reprinted in Colander (ed.), *The Lost Art of Economics*, 2001, pp. 123–35 (Chapter 2 of this volume).

[11]   1995, 'Marshallian General Equilibrium', *Eastern Economic Journal*, **21** (3), 281–93.

It is commonly believed by economists that the movement from Marshallian partial equilibrium to Walrasian general equilibrium was a major advancement in the history of economics. A key reason behind this belief is the fact that Walrasian general equilibrium involves much more complicated mathematical tools than does Marshallian partial equilibrium. This paper argues that Marshall in fact has an implicit general equilibrium theory, but he deliberately did not present it in mathematical form because the math at his time was not up for the task of guiding policy. According to this paper, for Marshall, Walras's specification of general equilibrium theory would be logically correct and precise, but irrelevant for most macroeconomic policy discussions. Right or wrong about the true reason why Marshall did not develop a general equilibrium theory, the conjecture of this paper highlights the problem that the status of computational technology and mathematic theories often plays a dominant role in the development of economic theorizing in the twentieth century. When the intuitive correspondence between theories and mathematics emphasized by Marshall was lost, technology, rather than economic reality, took the lead in shaping the development of economic science. By arguing why Marshall did not develop a general equilibrium theory like Walras's, this paper shows why Marshall's work can be seen not as a stepping stone to Walras, but instead is a stepping stone beyond Walras. Moreover, it presents a reflection of the role and function of mathematics in economic theories.

[12]   1996, *Beyond Microfoundations: Post Walrasian Macroeconomics*, Cambridge: Cambridge University Press.

Beyond Microfoundations collects thirteen essays by different authors. Colander provides a long introduction setting the stage for the articles. In it, Colander argues that a new approach to macro is needed, and explores what the essence of that new approach will be. Colander calls this new approach the Post Walrasian approach, in contrast to the standard approach, which he calls the Walrasian approach.

[13]   1998, 'Confessions of an Economic Gadfly', in Michael Szensberg (ed.), *Passion and Craft: Economists at Work*, Michigan: University of Michigan Press, pp. 39–56.

Colander's methodology is best understood within his development as an economist. This article captures some of that history. In it we see that Colander's path into economics was based on happenchance and the help of a number of top economists who did not fit within the mainstream methodologic approach. They allowed him freedom to explore economics in a different way than most economists are forced to do so. It was that different experience that led to his interest in methodology and economic education, which he sees as the way in which methodology is transferred to young economists.

[14]   1998, 'Beyond New Keynesian Economics: Post Walrasian Economics', in Roy Rotheim (ed.), *New Keynesian Economics/Post Keynesian Alternatives*, London and New York: Routledge, pp. 277–87.

This paper explains why a new classifier for macroeconomics other than ones following the traditional line of Classical/Keynesian classification is needed. It argues that what differentiates New Keynesian and New Classical is not so much their methodology, but more ideologies or policy standpoints. New Keynesian and New Classical approaches are essentially in the same methodological tradition, which Colander calls the Walrasian tradition, in contrast to the new classifier, Post Walrasian, which he proposes to refer to a new line of thinking about the macro economy which started to develop in the late twentieth century. One of the key differences between Walrasian and Post Walrasian economics is that the former treats economy as an equilibrium system whereas the latter views economy as an evolving complex system.

[15]   2000, 'The Death of Neoclassical Economics', *Journal of the History of Economic Thought*, **22** (2), 127–43 (Chapter 5 of this volume).

[16]   2000, 'Complexity and Policy' (with William Brock), in David Colander (ed.), *The Complexity Vision and the Teaching of Economics*, Cheltenham, UK and Northampton, MA, USA: Edward Elgar Publishing, pp. 73–96.

This article discusses the implications of complexity-based research on economic policy. It does so by suggesting how the change in economists' worldview from a simplified general equilibrium system to a complexity system would make a difference in policy analysis. It then turns to the question of complexity and the activism/laissez faire debate, arguing that complexity is neutral in that debate; it favors neither activism nor laissez faire. It concludes with a discussion of changes in the way complexity economists will actually do policy analysis, arguing that the different techniques complexity theorists can use are complementary to standard economics, not substitutes for it.

[17]   2001, *The Lost Art of Economics*, Cheltenham, UK and Northampton, MA, USA: Edward Elgar Publishing.

This is a collection of Colander's essays in the art of economics relating to both micro- and macroeconomics. Colander argues that much of economics attempts to be formally scientific, even when the problems and available empirical data do not allow a formal scientific analysis.

[18]   2003, 'Post Walrasian Macroeconomics and Heterodoxy: Thinking Outside the Heterodox Box', *International Journal of Political Economy*, **33** (2), 68–81.

This paper is a response to the heterodox criticisms of Colander's advocating the research agenda of Post Walrasian economics and his call for abandoning heterodoxy. The paper first makes a brief comparison between the difference in the assumptions of Walrasian and Post Walrasian economics. It then turns to explain why Post Walrasian economics is not subject to the problems attributed to it by heterodox critics. The paper focuses on two issues. First, the assumption of purposeful behavior in Post Walrasian economics is not the same thing as assuming optimization behavior. Second, Post Walrasian economics is not ideologically tainted; on the contrary, it is neutral about policy. The last part of the paper explains Colander's call for abandoning heterodoxy is not a call to stop the work heterodox economists are doing, nor a call to abandon the approaches heterodox economists are using. Instead, it is a call for heterodox economists to stop seeing their work as something that a good mainstream economist would not find interesting because of the mainstream's ideological blinders. In Colander's view, dropping the 'orthodox/heterodox' division can help jettison the 'us/them' mentality, and doing so would be conductive for those economists who see themselves as heterodox.

[19]   2004, 'The Changing Face of Mainstream Economics' (with Ric Holt and Barkley Rosser), *Review of Political Economy*, **16** (4), 485–99.

This article argues that economics is currently undergoing a fundamental shift in its *method*, away from neoclassical economics and into something new. Although that something new has not been fully developed, it is beginning to take form and is centered on dynamics, recursive methods and complexity theory. The foundation of this change is coming from economists who are doing cutting-edge work and influencing mainstream economics. These economists are defining and laying the theoretical groundwork for the fundamental shift that is occurring in the economics profession.

[20]   2004, *The Changing Face of Economics: Conversations with Cutting Edge Economists* (with Richard Holt and Barkley Rosser), Ann Arbor: University of Michigan Press.

This is a set of interviews with leading cutting-edge economists throughout the world. The interviews show an openness of these leading economists to new ideas that is often not found in the broader profession. In an introductory essay Colander and his co-authors argue that the 'action' in economics is in the cutting-edge of the profession, and if one wants to understand where the profession is going, one should focus on them, not on textbook economics, which significantly lags developments in the field.

[21]   2003, 'Post Walrasian Macro Policy and the Economics of Muddling Through', *International Journal of Political Economy*, **33** (2), 17–35 (Chapter 11 of this volume).

[22]   2005, 'The Making of an Economist Redux', *Journal of Economic Perspectives*, **19** (1), 175–98.

This article reports the results of a survey of graduate students at top graduate schools that replicates Colander's earlier study almost two decades earlier. The results show a substantial difference in the attitudes of students. They find mathematics less important and empirical work much more important. Colander attributes this change in part to developments in economics – in response to earlier complaints it became more empirical – and in part to a change in selection processes of top graduate schools. Programs now choose applicants for comfortableness with math, and thus current students do not find math as intimidating as did students in the earlier study.

[23] 2005, 'The Future of Economics: the Appropriately Educated in Pursuit of the Knowable', *Cambridge Journal of Economics*, **29**, 927–41.

This paper, initially entitled 'The Complexity Revolution and the Future of Economics', was written for the conference 'Economics for the Future' held at University of Cambridge in 2003. It offers a vision of the future of economics by analysing how and why economics changes under the forces that are inherent in economics institutional structure. Among various forces, this paper has a focus on how technological changes in analytic and computing methods are opening up new avenues of study. It explains how the increasing computing power makes it possible for economists to move away from the holy trinity assumptions of rationality, greed, and equilibrium to more realistic assumptions. With the technological advances, this paper envisages a fundamental change in the vision of economics taking place, from one seeing economics as the study of infinitely bright agents in information-rich environments to one seeing economics as the study of reasonably bright individuals in information-poor environments. While that happens, agent-based models and computer analysis of empirical data will increase in importance, and deductive analytics and axiomatic work will decrease in importance.

[24] 2005, 'From Muddling Through to the Economics of Control: Views of Applied Policy from J.N. Keynes to Abba Lerner', in Steven G. Medema and Peter Boettke (eds), The Role of Government in the History of Economic Thought, *History of Political Economy*, 2005 Supplement, **37**, 277–91.

This paper tells a story of changing methodological views regarding how theory should be used in thinking about policy. The paper considers three views. One is the view of J.N. Keynes and Lionel Robbins, who argue that pure economic theory has little or nothing to say about policy, but that a separate branch of economics exists that should consider such policy issues. A second view is that of Alfred Marshall and A.C. Pigou, who argue that a 'realistic' theory can be used to guide judgments on policy. These two views can be seen as a 'muddling through' approach, in which pure economic theory does not give much guidance for policy. The third view, which is most closely related to an 'economics of control' view set out by Abba Lerner, connects pure theory and policy in a more direct way, drawing implications about policy from pure theory. This paper discusses the evolution of these three views and concludes by arguing that the current textbook presentation of policy follows the third view and that while the first two are quite reasonable views, this third view is at best misleading and at worst simply wrong.

[25] 2005, 'Wild and Crazy Ideas: A Memorial to Ken Koford', *Eastern Economic Journal*, **31** (2), 159–64.

This article, written as a memorial to Colander's friend and colleague Ken Koford (then editor of the *Eastern Economic Journal*), discusses how economists relate and the discussion they had, and didn't have, after they learned that Ken was dying with incurable cancer. It tells a story about how an economist whose interests were ideas lived his life to the fullest – a life of ideas – and made the world a better place.

[26] 2005, 'What Economists Teach and What Economists Do', *The Journal of Economic Education*, **36** (3), 249–60.

There is a gulf between what economists do and what they teach. The development of computing technology is one of the reasons which result in the increasing gap. The computing technology has changed the approach of cutting-edge economic studies from deductive theoretical analysis to empirical work which has little reliance on theories and does not aim to test theories. The empirical studies these days are a type of highly sophisticated data mining. This paper considers that textbooks have two major purposes: first, to tell students what economic analysis is (that is, the economic way of thinking); second, to tell students how the economy operates. From the perspective of fulfilling these two goals, it might not be necessary to include the cutting-edge economic research into textbooks. Hence, the paper only suggests a couple of changes to be done in the micro textbook to reflect better the new work.

[27] 2006, 'Pluralism, Formalism, and American Economics' (with Harry Landreth) in Roger Koppl (ed.), *Money and Markets: Essays in Honor of Leland B. Yeager*, London and New York: Routledge, pp. 83–98.

This paper argues that methodological pluralism is not evolutionarily stable in the dynamic process of the economics profession and that the seeming pluralism in the early 1900s was simply a temporary part of a dynamic process in which the formalist and nonformalist methodological positions were of somewhat equal strength and neither had won out. It analyses the demise of institutionalists and Marshallians by explaining how they failed to meet the institutional requirements for survival, in a context of the enormous growth of universities during the post-World War II era. The paper argues that the rise and eventually dominance of formalism in the twentieth-century economics profession should not be seen as a movement away from pluralism, but merely a part of the swing of a pendulum, an analogy that also anticipates the return of pluralism and nonformalism in the early twenty-first century. It is important not to confuse the formalism of general equilibrium theory with the highly technical applied mathematics and econometrics that characterize much of the modern applied work in economics. By formalism, Colander means pure theorizing, namely, developing a grand theory by constructing a general solution to an abstract problem. In Colander's view, the methods used in much of modern applied economics, such as agent-based modeling or vector auto regression, are highly mathematical and technical but nonetheless informal.

[28] 2006, 'Introduction', in D. Colander (ed.), *Post Walrasian Macroeconomics: Beyond the DSGE Model*, Cambridge: Cambridge University Press, pp. 1–23.

Post Walrasian Macroeconomics is a collection of eighteen essays by different authors. It is a sequel of the 1996 book *Beyond Microfoundations*. This introductory chapter by Colander makes a clear contrast between what he calls Walrasian economics and Post Walrasian economics. They differ in visions, assumptions, questions asked, as well as tools and models used. It is notable that the DSGE models play a key role in Walrasian economics, while Post Walrasian economics sees the ad hoc assumptions in the DSGE models as flawed and prefers agent-based computational economics modeling. It is worth noting that this chapter was written before the 2008 financial crisis started. Colander's critical standpoint against the DSGE models can be traced back at least to the mid-1990s and is not a consequence of the crisis. Despite his belief that the timing of the crisis was unpredictable, its likelihood was predictable, and in this introductory article to the book Colander's criticisms of how the DSGE models have assumed away the inherent instability of the macro economy have anticipated that a crisis would occur.

[29]   2006, 'Post Walrasian Macroeconomics: Some Historic Links', in D. Colander (ed.), *Post Walrasian Macroeconomics: Beyond the DSGE Model*, Cambridge: Cambridge University Press, pp. 46–69.

This book chapter provides some historic links for the Post Walrasian economics by reviewing four key stages in the history of macroeconomics, including classical economics, the Keynesian Revolution, the Neoclassical/NeoKeynsian synthesis, and the New Classical Revolution. It argues that the Post Walrasian economics is more closely linked to classical economics than other predecessors in that they share a similar vision of economy as a complex system and similar approach to policy thinking. It considers the Post Walrasian work as a return to the broader classical question, with more advanced tools, that how reasonable agents with only bounded rationality operate in information-poor environments, in contrast to the Walrasian questions of how globally rational agents operate in information-rich environments.

[30]   2006, 'What We Taught and What We Did: The Evolution of US Economic Textbooks (1830–1930)', *Il Pensiero Economico Italiano*, **14** (2), 27–35.

This paper expands on the argument in his 'What Economists Teach and What Economists Do' (2005). That earlier paper argued that currently what economists do is different from what they teach and that over the past few decades the gulf between the two has widened. This paper considers the same question in historical perspective: Was there a difference between what economists taught and what they did in the mid-1800s and early 1900s, or is the divergence a recent phenomenon?

[31]   2007, *The Making of an Economist Redux*, Princeton, NJ: Princeton University Press.

This book updates *The Making of an Economist* (1990), a joint work with Arjo Klamer. It shows what is happening in elite US economics PhD programs. By examining these programs, the book gives a view of cutting-edge economics and a glimpse at its likely future. In addition, by comparing economics education today to the findings of the original book, the new book shows how much, and in what ways, the field has changed over the past two decades. In these conversations, the students – the next generation of elite economists – frankly describe what they think of their field and what graduate economics education is really like. Colander argues that understanding economic education is the key to understanding economists' methodology because graduate school significantly shapes the approach they take to economics throughout their career.

[32]   2007–2008, 'Live and Dead Issues in the Methodology of Economics' (with Ric Holt and Barkley Rosser), *Journal of Post Keynesian Economics*, **30** (2), 303–12.

This paper aims to clarify the arguments made by the authors in their previous works *The Changing Face of Economics* ([19] [20]) and respond to the remarks made by Dequech (2007–2008) on the divisions the authors made between 'orthodox, mainstream, and heterodox' in economics. The paper argues that making divisions is necessary for the purpose of its analysis, but it is not the authors' intention to use these divisions to paint a full picture of the economics profession. In fact, they cannot because the divisions are static in character, while the economics profession is seen by the authors as a complex adaptive system, in which new ideas are continually competing with old ones. Moreover, the authors find that their position is often seen as anti-heterodox, a position they emphasize they are not. On the contrary, they believe that heterodox ideas are important and the economics profession would be far better off if it took those ideas more seriously. By calling for abandoning the label of heterodoxy, what they are trying to do is to provide a different strategy which may avoid heterodox ideas being marginalized. At the end, the paper spells out some specific advice for young heterodox economists to follow.

[33]   2008, 'Beyond DSGE Models: Toward an Empirically Based Macroeconomics' (with Peter Howitt, Alan Kirman, Axel Leijonhufvud and Perry Mehrling), *American Economic Review*, **98** (2), 236–40 (Chapter 14 of this volume).

[34]   2008, 'The Making of a Global European Economist', *Kyklos*, **61** (2), 215–36.
This paper reports the results of a survey of top English speaking graduate programs in Europe, and argues that they are in the process of change, and that all change is not for the better.

[35]   2009, 'Economists, Incentives, Judgment, and the European CVAR Approach to Macroeconometrics', *Economics: The Open-Access, Open-Assessment E-Journal*, **3** (9), 1–21 (Chapter 13 of this volume).

[36]   2009, 'In Praise of Modern Economics', *Eastern Economics Journal*, **35** (1), 10–13.
This paper is an invited response to criticisms of modern economics by Barbara Bergman. It compares economics in the early twentieth century with economics in the 1970s. It argues that economics had serious problems in the 1970s: there was a limiting orthodoxy; students were cynical and treated economics like a game; and there was a notable lack of intellectual excitement within the field. In comparison, modern economics today is a vibrant and advancing field that is intellectually alive and open to discovery, and the so-called neoclassical orthodoxy no longer exists. While recognizing economics today has many problems, this paper, by taking all aspects into account, concludes that modern economics is progressive and deserves praise, not nagging.

[37]   2009, 'The Complexity Vision as a Bridge between Graduate School and Undergraduate Macro' (with Casey Rothschild), in Mark Setterfield (ed.), *Macroeconomic Theory and Macro Pedagogy*, London: Palgrave Macmillan, pp. 118–28.
The paper argues that the current teaching at the undergraduate level and that at the graduate levels both unduly downplay the complexity of macro economy, but in very different ways. This has led to the lack of connection between the formal graduate teaching and the rough-and-ready teaching of macro at the undergraduate level and has been detrimental to pedagogy at both levels. The paper suggests that the connection can be easily made by bringing a vision of the macro economy as a complex system to the fore of both graduate and undergraduate instruction. Once this is done, the engineering approach taught at the undergraduate level and the pure theoretical approach taught at the graduate level can both be seen as reasonable ways of dealing with that complexity, albeit with different aims in mind.

[38]   2009, 'The Financial Crisis and the Systemic Failure of Academic Economics' (with Alan Kirman, Hans Follmer, Michael Goldberg, Brigitte Sloth, Katarina Juselius,

Armin Haas, and Thomas Lux) appeared first on the web and was widely discussed. The authors allow anyone to reprint it, and it has been reprinted in a variety of journals and books including *Critical Review*, 2009, **21** (2–3), 249–67.

This paper is a report by a group of economists exploring the role of mathematics in financial economics and is often called the Dahlem Report. It argues that economists not only failed to anticipate and understand the 2008 financial crisis; they may also have contributed to it – with risk and derivatives models that, through spurious precision and untested theoretical assumptions, encouraged policy makers and market participants to see more stability and risk sharing than was actually present. Moreover, once the crisis occurred, it was met with incomprehension by most economists because of models that, on the one hand, downplay the possibility that economic actors may exhibit highly interactive behavior; and, on the other, assume that any homogeneity will involve economic actors sharing the economist's own putatively correct model of the economy, so that error can stem only from an exogenous shock. The financial crisis presents not only an intellectual challenge, but also an ethical challenge to economics. This paper suggests that it should be an ethical responsibility for economists to communicate the limitations of the models that they construct. Failing to do so will lead to a failure of the economics profession. Devastating as it is, the financial crisis also presents an opportunity to reform its study by grounding it more solidly in reality. Its underlying theme is that the macro economy is best seen as an evolving complex system that is in many ways unpredictable.

[39] 2009, 'Mathematics, Methods, and Modern Economics' (with Hans Follmer, Armin Haas, Alan Kirman, Katarina Juselius, Brigitte Sloth, and Thomas Lux), *Real-world Economics Review*, **50**, 118–21.

This short essay takes up the following question raised by the editor of *Real-world Economics Review*: 'It is agreed that the current economic crisis has shown that the standard models of academic economics are seriously wanting. Should the main emphasis of reform be on developing new formal models or to an opening up of economics to methods other than traditional modeling?'

The essay argues that mathematical models per se are not the problem of economics. The real problem is the inappropriate use and interpretation of mathematical models. The solution to this is to be careful with the limitations of the models while using or interpreting the models. The same question is also answered by Tony Lawson from a different perspective in the same issue of the journal.

[40] 2009, 'What Was "It" that Robbins was Defining?', *Journal of the History of Economic Thought*, **31** (4), 437–48.

By reexamining Robbins's definition of economics, this paper provides a different interpretation of Robbins's *Essay on the Nature and Significance of Economic Science* than that which most economists hold. The paper argues that, for Robbins, the scientific branch of economics and the entire field of economics were quite different and what he defined in the *Essay* included only the 'economic science' portion of what economists did. The line of demarcation was drawn by Robbins to make the point that economists needed to distinguish economics science, which should avoid value judgments, from political economy, which should necessarily embrace them. This paper argues that the prescriptive message Robbins hoped to convey was that value judgments and policy analysis belonged in the political economy branch of economics, not in the economic science branch of economics. This is quite different than saying that economists need to eliminate value judgments from the field of economics. Value judgments are a necessary part of policy analysis. The paper analyses Robbins's view and argues that Robbins thought of economics in the same way as did J.N. Keynes, Marshall, and Pigou, where economic science was only one part of economics. It concludes with an emphasis on Robbins's prescriptive advice about the need for two clearly distinguished separate tracks in economics – one a science track designed for questions of understanding the economy, and one an applied policy track designed for guiding policy.

[41] 2009, 'Written Testimony submitted to the Congress of the United States, House Science and Technology Committee, for the Hearing on: The Risks of Financial Modeling: VaR and the Economic Meltdown', September **10**, 2009.

This is the first of two testimonies given by Colander to the Congress of the US, House Science and Technology Committee. It was set to answer two questions. First, why didn't economists recognize the financial system was in trouble, and warn society about it? Second, what changes can be made to avoid fiascos like a financial crisis? In answering the first question, the testimony suggests that the dominance of the dynamic stochastic general equilibrium (DSGE) model should take the blame. It explains how the DSGE model assumes away strategic coordination problems and denies the possibility of financial crises even to occur. It is important to note that for Colander, the problem is not the models per se, but the way economic models are used, which is a problem of incentives rooted in the institutional structure of academia. In answering the second questions, two suggestions are made to the National Science Foundation: first, include a wider range of peers in the reviewing process of NSF grants in the social sciences; second, increase the number of researchers trained to interpret, rather than develop, models.

[42] 2010, *The Making of a European Economist*, Cheltenham, UK and Northampton, MA, USA: Edward Elgar Publishing.

The book expands upon Colander's 2008 article on European graduate economics education. It reports the results of a survey of European graduate students in economics at top European programs and also interviews students about the results. It uses the same survey that Colander used to study US graduate programs. He finds that European programs are more likely to be open to different views, but that they are becoming more US-like in part because they have adopted the US ranking system of economic research output. He argues that, to retain its originality, Europe should consider using a different way of ranking research, and he offers some suggestions.

[43] 2010, 'How to Win Friends and (Possibly) Influence Mainstream Economists' (with Ric Holt and Barkley Rosser), *Journal of Post Keynesian Economics*, **32** (3), 397–409.

This paper responds to two central arguments made by Matías Vernengo in his paper 'Conversation or Monologue: On Advising Heterodox Economists', and stands by the authors' earlier arguments ([20] [32]) that (1) heterodox economists hurt themselves by self-labeling themselves as heterodox because mainstream economics no longer is limited to a neoclassical orthodoxy; and that (2) heterodox economists would be well served to spend less time writing about methodology and more time writing about policy issues.

[44]   2010, 'The Domain of Austrian Economics', in Roger Koppl, Steven Horwitz and Pierre Desrochers (eds), *What is so Austrian about Austrian Economics? (Advances in Austrian Economics, Volume 14)*, London: Emerald Group Publishing, pp. 29–41.
Modern mainstream economics is a plurocracy in which there is no orthodoxy of ideas, only an orthodoxy of method. Given the training it provides its students, mainstream economics' natural domain is science. With the mainstream's acceptance of complexity views of the economy, Austrian economists' views can now get a hearing within the mainstream. Thus, within the science of economics, there is no need for a separate Austrian economics. However, there is a need for Austrian economics in political economy, the branch of economics that takes the insights of science and relates them to policy. The paper urges Austrian economics to embrace political economy as its domain and to position its work within political economy.

[45]   2010, 'The Economics Profession, the Financial Crisis, and Method', *Journal of Economic Methodology*, **17** (4), 419–27.
This paper clarifies the points made in the paper 'The Financial Crisis and the Systemic Failure of Academic Economics' (2009). In 2007–2008, the world economy came perilously close to a systemic failure in which a financial system collapse almost undermined the entire world economy as we know it. These events have led some to fault the economics profession for its failure to predict the crisis, and to ask whether the crisis will lead the economics profession to change its ways. This paper discusses these two issues, and then turns to some suggestions for institutional changes in the economics profession that might lead to better outcomes in the future.

[46]   2010, 'The Sins of the Sons of Samuelson: Vision, Pedagogy and the Zig Zag Windings of Complex Dynamics' (with Casey Rothschild), *Journal of Economic Behavior and Organization*, **74** (3), 277–90.
This paper describes the transition of economic methodology from classical to neoclassical. The methodology under discussion is with a focus on applied economics. The standard economics text is centered on a vision of a naturally self-regulated, dynamically stable system with a unique global attractor. This paper discusses how we got there and how recent developments in the study of dynamical systems allow us to go beyond that. It traces the evolution of the teaching of economics from Alfred Marshall, who built his supply-and-demand framework within a complexity vision of the economy. It suggests that that complexity vision was lost as economists formalized the supply–demand framework and extended it to the entire economy. This paper argues that the current textbook presentation of economics should not and cannot serve as the only intellectual frame we provide to our students.

[47]   2010, 'Written Testimony submitted to the Congress of the United States, House Science and Technology Committee, for the hearing on: How Economists Failed Society', July 20, 2010, republished in *Institutional Risk Analyst*. (Chapter 15 of this volume)

[48]   2011, 'Applied Policy, Welfare Economics, and Mill's Half-truths', in John Davis and Wade Hands (eds), *The Elgar Companion to Recent Economic Methodology*, Cheltenham, UK and Northampton, MA, USA: Edward Elgar Publishing, pp. 173–87 (Chapter 6 of this volume).

[49]   2011, 'How Economists Got It Wrong: A Nuanced Account', *Critical Review*, **23** (1–2), 1–27 (Chapter 12 of this volume).

[50]   2011, 'Is the Fundamental Science of Macroeconomics Sound?', *Review of Radical Political Economy*, **43** (3), 302–9.

Not long after the 2008 financial crisis, Ben Bernanke argued that in the events leading up to the financial crisis, mistakes were made, but they were primarily engineering or management mistakes, not mistakes in the fundamental science of macroeconomics, which he sees as sound. This paper argues that Bernanke is wrong and that standard macroeconomics has not recognized, and still does not recognize, the limits of science and of formal modeling when studying something as complex as the macro economy. This failure to recognize, and adequately convey to policy makers, the limits of our scientific understanding of the macro economy, has led standard macroeconomics to combine fundamental science and policy applications in ways that undermine both. This paper advocates a classical methodological approach, which Keynes followed as well, that strictly separates fundamental science from policy analysis. Policy does not directly follow from models; it follows from reasoned analysis which uses models, but which combines models with institutional knowledge, intuition, and common sense.

[51]   2011, 'The Keynesian Method, Complexity, and the Training of Economists', in Arie Arnon, Jimmy Weinblatt, and Warren Young (eds), *Perspectives on Keynesian Economics*, Heidelberg: Springer, pp. 183–201.

This paper explains how the grand Keynesian synthesis macro and modern DSGE macro have deviated from the Keynesian method and why the loss of the Keynesian method is of concern. It analyses how the profession moved from Keynes's writings to the modern DSGE approach from the perspective of academic incentives. It also explores how the change to the central bank training approach led the Keynesian method to fade away and allowed the DSGE approach to gain its place in influencing macro policymaking today. It concludes with a call for changes in training, especially the training of policy economists, whose job requires not only the knowledge of technical models, but also judgment, intuition and deep institutional knowledge.

[52]   2012, 'What Makes a Good Economist', in Diane Coyle (ed.), *What's the Use of Economics? Teaching the Dismal Science after the Crisis*, London: London Publishing Partnership, pp. 11–14.

This short article was initially written for an international conference discussing the state of economics and economics education, organized by the UK Government Economic Service and the Bank of England in 2012. It responds to the theme of the conference by reflecting the question: what makes a good economist? Following J.M. Keynes, this article argues that it is the blending of skills, not the particular skills that is essential for making a good economist. It sees an ideal curriculum as one in which teachers are passionately teaching the approach and specialty that they know, but teaching it with humility, an attitude beginning with recognition that no single approach is sufficient.

[53]   2013, 'A Failure to Communicate: The Fact–Value Divide and the Putnam–Dasgupta Debate' (with Hiue-chun Su), *Erasmus Journal of Economics and Philosophy*, **6** (2), 1–23 (Chapter 7 of this volume).

[54]   2013, 'Moving Beyond the Rhetoric of Pluralism: Suggestions for an "Inside-the-Mainstream" Heterodoxy', in Robert Garnett, Erik K. Olsen and Martha Starr (eds), *Economic Pluralism*, London: Routledge, pp. 36–47 (Chapter 16 of this volume).

[55]   2013, 'Creating Humble Economists: A Code of Ethics for Economists', in George DeMartino and Dierdre McCloskey (eds), *Handbook on Professional Economic Ethics*, Cambridge: Cambridge University Press, pp. 737–49 (Chapter 17 of this volume).

[56]   2013, 'The Systemic Failure of Economic Methodologists', *Journal of Economic Methodology*, **20** (1), 56–68 (Chapter 4 of this volume).

[57]   2013, 'What Should Turkish Economists Do and How Should They Do It?', *Ekonomi-Tek – International Economics Journal*, **2** (2), 1–12.

It is Colander's view that institutional incentives play a crucial role in determining economists' research agenda. This paper is an application of this theory to the case of Turkey. Like the academic economics profession in many countries, Turkey faces the problem that the research which Turkish economists do helps Turkey far less than it should, and too often is done merely to get published and not to most effectively solve real-world economic problems that Turkey faces. This paper suggests two ways of dealing with such problems: one is for Turkish universities to develop a new journal-ranking method focusing on a particular research niche, and to use that ranking to evaluate research; the second is a voucher system that would give Turkish demanders of Turkish economic research more direct control over what research is done. Each proposal would change the incentive structure confronting Turkish economists, making what Turkish economists want to do much more consistent with what Turkish society wants them to do.

[58]   2013, 'Why are there no Milton Friedmans Today?', *Econ Journal Watch*, **10** (2), 167–71.

The question of why are there no Milton Friedmans today can be approached in a number of different ways. For example, it might be approached as a question about economists' roles as public intellectuals: Are there fewer economist public intellectuals today than previously, and if so why? Alternatively, it might be approached as a question about Friedman's support of free markets: Are there fewer economists who support free markets today, and, if so, why? This paper provides brief answers for each. Colander's answer to the first question is affirmative and the reason why is that economist public intellectuals are filtered out of the profession by its institutional selection process. It is more difficult to give the second question a straightforward answer. An economist's view on markets often reflects their morality and ideology, and their pragmatic assessments of institutions and politics, much more than any conclusions of economic theory. However, instead of debating the deeper philosophical, practical, and moral arguments against markets as classical liberals did, modern economists structure the debates around technical models and draw policy conclusions directly from the models. Given the blending of theory and policy, economists' positions on policy issues became blurred.

[59]   2014, 'Achieving a Brighter Future from the Bottom Up: Activist Laissez-Faire Social Policy', in Richard P.F. Holt and Daphne T. Greenwood (eds), *A Brighter Future: Improving the Standard of Living Now and for the Next Generation*, London and New York: Routledge, pp. 73–90.

The central argument of this paper is that our current operating economic system is obsolete and has not adjusted for the successes of the system in achieving material welfare. In a complex environment bottom-up policy that relies on individual initiative works better than direct top-down policy, and changing the environment to encourage bottom-up social policy is our best chance at achieving a better society. It further argues that we need to bring the same incentive dynamic that for-profit corporations and private entrepreneurship brought to the achievement of material welfare to social problems. We can only do that by changing the operating system of capitalism to direct social entrepreneurship toward solving social problems. Doing so will involve changes in law, accounting procedures, and more generally in our vision of what organizations' goals are. It won't be easy, but it is the direction in which we should be moving.

[60] 2014, 'Can European Economics Compete with U.S. Economics? And Should It?', in Alessandro Lanteri and Jack Vroman (eds), *The Economics of Economists: Institutional Settings, Individual Incentives, and Future Prospects*, Cambridge: Cambridge University Press, pp. 153–73.

This paper starts with recognizing the undergoing process of changing incentives in the research environment taking place in the European economics profession in recent years. It agrees that change to the current system is necessary, yet argues that the metrics with almost unidimensional focus on the quality-weighted journal article rankings and citations, if used, will likely undermine the traditional European economics professions strengths. This paper argues that the traditional European system has several advantages over the US system, including giving researchers a larger incentive to work on thoughtful research over publishable research, and allowing more diversity in research topics and approaches as well as in teaching. The paper offers some suggestions for developing an assessment system other than using unidimensional metrics and formal rankings.

[61] 2014, 'The Economics of Influence', *Journal of Economic Issues*, **48** (2), 485–91.

The economics profession has fallen into the habit of telling a limited 'economics of control' policy story in their teaching of economics. While it is a useful story, it leaves out important elements of policy. This paper briefly analyses the history of the profession's current policy story, and argues that a newly developed complexity theory offers a richer policy narrative. It is a policy story in which the government and market coevolve, and the role of government policy is to positively influence that evolution, not to control the system. The paper concludes with a discussion of some implications that the acceptance of an economics-of-influence approach to policy would have for the story economists tell about policy.

[62] 2014, 'The Wrong Type of Pluralism: Toward a Transdisciplinary Social Science', *Review of Political Economy*, **26** (4), 516–25.

When heterodox economists talk of pluralism they are generally talking about pluralism within the economics profession – they are asking: how can we have a more pluralistic economics profession? This paper argues that another, perhaps more useful, way to think of pluralism and economics is from the perspective of all the social sciences. When considered in reference to the social science profession rather than in reference to the economics profession, the amount of pluralism increases significantly, since different social sciences follow quite different methodologies. However, looking at pluralism from the social science perspective reveals a different type of pluralism problem in social science. While there may be plenty of pluralism within social science as a whole, there is a serious question about whether it is appropriately distributed. This paper argues that heterodox economists' agenda should be a greater blending of all the social science departments. It summarizes proposals to do so on both the undergraduate level and graduate level, and explains why supporting variations of these proposals would be a strategy that would further the objectives of most heterodox economists more than would their current strategy of pushing for more pluralism in economics.

[63]   2014, *Complexity and the Art of Public Policy: Solving Society's Problems from the Bottom Up* (with Roland Kupers), Princeton, NJ: Princeton University Press.

In contrast to economists' standard policy models which are stuck in either a market fundamentalist or government control narrative, this book outlines a new, more flexible policy narrative, which envisions society as a complex evolving system that is uncontrollable but can be influenced. This new policy narrative changes the way of framing policy questions. It offers innovative bottom-up solutions that, through new institutional structures such as for-benefit corporations, channel individuals' social instincts into solving societal problems, making profits a tool for change rather than a goal. The book argues that a central role for government in this complexity framework is to foster an ecostructure within which diverse forms of social entrepreneurship can emerge and blossom.

[64]   2015, 'Framing the Economic Policy Debate', *History of Political Economy*, **47** (annual suppl.), 253–66 (Chapter 8 of this volume).

[65]   2015, 'Making Sense of Economist's Positive Normative Distinction' (with Huei-Chun Su), *Journal of Economic Methodology*, **22** (2), 157–70.

The goal of this article is to provide a slightly different spin on economists' use of the positive–normative distinction by providing some context for its use. The major difference is the following: philosophers and philosophically oriented economists, such as Hilary Putnam and John Davis, see the positive–normative distinction in economics as following from the logical positivist position, and they interpret comments made by economists as reflecting scientific methodological positions that have long since been repudiated by philosophers of science. This article argues that economists' use of the positive–normative distinction developed from the Mill–Keynes methodological tradition, which did not hold logical positivist views. Instead, it had pragmatic purposes and was designed to encourage economists to be more modest in their claims for the implications of economic theory. This paper concludes by arguing that economist's current use of the positive–normative distinction is problematic, but that the best way forward is not to eliminate it, but to reposition it within the Mill–Keynes tradition from which it initially developed. Doing so avoids the problems of associating it with logical positivism, while simultaneously using the distinction to remind economists about the limitations of applying economic theorizing to real world problems.

[66]   2016, 'Complexity Economics and Workday Economic Policy', in David Wilson and Alan Kirman (eds), *Complexity and Evolution: Toward a New Synthesis for Economics*, Cambridge, MA: MIT Press Cambridge, pp. 285–98 (Chapter 9 of this volume).

List of book reviews

1. 1988, review of *A Search for a Synthesis in Economic Theory* by Ching-Yao Hsieh and Stephen L. Mangum, Armonk, NY and London: Sharpe, 1986, in *Journal of Economic Literature*, **20** (2), 321–2.
2. 1988, review of *Methodology for a New Microeconomics* by Lawrence A. Boland, Boston, London, and Sydney: Allen & Unwin, 1986, in *History of Political Economy*, **20** (2), 321–2.
3. 1989, review of *The Political Economy of Rent-Seeking* edited by C. Rowley, R. Tollison and G. Tullock, Boston, Dordrecht, Lancaster: Kluwer Academic Publishers, 1987, in *Public Choice*, **61** (3), 295–6.
4. 1990, review of *Economists and the Economy: The Evolution of Economic Ideas, 1600 to the Present Day* by Roger Backhouse, New York: Basil Blackwell, 1988, in *Journal of Economic History*, **50** (1), 241–2.
5. 1990, review of *The Keynesian Revolution in the Making: 1924–1936* by Peter Clarke, Oxford, New York, Toronto, and Melbourne: Oxford University Press, Clarendon Press, 1988, in *Journal of Economic Literature*, **28** (3), 1201–2.
6. 1991, review of *The State of Economic Science: Views of Six Nobel Laureates* edited by Werner Sichel, Kalamazoo, MI: W.E. Upjohn Institute for Employment Research, 1989, in *Eastern Economic Journal*, **17** (1), 135–6.
7. 1992, review of *Economics on Trial: Lies, Myths and Realities* by Mark Skousen, Homewood, IL: Business One Irwin, 1991, in *Journal of Economic Literature*, **30** (1), 178–9.
8. 1992, 'The New, the Neo, and New-Neo', a review of *New Keynesian Economics* edited by N. Gregory Mankiw and David Romer, Cambridge, MA: the MIT Press, 1991, in *Methodus*, 166–70.
9. 1993, review of *The Principles of Economics: Some Lies my Teacher Told Me* by Larry Boland, London and New York: Routledge, 1992, in *Journal of Economics Literature*, **31** (3), 1435–89.
10. 1993, review of *Striking the Mother Lode in Science: The Importance of Age, Place and Time* by Paula E. Stephan and Sharon G. Levin, New York: Oxford University Press, 1992, in *Southern Economic Journal*, **60** (2), 509–10.
11. 1994, review of *A History of Macroeconometric Model-Building* by Ronald Bodkin, Lawrence R. Klein and Kanta Marwah, Aldershot, UK and Brookfield, VT, USA: Edward Elgar Publishing, 1991, in *History of Political Economy*, Spring, 169–71.
12. 1994, review of *Economics–Mathematical Politics or Science of Diminishing Returns?* by Alexander Rosenberg, Chicago: University of Chicago Press, 1992, in *Southern Economics Journal*, **60** (3), 767–8.
13. 1995, review of *Post Keynesian Macroeconomic Theory: A Foundation for Successful Economic Policies for the Twenty-first Century* by Paul Davidson, Aldershot, UK and Brookfield, VT, USA: Edward Elgar Publishing, 1994, in *Journal of Economic Literature*, **33** (4), 1986–87.

14. 1996, review of *Ethics and Economic Theory: Ideas–Models–Theories* by Kurt W. Rothschild, Cheltenham, UK and Brookfield, VT, USA: Edward Elgar Publishing, 1993, *Review of Political Economy*, **8** (2), 248–51.
15. 1997, review of *Beyond Rhetoric and Realism in Economics: Towards a Reformulation of Economic Methodology* by Thomas A. Boylan and Paschal F. O'Gorman, London: Routledge, 1995, in *Economics and Philosophy*, **13** (1), 140–42.
16. 2000, review of *Foundations of Complex-System Theories: in Economics, Evolutionary Biology, and Statistical Physics* by Sunny Y. Auyang, Cambridge, UK: Cambridge University Press, 1999, in *Metascience*, **9** (1), 62–70.
17. 2003, review of *Economics and its Enemies: Two Centuries of Anti-Economics* by William Oliver Coleman, Basingstoke, UK and New York: Palgrave Macmillan, 2002, in *Journal of Economic Literature*, **41** (4), 1275–6.
18. 2003, review of *Economics as Religion: From Samuelson to Chicago and Beyond* by Robert Nelson, University Park, PA: Penn State University Press, 2001, in *History of Political Economy*, **35** (2), 336–40.
19. 2003, review of *How Economics Became a Mathematical Science* by Roy Weintraub, Durham, NC: Duke University Press, 2002, in *Journal of Economic History*, **63** (2), 514–16.
20. 2004, review of *Rationalizing Capitalist Democracy: The Cold War Origins of Rational Choice Liberalism* by S.M. Amadae, Chicago: University of Chicago Press, 2003, in *Journal of Economic History*, **64** (1), 281–2.
21. 2005, 'Revolution or Evolution: Reflections on the Post-Autistic Movement', a review of *The Crisis in Economics: The Post-Autistic Economics Movement: The First 600 Days* edited by Edward Fullbrook, London: Routledge, 2003, in *Journal of Economic Methodology*, **12** (2), 336–42.
22. 2005, review of *The Classical Economists Revisited* by D.P. O'Brien, Princeton, NJ: Princeton University Press, 2004, in *History of Economic Ideas*, **13** (1), 161–3.
23. 2006, review of *Macroeconomic Foundations of Macroeconomics* by Alvaro Cencini, London: Routledge, 2005, in *Economica*, **73** (291), 548–9.
24. 2008, 'Confronting Economists who are Confronting Economics', a review of *Economics Confronts the Economy* by Philip A. Klein, Cheltenham, UK and Northampton, MA, USA: Edward Elgar Publishing, 2006, in *Research in the History of Economic Thought and Methodology*, **26** (A), 147–52.
25. 2007, review of *Economics and Happiness: Framing the Analysis* edited by Luigino Bruni and Pier Luigi Porta, Oxford and New York: Oxford University Press, 2005, in *Journal of Economic Literature*, **45** (1), 192–5.
26. 2008, review of *The Economy as an Evolving Complex System III: Current Perspectives and Future Directions* edited by Lawarene Blume and Steven Durlauf, Oxford: Oxford University Press, 2005, in *Economica*, **75** (297), 191–2.
27. 2008, review of *Do Economists Make Markets? On the Performativity of Economics* edited by Donald Mackenzie, Fabian Muniesa and Lucia Siu, Princeton, NJ and Oxford: Princeton University Press, 2007, in *Journal of Economic Literature*, **46** (3), 720–24.
28. 2010, review of *The Romantic Economist: Imagination in Economics* by Richard Bronk, Cambridge: Cambridge University Press, 2009, in *History of Political Economy*, **42** (2), 385–6.

29. 2013, review of *Reckoning with Markets: Moral Reflections in Economics* by James Halteman and Edd Noell, Oxford: Oxford University Press, 2012, in *History of Political Economy*, **45** (4), 750–51.
30. 2015, review of *Big Ideas in Macroeconomics: A Nontechnical View* by Kartik Arhreya, Cambridge, MA: MIT Press, 2014, *Economica*, **82** (326), 391–2.